Communications
in Computer and Information Science 350

Tai-hoon Kim   Dae-sik Ko
Thanos Vasilakos   Adrian Stoica
Jemal Abawajy (Eds.)

Computer Applications for Communication, Networking, and Digital Contents

International Conferences, FGCN and DCA 2012
Held as Part of the Future Generation
Information Technology Conference, FGIT 2012
Gangneug, Korea, December 16-19, 2012
Proceedings

Volume Editors

Tai-hoon Kim
GVSA and University of Tasmania, Hobart, TAS, Australia
E-mail: taihoonn@hanmail.net

Dae-sik Ko
Mokwon University, Daejeon, Korea
E-mail: kds@mokwon.ac.kr

Thanos Vasilakos
University of Western Macedonia, Kozani, Greece
E-mail: vasilako@ath.forthnet.gr

Adrian Stoica
NASA JPL, Caltech, Pasadena, CA, USA
E-mail: adrian.stoica@jpl.nasa.gov

Jemal Abawajy
Deakin University, Waurn Ponds, VIC, Australia
E-mail: jemal.abawajy@deakin.edu.au

ISSN 1865-0929   e-ISSN 1865-0937
ISBN 978-3-642-35593-6   e-ISBN 978-3-642-35594-3
DOI 10.1007/978-3-642-35594-3
Springer Heidelberg Dordrecht London New York

Library of Congress Control Number: 2012953665

CR Subject Classification (1998): C.2, H.4, D.2, H.3, H.5, I.2

Typesetting: Camera-ready by author, data conversion by Scientific Publishing Services, Chennai, India

Printed on acid-free paper

Springer is part of Springer Science+Business Media (www.springer.com)

Foreword

Future-generation communication and networking and digital contents and applications are areas that attract many academics and industry professionals. The goal of the FGCN and DCA conferences is to bring together researchers from academia and industry as well as practitioners to share ideas, problems, and solutions relating to the multifaceted aspects of these areas.

We would like to express our gratitude to all of the authors of submitted papers and to all attendees for their contributions and participation.

We acknowledge the great effort of all the Chairs and the members of the Advisory Boards and Program Committees of the above-listed events. Special thanks go to SERSC (Science & Engineering Research Support Society) for supporting this conference.

We are grateful in particular to the following speakers who kindly accepted our invitation and, in this way, helped to meet the objectives of the conference: Zita Maria Almeida do Vale, Hai Jin, Goreti Marreiros, Alfredo Cuzzocrea and Osvaldo Gervasi.

We wish to express our special thanks to Yvette E. Gelogo for helping with the editing of this volume.

December 2012

Chairs of FGCN 2012
DCA 2012

Preface

We would like to welcome you to the proceedings of the 2012 International Conference on Future-Generation Communication and Networking (FGCN 2012) and the 2012 International Conference on Digital Contents and Applications (DCA 2012), which were held during December 16–19, 2012, at the Korea Woman Training Center, Kangwondo, Korea.

FGCN 2012 and DCA 2012 provided a chance for academics and industry professionals to discuss recent progress in related areas. We expect that the conference and its publications will be a trigger for further research and technology improvements in this important field. We would like to acknowledge the great effort of all the Chairs and members of the Program Committee.

We would like to express our gratitude to all of the authors of submitted papers and to all attendees for their contributions and participation. We believe in the need for continuing this undertaking in the future.

Once more, we would like to thank all the organizations and individuals who supported this event and helped in the success of FGCN 2012 and DCA 2012.

December 2012   Tai-hoon Kim on behalf of the Volume Editors

Organization

Honorary Chair

Dae-sik Ko   Mokwon University, Korea

General Co-chairs

Adrian Stoica   NASA JPL, USA
Haengkon Kim   Catholic University of Daegu, Korea
Thanos Vasilakos   University of Western Macedonia, Greece
Wai-chi Fang   National Chiao Tung University, Taiwan

Program Co-chairs

Charalampos Z. Patrikakis   National Technical University of Athens, Greece
Gansen Zhao   Sun Yat-sen University, China
Javier Garcia Villalba   Universidad Complutense de Madrid, Spain
Jemal Abawajy   Deakin University, Australia
Tai-hoon Kim   GVSA and UTAS, Australia
Yang Xiao   University of Alabama, USA

Workshop Chair

Yoonsik Kwak   Korea National University of Transportation, Korea

Publicity Co-chairs

Bonghwa Hong   Kyung Hee Cyber University, Korea
Byungjoo Park   Hannam University, Korea
Damien Sauveron   University of Limoges, France
Houcine Hassan   Polytechnic University of Valencia, Spain
Irfan Awan   University of Bradford, UK
J.H. Abawajy   Deakin University, Australia
Muhammad Khurram Khan   King Saud University, Saudi Arabia
Qun Jin   Waseda University, Japan
Yang Xiao   University of Alabama, USA

Publication Chair

Maria Lee   Shih Chien University, Taiwan

International Advisory Board

Aboul Ella Hassanien	Cairo University, Egypt
Byeong-Ho Kang	University of Tasmania, Australia
Frode Eika Sandnes	Oslo University College, Norway
Gansen Zhao	Sun Yat-sen University, China
Gongzhu Hu	Central Michigan University, USA
Hamid R. Arabnia	University of Georgia, USA
Han-Chieh Chao	National Ilan University, Taiwan
Hsiao-Hwa Chen	National Sun Yat-Sen University, Taiwan
Jianhua Ma	Hosei University, Japan
Sankar K. Pal	Indian Statistical Institute, India
SeungKook Cheong	Advanced Communications Research Laboratory, ETRI, Korea
Tughrul Arslan	University of Edinburgh, UK
Xiaofeng Song	Nanjing University of Aeronautics and Astronautics, China

Program Committee

A.V. Senthil Kumar	Bharathiar University, India
Abbas M. Al-Bakry	Babylon University, Iraq
Aboul Ella Hassanien	Cairo University, Egypt
Adel Al-Jumaily	University of Technology, Sydney, Australia
Adnan Al-Rabea	Albalqa Applied University, Jordan
Aggeliki Sgora	University of Piraeus, Greece
Ai-Chun Pang	National Taiwan University, Taiwan
Albert Banchs	Universidad Carlos III de Madrid, Spain
Ali Sher	American University of Ras Al Khaimah, UAE
Amparo Fuster-Sabater	Institute of Applied Physics (CSIC), Spain
Anan Liu	Tianjin University, China
Andreas Riener	Johannes Kepler University Linz, Austria
Andres Iglesias Prieto	University of Cantabria, Spain
Andrzej Jajszczyk	AGH University of Science and Technology, Poland
Anirban Kundu	West Bengal University of Technology, India
Antonio Lagana	University of Perugia, Italy
Arash Habibi Lashkari	University Technology Malaysia (UTM), Malaysia
Aroop Mukherjee	King Saud University, Saudi Arabia
Asoke Nath	St. Xavier's College, India
Azzam Sleit	University of Jordan, Jordan
Azzouzi Messaouda	Ziane Achour University of Djelfa, Algeria
Benahmed Khelifa	University of Bechar , Algeria
Beomjin Kim	Indiana University Purdue University Fort Wayne, USA

Bin Guo   Institut TELECOM SudParis, France
Bo Meng   South-Center University for Nationalities,
    China
Bogdan Ghita   The University of Plymouth, UK
Brajesh Kumar Singh   FET, R.B.S. College, Bichpuri, India
Cai Linqin   Chongqing University of Posts and
    Telecommunications, China
Cesar Andres Sanchez   Universidad Complutense de Madrid, Spain
Chandrasekaran Subramaniam   Anna University, India
Changjiang Zhang   Zhejiang Normal University, China
Chao-Hung Lin   National Cheng-Kung University, Taiwan
Chao-Tung Yang   Tunghai University, Taiwan
Chee Siong   Universiti Malaysia Sarawak (UNIMAS),
    Malaysia
Chia-Chen Lin   Providence University, Taiwan
Chi-Man Pun   University of Macau, SAR China
Chin-Chen Chang   Feng Chia University, Taiwan
Ching-seh Wu   Oakland University, USA
Cho Siu Yeung David   Nanyang Technological University, Singapore
Christophe Fouquere   University of Paris, France
Chu-Hsing Lin   Tunghai University, Taiwan
Chun-Wei Lin   National Cheng Kung University, Taiwan
Ciprian Dobre   University Politehnica of Bucharest, Romania
Clement Leung   Hong Kong Baptist University, SAR China
Dae-Ki Kang   Dongseo University, Korea
Damien Sauveron   Université de Limoges, France
Danda B. Rawat   Eastern Kentucky University, USA
Dhananjay Singh   National Institute for Mathematical Sciences,
    Korea
Dimitrios D. Vergados   University of Piraeus, Greece
Dirk Thorleuchter   Fraunhofer INT, Germany
Doinita Ariton   Danubius University of Galati, Romania
Dominique Decouchant   Universidad Autonoma Metropolitana, Mexico
    and Laboratoire LIG de Grenoble, France
Dong Hyun Jeong   University of the District of Columbia, USA
Don-Lin Yang   Feng Chia University, Taiwan
Arun Sharma   Krishna Institute of Engineering and
    Technology, Ghaziabad, India
Ousmane Thiare   University Gaston Berger of Saint-Louis,
    Senegal
Saurabh Mukherjee   Banasthali University, Rajasthan, India
Driss Mammass   Ibn Zohr University, Morocco
E. George Dharma Prakash
  Raj   Bharathidasan University, India
Eleonora Pantano   University of Calabria, Italy

Ezendu Ariwa	London Metropolitan University, UK
Farrukh A. Khan	FAST National University of Computer and Emerging Sciences, Pakistan
Fernando Berzal	University of Granada, Spain
Florian Nuta	Danubius University of Galati, Romania
G. Ganesan	Adikavi Nannaya University, India
Ganesan R.	PSG College of Arts and Science, India
Ganesh Naik	RMIT University, Australia
Gang Wu	Southeast University, China
Genge Bela	Petru Maior University, Romania
George A. Gravvanis	Democritus University of Thrace, Greece
Gianluigi Ferrari	University of Parma, Italy
Giner Alor Hdez	Instituto Tecnologico de Orizaba, Mexico
Guimin Chen	Xidian University, China
Hocine Cherifi	University of Burgundy, France
Hong Jer Lang	Taylor's University, Malaysia
Hong Sun	AGFA Healthcare, Belgium
Hosam El-Ocla	Lakehead University, Canada
Hsiang-Cheh Huang	National University of Kaohsiung, Taiwan
Hsin-Hung Chou	Chang Jung Christian University, Taiwan
Hui Chen	Virginia State University, USA
Hui-Kai Su	National Formosa University, Taiwan
Huirong Fu	Oakland University, USA
Hung-Min Sun	National Tsing Hua University, Taiwan
Hyun-A Park	University of Arizona, USA
I-Ching Hsu	National Formosa University, Taiwan
Iosif Androulidakis	University of Ioannina, Greece
J. Octavio Gutierrez-Garcia	CINVESTAV del IPN, Mexico
J. Vigo-Aguiar	Universidad de Salamanca, Spain
Jaime Lloret Mauri	Polytechnic University of Valencia, Spain
Janusz Szczepanski	Polish Academy of Science, Poland
Jasni Mohamad Zain	Universiti Malaysia Pahang, Malaysia
Jatinderkumar Saini	Gujarat Technological University, India
Jayadev Gyani	Jayamukhi Institute of Technological Sciences, India
Jiann-Liang	National Dong Hwa University, Taiwan
Jieh-Shan George Yeh	Providence University, Taiwan
Jiming Chen	Zhejiang University, China
Juha Röning	University of Oulu, Finland
Junbin Fang	University of Hong Kong, SAR China
Jungpil Shin	University of Aizu, Japan
Jun-Ki Min	Korea University of Technology and Education, Republic of Korea
Ka Lok Man	Xi'an Jiaotong-Liverpool University, China

Kaori Fujinami	Tokyo University of Agriculture and Technology, Japan
Kenji Suzuki	The University of Chicago, USA
Ki Jun Han	Kyungbook National University, Korea
Kia Ng	University of Leeds, UK
Kin Keung Lai	City University of Hong Kong, SAR China
Ko Chi Chung	National University of Singapore, Singapore
Kuo-Hung Huang	National Chiayi University, Taiwan
Kwok-Yan Lam	Tsinghua University, China
Ladislav Huraj	University of SS Cyril and Methodius in Trnava, Slovakia
Lansheng Han	Huazhong University of Science and Technology, China
Le Thi Lan	Hanoi University of Technology, Vietnam
Li Shijian	Zhejiang University, China
Ling Pei	Finnish Geodetic Institute, Finland
Lixin Han	Hohai University, China
Luigi Gallo	ICAR-CNR, Italy
Luis Alvarez Sabucedo	Universidade de Vigo, Spain
Luis Javier Garcia Villalba	Universidad Complutense de Madrid, Spain
M. Hemalatha	Karpagam University, Indonesia
Manuel Fernando dos Santos Silva	ISEP Instituto Superior de Engenharia do Porto, Portugal
Marc Lacoste	Orange Labs, France
Marcelo de Carvalho Alves	Federal University of Mato Grosso, Brazil
Matthias Reuter	Clausthal University of Technology, Germany
Mayyada Hammoshi	Technical Institute of Mosul, Iraq
Mezghani Ben Ayed Dorra	National School of Engineer of Tunis, Tunisia
Michael N. Vrahatis	University of Patras, Greece
Michel-Marie Deza	Laboratoire de Geometrie Appliquee, France
Miguel A. Garcia-Ruiz	University of Colima, College of Telematics, Mexico
Ming-Huwi Horng	National PingTung Institute of Commerce, Taiwan
Ming-Yen Lin	Feng Chia University, Taiwan
Mohammad Awrangjeb	University of Melbourne, Australia
Mohammad Moghal	University of Bedfordshire, UK
Mohammad Rakibul Islam	Islamic University of Technology, Bangladesh
Mohammed Ali Hussain	Sri Sai Madhavi Institute of Science and Technology, India
Mohd Helmy Abd Wahab	Universiti Tun Hussein Onn Malaysia, Malaysia
Muhammad Khurram Khan	King Saud University, Saudi Arabia
N. Jaisankar	VIT University, India

Nashwa El-Bendary	Arab Academy for Science and Technology and Maritime Transport, Egypt
Natarajan Meghanathan	Jackson State University, USA
Neveen I. Ghalii	Al-Azhar University, Egypt
Nikolaos Pantazis	Technological Educational Institution (TEI) of Athens, Greece
Ning Chen	Xi'an Polytechnic University, China
Ning Gui	University of Antwerp, Belgium
Nistor Grozavu	Paris 13 University, France
Noraziah Ahmad	University of Malaysia Pahang, Malaysia
Nursuriati Jamil	Universiti Teknologi MARA, Malaysia
Omar Soluiman	Cairo University, Egypt
P.R. Parthasarathy	Indian Institute of Technology, India
Panos Kudumakis	Queen Mary University of London, UK
Patrizia Grifoni	National Research Council, IRPPS, Italy
Peiquan Jin	University of Science and Technology of China, China
Phuc V. Nguyen	Asian Institute of Technology and Management, Vietnam
Pin Ng	HKCC Hong Kong Polytechnic University, SAR China
Ping-Tsai Chung	Long Island University, USA
Abraham T. Mathew	National Institute of Technology Calicut, India
Qiu Chen	Tohoku University, Japan
Qutaiba Ibrahem Ali	Mosul University, Iraq
Radek Oslejsek	Masaryk University, Czech Republic
Ren Xun-yi	Nanjing University of Posts and Telecommunications, China
Richard Y.K. Fung	City University of Hong Kong, SAR China
Ricky Yu-Kwong Kwok	Colorado State University, USA
Rita Yi Man Li	Hong Kong Shue Yan University, SAR China
Ritesh Chugh	University of Melbourne, Australia
Robert C. Hsu	Chung Hua University, Taiwan
Robert C. Meurant	Sejong University, Korea
Robert Goutte	University of Lyon, France
Rocio Abascal Mena	Universidad Autonoma Metropolitana Cuajimalpa, Mexico
Rohaya Latip	University Putra Malaysia, Malaysia
Ruay-Shiung Chang	National Dong Hwa University, Taiwan
Rui L. Aguiar	Universidade de Aveiro, Portugal
Ruzaini Abdullah Arshah	Universiti Malaysia Pahang, Malaysia
S. Santhosh Baboo	D.G. Vaishnav College, India
S. Hariharan	Pavendar Bharathidasan College of Engineering and Technology, India
Sabira Khatun	Universiti Malaysia Pahang, Malaysia

Saleh Alwahaishi	King Fahd University of Petroleum and Minerals, Saudi Arabia
Samad Kolahi	Unitec Institute of Technology, New Zealand
Sanghyuk Lee	Xi'an Jiaotong-Liverpool University, China
Seyed Zeinolabedin Moussavi	Shahid Rajaee University, Iran
Shahab Shamshirband	Islamic Azad University, Iran
Shahrul Azmi bin Mohd Yusof	Universiti Utara Malaysia, Malaysia
Shaojie Qiao	Southwest Jiaotong University, China
Shun-Ren Yang	National Tsing Hua University, Taiwan
Simon Fong	University of Macau, SAR China
Soon Ae Chun	City University of New York, USA
Soo-Yeon Ji	Bowie State University, USA
Sotirios Ziavras	New Jersey Institute of Technology, USA
Stephen Huang	University of Houston, USA
Sulieman Bani-Ahmad	Al-Balqa Applied University, Jordan
Sun-Yuan Hsieh	National Cheng Kung University, Taiwan
Syed Nadeem Ahsan	IST, Austria
T. Ramayah	Universiti Sains Malaysia, Malaysia
Tae (Tom) Oh	Rochester Institute of Technology, USA
Talib Mohammad	University of Botswana, Botswana
Terence D. Todd	McMaster University, Canada
Te-Shun Chou	East Carolina University, USA
Tian Xueying	Suzhou University of Science and Technology, China
Tsung-Chih Lin	Feng-Chia University, Taiwan
Tutut Herawan	Universiti Malaysia Pahang, Malaysia
Valentina E. Balas	Aurel Vlaicu University of Arad, Romania
Veselina Jecheva	Burgas Free University, Bulgaria
Victor C. M. Leung	University of British Columbia, Canada
Vijay H. Mankar	Govt. Polytechnic, India
Vijayalakshmi Saravanan	VIT University, Vellore, India
Viktor Yarmolenko	Intetech Ltd., UK
Vincent Oria	NJIT, USA
Vincenzo De Florio	University of Antwerp, Belgium
Vladimir Siladi	Matej Bel University, Slovakia
Wan Haslina Hassan	Sunway University College, Malaysia
Waralak V. Siricharoen	UTCC, Thailand
Weili Han	Fudan University, China
Weirong Jiang	Juniper Networks Inc., USA
Wenqian Shang	Communication University of China, China
Witold Pedrycz	University of Alberta, Canada
Wuyi Yue	Konan University, Japan
Yeonseung Ryu	Myongji University, Korea
Yilun Shang	University of Texas at San Antonio, USA
Yingyuan Xiao	Tianjin University of Technology, China

Table of Contents

Carrier Aggregation Receiver with Beamformer and Compensation of Doppler Effects and Timing Offset

Xin Wang and Heung-Gyoon Ryu

Department of Electronic Engineering Chungbuk National University
Cheongju, Korea 361-763
wxzf007@naver.com, ecomm@cbu.ac.kr

Abstract. Due to limitations in sampling capabilities for high frequency systems, the universal receiver at this time cannot sample the incoming signals just after a RF stage process. As one way, using sub-sampling technique can convert multi-band signals from RF band to IF band without oscillators. But as the filter performance in RF bands, signals converted to low bands possibly cause interference and degrade performances. In this paper, we extend a sub-sampling method to the case of multi-band receiver using pre-FFT beamformer, and a new approach is proposed to avoid interference by TDM method. The purpose of designing the pre-FFT beamformer is to coherently combine the desired signals and suppress the undesired signals so that it is able to provide medium to high gains in a mobile environment. Simulation results show that after compensating the Doppler effects and timing offset the approach works effectively and we can get optimal performances in the multi-band receiver.

Keywords: Sub-Sampling, TDM, Multi-band receiver, Offset compensation, timing Synchronization, Beamforming, LMS.

1   Introduction

In uplink OFDMA systems, available subcarriers are divided into groups and assigned to multiple users for simultaneous transmissions. [1] The ideal universal receiver sampling the incoming signals just after a RF stage is very seducing but not realistic at this time due to limitations in sampling capabilities for high frequency systems. A multiple antenna array can be used at the receiver, not only for spectral efficiency or gain enhancement, but also for interference suppression. Software-defined radio (SDR) [2] principles have attracted more and more attention.

To meet requirement of IMT-Advanced, carrier aggregation (CA) is used in LTE-Advanced [3]. That is one method that combines carrier component (CC). So in this paper to get some CC, sub-sampling technique is used.

Sub-Sampling is a technique that samples high data rate signals with smaller sampling rate than Nyquist sampling rate. There have been studied about Sub-Sampling [4]. After down-sampling about over 2 band signals using sub-sampling, the signals are digitized, and then over 2 band signals can be received [5]. Based on pilot-based transmission, the information of pilot is used to estimate optimum weights for

T.-h. Kim et al. (Eds.): FGCN/DCA 2012, CCIS 350, pp. 1–9, 2012.
© Springer-Verlag Berlin Heidelberg 2012

the spatial filtering operated by smart antenna. Beamforming process is performed using a pre-FFT method[6] based on VSS-LMS(Variable Step Size)[7,8].

In this paper, we propose sub-sampling with TDM that can avoid previous problems to separate over 2 signals in time. The purpose of designing the pre-FFT beamformer is to coherently combine the desired signals and suppress the undesired signals so that it is able to provide medium to high gains in a mobile environment. Simulation results show that after compensating the Doppler effects and timing offset the approach works effectively and we can get optimal performances in the multi-band receiver.

2   System Model

In this paper we consider 2 signals that have different center frequency. Transmitted signals are based on OFDM. Eq. (1) is the signals in time domain. We assume that there are two received bands. $X^A_{k,m}$ and $X^B_{k,m}$ are transmitted signals respectively. As in eq. (1), the signals is represented after IFFT in time domain.

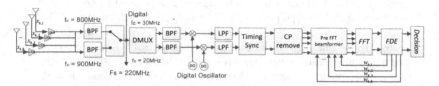

Fig. 1. Multi-band receiver structure with Pre-FFT beamformer using sub-sampling and TDM

$$x(t) = \begin{cases} \dfrac{1}{\sqrt{N}} \displaystyle\sum_{k=0}^{N-1} X^A_{k,m} e^{j(\frac{2\pi k}{N} + f_A)t}, & x_A(t) \\ \dfrac{1}{\sqrt{N}} \displaystyle\sum_{k=0}^{N-1} X^B_{k,m} e^{j(\frac{2\pi k}{N} + f_B)t}, & x_B(t) \end{cases} \tag{1}$$

Each band is represented as $x_A(t)$ and $x_B(t)$ in time domain and has center frequencies as f_A and f_B. The channel is considered affected by AWGN, multipath and Doppler shift[12]:

$$h(t) = \beta_0(t)\delta(t) + \sum_{m=1}^{M} \beta_i(t) \cdot \delta(t - \tau_i) \tag{2}$$

where M is the number of multipaths and τ_i is the delay of arrival of the m-th path. $\beta_0(t)$ and $\beta_i(t)$ are complex values that take into account attenuation and Doppler shift.

The receiver is equipped with an uniform linear array(ULA) of L sensors located along a straight line. The signal received by the ULA can be written by a $L \times N_T$ matrix

$$X = a(\theta_d) \cdot s^T + \sum_{m=1}^{M} a(\theta_m) \cdot r_m^T + M \tag{3}$$

where s and r_m are the column vectors of the direct and reflected rays attenuated by the Doppler shift. θ_d and θ_m are the respective angles of arrival and $a(\cdot)$ is the column steering vector

$$a(\theta) = \begin{bmatrix} 1 & e^{j\pi \sin\theta} & .. & e^{j\pi(L-1)\sin\theta} \end{bmatrix}^T. \tag{4}$$

The AWGN effect is represented by the matrix M. And since it can be considered omnidirectional, it affect every antenna and M is generated independently.

3   Beamforming Algorithm

The beamforming algorithm exploits the spatial diversification of the incoming signal replicas by a multiplicity of sensors. For our system we have adopted an LMS(least mean square) algorithm. The basic idea of the LMS algorithm is to evaluate the vector w_k with an iterative approach. Filter coefficients are updated to approach the minimum squared error(MSE) value with null gradient. The updating is performed by

$$w_{k+1} = w_k - \mu \cdot g(w_k) \tag{5}$$

where $g(\cdot)$ is the stochastic gradient of the estimated MSE calculated at the k-th due to w_k:

$$g(w_k) = \nabla_{w_k}(M \hat{S} E_k) . \tag{6}$$

The convergence characteristics of the algorithm depend on the positive scalar μ [9].We have opted for the pre-FFT method for its much lower complex for needing only one FFT per OFDM symbol is required while the post-FFT method needs L times FFT[6]. We use the symbol "~" to indicate a FFT operation. And we define that

- $\bar{s}$, the vector of dimensions $J \times 1$, with J = the number of pilot tones containing the reference signal.
- w_k, $L \times 1$ vector containing the complex gains.
- $\tilde{X}_k$, the $L \times N$ matrix whose every row is the FFT of corresponding row of X_k where is the k-frame received data matrix without CP.
- D, the $J \times N$ matrix indicating the pilots position.

The instantaneous estimation of MSE can be written as:

$$M \hat{S} E_k = \left\| \bar{s}^T - w_k^H \tilde{X}_k D^T \right\|^2 . \tag{7}$$

Using the generalized derivative rules, the gradient can be rewritten as:

$$g(w_k) = 2\tilde{X}_k D^T (D\tilde{X}_k^H w_k - \bar{s}^*) = 2\tilde{X}_k \tilde{e}_k \tag{8}$$

where

$$\tilde{e}_k = D^T (D\tilde{X}_k^H w_k - \overline{s}^*) \ .$$

Using the generalized Parceval equality to rewrite (8) as:

$$\begin{aligned}
e_k &= IFFT\left\{D^T(D\tilde{X}_k^H w_k - \overline{s}^*)\right\} \\
&= IFFT\left\{D^T(\overline{y}_k - \overline{s})^*\right\}.
\end{aligned} \tag{9}$$

4   Timing and Frequency Synchronization

The orthogonally among subcarriers is often destroyed by the CFOs due to oscillator mismatches and it degrades performance. Signal x(t) is like (10) due to Doppler effect.

$$y_n = \sum_{k=0}^{N-1} H_k \cdot X_k \cdot e^{i2\pi\frac{k+\varepsilon}{N}} + z_n \tag{10}$$

Signal x(t) is like (11) due to Doppler effect in time domain.

Doppler effect is represented phase rotation in frequency domain. k , n, ε are sub-carrier, symbol, normalized Doffer frequency respectively in (10).

$$\begin{aligned}
Y_p &= \sum_{m=0}^{N-1}\sum_{k=0}^{N-1} H_{k,m} \cdot X_{k,m} \cdot e^{i2\pi\frac{(k+\varepsilon)}{N}} \cdot e^{-i2\pi\frac{m}{N}} + Z_p \\
&= H_p \cdot X_p\, e^{i2\pi\varepsilon p} + \sum_{\substack{m=0 \\ m\neq k}}^{N-1}\sum_{k=0}^{N-1} H_{k,m} \cdot X_{k,m} \cdot e^{i2\pi\frac{(k-m)}{N}} \cdot e^{i2\pi\frac{\varepsilon}{N}} + Z_p
\end{aligned} \tag{11}$$

In (11), first stage is phase rotation and second stage is ICI. Where p is symbol in frequency domain and k, m are sub-carrier before IFFT in transmitter and sample before FFT in receiver.

In this system, we compensate those problems with synchronization signal and block type pilot and assume that the receiver speed is constant.

$$Y_p = H_p \cdot X_p\, e^{i2\pi\varepsilon p} + Z_p \ . \tag{12}$$

Phase rotation is estimated using received pilot signals.

$$P(i) = \sum_{i=1}^{N} mean\left\{\sum_{n=1}^{64} Block\_Pilot(i+n-1)\right\} \tag{13}$$

$$\begin{aligned}
&\frac{angle\{P(i)\} - angle\{P(i+1)\}}{pilot\_interval} \cdot ([1 : pilot\_interval - 1]) \\
&i = 1, 2, \ldots
\end{aligned} \tag{14}$$

P is average of block type pilot. Eq. (14) represents linear interpolation using P, so the symbols that have not pilots is estimated.

A signal that has N samples is a symbol. If the symbol is delayed, the symbol affects next a symbol. So ISI occurs. But ISI is removed by cyclic prefix (CP). Eq. (15) represents phase error and ISI.

$$y_n = h_n \otimes x_{n+\delta} + z_n$$

$$Y_p = \sum_{m=0}^{N-1} \sum_{k=0}^{N-1} H_{k,m} \cdot X_{k,m} \cdot e^{i2\pi\frac{k-m}{N}} \cdot e^{i2\pi\frac{\delta_m}{N}} + Z_p$$

$$= H_p \cdot X_p \sum_{m=0}^{N-1} e^{i2\pi\frac{\delta_m}{N}} + \sum_{\substack{m=0 \\ m \neq k}}^{N-1} \sum_{k=0}^{N-1} H_{k,m} \cdot X_{k,m} \cdot e^{i2\pi\frac{k-m}{N}} \cdot e^{i2\pi\frac{(\delta_m)}{N}} + Z_p \tag{15}$$

But TDM method can't sample two bands at the same time. So it is possible to generate delay at second band. Sample timing offset is like (16).

$$Y_p = H_p \cdot X_p \sum_{m=0}^{N-1} e^{-i2\pi\frac{\delta_m}{N}} \tag{16}$$

Phase error of sample timing offset has different phase degree per sub-carrier because of orthogonality of OFDM. So using synchronization signal, the offset value is estimated [13].We use constant amplitude zero autocorrelation (CAZAC) sequence as synchronization signals for its good self-correlation to get fine timing and dropper offset. The CAZAC is used to design the training sequence (TS). Assume S is the TS of the OFDM systems, according to [14], it can be represented as

$$S(k) = e^{j\frac{M\pi k^2}{N}}, k = 0,1,2 \cdots N-1 \tag{17}$$

Where M is relative-prime to N. Assume H(k)=1,M=1 when there has a frequency offset in the system, the received signal of the TS is

$$r_s(k) = e^{-j\frac{\pi\varepsilon^2\pi}{N}} e^{j\frac{\pi(k+\varepsilon)^2}{N}} + z_n, \tag{18}$$
$$k = 0,1,2 \cdots N-1.$$

The property of auto-correlation of the TS is used in this part get the timing [13]

$$M(d) = \sum_{k=1}^{N} r_s(d+k)s^*(k)$$
$$= \left[e^{-j\pi\varepsilon_i^2/N} e^{j\pi(d+k+\varepsilon_i)^2/N} e^{-j\pi\varepsilon_f^2/N} + z(k) \right]^* e^{-j\pi k^2/N} \tag{19}$$

$$\hat{\delta} = \arg\max(M(d)) \tag{20}$$

Where $M(d)$ is the cross-correlation of the received TS and the know TS in the receiver, $\hat{\delta}$ is the coarse timing start point. Assume ε_i and ε_f is the integer and fractional CFO.

5   Proposed Sub-sampling Method

Sub-sampling is a method that makes aliasing deliberate to move frequency of signal.

5.1   Existing Structure

Existing multi-band system with Sub-Sampling finds sampling frequency that doesn't overlap signals between multi-band signals according to (10). But to select multi-band signals respectively, RF filter is used. Although RF filter has good Q value, the RF filter can't remove all adjacent signals.

Fig. 2. Problem when signals are sub-sampled from RF band

Sub-Sampling about multi-band of over 2 bands meet condition like (21) [10].

$$0 < F_{IF,A} - BW_A / 2, \quad F_S > F_{IF,A} - BW_A / 2$$
$$0 < F_{IF,B} - BW_B / 2, \quad F_S > F_{IF,B} - BW_B / 2$$
$$\text{if } F_{IF,B} > F_{IF,A}$$
$$F_{IF,B} - BW_B / 2 > F_{IF,A} + BW_A / 2$$
$$\text{if } F_{IF,A} > F_{IF,B}$$
$$F_{IF,A} - BW_A / 2 > F_{IF,B} + BW_B / 2 \tag{21}$$

First, the signals that are converted in low frequency band are large than 0 and smaller than Fs/2 respectively. Second, the low frequency part of $F_{IF,A}$ is larger than the high frequency part of $F_{IF,B}$ ($F_{IF,B} < F_{IF,A}$)or, the low frequency part of $F_{IF,B}$ ($F_{IF,A} > F_{IF,A}$) is larger than the high frequency part of $F_{IF,A}$ ($F_{IF,B} > F_{IF,A}$).

5.2   Proposed Structure

We propose a method that adds TDM method in Sub-Sampling method.

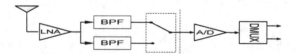

Fig. 3. Multi-band receiver structure with joint sub-sampling and TDM method

The proposed structure is like Fig 3.

$$0 < F_{IF,A} - BW_A / 2, \quad F_S > F_{IF,A} - BW_A / 2$$
$$0 < F_{IF,B} - BW_B / 2, \quad F_S > F_{IF,B} - BW_B / 2 \tag{22}$$

Multi-band signals are received the signals pass through LNA. Afterward, the multi-band signals are divided into two signals by filter. And each signal is sampled twice faster than the existing sub-sampling frequency. Hence TDM and sub-sampling are performed at the same time. The signals that are received with TDM has no interference between receiving singles as signals is divided by time.

6   Simulation and Discuss

Fig. 4 shows that a polar spatial pattern which indicates a strong signal pattern we want and ignore the weak ones. Fig. 5 indicates BER performance when Doppler occurs. We can see the performance according to Doppler scale. The two bands have no difference according to Doppler scale. The two bands have no difference due to TDM. In case of A,B band w/o comp for Doppler=0.01 , we can't communicate because of phase rotation. And when the Doppler=0.05, we can't communicate because we use block type pilot and do linear interpolation. It is difficult to estimate fast phase rotation.

Table 1. Simulation Parameters

OFDM system	
The number of Subcarriers	64
Bandwidth	20MHz
Symbol Period	4 μs
The number of Sensors	8
CP Length	0.8 μs
Pilot Type	Block Type Pilot
Modulation	QAM
Channel	AWGN

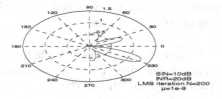

Fig. 4. Polar spatial pattern

Fig. 6 indicates result about timing offset. Here, Delay1 is 3ns, Delay 2 : 0.125us, Delay 3 : 0.5us. We can see two bands can communicate due to Delay 1 and Delay 2 after compensation. And in case of Delay 3 we can't communicate with comp for it is difficult to estimate fast phase rotation.

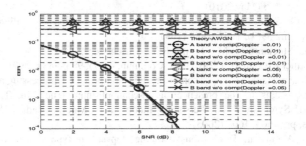

Fig. 5. BER performance with Doppler effect

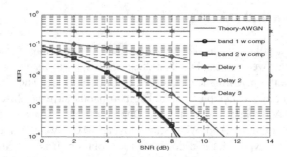

Fig. 6. BER performance with different timing offset

7 Conclusions

In this paper, we propose a downlink OFDMA that can receive multi-band and multi-mode signals using sub-sampling method with TDM in the same time combined with beamforming technology. Sub-sampling is a method that can convert high frequency band signals to low frequency band signals. It also is able to receive over 2 bands signals with one sample & holder and ADC. The sampling frequency need not very high due to (16). It also has an advantage that each signal is individually divided which means undesired signals that occurs due to RF filter characteristic don't affect the others signals. Simulations illustrate the BER performance by compensating the frequency offset and timing offset of the system.

Acknowledgement. This research was supported by Basic Science Research Program through the National Research Foundation of Korea(NRF) funded by the Ministry of Education, Science and Technology(No. 2010-0007567).

References

1. Huang, D., Letaief, K.B.: An Interference-Cancellation Scheme for Carrier Frequency Offsets Correction in OFDMA Systems. IEEE Trans. Commun. 53(7), 1155–1165 (2005)
2. Mitola, J.: The software radio architecture. IEEE Commun. Mag. 33(5), 26–38 (1995)
3. Ratasuk, R., Tolli, D., Ghosh, A.: Carrier Aggregation in LTE- Advanced. In: IEEE VTC 2010-Sping, pp. 1–5 (May 2010)
4. Vaughan, R.G., Scott, N.L., White, D.R.: The theory of bandpass sampling. IEEE Trans. Signal Processing 39(9), 1973–1984 (1991)
5. Akos, D.M., Stockmaster, M., Tsui, J.B.Y., Caschera, J.: Direct bandpass sampling of multiple distinct RF signals. IEEE Trans. Commun. 47(7), 983–988 (1999)
6. Shoki, H., Matsuoka, H.: Comparison of pre-FFT and post-FFT processing adaptive arrays for OFDM systems in the presence of co-channel interference. In: The 14th IEEE International Symposium on Personal, Indoor and Mobile Radio Communication Proceedings, pp. 1603–1607 (2003)
7. Mayyas, K., Aboulsnar, T.: A robust variable step sizelmstype algorithm: analysis and simulations. IEEE Transactions on Signal Processing 45, 631–649 (1997)

8. Farhang-Boroujeny, B., Ang, W.P.: Gradient adaptive stepsize LMS algorithms: past results and new developments. In: IEEE Adaptive Systems for Signal Processing, Communications, and Control Symposium, pp. 278–282 (2000)
9. Johnston, E.W., Kwong, R.: A variable step size lms algorithm. IEEE Transactions on Signal Processing 40, 1633–1642 (1992)
10. Tseng, C.-H., Chou, S.-C.: Direct Downconversion of Multiband RF Signals Using BandPass Sampling. IEEE Trans.Commun. 5(1)
11. Speth, M., Classen, F., Meyr, H.: Frame Synchronization of OFDM systems in frequency selective fading channels. In: IEEE VTC 1997, pp. 1807–1811 (May 1997)
12. Borio, D., Camoriano, L., Presti, L.L., Mondin, M.: Beamforming and Synchronization Algorithms Integration for OFDM HAP-Based Communication. Journal on Wireless Information Networks 13(1) (January 2006)
13. Meng, J., Kang, G.: A Novel OFDM synchronization Algorithm Based On CAZAC Sequence. In: IEEE ICCASM 2010, vol. 14, pp. 634–637 (November 2010)
14. Chu, D.C.: Polyphase codes with good periodic correlation properties. IEEE Trans on IT 45(7), 531–532 (1972)

Source Localization for Uniform Noise Maximum Likelihood Estimation Method and Iterative Algorithm Based on AOA

An Qin-li[1,2], Chen Jian-feng[1], and Yin Zhong-hai[2]

[1] College of Marine, Northwestern Polytechnical University, Xi'an, 710072, China
[2] College of Science, Air Force Engineering University, Xi'an, 710051, China
an_qinli@126.com

Abstract. maximum likelihood estimation(MLE) method and iterative algorithm based on Uniform noise ,which is the same for every sensor in the network, for localizing a source based on angle of arrival (AOA) measurements are presented. We compare MLE iterative method along with least squares estimation(LSE) approach through a number of simulations at various signal to noise levels and target to localization. We find that MLE iterative algorithm is less error and more robust to noise disturbance than LSE method.

Keywords: target localization, uniform noise, least squares estimation(LSE), maximum likelihood estimation(MLE), angle of arrival (AOA), root mean square(RMS).

1   Introduction

With the development of wireless system and the increasing of mobile subscribers, the demand of Location Based Services is become higher and higher. It is remarkable application that wireless location is demanded in one hundred meters by Federal Communications Commission(FCC). In the application, the signal is transmitted between Mobile Terminal and a series of Base Stations. The localization based on angle of arrival (AOA) usual adopts array antennas for gauging angle of arrival of target, by which the number of base station is less than time of arrival(TOA) and time difference of arrival(TDOA) [1-4].   The error of AOA mostly results from the error of discrete angle which obeys uniform distribution.

In this paper, we investigate geometric localization of static target based on AOA. Assumed that the error of AOA obeys uniform distribution. A iterative algorithm is given through analysing MLE of uniform ditribution. We compare MLE iterative method along with least squares estimation(LSE) through simulation experiments.

2   Least Squares Estimation(LSE)

Assumed that observation data from AOA are presented as follows

T.-h. Kim et al. (Eds.): FGCN/DCA 2012, CCIS 350, pp. 10–16, 2012.

$$\hat{\theta}_i - \theta_i = n_i (i = 1, \cdots, n) \tag{1}$$

$$n_i \sim U(-\Delta\theta, \Delta\theta)(i = 1, \cdots, n)$$

$$\tan\theta_i = \frac{y - y_i}{x - x_i}(i = 1, \cdots, n)$$

Rewriten as

$$x\sin\theta_i - y\cos\theta_i = x_i \sin\theta_i - y_i \cos\theta_i (i = 1, \cdots, n) \tag{2}$$

Where (x, y) and (x_i, y_i) are coordinates of target and base station i.

By (2), we have LSE of target localization[5] as

$$\begin{pmatrix} x \\ y \end{pmatrix} = \left(A_L^T A\right)^{-1} A_L^T b_L \tag{3}$$

where

$$A_L = \begin{bmatrix} \sin\hat{\theta}_1 & -\cos\hat{\theta}_1 \\ \vdots & \vdots \\ \sin\hat{\theta}_i & -\cos\hat{\theta}_i \\ \vdots & \vdots \\ \sin\hat{\theta}_n & -\cos\hat{\theta}_n \end{bmatrix}, \quad b_L = \begin{pmatrix} x_1 \sin\hat{\theta}_1 - y_1 \cos\hat{\theta}_1 \\ \vdots \\ x_i \sin\hat{\theta}_i - y_i \cos\hat{\theta}_i \\ \vdots \\ x_n \sin\hat{\theta}_n - y_n \cos\hat{\theta}_n \end{pmatrix}$$

3   Maximum Likelihood Estimation(MLE)

The cost function of MLE is prevented as

$$L(x, y, \Delta\theta; \hat{\theta}_1, \cdots, \hat{\theta}_n) = \frac{1}{(2\Delta\theta)^n} \leq \min_{1 \leq i \leq n} \frac{1}{(2|\hat{\theta}_i - \theta_i|)^n}$$

$$= \min_{1 \leq i \leq n} \frac{1}{(2|\hat{\theta}_i - \arctan\frac{y - y_i}{x - x_i}|)^n}$$

where

$$-\Delta\theta < \hat{\theta}_i - \arg\tan\frac{y - y_i}{x - x_i} < \Delta\theta (i = 1, \cdots, n)$$

Let $\Delta = \tan \Delta\theta$, the tangent of inequation above is given by

$$-\Delta(1 + \frac{y - y_i}{x - x_i} \tan \hat{\theta}_i) < \tan \hat{\theta}_i - \frac{y - y_i}{x - x_i} (i = 1, \cdots, n)$$

$$\tan \hat{\theta}_i - \frac{y - y_i}{x - x_i} < \Delta(1 + \frac{y - y_i}{x - x_i} \tan \hat{\theta}_i)(i = 1, \cdots, n)$$

The inequations are multiplied by $(x - x_i)\cos \hat{\theta}_i$, we have

$$(x - x_i)(-\sin \hat{\theta}_i - \Delta \cos \hat{\theta}_i) + (y - y_i)(\cos \hat{\theta}_i - \Delta \sin \hat{\theta}_i) < 0(i = 1, \cdots, n)$$

$$(x - x_i)(\sin \hat{\theta}_i - \Delta \cos \hat{\theta}_i) + (y - y_i)(-\cos \hat{\theta}_i - \Delta \sin \hat{\theta}_i) < 0(i = 1, \cdots, n)$$

Therefore, the model is presented as

$$\min \Delta$$

s.t.

$$(x - x_i)(-\sin \hat{\theta}_i - \Delta \cos \hat{\theta}_i) + (y - y_i)(\cos \hat{\theta}_i - \Delta \sin \hat{\theta}_i) < 0(i = 1, \cdots, n) \qquad (4)$$

$$(x - x_i)(\sin \hat{\theta}_i - \Delta \cos \hat{\theta}_i) + (y - y_i)(-\cos \hat{\theta}_i - \Delta \sin \hat{\theta}_i) < 0(i = 1, \cdots, n) \qquad (5)$$

4 Iterative Algorithm of MLE

Note that the solution of MLE is a nonlinear programming. The time complexity is high. Now the iterative algorithm of MLE is given as follows.

Rewrite (4)(5) as

$$-x\sin \hat{\theta}_i + y\cos \hat{\theta}_i - \Delta((x - x_i)\cos \hat{\theta}_i + (y - y_i)\sin \hat{\theta}_i) < -x_i \sin \hat{\theta}_i + y_i \cos \hat{\theta}_i (i = 1, \cdots, n) \qquad (6)$$

$$x\sin \hat{\theta}_i - y\cos \hat{\theta}_i - \Delta((x - x_i)\cos \hat{\theta}_i + (y - y_i)\sin \hat{\theta}_i) < x_i \sin \hat{\theta}_i - y_i \cos \hat{\theta}_i (i = 1, \cdots, n) \qquad (7)$$

approximate (6)(7) as

$$-x\sin \hat{\theta}_i + y\cos \hat{\theta}_i - \Delta((x_p - x_i)\cos \hat{\theta}_i + (y_p - y_i)\sin \hat{\theta}_i) < -x_i \sin \hat{\theta}_i + y_i \cos \hat{\theta}_i (i = 1, \cdots, n)$$

$$x\sin \hat{\theta}_i - y\cos \hat{\theta}_i - \Delta((x_p - x_i)\cos \hat{\theta}_i + (y_p - y_i)\sin \hat{\theta}_i) < x_i \sin \hat{\theta}_i - y_i \cos \hat{\theta}_i (i = 1, \cdots, n)$$

$\begin{pmatrix} x_p \\ y_p \end{pmatrix}$ is given as initial coordinate of the target, which is given

by $p = \begin{pmatrix} x_p \\ y_p \end{pmatrix} = (A_L^T A)^{-1} A_L^T b_L$.

The linear programming model is given by

$$\min \Delta$$

$$-x\sin\hat{\theta_i} + y\cos\hat{\theta_i} - \Delta((x_p - x_i)\cos\hat{\theta_i} + (y_p - y_i)\sin\hat{\theta_i}) < -x_i\sin\hat{\theta_i} + y_i\cos\hat{\theta_i} (i=1,\cdots,n)$$

$$x\sin\hat{\theta_i} - y\cos\hat{\theta_i} - \Delta((x_p - x_i)\cos\hat{\theta_i} + (y_p - y_i)\sin\hat{\theta_i}) < x_i\sin\hat{\theta_i} - y_i\cos\hat{\theta_i} (i=1,\cdots,n)$$

where

$$A_1 = \begin{pmatrix} -\sin\hat{\theta_1} & \cos\hat{\theta_1} & -((x_p - x_1)\cos\hat{\theta_i} + (y_p - y_1)\sin\hat{\theta_i}) \\ \vdots & \vdots & \vdots \\ -\sin\hat{\theta_i} & \cos\hat{\theta_i} & -((x_p - x_i)\cos\hat{\theta_i} + (y_p - y_i)\sin\hat{\theta_i}) \\ \vdots & \vdots & \vdots \\ -\sin\hat{\theta_n} & \cos\hat{\theta_n} & -((x_p - x_n)\cos\hat{\theta_i} + (y_p - y_n)\sin\hat{\theta_i}) \end{pmatrix}$$

$$A_2 = \begin{pmatrix} \sin\hat{\theta_1} & -\cos\hat{\theta_1} & -((x_p - x_1)\cos\hat{\theta_i} + (y_p - y_1)\sin\hat{\theta_i}) \\ \vdots & \vdots & \vdots \\ \sin\hat{\theta_i} & -\cos\hat{\theta_i} & -((x_p - x_i)\cos\hat{\theta_i} + (y_p - y_i)\sin\hat{\theta_i}) \\ \vdots & \vdots & \vdots \\ \sin\hat{\theta_n} & -\cos\hat{\theta_n} & -((x_p - x_n)\cos\hat{\theta_i} + (y_p - y_n)\sin\hat{\theta_i}) \end{pmatrix}$$

$$A_p = \begin{pmatrix} A_1 \\ A_2 \end{pmatrix}$$

$$b_1 = \begin{pmatrix} -x_1\sin\hat{\theta_1} + y_1\cos\hat{\theta_1} \\ \vdots \\ -x_i\sin\hat{\theta_i} + y_i\cos\hat{\theta_i} \\ \vdots \\ -x_n\sin\hat{\theta_n} + y_n\cos\hat{\theta_n} \end{pmatrix}, \quad b_p = \begin{pmatrix} b_1 \\ -b_1 \end{pmatrix}$$

The iterative algorithm of MLE is presented as

Input: $p = \begin{pmatrix} x_p \\ y_p \end{pmatrix} = \left(A_L^T A\right)^{-1} A_L^T b_L$, A_p, b_p, error bound $\varepsilon > 0$;

Output: target coordinate $p = \begin{pmatrix} x_p \\ y_p \end{pmatrix}$.

(1) If $\left\|p - linprog(\Delta, A_p, b_p)\right\| < \varepsilon$, stop and output $p = linprog(\Delta, A_p, b_p)$; otherwise, goto(2).

(2) Let $p = linprog(\Delta, A_p, b_p)$, goto(1).

5   Simulation Experiment

Assume that the coordinates of Base Stations are presented as follows(Figure.1): $(0,0)$; $(0,R)$; $(0,-R)$; $(R\cos(\pi/6), R\sin(\pi/6))$; $(R\cos(\pi/6), -R\sin(\pi/6))$; $(-R\cos(\pi/6), -R\sin(\pi/6))$; $(-R\cos(\pi/6), R\sin(\pi/6))$. Assume that the coordinates of target are presented as follows(figure.1): $(\dfrac{R}{2}\cos\dfrac{k\pi}{30}, \dfrac{R}{3}\sin\dfrac{k\pi}{30})$ $(k = 0, \cdots, 59)$.

Assume that $\varepsilon = 0.001$, $R = 1$, $n_i \sim U(-\dfrac{k\pi}{360}, -\dfrac{k\pi}{360})$ ($k = 1, \cdots, 10$). Our simulations were run using 60 target positions and 10 noise levels each of which is tested 10 times. The RMSs of error and means of error between MLE iterative algorithm and LSE are compared as Figure.2 and Figure.3

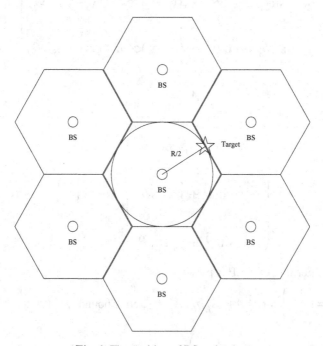

Fig. 1. The position of BS and target

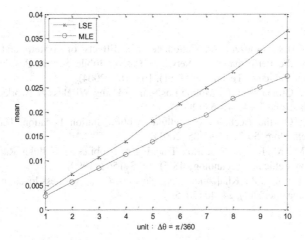

Fig. 2. The means of error between LSE and MSE iterative algorithm to variant noise levels

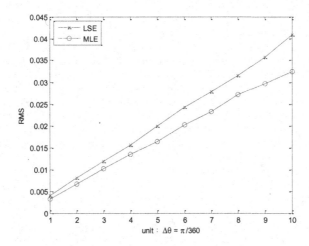

Fig. 3. The RMSs of error between LSE and MSE iterative algorithm to variant noise levels

6   Conclusion and Future

Figure.2 and Figure.3 show RMS and mean of error by MLE iterative method are less than those of LSE, which is clear in accordance with various noise levels. To conclude, the method we proposed is less error and more robust to noise disturbance than LSE method.

References

1. Botteron, C., Host Madsen, A., Fattouche, M.: Effects of System and environment Parameters on the Performance of Network- Based Mobile Station Position Estimators. IEEE Trans. on Vehicular Technology 53(1), 163–180 (2004)
2. Gustafsson, F., Gunnarsson, F.: Mobile Positioning Using Wireless Networks. IEEE Signal Processing Magazine 22(4), 41–53 (2005)
3. Spirito, M.A.: On the Accuracy of Cellular Mobile Station Location. IEEE Trans. on Vehicular Technology 50(3), 674–685 (2001)
4. Hellebrandt, M., Mathar, R.: Location Tracking of Mobiles in Cellular Radio Networks. IEEE Trans. on Vehicular Technology 48(5), 1558–1562 (1999)
5. Sayed, A.H., Tarighat, A., Khajehnouri, N.: Network-Based wireless location. IEEE Signal Processing Magazine 22(4), 24–40 (2005)

Design and Implementation of Resource Management Tool for Virtual Machine

Byung Ki Kim[1,*], Young Jun Yoo[1], Chuck Yoo[2], and Young Woong Ko[1]

[1] Dept. of Computer Engineering, Hallym University, Chuncheon, Korea
{bkkim,willow72,yuko}@hallym.ac.kr
[2] Dept. of Computer Science and Engineering, Korea University, Seoul, Korea
hxy@os.korea.ac.kr

Abstract. To support real time task in a virtual machine, hypervisor have to monitor system resource and provide exact resource for real time task. There are several monitor tools running on virtual machine, however, it has limitations on supporting detailed information for monitoring real time workload, performance degradation and difficult for controlling user interface. In this work, we proposed a resource monitoring and feedback tool for Xen virtual machine called XMM. XMM provides accurate resource monitoring in a hypervisor level without incurring much overhead. We also provide a GUI based control tool adjusting system resources based on user intervention, which can be useful in a multimedia system where user preference is important. XMM shows lots of information reflecting system behavior and it can give scheduling feedback for handling real time task. We believe XMM can be a useful tool for Xen virtual machine for various purposes.

Keywords: Xen, realtime, scheduler, QoS, resource monitor.

1 Introduction

Virtualization is gaining popularity in enterprise environments, embedded systems, and desktop systems as a software solution [1]. Virtualization reduces hardware costs by consolidating the workloads of several under utilized servers to fewer machines. Especially, much attention has been given to supporting time critical workloads in virtualization systems. However, current virtualization systems have difficulty supporting real time workloads, such as streaming servers, game servers, and telephone servers. In virtualization environments, it is difficult to support real time guarantees because virtualization systems experience long delays when domains switch between CPUs [2]. A delay can be generated when a domain does not have access to a CPU. Therefore, to guarantee real time execution of a task, we have to minimize the delay in virtualization. In a VM, there

---

* This work was supported by the National Research Foundation of Korea(NRF) grant funded by the Korea government(MEST) (No. 2011-0029848), and Basic Science Research Program through the National Research Foundation of Korea(NRF) funded by the Ministry of Education, Science and Technology(2010-0005442).

T.-h. Kim et al. (Eds.): FGCN/DCA 2012, CCIS 350, pp. 17–24, 2012.
© Springer-Verlag Berlin Heidelberg 2012

are many requirements for supporting real time characteristics. To support real time tasks in a VM, it is necessary to monitor and control resources, including CPUs, memory, and I/O devices. Recently, several monitoring tools, including Xenmon, have been released to run on virtual machines. However, there are limitations on supporting detailed information for monitoring real time workloads. Furthermore, frequent access to trace buffers severely degrades overall system performance. In this chapter, we propose a light weight monitoring tool for a Xen VM, which provides high accuracy workload monitoring; users can monitor high volumes of system information with low overhead. We also provide user friendly GUI tools.

2   Related Work

To support predictable resource monitoring, the Xen hypervisor must provide monitoring and controlling tools to trace physical resources, such as memory, disks, and CPUs. Currently, many research groups are actively working on implementing resource monitoring tools, including Gprof [3], Oprofile [4], XenOprof [5], and Xenmon [6]. Gprof is a call graph execution profiler, which creates a call graph that functions in a program call in detail, measure the processing time in each program. Although Gprof takes a significant amount of time because it is called at fairly frequent intervals, it is useful for optimization. To construct the call graph properly, Gprof infers symbolic information from the source code. Oprofile is a system wide profiler for Linux systems, capable of profiling all running code at low overhead. It profiles various hardware events, such as clock cycles, instructions, cache misses, etc. Oprofile consists of a kernel driver and a daemon for collecting sample data, and several post profiling tools for turning data into information. Xenoprof is an extended Oprofile with a Xen specific driver. Xenoprof is a system wide statistical profiling toolkit implemented for Xen virtual machine environments. Xenoprof maps performance events to specific H/W performance counters. It supports system wide coordinated profiling in a Xen environment to obtain the hypercalls for setup, stop, and start event sampling. Xenoprof allows profiling of concurrently executing VMs and the Xen VMM. Xen provides management user interfaces. The xm program is the main interface for managing Xen guest domains. The xm with various options may be invoked individually as command line arguments in shell mode. This can be used to create, pause, and shutdown domains. It can also be used to list current domains, enable or pin VCPUs, and attach or detach virtual block devices. Because of its interface, there is a need for handy tools . XenMon periodically aggregates a variety of metrics across all VMs. They use Xentrace, which is a light weight event logging facility present in Xen. Xentrace is used to capture trace buffer data from Xen. All of the events that have occurred in Xen are logged into trace buffers. Their contribution is to determine the right set of events to monitor. Logs generated by Xentrace are too big to use efficiently. Therefore, they provide a user space processing tool that polls the trace buffers for new events and processes them into meaningful information called xenbaked.

Information processed by xenbaked displays and logs data through Xenmon. But Xenmon often requires a significant amount of time to access trace buffers. Other researchers are working on the tracing performance of Virtual systems. Although these approaches provide a great deal of information to virtualization systems, they have limitations in supporting real time workloads executed in guest operating systems. Also, these tools are displayed in console mode only and are not easy to use. Furthermore, it is uncomfortable to monitor and adjust system resources with them. For example, in Xenmon, one typical monitoring tool, if administrators want to adjust domain resource allocation in real time, it is difficult to change the system configuration while watching system information. We proposed a resource monitoring and feedback tool for the Xen VMM, called Xen Monitor and Manager (XMM). Our primary goal is to provide accurate resource monitoring on a hypervisor level without incurring much overhead. We also provided a GUI based control tool, adjusting system resources based on user intervention, which can be useful in a multimedia system where user preference is important. If a domain needs more CPU resources for handling multimedia tasks, XMM can boost up the domain through the simple click of a button. In this work, to show that our prototype monitor is practical, we implemented QoS monitoring interfaces and control mechanisms for scheduling parameters.

3   Design and Implementation of the Monitoring Tool

In Figure 1, we described the overall architecture of the proposed system. The grey colored boxes represent extended parts of the previous Xen VM. We implemented an XMM module on Dom0 and modified the Xentrace module to

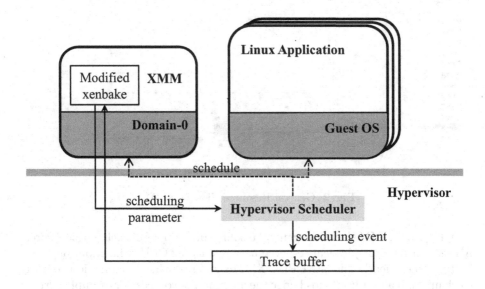

Fig. 1. The general architecture of XMM

provide more information for XMM. XMM can control and collect information from the hypervisor using the hypercall interface. XMM can provide convenient monitoring and profiling using xenbaked. We extended Xentrace to provide more information and utilized trace buffer information to collect Xen hypercalls, such as scheduling information, IRQs, and the number of hypercall counts. The extended Xentrace includes the creation and deletion of domains, and switching and paging information, which is not supported in Xenmon. Furthermore, we implemented a scheduler statistic module in the Credit scheduler so that the XMM can trace scheduling events to characterize domains. With this information, it is possible to easily recognize the characteristics of a domain. For example, if a domain frequently uses network related hypercall and interrupt, we assume this domain is network intensive. Otherwise, we can assume it is I/O bound or CPU intensive. This information can be used to select scheduling policies for future work.

3.1   Monitoring Tool

The XMM is not only used for resource monitoring but also for controlling a domains resources. To control a domains resources, Xen provides xm tools for general purposes, such as boot, shutdown, suspend, and so on. But this traditional control interface via the console user interface has difficulty allocating resources properly while monitoring in real time. Therefore, we propose a combination of its monitoring tool and controllers through a graphical display and interface.

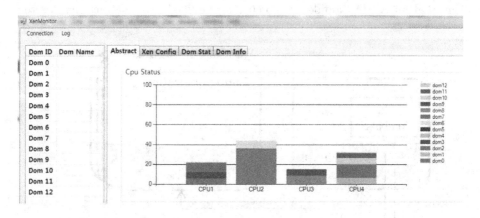

Fig. 2. General Resource View of XMM

In Figure 2, XMM shows the general resource utilizations of each physical core. A user can monitor physical resource usages, such as CPU utilization, on each PCPU. To efficiently allocate CPUs, XMM should provide an admission control mechanism. If a user wants to change the amount of resources, for example period and slice in the SEDF scheduler, there is an interface where the user can select a domain ID and input the scheduling parameter. Figure 3 shows the XMM resource control module, where the user can see domain specific workloads and control scheduling information.

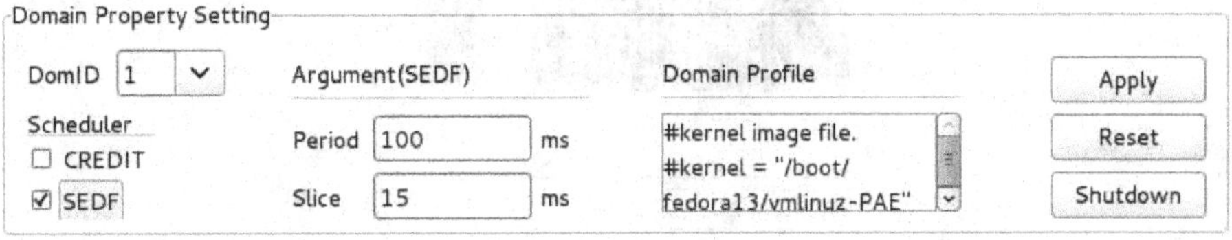

Fig. 3. Interface for control the schedule parameter

In our work, if we click on scheduling information, such as period and slice, we can change the amounts for the domain resources. XMM will sends domctl hypercall to update the scheduling parameters. If we specify a domain as real time, XMM increases or decreases the amount of CPU allocation for a domain.

3.2 Scheduler Monitor

XMM provides detailed scheduler information. Figure 4 presents the results of the analysis of scheduling events. From these scheduler profiling results, we can determine the characteristics of the domain behavior. It presents the four important characterization features to the VM. A VM can have one or more VCPU(s), so the XMM presents the scheduling events of a VCPU as a unit. Firstly, the CPU utilization of each VCPU is considered. Secondly, the load balance count shows the number of times the VCPU migrates across the physical cores. Thirdly, the schedule count number with different priorities is represented. Finally, the CPU usage of each priority is provided. In the credit scheduler, this information is useful to characterize the VM.

4 Scheduling Events Analysis

For this experiment, we classified the domains for CPUs, disks, and networks and measured the scheduling events within the hypervisor. We booted up four domains with one VCPU allocated. All domains were pinned to a PCPU, not to be moved to another PCPU through load balancing. Three domains had CPU intensive jobs that consumed 25% of their CPU share by periodically calculating MD5 hash. We examined the target domains running information from the hypervisor view using Xentrace.

- CPU : Calculate 1.2MB MD5 hash for every 30ms (25% of CPU share)
- Disk I/O : Copy a file from disk
- Network I/O : Send a file to the external server (read from disk and send packets through the network)

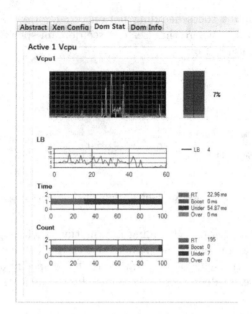

Fig. 4. Tracing scheduler information

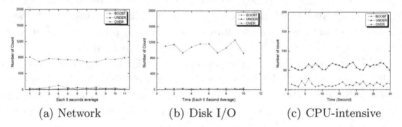

| (a) Network | (b) Disk I/O | (c) CPU-intensive |

Fig. 5. Scheduling count for different workload

Figure 5(a) shows the scheduled count number that the target domain scheduled while using the network . This domain will increase network I/O requests through Dom0. We can see that Credit schedules the domain with BOOST priority most of the time. Figure 6(a) represents the runtime for each priority. Compared to the scheduled number, the domain with BOOST priority consumed CPUs quickly, but Dom0 CPU utilization increased. Because of Xens split driver model, I/O requests were handled by Dom0. Furthermore, an idle domain was scheduled and spent more than the target domain; the target domain was underutilized. We know that network intensive domains are scheduled with BOOST priority most of time but do not spend a lot of their CPU shares.

To analyze the I/O intensive domains, we collected domain scheduling information while domains copy a file using the cp command. In Figure 5(b), the domain was scheduled with BOOST priority. It was scheduled with the BOOST state many times but expended short time periods (less than 1 ms). Similar

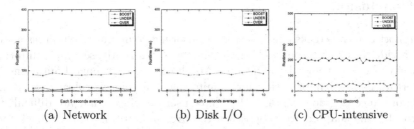

(a) Network   (b) Disk I/O   (c) CPU-intensive

Fig. 6. Running time for different workload

to Figure 5(a), target domains were scheduled often, but CPU utilization was very low because these domains quickly blocked after requests for I/O and after Dom0 processed the I/O requests, the Xen scheduler changed the priorities of these domains to BOOST. Although the domains were in the UNDER state, they spent a short period of time compared to CPU intensive domains. If two or more CPU intensive domains were mapped on the same PCPU, there was CPU contention because the domains compete for scheduling. In this situation, the Credit scheduler will schedule domains fairly.

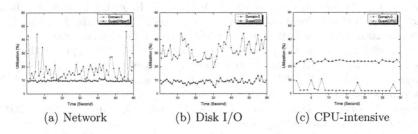

(a) Network   (b) Disk I/O   (c) CPU-intensive

Fig. 7. CPU utilization

We measured the CPU intensive domains scheduling information. Figure 5(c) shows the time schedule counts for each priority per second. Figure 6(c) shows the average time spent in each priority per second. In this result, we see that most of the time, this VCPU spent CPUs (credits) with UNDER priority. Because this domain did not request I/O, there was less of the BOOST state. And because this domain spent most of its CPU time in the UNDER priority, it is CPU intensive. CPU intensive domains have a lower context switch rate than I/O intensive domains. Figure 7(c) indicates that the CPU intensive domain was scheduled with UNDER priority most of the time. This domain consumed CPUs more than the BOOST priority. Because of the periodic tasks in the target domain, there was BOOST priority but only a short period of time was spent. The other domains consumed CPUs periodically. There was a low context switch rate and CPU shares were consumed stably.

5 Conclusion

To support real time tasks in a VM, a hypervisor has to monitor system resources and provide the exact resources for real time tasks. Currently, several monitoring tools have been developed to run on VMs, however, they have limitations in supporting detailed information for monitoring real time workloads, resulting in performance degradation, and they have user interfaces that are difficult to control. In this chapter, we proposed a resource monitoring and feedback tool for a Xen VM, called XMM. XMM provides accurate resource monitoring on a hypervisor level without incurring much overhead. We also provide a GUI based control tool that can adjust system resources based on user intervention, which can be useful in a multimedia system where user preference is important. XMM provides a great deal of information reflecting system behavior and scheduling feedback for handling real time tasks. XMM can detect resource overload and control resource allocation for each VM. We believe that XMM can be a useful tool for the Xen virtual machine, fulfilling various purposes.

References

1. Gupta, D., Cherkasova, L., Gardner, R., Vahdat, A.: Enforcing Performance Isolation Across Virtual Machines in Xen. In: van Steen, M., Henning, M. (eds.) Middleware 2006. LNCS, vol. 4290, pp. 342–362. Springer, Heidelberg (2006)
2. Cherkasova, L., Gupta, D., Vahdat, A.: Comparison of the three cpu schedulers in xen. ACM SIGMETRICS Performance Evaluation Review 35(2), 42–51 (2007)
3. Graham, S., Kessler, P., Mckusick, M.: Gprof: A call graph execution profiler. ACM Sigplan Notices 17(6), 120–126 (1982)
4. Levon, J., Elie, P.: Oprofile, a system-wide profiler for linux systems (2008), http://oprofile.sourceforge.net
5. Menon, A., Santos, J., Turner, Y., Janakiraman, G., Zwaenepoel, W.: Diagnosing performance overheads in the xen virtual machine environment. In: Proceedings of the 1st ACM/USENIX International Conference on Virtual Execution Environments, pp. 13–23. ACM (2005)
6. Gupta, D., Gardner, R., Cherkasova, L.: Xenmon: Qos monitoring and performance profiling tool. Architecture (Technical Report HPL-2005-187), pp. 1–13 (2005)

Data Link Layer' Security Analysis
for Wireless Sensor Networks

Ndibanje Bruce[1], Tae-Yong Kim[2], and Hoon Jae Lee[2]

[1] Department of Ubiquitous IT, Graduate School of General, Dongseo University,
Busan, 617-716, South Korea
[2] Division of Computer and Engineering, Dongseo University, Busan, 617-716, South Korea
bruce.dongseo.korea@gmail.com, tykimw2k@gdsu.dongseo.ac.kr,
hjlee@dongseo.ac.kr

Abstract. Nowadays, the most exciting and challenging research domain remains Wireless Sensor Networks due to their rapidly progress in Information and Communication Technology. Follow-on different debates over the most effective means of securing wireless sensor networks, the intent of this paper is to investigate the security issues and challenges as well as solutions in WSN. Authentication is the primary focus, as the most malicious attacks on a network are the work of imposters, such as DOS attacks. Nevertheless, the data link layer is not spared, in this paper we emphasized on it for the reason that it handles everything within one hop such as the media access control (MAC), the error control (EC) and the power control (PC) while the link layer specifies the handshakes and handles retransmissions.

Keywords: Data Link Layer, WSN, Issues, Sensors Nodes, Attacks, Countermeasure.

1 Introduction

A WSN is a large network of resource-constrained sensor nodes with multiple preset functions, such as sensing and processing, for fulfilling different application objectives. The major elements of WSN are the sensor nodes and the base stations. In fact, they can be abstracted as the "sensing cells" and the "brain" of the network, respectively. Sensor nodes are static most of the time, whereas mobile nodes can be deployed according to application requirements. After an event of interest occurs, one of the surrounding sensor nodes can detect it, generate a report, and transmit the report to a BS through multi hop wireless links. In wireless sensor networks, it is critical to restrict the network access only to eligible sensor nodes, while messages from outsiders should not be forwarded in the networks. Moreover, outsiders cannot eavesdrop, modify or forge packets from eligible nodes inside the sensor network. Since sensor nodes are highly constrained in terms of resources, satisfying the security protocols in an efficient way (using less energy [1], computational time and memory space) without sacrificing the strength of their security properties is one of the major challenges.

T.-h. Kim et al. (Eds.): FGCN/DCA 2012, CCIS 350, pp. 25–32, 2012.
© Springer-Verlag Berlin Heidelberg 2012

A WSN protocol stack is typically presented by five layers, as presented in Fig. 1. Most notably, session layer is not usually utilized and a WSN transport protocol rarely utilizes end-to-end flow control. The middleware layer implements API for WSN applications and may contain sophisticated functionality for task allocation and resource sharing. It is often seen as a part of application layer [2-3].

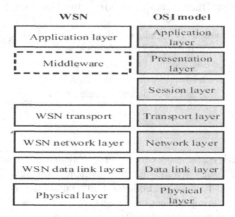

Fig. 1. OSI model and WSN protocol layers [2]

In this work, we discuss the security issues and challenges on the most attacks and proposed solutions in WSN. In particular, we emphasize on the security issues of the Data Link Layer.

Organization. The paper is organized as follows. Section 2 describes the communication in WSN on protocol layers. The Section 3 details the issues and challenges in WSN and countermeasure. We present the secure Data Link Layer in Section 4 and make an examination to the countermeasures against susceptible attacks. Section 5 presents the evaluation of the security performance given by the countermeasures in WSN. Finally we conclude in Section 6 where we provide some direction for future work regarding the emergence of the WNS and their vulnerabilities.

2   Communication in Wireless Sensor Networks

2.1   Sensor Node Components

A sensor node consists of five basic parts: sensing unit, central processing unit (CPU), storage unit, transceiver unit, and power unit [4] as shown in Fig. 2. It may also have additional application dependent components attached, such as location finding system (GPS), mobilize and power generator. The lifetime of a sensor node depends to a large extent on the battery lifetime; hence it is extremely important to adopt energy-efficient strategies for information processing. By definition, a sensor node is a device that can observe or control physical parameters of the environment which is converted to digital signals by the ADC, and then fed into the processing unit. A transceiver unit connects the node to the network. Power units may be supported by power scavenging units such as solar cells.

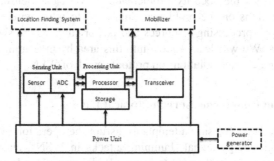

Fig. 2. The Sensor Node components

A mobilizer may sometimes be needed to move sensor nodes when it is required to carry out the assigned tasks. The sensor nodes rely on wireless channels via transceiver for transmitting data to and receiving data from other nodes.

2.2   Communication Protocol Stack

The protocol stack used in sensor nodes contains main protocols such as management and communication protocols. Those protocols include the physical, data link, network, transport, and application layers for the communication protocol combining task, mobility and power management plane for the management protocol as defined in Fig. 3.

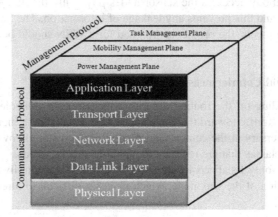

Fig. 3. Generic Protocol Stack for Sensor Networks [5]

The task management plane balances and schedules the sensing tasks given to a specific region. These management planes are needed so that sensor nodes can work together in a power efficient way, route data in a mobile sensor network, and share resources between sensor nodes [5].

3   WSN Security Issues and Challenges

This section describes the security problematic in Wireless Sensor Networks and presents some solutions on the problems. Compared to other wireless technologies, such as WLANs [6], processing resources and power supplies are significantly more stringent in WSNs. We will lead readers into this area by presenting a review [7] of various potential attacks and solutions on protocol stack of WSN.

3.1   Attacks and Countermeasure in Physical Layer

Jamming Attack. The adversary attempts to disrupt the operation of the network by broadcasting a high-energy signal. Jamming attacks in WSNs, classifying them as constant (corrupts packets as they are transmitted), deceptive (sends a constant stream of bytes into the network to make it look like legitimate traffic), random (randomly alternates between sleep and jamming to save energy), and reactive (transmits a jam signal when it senses traffic). To defense against this attack, use spread spectrum techniques for radio communication

Tempering Attack. The simplest way to attack is to damage or modify sensors physically and thus stop or alter their services given physical access to a node. The negative impact will be greater if base stations or aggregation points are attacked, since the former carry more responsibility of communications and/or data processing. Another way to attack is to capture sensors and extract sensitive data from them such as cryptographic keys or other data on the node. One defense to this attack involves tamper-proofing the node's physical package, self destruction (tamper-proofing packages) – whenever somebody accesses the sensor nodes physically the nodes vaporize their memory contents and this prevents any leakage of information. The Second defense is Fault Tolerant Protocols; the protocols designed for a WSN should be resilient to this type of attacks.

3.2   Attacks and Countermeasure in Network Layer

Sinkhole. Depending on the routing algorithm technique, a sinkhole attack tries to lure almost all the traffic toward the compromised node, creating a metaphorical sinkhole with the adversary at the center. Geo-routing protocols are known as one of the routing protocol classes that are resistant to sinkhole attacks, because that topology is constructed using only localized information, and traffic is naturally routed through the physical location of the sink node, which makes it difficult to lure it elsewhere to create a sinkhole.

Selective Forwarding/ Black Hole Attack (Neglect and Greed). WSNs are usually multi-hop networks and hence based on the assumption that the participating nodes will forward the messages faithfully. Malicious or attacking nodes can however refuse to route certain messages and drop them. If they drop all the packets through them, then it is called a Black Hole Attack. However if they selectively forward the packets, then it is called selective forwarding. To overcome this, Multi path routing can be used in combination with random selection of paths to destination, or braided paths can be used which represent paths which have no common link or which do not have two consecutive common nodes, or use implicit acknowledgments, which ensure that packets are forwarded as they were sent.

3.3   Attacks and Countermeasure in Transport Layer

Flooding. An attacker may repeatedly make new connection requests until the re-sources required by each connection are exhausted or reach a maximum limit. It pro-duces severe resource constraints for legitimate nodes. One proposed solution to this problem is to require that each connecting client demonstrate its commitment to the connection by solving a puzzle. As a defense against this class of attack, a limit can be put on the number of connections from a particular node.

De-synchronization Attacks. In this attack, the adversary repeatedly forges messages to one or both end points which request transmission of missed frames. Hence, these messages are again transmitted and if the adversary maintains a proper timing, it can prevent the end points from exchanging any useful information. This will cause a considerable drainage of energy of legitimate nodes in the network in an endless syn-chronization-recovery protocol. A possible solution to this type of attack is to require authentication of all packets including control fields communicated between hosts. Header or full packet authentication can defeat such an attack.

4   Secure Data Link Layer for WSN

4.1   Attacks and Countermeasure in Data Link Layer

Continuous Channel Access (Exhaustion). A malicious node disrupts the Media Access Control protocol, by continuously requesting or transmitting over the channel. This eventually leads a starvation for other nodes in the network with respect to channel access. One of the countermeasures to such an attack is Rate Limiting to the MAC ad-mission control such that the network can ignore excessive requests, thus preventing the energy drain caused by repeated transmissions. A second technique is to use time divi-sion multiplexing where each node is allotted a time slot in which it can transmit.

Collision. This is very much similar to the continuous channel attack. A collision occurs when two nodes attempt to transmit on the same frequency simultaneously. When packets collide, a change will likely occur in the data portion, causing a check-sum mismatch at the receiving end. The packet will then be discarded as invalid. A typical defense against collisions is the use of error-correcting codes.

Interrogation. Exploits the two-way request-to send/ clear to send (RTS/CTS) hand-shake that many MAC protocols use to mitigate the hidden-node problem. An attacker can exhaust a node's resources by repeatedly sending RTS messages to elicit CTS responses from a targeted neighbor node. To put a defense against such type of at-tacks a node can limit itself in accepting connections from same identity or use Anti replay protection and strong link-layer authentication.

Table 1. Data Link Layer MAC Protocols and their impacts to WSN

MAC Protocol	Impact to WSN
IEEE 802.11 with distributed coordination function using (DCF) [8]	The nodes use CSMA / CA mechanism and avoid time at random to realize the wireless channel share when the wireless channels are busy.
IEEE 802.11 with point coordination function using (PCF)[9]	It coordinates node data transmission through the access points, queries which nodes currently have the request of data transmission by polling mode, and gives the right to send data when it is necessary.
S-MAC (sensor-medium access control) protocol[10]	S-MAC aims at reducing energy consumption from all possible sources which cause energy waste, and provide a good expandability through the cyclical mechanism periodically. Nodes are synchronized to go to sleep and wake up at the same time
T-MAC (timeout MAC) protocol [11]	T-MAC protocol uses the periodicity interception or sleep mechanism to reduce energy consumption on the circumstances of lower information transmission frequency
DMAC protocol[12]	DMAC protocol is presented according to data gathering tree structure, which adopts a staggered scheduling mechanism; data are continuously transmitted from the data source node to clustering node, which reduce the transmission delay in the network, so the network energy consumption and data transmission delay are greatly reduced.

5   Security Analysis Performances

In shortly, the goal of security is to provide security services to defend against all the kinds of threat explained in this paper. This section present the security analysis performance regarding the security issues discussed above.   The analysis of security and survivability requirements of the WSN is done based on the design goals of scalability, efficiency, key connectivity, resilience and reliability [13]. Security services include the following [14]:

Authentication ensures that the other end of a connection or the originator of a packet is the node that is claimed.

Access-control prevents unauthorized access to a resource.

Confidentiality protects overall content or a field in a message. Confidentiality can also be required to prevent an adversary from undertaking traffic analysis.

Privacy prevents adversaries from obtaining information that may have private content. The private information may be obtained through the analysis of traffic patterns, i.e. frequency, source node, routes, etc.

Authorization: authorizes another node to update information (import authorization) or to receive information (export authorization).

Anonymity hides the source of a packet or frame. It is a service that can help with data confidentiality and privacy.

Non-repudiation proves the source of a packet. In authentication the source proves its identity. Non repudiation prevents the source from denying that it sent a packet.

Freshness ensures that a malicious node does not resend previously captured packets.

Availability mainly targets DoS attacks and is the ability to sustain the networking functionalities without any interruption due to security threats.

Resilience to attacks required to sustain the network functionalities when a portion of nodes is compromised or destroyed.

Forward secrecy a sensor should not be able to read any future messages after it leaves the network.

6   Conclusions and Future Work

This paper investigates on the security related issues and challenges with solutions in WSN. The attacks classifications and countermeasures   in wireless sensor have been presented and we explored attacks and countermeasures on the data link layer. This work motivates researchers and designers to come up with smarter and more robust security mechanisms and make their network safer. What is certain is that, security is playing a pivotal role in this eventual ubiquity of wireless sensor networks, and therefore will continue to be a major research area for the foreseeable future. Continued research into the suitability and efficiency of security architectures for WSNs will be carried out through both implementation and simulation. The focus is on making the scheme suitable in general for all layers of WSNs and in particular for the data link layer, whether security dependant or not, in a manner accessible to all network designers.

Acknowledgements. This research was supported by Basic Science Research Program through the National Research Foundation of Korea (NRF) funded by the Ministry of Education, Science and Technology (grant number: 2012-0008447). And it also supported by the IT R&D program of MKE/KEIT (10041682).

References

1. Sharma, A., Shinghal, K., Srivastava, N., Singh, R.: Energy Management for Wireless Sensor Network Nodes. International Journal of Advances in Engineering & Technology 1(1), 7–13 (2011)
2. Kuorilehto, M., Kohvakka, M., Suhonen, J., Hamalainen, P., Hannikainen, M., Hamalainen, T.D.: Ultra-Low Energy Wireless Sensor Networks in Practice: Theory, Realization and Deployment. Tampere University of Technology, Finland (2007)

3. Hassanzdeh, N.: Scalable Data Collection for Wireless Sensors Networks. Swedish Institute of Computer Science, Stockholm, Sweden XR-EE-LCN (2012)
4. Akyildiz, I.F., Su, W., Sankarasubramaniam, Y., Cayirci, E.: A survey on sensor networks. IEEE Commun. Mag., 102–114 (August 2002)
5. Zheng, J., Jamallipour, A.: Wireless Sensor Network. A Networking Perspective. IEEE (2009) ISBN: 178-0-470-16763-2
6. Souppaya, M., Scarfone, K.: Recommendations of the National Institute of Standards and Technology (NIST). Guidelines for Securing Wireless Local Area Networks (WLANs), U.S Department of Commerce, Special Publication 800-153 (February 2012)
7. Xing, K., Sundhar, S., Srinivasan, R., Rivera, M., Li, J., Cheng, X.: Attacks and Countermeasures in Sensor Networks: A Survey. Network Security (2005)
8. Van Dam, T., Langendoen, K.: An adaptive energy-efficient MAC protocol for wireless sensor networks. In: Proc 1st Ibt'l Conf. on Embedded Networked Sensor Systems, Los Angeles (2003)
9. Lu, G., Machari, K., Raghavendra, C.: An adaptive energy efficient and low-latency MAC for data gathering in wireless sensor networks. In: Proc 18th Int'l Parallel and Distributed Processing Symp. (IPDPS 2004), New Mexico (2004)
10. Mahajan, L., Kaur, S.: Medium Access Control Optimization for Wireless Sensor Networks. International Journal of Computer Science and Technology 1(1), 8 (2010)
11. Ganeriwal, S., Kumar, R., Srivastava, M.: Timing2sync protocol for sensor networks. In: Proceedings of t he 1st ACM Conference on Embedded Networked Sensor Systems, Los Angeles (2003)
12. Van Dam, T., Langendoen, K.: An adaptive energy-efficient MAC protocol for wireless sensor networks. In: Proc 1st Ibt'l Conf. on Embedded Networked Sensor Systems, Los Angeles (2003)
13. Camtepe, S.A., Yener, B.: Key management in wireless sensor network. In: Lopez, J., Zhou, J.Y. (eds.) Wireless Sensor Network Security. IOS Press (2008)
14. Altisen, K., Devismes, S., Lafourcade, P., Ponsonnet, C.: Secure Probabilistic Routing in Wireless Sensor Networks, Verimag Research Report, TR-2011-15g, ADPP-RR-2011

Design and Implementation of Packet Analyzer for IEC 61850 Communication Networks in Smart Grid

Changhun Lee, Myungoh Park, Jiyoung Lee, and Inwhee Joe

Division of Computer Science and Engineering
Hanyang University
iwjoe@hanyang.ac.kr

Abstract. In the aspect of stable operation for smart grid, the combination of communication technology is an important component. This paper proposes the design and implementation of a packet analyzer dedicated to IEC 61850 for effectively analyzing standard protocols for IEC 61850 communication networks. A substation automation system consists of a station, bay, and process level. Since the amount of packets is massive in IEC 61850, we need to develop a packet analyzer for analyzing communications between the substation automation system server and client, which demands real-time operation and high reliability. Our packet analyzer is implemented with FLA (fast later access) and DPI (deep packet inspection) features as a network application analyzing only IEC 61850 communication protocols. The experimental results show that our packet analyzer outperforms the existing Wireshark program significantly in terms of the packet analysis time.

Keywords: IEC 61850, Packet Analyzer, GOOSE, MMS, FLA, DPI.

1   Introduction

Recently, research on substation systems has been progressing towards automation: IEC 61850 is the international standard for a communication network in substation system [1]. Information Technology (IT) is necessary to the existing substation for automation and remote monitoring. These two new control systems associate with replacing existing electronic devices for an Intelligent Electronic Device (IED) [2] with the communication function of a microprocessor.

IEC 61850 standard substations consist of apparatus such as IED, network switches, Merging Unit (MU), and Human Machine Interface (HMI). Network protocols used in substation automation systems are indicated in related papers [3]. Stability of communication networks is one of the most important components in communication networks which automatically control electricity transmission and distribution. For stability, it is required to conduct research on analyzing traffic and packets on networks and operating internal substation networks safely and effectively [4]. Also, this analysis would be useful information when the scalability of equipment

T.-h. Kim et al. (Eds.): FGCN/DCA 2012, CCIS 350, pp. 33–40, 2012.

and system is needed. On substation networks where real-time operation and high reliability are required, there is a limitation for universal packet analyzer that analyzes all kinds of packets to classify and analyze large-capacity packets.

Manufacturing Message Specification (MMS), Generic Object Oriented Substation Event (GOOSE), Sampled Value (SV) messages on IEC 61850 networks transmit system operation, status information, warning message, and measured values, and levels where these messages are communicated are separated. These data consist of a large amount of information and include unique information classified by the type of messages. This information is crucial to maintain a transmission and distribution system.

A general purpose packet analyzer is implemented to analyze all kinds of packets and only provides simple traffic analysis. By using this packet analyzer, there are several problems that consume considerable analysis time while analyzing all packets and occupying system resources such as memory to maintain and control contents of analyzed packets. Also, this kind of packet analyzer cannot analyze several packets, but merely has a function of decomposing and arranging contents of a single packet one by one. Thus, extra programming works are required in order to analyze communication network with high reliability and stability like IEC 61850.

Packet analyzer dedicated IEC 61850 proposed in this paper analyzes only MMS, GOOSE, and SV, separating from other messages. We propose the Fast Later Access (FLA) method to solve re-decomposition problem, limitation of existing general-purpose analyzers, generated when analysis contents of packets are referred. Also, Deep Packet Inspection (DPI) analyzes payload of packets, extracts meaningful data, so that we can implement improved packet analysis function and enhance traffic analysis efficiency from this.

2   Features of IEC 61850

2.1   Substation Automation System

Electrical data are located into a database to operate, manage, and monitor in Substation Automation System (SAS) [5]. There are three levels in SAS based on IEC 61850: process level, bay level, station level. Current and voltage values are acquired in the process level and transmitted to the bay level. There are IEDs which operate like relay and controllers dealing with IEDs and communicates to lower levels, block commands to actuator, and station level transmits the result. Station level monitors and controls all systems in the substation.

IEC 61850 standard protocol is easy to integrate and manage systems and able to actively adapt to technical change since the protocol defines data level and communication level respectively [6]. Buses connect levels: a bus connecting between station level and level is called a station bus, and a bus connecting between the bay level and process level is called a process bus.

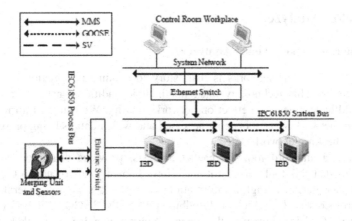

Fig. 1. Substation Automation System

2.2   Structure of Packets

GOOSE

GOOSE messages multicast and transmit errors or warning messages for trip command, interlocking information or status information of IED. Also, GOOSE messages have high priority. Information comprised in the GOOSE messages allows receivers to recognize what and when the device status changes. The time of the last status change makes a receiver response the related event that is previously inputted. The IEDs related to receiving messages make use of reports in order to decide proper protection response for the given state.

MMS

MMS messages contain general operation and information and have medium priority. A set of services and the responses is defined for all IEDs to behave in the same way as the network behavior perspective by The Abstract Communication Service Interface (ACSI) models of IEC 61850. MMS is the only public (ISO standard) protocol with proven implementation track record to assist with complex naming and service models of IEC 61850. MMS supports intricate named items and an abundant set of changeable services to map IEC 61850 directly. The performance of mapping IEC 61850 object and service models of MMS is based on implementing a variety of services of ACSI. As an example of this performance, the control model, one of services of ACSI, is mapped to read and write services of MMS.

MMS messages consist of unconfirmed service messages collecting periodic information, confirmed service messages transmitting more than 70 kinds of service messages, and initiate messages concerning with initial session setting. Confirmed service PDU basically consists of Request/Response TAG, InvokeID, Confirmed Service Tag, and Service Specific, and Service Specific follows MMS standard.

3   Packet Analyzer

3.1   General-Purpose Packet Analyzer

Analysis of packets on networks is mandatory to acquire information on network communications. This technology must not include additional network traffic and which would have a negative effect on network stability. We can get information on what kind of network service is being accessed and which data is being passed in the network by checking network traffic.

Wireshark, a standard tool for packet analysis, provides dissection capability, which means that this tool parses out and shows known fields of network traffic so that users can get meaningful information. Wireshark supports general-purpose SCADA protocols such as Fieldbus/Modbus, OPC, DNP3, GOOSE, IEC 60870-5-104, and IEEE C37.118; however, these general-purpose analyzers are likely to cause a significant load and are limited when traffic analysis of a special-purpose is required.

3.2   Packet Analysis Requirements for IEC 61850

For IEC 61850 communication protocols, communication layers are divided by characteristics of each layer, and message mapping or transmission method is divided by service or standard as mentioned above. Communication in the process bus requires high speed process. GOOSE message transmitting trip command communicates in station bus as well and should satisfy communication requirements under 3 ms. In a process bus, more rigorous high speed process is required than in real situation [7].

SAS should operate transmission and distribution systems stably with high speed message communication. In the process bus, a large load of traffic is generated because of rapid transmission of packets. In station bus as well, it is frequent to transmit relatively large capacity of packets such as periodic reporting and requirement of clients: thus, traffic load would be massive.

Messages guaranteeing real-time transmission such as GOOSE messages must assure a stable communication environment regardless of traffic generation. Because these messages may contain a trip command processing error or warning, packet loss should not occur even when packets are being dissected. When serious situation such as network collision is occurred, the overall system is likely to collapse as well since communication in IEC 61850 is for transmission and distribution system; thus, packet analysis and traffic analysis should be performed in parallel.

4   Proposed Packet Analyzer Dedicated to IEC61850

We implemented the core module of this packet analyzer by C++ using Nokia's Qt. The packet analyzer proposed in this research has the following properties in order to enhance efficiency of packet analysis:

- First, this program dissects only IEC 61850 protocol messages to avoid a massive amount of packet analysis. This offers more resource to packet analyzer for efficient operation and control of network.
- In addition, Fast Later Access (FLA) method is proposed, by which packets captured and analyzed previously do not have to reanalysis for speed improvement.
- Finally, analysis of according to characteristics of packets and traffic are provided, analyzed meaningful information in payload using DPI.

4.1   Dedicated Packet Analyzer

Since the proposed packet analyzer is based on Libpcap in Linux, all packets received by the Ethernet card are captured. In the filtering process, this packet analyzer checks Ethertype header of layer 2 and only passes packets with a payload of GOOSE messages and IP header. GOOSE messages are conveyed to the dissector module in this process. Among packets containing IP header payload, the packets of which upper layer protocol in IP header is TCP are chosen to dissect. MMS packets are dissected and passed to the decomposition module on consecutive process. The difference between general-purpose and proposed packet analyzer is that all the packets go through with the former, while for the latter, packets not qualified are dissected. Proposed packet analyzer dissects unassociated packets in medium step, while the general-purpose packet analyzers let all the packets go through this process. The packet analyzer dedicated to IEC 61850 eliminates analysis and maintenance of unnecessary packets and enhances packet dissect speed.

4.2   Fast Later Access

Existing packet analyzers have their own algorithms in order to analyze a significant amount of packets. Since these packet analyzers are not able to store entire contents of analyzed packets on memory, list of captured packets is on screen. Also, some parts of packet contents are only managed by memory, and the others are temporarily stored in a general way. Whenever detail information of packets is required, Wireshark reads over temporarily stored packets and packet dissecting process has to be performed once again in this process; thus, although packets are already dissected, packet dissecting process is performed again because general-purpose packet analyzer cannot recognize which packet would be required by a user.

In this research, we propose an offset storing method to resolve this problem. After capturing and analyzing packets, this method stores offset in index table, which has dissected packet contents, and then directly read the contents using offset information of Data Table without re-decomposition process. In this way, Fast Later Access (FLA) does not need to process packet dissection again when specific information of packets is required.

Fast Later Access (FLA) exploits the index and data tables. The index table has memory address information where analyzed data of packets is stored, calculating index and length of corresponding packets. When a user demands details of the packets or re-demands using screen scroll, an analyzed packet data has only to be read by the data table offset contained in the index table.

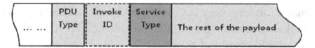

Fig. 2. Payload of MMS

4.3   Packet and Traffic Analysis Using DPI

For general traffic analysis, DPI traffic analysis is restricted due to the possibility of invading privacy and anonymity; however, traffic analysis suitable for managing an electric power network is needed to protect the network from danger in case of IEC 61850. To manage and protect the transmission and distribution system, it is mandatory to detect risk elements and possible disorder in the network in advance and control unnecessary traffic occurrence. IEDs in the bay level collect measurements of process level and transmit them according to demand of clients.

The proposed method of this research dissects the payload of an MMS message and represents information of voltage and current measurements. On IEC 61850 research, it is general for GOOSE message to have high priority in the transmission to guarantee real-time operation, while MMS message is given low priority. However, MMS has more than 70 kinds of services, and the system should consider messages which demand rapid processing among these services.

Figure 2 roughly indicates payload of MMS. Implemented packet analyzer discovers the service type through payload analysis of MMS and separately represents MMS with measurements.

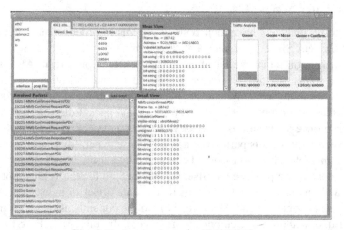

Fig. 3. Packet Analyzer for IEC 61850

Traffic analysis of general-purpose packet analyzer only provides the number of corresponding packets among all. However, dissecting all packets cannot obtain accurate results, so traffic analysis is needed, considering the characteristic of the network. In Figure 3, packet analyzer implemented on this research dissects only GOOSE and MMS messages and traffic according to importance. This packet analyzer provides information on not only the number of GOOSE, but also measurement value among MMS messages. Also, it represents how many MMS messages communicate among all not periodically, but only when client requires. It classifies packets transmitting voltage and current measurements to clients, dissecting payload of MMS messages.

5   Performance Evaluation

IED equipment in real substation collected packets in order to evaluate performance of packet analyzing method dedicated IEC 61850 in this paper. We compared performance to Wireshark, a general-purpose packet analysis program, used the most: the first evaluation is comparison of time to analyze the same amount of packets, and we analyzed time consumed to bring already dissected packet contents for the second evaluation. Since packet analyzer dedicated IEC 61850 filters certain communication standards such as MMS and GOOSE, we analyzed and compared filter function of Wireshark as well when the function is activated or deactivated.

Figure 4 represents the time consumed in analyzing the same amount of packets. We were able to discover that dedicated packet analyzer dissects much faster than Wireshark with both general-purpose and filtering functions.

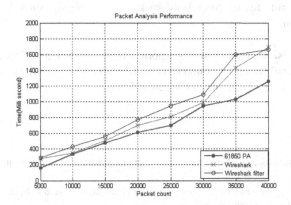

Fig. 4. Performance Comparison of Packet Analyzer According to Packet Size

Figures 5 and 6 illustrate performance of the proposed algorithm to reduce time consumption to bring already analyzed packets. Various lengths of MMS and GOOSE packets were used for evaluation. A dedicated packet analyzer takes a short time to transfer dissected packets since a dedicated packet analyzer at once analyzes packets and stores the contents. Whenever the Wireshark analyzes, packets have to pass parsing module; thus, it takes analogous time as first analysis when reanalysis is required. Also, analyzing time differs according to the length and complexity of packets.

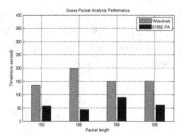
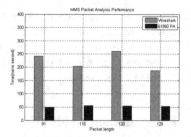

Fig. 5. GOOSE Packet Analysis Performance when re-analyzed

Fig. 6. MMS Packet Analysis Performance when re-analyzed

6   Conclusion

IEC communication networks require high reliability. In this paper, we addressed problems of network analysis when an existing packet analyzer is applied according to the characteristics of communication networks. Also, we proposed an algorithm in order to resolve the problems and improve performance. We implemented a dedicated packet analyzer based on Libpcap and Qt Creator in Linux and evaluated the performance of the packet analyzer. The experimental results showed that our packet analyzer outperforms the existing Wireshark program significantly in terms of the packet analysis time.

Acknowledgments. This work was supported by Basic Science Research Program through the National Research Foundation by Korea (NRF) funded by the Ministry of Education, Science and Technology (2012-0005507).

References

1. IEC 61850 Communication Networks and System in Substation Automation, http://www.iec.ch
2. Zaijun, W., Minqiang, H.: Research on a substation automation system based on IEC 61850. Power System Technology (10), 61–65 (2003)
3. Jang, H., Raza, A., Qureshi, M., Kumar, D., Yang, H.: A Survey of Communication Network Paradigm for Substation Automation. In: IEEE ISPLC, pp. 310–315 (2008)
4. Mo, J., Liu, B., Tan, J.C.: Dynamic Simulation and Test of IEC 61850-9-2 Process Bus Applications. Advanced Materials Research, 433–440 (2012)
5. Roostaee, S., Hooshmand, R., Ataei, M.: Substation Automation System Using IEC 61850. In: Power Engineering and Optimization Conference (PEOCO), pp. 393–397 (2011)
6. Sidhu, T.S., Gangadharan, P.K.: Control and Automation of Power System Substation using IEC 61850 Communication, Control Applications. In: Proceeding of 2005 IEEE Conference, pp. 1331–1336 (2005)
7. Xu, L.: Industry Network QoS Approach Based on New Ethernet Standards. In: Proceedings of International Conference on Computer Science & Education (2009)

An Efficient AP Selection Scheme for Wireless Distributed Systems

Seok-woo Hong[1], Min Choi[2], and Namgi Kim[1,*]

[1] Computer Science Department, University of Kyonggi
Suwon, Kyonggi, Korea
[2] University of Chungbuk
Heungdeok-gu, Chungbuk, Korea
{swhong,ngkim}@kgu.ac.kr, mchoi@cbnu.ac.kr

Abstract. In this paper, we propose an efficient access point (AP) selection scheme for wireless multi-hop networks. Some previous IEEE 802.11 studies have used multi-hop techniques to solve the shadow region and to cover the wide region in the area where the AP is deployed. However, users employing these techniques are unable to determine which AP is more efficient among the number of APs in the wireless multi-hop networks. In addition, it is very difficult to capture the status of the current channel using only the received signal strength indication (RSSI) in the existing AP selection scheme. Therefore, in this paper, we propose a new AP selection algorithm with the hop count for wireless multi-hop networks. We built a wireless distributed system (WDS) that can be easily constructed as a wireless multi-hop network without expert knowledge. Then, we measured the throughput and evaluated the performance of our AP selection scheme in UDP Downlink and UDP Uplink. Based on the results of our measurements, our AP selection scheme can increase the performance of all stations in wireless multi-hop networks.

Keywords: AP selection, Wifi, IEEE 802.11, Multihop.

1 Introduction

Due to the popularization of new handheld smart devices, many IEEE 802.11 wireless LAN systems have been built [1][2]. With the propagation of these wireless LAN systems, people can easily use wireless networks anytime and anywhere. By using the IEEE 802.11 wireless networks, they can communicate while freely moving within the scope of the access point (AP) without being restricted by wired lines. However, wireless networks are greatly affected by their surrounding environments, with the signal strength decreasing in areas where obstacles exist, and they are unable to provide access in a wide area [3]. To solve these problems, the IEEE 802.11 standard supports wireless multi-hop network technologies, which wirelessly connect APs with each other in order to construct an extended wireless network [4].

In multi-hop networks, each user is connected with only one AP. Existing connection schemes check only the strength of the received signals from the beacons

---

* Corresponding author.

T.-h. Kim et al. (Eds.): FGCN/DCA 2012, CCIS 350, pp. 41–47, 2012.
© Springer-Verlag Berlin Heidelberg 2012

transmitted from the APs and select the AP that has sent the strongest signal. However, if the APs are selected based only on the received signal strength in multi-hop networks, APs that have slightly weaker signals but can be connected at the same transmission rate and are closer to the backbone network may not be selected in some cases. Figure 1 shows an example of inefficient AP selection with the existing connection scheme.

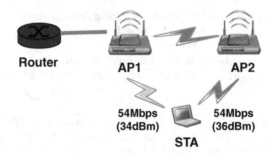

Fig. 1. An example of inefficient AP selection

Therefore, in the present paper, to solve this problem, an efficient AP selection scheme is proposed to select an AP closer to the backbone network. This scheme chooses a closer AP among APs with the same transmission rate using packet sniffing. The proposed scheme has the advantage of being completely backward compatible with existing APs because the device selects APs through self-organization without changing the IEEE 802.11 standards.

2   Related Works

Server-based AP selection schemes store information on APs in the central server by region. They recommend the most appropriate AP in the relevant region when a station wishes to select an AP [5]. When using these schemes, a station can select APs efficiently because the selection process is not passive. However, these schemes are disadvantageous in that the station must be connectable to the server, and the cost to collect prior data for individual regions is high.

On the other hand, schemes where the stations can select the APs themselves without using any server have not been studied sufficiently. In such schemes, the APs should provide additional information to the stations [6][7]. The additional information that can be provided by APs includes the number of users currently connected and the APs' packet error rates (PER). However, the IEEE 802.11 standard does not currently support these options. Moreover, even if the IEEE 802.11 standard supports these at a later stage, the new scheme will not be backward compatible because the transmission frame structures of APs that have already been installed would have to be changed.

Finally, among those schemes in which no central server is used and APs do not provide additional information either, there is a scheme to measure the time between the probe request of each AP and the relevant probe response message to estimate the amount of traffic [8]. This is possible because if a probe response comes after a long period of time after a wireless probe request was sent, it can be assumed that there is a large amount of traffic in the relevant AP. However, this scheme can only be used when selecting APs with small loads in single-hop networks and cannot be used when selecting APs closer to the backbone network in multi-hop networks.

3   Proposed Scheme

Infrastructures where wireless multi-hop networks are deployed include ad hoc, mesh networks, and WDS. In the present study, we use the WDS infrastructure, where APs are easily connected each other to expand the scopes of the service regions without any additional overheads. The MAC frame structure used in the WDS infrastructure is shown in Figure 2. The ToDS and FromDS fields shown in the figure determine how the address field is used. If both the ToDS and the FromDS fields set 1, the frame, which includes the fields, is relayed from an AP to another AP. In this case, Address1 represents the MAC address of the station that sent the data as a source address, Address2 represents the MAC address of the station that receives the data as a destination address, Address3 represents the MAC address of the AP that relays the data as a transmitter address (TA) and, finally, Address4 represents the MAC address of the AP that receives the data relayed as a receiver address (RA) [9].

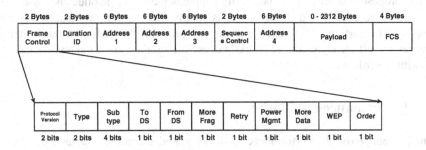

Fig. 2. IEEE 802.11 MAC frame structure

Figure 3(a) shows an overall system flowchart of the proposed selection scheme. The user's station selects the APs and checks the APs to find new APs at regular intervals. When new APs have been found, the user's station sends a ping request message to the gateway and then watches a ping reply message via packet sniffing to select an AP closer to the backbone network. Figure 3(b) shows the pseudo code of the proposed scheme. To find an AP closer to the backbone network, the packets relayed between the APs is analyzed. Relay packets can be seen through the FromDS and the ToDS fields on the frame header. If a packet is identified as a relay packet, four address fields are analyzed to select a closer AP. A closer AP to the backbone network can be found because changes in the RA and the TA at each step are recorded in the relayed packet. As only one packet moves at a time in wireless communications, the order of the detection of the packets can be recorded to easily identify APs closer to the backbone network. Based on this information, the AP closest to the backbone network can be selected to reduce the number of hops.

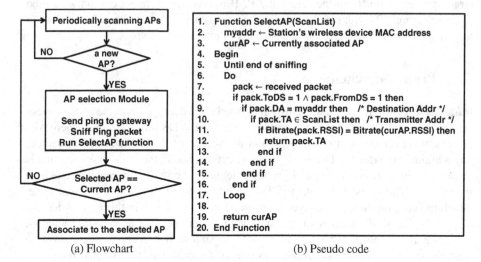

(a) Flowchart   (b) Pseudo code

Fig. 3. Proposed scheme

The proposed scheme can be easily implemented and applied because the information recorded in the frame header is simply used so that the structure of the entire system and the algorithm are not complicated. In addition, our scheme increases the efficiency of the network because the user's station moves toward the APs with fewer hops.

4   Performance Evaluation

In the present study, the performance of the proposed scheme was assessed through real experiments conducted using three APs and three laptops, as shown in Figure 4(a). The three APs were connected with each other with bridges to configure a WDS for static routing of the chain's topology, as shown in Figure 4(b).

To facilitate the analysis in the present experiments, the IEEE 802.11b standard, which has a maximum transmission rate of 11 Mbps, was used. This is because the faster wireless LAN standards generate a large number of traffics and it is not easy to capture and analyze them all simply. The MTU of the traffic used in the experiments was 1500 bytes, and the transmission interval was 3 ms.

Figure 5 shows the four topologies of the stations used in the experiments. The individual topologies were selected to gradually show the view of the stations when the proposed scheme was applied and to demonstrate the improved performance as they gradually approached the AP close to the backbone network.

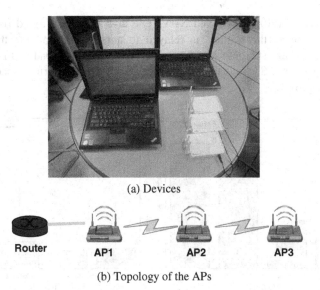

(a) Devices

(b) Topology of the APs

Fig. 4. Experimental environment

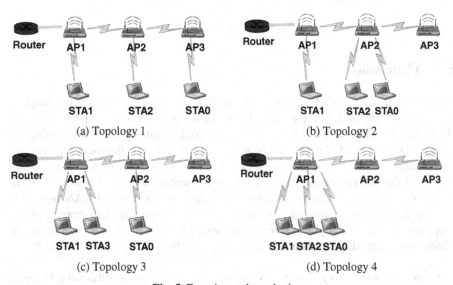

(a) Topology 1

(b) Topology 2

(c) Topology 3

(d) Topology 4

Fig. 5. Experimental topologies

Figure 6 shows the results of experiments of the STA0 in Topology 1 through Topology 4 with the Uplink/Downlink of UDP traffic. In the UDP Uplink, the performance of STA0 improved as it came closer to AP1, which was close to the backbone network. In the UDP Downlink, STA0 showed a minor improvement in performance up to Topology 3, but showed a large improvement in performance in Topology 4, where all the stations were connected to AP1. This is because if the packets are transmitted through the Downlink, AP1 cannot but service packets traveling toward STA0, STA1, and STA2 one at a time in a round robin method. Therefore, if one of the stations is relayed to another AP and the throughput is reduced, the other stations are also affected due to head-of-line blocking. Consequently, even if STA0 is directly connected to AP1, the performance will not be very much improved.

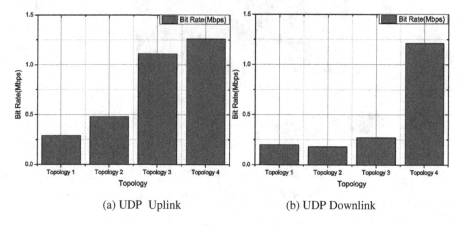

(a) UDP Uplink   (b) UDP Downlink

Fig. 6. Experimental results

5   Conclusion

In the present paper, an AP selection scheme that is effective in a wireless multi-hop network was proposed. In the proposed scheme, the user's station connects with APs closer to the backbone network through simple packet sniffing without changing the existing IEEE 802.11 wireless LAN standard. To test the proposed scheme, the performance improvement was assessed through real experiments. The results suggested that the proposed scheme improves the performance of the entire network by enabling the users' stations to efficiently select APs in wireless LAN networks. For the future work, more stations will be added to test the performance of the proposed scheme in a more complicated network topology. Furthermore, schemes to effectively select APs when transmission speeds are different will also be studied.

Acknowledgment. This research was supported by Basic Science Research Program through the National Research Foundation of Korea (NRF) funded by the Ministry of Education, Science and Technology (grant number 2012R1A1A1002133).

References

1. IEEE: Information technology - Telecommunications and information exchange between systems - Local and metropolitan area networks - Specific requirements - Part 11: Wireless LAN Medium Access Control (MAC) and Physical Layer (PHY) Specifications, IEEE Standard 802.11 (1999)

2. Crow, B.P., Widjaja, I., Kim, J.G., Sakai, P.T.: IEEE 802.11 Wireless Local Area Networks. IEEE Communications Magazine 35(9), 116–126 (1997)
3. Schiller, J.: Mobile Communications. Addison-Wesley, England (2003)
4. Kim, T., Kim, S., Kim, M., Lee, H., Cho, C.: Performance Evaluation and Analysis of Transport Layer Protocol in Wireless Distribution System. In: Proc. of KCC, vol. 35(1D), pp. 230–235 (2008)
5. Nicholson, A.J., Chawathe, Y., Chen, M.Y., Noble, B.D., Wetherall, D.: Improved Access Point Selection. In: Proc. of MobiSys 2006, Uppsala, Sweden (2006)
6. Fukuda, Y., Abe, T., Oie, Y.: Decentralized Access Point Selection Architecture for Wireless LANs - Deployability and Robustness for Wireless LANs. In: Proc. of IEEE VTC (2004)
7. Abusubaih, M., Gross, J., Wiethoelter, S., Wolisz, A.: On Access Point Selection in IEEE 802.11 Wireless Local Area Networks. In: Proc. of WLN (2006)
8. Chen, J.-C., Chen, T.-C., Zhang, T., Berg, E.: Effective AP Selection and Load Balancing in IEEE 802.11 Wireless LANs. In: Proc. of Global Telecommunications Conference, pp. 1–6 (2006)
9. Gupta, D., LeBrun, J., Mohapatra, P., Chuah, C.-N.: WDS-Based Layer 2 Routing for Wireless Mesh Networks. In: Proc. of WiNTECH (2006)

Call Admission Control Satisfying Delay Constraint for Machine-to-Machine Communications in LTE-Advanced

Kyungkoo Jun

Dept. of Embedded Systems Engineering
University of Incheon, Korea
kjun@incheon.ac.kr

Abstract. Complex and large systems such as smart grid and intelligent transportation systems consist of a large number of sensors, actuators and controllers. Hence machine–to–machine (M2M) communications between them are essential for full automatic control of the systems. The M2M communications is typical in the sense that it involves an enormous number of machine–type–communication (MTC) devices and data traffic patterns as well as QoS requirements vary widely depending on applications. LTE–Advanced of 3GPP is preparing a list of supportive functions for the M2M communications. To this end, a massive admission control scheme for the M2M communications was proposed. However, it poorly handles the call admission requests when the transmission interval of a device is relatively longer than its delay constraint, resulting in higher call blocking probability. This paper proposes a method that is free from such limitation and furthermore can reduce the computational overhead required for determining the call admission as long as the transmission interval and the delay meet certain conditions. The improvement in the call blocking probability and the proofs that the proposed method can satisfy the delay constraint were provided along with the simulation results.

Keywords: M2M communications, LTE-Advanced, call admission control, delay constraint, QoS.

1 Introduction

Green technologies such as smart grid systems[1] and intelligent transportation systems[2] draw interest as energy efficiency becomes of the first importance. Such systems are designed to collect data from a huge number of sensors and then determine actions after analyzing the data, which are then carried out by an enormous number of actuators. It is, however, almost impossible to manage the sensors and actuators manually because of their excessively large quantity. Hence, the provision of full automatic control mechanisms for such systems is essential. To this end, machine–to–machine (M2M) communications is considered as one of the enabling technologies for automatic control.

T.-h. Kim et al. (Eds.): FGCN/DCA 2012, CCIS 350, pp. 48–55, 2012.
© Springer-Verlag Berlin Heidelberg 2012

The M2M communications in various applications have the following common characteristics. The number of involved machine–type–communication (MTC) devices such as sensors and actuators is enormously large. And the patterns of data traffic between MTC devices and controllers are diverse. For example, the intervals between data transmissions range from 10 ms to several minutes. In addition QoS requirements are quite different depending on applications.

Cellular mobile networks have several critical issues regarding the support of M2M communications. One of the issues is how to efficiently handle the massive number of the call admission control requests from a large number of MTC devices, which occur randomly and simultaneously. The radio resource management is also complicated because of a broad range of the QoS requirements. Typically, the guarantee of time–related constraints is important in control systems because it determines the reliability and safety of whole systems.

LTE–Advanced[3] of 3GPP proposes a list of desirable functions[4][5] to support the M2M communications. Among them, the three functions which are related with this paper are introduced here. Firstly, it should be able to allocate a small number of physical resource blocks (PRB) to MTC devices because they often need to transmit a tiny size of data. Secondly, the time–controlled access should be provided; MTC devices are allowed to access the radio resources only during the granted time interval (GTI). Otherwise it would be complex and hard to manage the resource allocation for a large number of MTC devices. Thirdly, the group-based management should be supported; a set of MTC devices are grouped together by certain categories and they are managed as a whole group rather than individual devices. Such grouping is helpful to manage a large quantity of MTC devices efficiently.

By assuming the provision of these three functions, a massive call admission control scheme[6][7] was proposed. In the scheme, MTC devices are assumed to transmit data periodically with a maximum jitter constraint. It proposes a sufficient condition that can check whether a new call admission can be granted without violating the jitter constraints of existing calls. It employs a cluster–based approach; it groups MTC devices into clusters according to QoS requirements, requiring that all newly admitted MTC devices should belong to one of the clusters. For the radio resource allocation, the GTIs are allocated to the clusters by base stations, which is eNodeB in LTE systems, and the MTC devices in a cluster can send or receive data by sharing the slots within the GTI.

Since this scheme, however, priorities the clusters as they have shorter interval of transmission, the clusters that have a long interval but its delay constraint is relatively short are poorly handled, being rejected at the call admission. Such improper management of the priority results in the increased call block probability.

This paper proposes a call admission method that employs a different sufficient condition that priorities in the order of delay. It also proposes an optimized sufficient condition that can reduce the computational overhead of the call admission procedure if the interval and the delay meet certain conditions.

This paper is organized as follows. Section 2 describes the proposed method in detail and proves its validity. Section 3 presents the simulation results and Section 4 concludes the paper.

2   Proposed Call Admission Control for the MTC Devices in LTE–Advanced Systems

The proposed method assumes that all MTC devices reside within a same eNodeB and they create data and transmit it periodically to MTC controllers on external networks via the eNodeB. Thus the first step the MTC devices take to communicate with the MTC controllers is to ask the eNodeB for the call admission. Once admitted, the eNodeB allocates the MTC devices with radio resources for them to transmit the data. Also it is assumed that there is delay constraints; the elapsed time from the data creation of an MTC device until it finishes its transmission to an eNodeB is bounded by a maximum allowable delay. Therefore, the QoS requirement for an MTC device can be expressed as (p, d) where p is the interval of the data creation and d is the delay constraint.

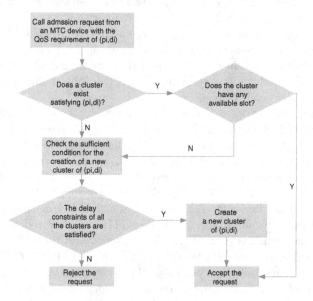

Fig. 1. The algorithm of the proposed call admission control

The proposed method manages the MTC devices in a group–based way; a set of the MTC devices with the same QoS requirement is grouped together as a cluster, which then are numbered as $i = 1, \ldots, N$. The QoS requirement of cluster i is (p_i, d_i) and the number of the MTC devices within cluster i is n_i. The eNodeB allocates to the clusters the GTI which is a set of the PRBs having both time and frequency elements. The duration of the GTI is set to τ. Since maximum L MTC devices can transmit during one GTI, n_i should be less than or equal to L for all the clusters.

If the GTIs for different clusters are overlapped at the same time, the cluster that has a shorter d_i is given a higher priority. The clusters with lower priorities are allocated the GTIs at subsequent available times. In the case that d_is of two or more clusters are same, the cluster that has a longer p_i is prioritized; it can avoid the repetitive delay of the longer–period clusters by the shorter–period ones because a shorter period can occur multiple times within a longer period. Throughout the paper, it is assumed that the cluster number $i = 1, \ldots, N$ denotes the priority; the lower the number, the higher the priority.

The GTI allocation to a cluster is informed to the MTC devices through physical downlink control channel (PDCCH). The allocation information also carries the slot locations within GTI that each MTC device can occupy. Non–GTI time frames and the non–occupied slots in the GTIs are allocated to user equipments (UE).

When the MTC devices terminate the calls, they informs the eNodeB, which then reclaims corresponding slots to reallocate them for UEs or other MTC devices. In the case that such notification is not made due to some reasons such as abrupt breakdown of the MTC devices, the eNodeB can still check the slot occupancy by monitoring physical uplink control channel (PUCCH) that carries the information about which devices use which slots. If a slot is detected as being not used more than n times without notification, the corresponding call is determined as being terminated and the slot is regained. Once all the MTC devices in a cluster terminate the calls, the cluster is removed and the GTI is not allocated any more.

Figure 1 shows the algorithm of the proposed call admission control. An MTC device asks the call admission by sending a request of (p_i, d_i) to the eNodeB through random access channel (RACH). If there already exists a cluster satisfying (p_i, d_i) and the associated GTI has at least one available slot, the request is accepted and the MTC device joins the cluster. Otherwise, it is necessary to create a new cluster. However it should be checked in advance that the creation of the new cluster does not affect the delay satisfaction of the existing clusters. The check procedure is discussed in detail shortly. The new cluster is created only if the delays of existing clusters are not violated. If the created cluster happens to have the same (p_i, d_i) as existing clusters, the new cluster is assigned a lower priority.

Before creating a new cluster, the analysis about the satisfiability of the delay constraints is performed by checking a sufficient condition for all the existing clusters including a new yet–to–be–created cluster. Let $w(i)$ the worst case time that cluster i takes to finish its transmission, then

$$w(i) = \sum_{k=1}^{i} \tau \left\lceil \frac{p_i}{p_k} \right\rceil \tag{1}$$

Regarding Eq. 1, when the transmission timings of two or more clusters overlap, the clusters with lower priorities postpone their transmission until the higher priority ones finish. Thus, the maximum time cluster i takes for its transmission must include delays by the clusters of higher priority. Since the duration of GTI per cluster is τ, cluster i which is delayed by cluster k should wait for maximum $\tau \left\lceil \frac{p_i}{p_k} \right\rceil$ where p_i and p_k are the transmission interval of cluster i and k, respectively and $k \leq i$. Thus the maximum transmission time $w(i)$ of cluster i becomes the sum of all the delays from cluster $k = 1, \ldots, i-1$ plus its transmission time.

Based on $w(i)$, the following theorem proposes a sufficient condition that guarantees the satisfaction of d_i of all the clusters. The proof is omitted since it is evident and self–explainable.

Theorem 1. *The delay constraint d_i of all the cluster $i = 1, \ldots, N$ can be satisfied if*

$$w(i) \leq d_i, \forall i \in \{1, \ldots, N\} \tag{2}$$

Interestingly, theorem 1 can be further optimized as theorem 2 if p_i and d_i of all the clusters meet the following two conditions.

$$p_i = d_i, \forall i \in \{1, \ldots, N\} \tag{3}$$

$$p_i > p_k \implies p_i = n \times p_k, \quad \forall i, k \in \{1, \ldots, N\} \tag{4}$$

where n is an integer bigger than 1. Since MTC devices are usually deployed under the supervision of one purpose–specific organization, their p_i and d_i can be adjusted in a certain pattern in order to meet the conditions of (3) and (4)

Theorem 2. *If (3) and (4) hold, the delay constraint d_i of all the clusters are satisfied if*

$$\sum_{k=1}^{N} \frac{1}{p_k} \leq \frac{1}{\tau} \tag{5}$$

Proof. (2) can be expressed as

$$\sum_{k=1}^{i} \tau \left\lceil \frac{p_i}{p_k} \right\rceil \leq d_i, \forall i \in \{1, \ldots, N\} \tag{6}$$

By applying (3) to (6), the following is obtained.

$$\sum_{k=1}^{i} \tau \left\lceil \frac{p_i}{p_k} \right\rceil \leq p_i, \forall i \in \{1, \ldots, N\} \tag{7}$$

Since $\left\lceil \frac{p_i}{p_k} \right\rceil = \frac{p_i}{p_k}$ due to (4), (7) can be

$$\sum_{k=1}^{i} \tau \frac{p_i}{p_k} \leq p_i, \forall i \in \{1, \ldots, N\} \tag{8}$$

By dividing both sides of (8) by τ and p_i, the following is obtained.

$$\sum_{k=1}^{i} \frac{1}{p_k} \leq \frac{1}{\tau}, \forall i \in \{1, \ldots, N\} \tag{9}$$

Since $\sum_{k=1}^{i} \frac{1}{p_k}$ increases monotonically as i increases and $\frac{1}{\tau}$ is a constant, if (9) holds for the case of $k = N$, then it also holds for all i. Thus, i can be substituted by N, which leads to (5).

The admission decision based on theorem 2 can reduce the computational overhead compared with theorem 1. The call admission based on theorem 1 requires $\frac{N(N+1)}{2}$ times of multiplications, $\frac{N(N+1)}{2}$ divisions, $\frac{N(N-1)}{2}$ additions and N comparisons because (1) and (2) are computed for $\forall i \in \{1, \ldots, N\}$. On contrary, theorem 2 requires only N divisions, $N - 1$ additions and 1 comparison because it checks only the case of N. When an enormous number of the MTC devices are involved resulting in a very large number of N, the difference in the required amount of computations would be notable between theorem 1 and 2.

The optimized method of theorem 2 is also more efficient than the method of [6][7] which does not take advantage of the conditions of (3) and (4). When analyzing [6] and [7], it requires $\frac{N(N+1)}{2}$ times of multiplications, $\frac{N(N+1)}{2}$ divisions, $\frac{N(N-1)}{2}$ additions and N comparisons.

3   Performance Evaluation

This section evaluates the proposed method by the simulations. The simulations assume there is one eNodeB and its bandwidth is 20 MHz. One GTI consists of 100 PRBs and its duration τ is 1 ms. Within one GTI, maximum 20 MTC devices can transmit, allocating 5 PRBs for each device. It is also assumed that 5 PRBs are enough resources for one MTC device to transmit data.

Table 1. The list of (p_i, d_i) and cluster priority

Priority	p_i (ms)	d_i (ms)
1	500	2
2	500	4
3	250	5
4	200	5
5	100	6
6	100	10
7	40	10
8	20	10
9	10	10
10	20	15

The simulations create MTC devices one by one with the intervals that follow the exponential distribution of the average of 1 ms. Once created, the MTC devices choose randomly one of (p_i, d_i) shown in Table 1 as the QoS requirement. And the MTC devices that are admitted by the eNodeB have the call duration that follows the exponential distribution with the average of 15 ms. Only uplink data transmission is assumed. Once the calls are terminated, the MTC devices stop their operation, not requesting any more calls. The simulations each of which lasts 1000 ms are repeated several times and the results are averaged.

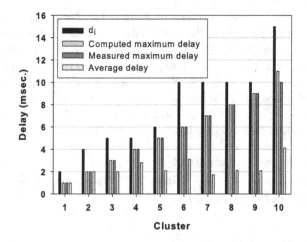

Fig. 2. The delay constraints of the clusters and the simulation results

Figure 2 shows the four types of delays per cluster when the proposed method was used. d_is are the delay constraints of clusters, the computed maximum delays are the analytical results from equation (1), and the measured maximum delay and the average delay are from the simulation results. The X axis shows the cluster numbers shown in Table 1 and the Y axis is the time in milliseconds. It shows that the proposed method has all the clusters meet their delay constraints; all the measured maximum delays are lower than the corresponding d_is.

4   Conclusions

This paper proposed a call admission control method for the M2M communications in LTE–Advanced systems. It improves the call admission probability compared with the conventional method by using the delay based priority assignment scheme. Furthermore it suggests that the computation overhead required for the call admission can be reduced if the transmission interval and the required delay meet the certain conditions. The proofs that the proposed method can satisfy the delay constraint were provided and the simulation results confirmed it, showing also the comparison of the blocking probability.

Acknowledgements. This work was supported by the University of Incheon research grant in 2011.

References

1. Gellings, C.: The Smart Grid: Enabling Energy Efficiency and Demand Response. CRC Press
2. Chowdhury, M., Sadek, A.: Fundamentals of Intelligent Transportation Ssytems Planning. Artech House
3. http://www.3gpp.org
4. 3GPP TS 22.368 V11.1.0: Service Requirements for Machine Type Communications (March 2011)
5. 3GPP TS 23.888 V1.1.1: System Improvements for Machine Type Communications (April 2011)
6. Lien, S., Chen, K.: Massive Access Management for QoS Guarantees in 3GPP Machine–to–Machine Communications. IEEE Comm. Letters 15(3) (March 2011)
7. Lien, S., Chen, K., Lin, Y.: Toward Ubiquitous Massive Accesses in 3GPP Machine to Machine Communications. IEEE Comm. Mag. (April 2011)

A Trustworthy and Interoperable Identity Authentication Sharing Architecture

Seungchul Park

School of Computer Science and Engineering, Korea University of Technology and Education,
1800 Chungjeol-ro, Byeongcheon-Myun, Dongnam-gu, Cheonan, Chungnam, 330-708, Korea
scpark@kut.ac.kr

Abstract. Identity authentication sharing technologies which allow many service providers to share the result of identity authentication of an identity provider receive high attention as alternatives for current problematic identity authentications in the future Internet environment, owing to their advantages including high usability, cost effectiveness of service providers, and privacy protection. However, in order for the identity authentication sharing technologies to be widely deployed in global Internet scale, the interoperability problem among the different identity authentication sharing protocols and the trustworthiness issue among the participating identity providers, service providers, and users should be resolved in advance. This paper firstly analyzes current status of the protocol interoperability issue and existing trust frameworks for identity authentication sharing. And then, based on the result of analysis, this paper proposes a trustworthy and interoperable identity authentication sharing architecture for future global Internet.

Keywords: Identity Management, Authentication Sharing, Interoperable Identity, Trust Framework.

1   Introduction

During the past decade, several identity authentication sharing technologies such as OpenID[1], Information Card/IMI(Identity Metasystem Interoperability)[2,3], and SAML(Security Assertion Markup Language)[4] have been actively developed in order to solve the problems of current Internet identity authentication systems. The identity authentication sharing technologies allow many service providers to share the result of authentication performed by an identity provider. In the identity authentication sharing environment, each Internet user registers his or her identity information to only small number of identity providers that are trusted, instead of repeated registration to many service providers, and needs to manage only the credentials issued by the identity providers. The single sign-on functionality of the identity authentication sharing technology, which enables the authenticated users of an identity provider to visit other service providers without additional authentications, allows Internet users to avoid current authentication systems' repeated login and logout. Furthermore, since the service providers, in the identity authentication sharing environments, can

T.-h. Kim et al. (Eds.): FGCN/DCA 2012, CCIS 350, pp. 56–63, 2012.

outsource the authentication services from the identity providers, the development and maintenance cost of service providers can be accordingly reduced[5,6,7].

In order for the identity authentication sharing technologies which have many advantages to be widely deployed in real Internet environments, the interoperability problem among the corresponding identity authentication sharing protocols and the trustworthiness problem among the participating identity providers, service providers, and users need to be resolved in advance[7,8].This paper analyzes current status of the protocol interoperability and the trust frameworks for the identity authentication sharing. And then, based on the result of the analysis, this paper proposes an identity authentication sharing architecture which is sufficiently scalable, flexible and interoperable enough to be adopted in future global Internet. The proposed architecture was designed to be based on the open and dynamic trust framework so as to support high scalability and flexibility. And the architecture was designed to support the interoperability effectively for newly emerging protocols as well as the existing protocols for identity authentication sharing.

2   Interoperability Status of Identity Authentication Sharing

2.1   Identity Authentication Sharing Protocols

Among many identity authentication sharing protocols developed during the past decade, Passport/LiveID, OpenID, Information Card/IMI, and SAML are most well-known. In the Passport(currently LiveID) developed by Microsoft, all users' identity information is maintained and managed by the central Passport server. When a user wants to logon a service provider associated with the Passport/LiveID, the identity authentication request for the user is redirected to the Passport server via the web browser. The authentication result of the Passport server is then forwarded to the service provider[9,10]. On the other hand, the OpenID was developed as a simple, open and distributed identity authentication sharing protocol so that users can use self-selected URL style identity ID(called OpenID)s, which are authenticated by corresponding identity provider(called OpenID provider)s easily discovered through the URL, for all OpenID-enabled web sites[11]. OpenID 2.0[12] allows users to offer URLs of their identity providers to the visiting service providers instead of offering their OpenIds. Then, OpenID 2.0 identity providers issue pseudonym-style IDs to the users, each of which is differently applicable to the OpenID-enabled websites without being exposed to other websites, so that the privacy protection is enhanced. In the OpenID, identity authentication policies can be communicated between the identity provider(s) and service provider(s) through OpenID PAPE(Provider Authentication Policy Extension). Information Card/IMI[13] standardized by OASIS[14] in May 2009 is actively promoted and deployed mainly by ICF(Information Card Foundation)[15]. Information card of IMI is a XML-style digital identity card which includes information about card issuer, authentication token type, and other attributes such as card identifier, date of issue, and so on. The card selector of user agent manages various information cards issued by different identity providers. When a user visits an IMI-enabled service provider, the service provider delivers the authentication requirement for the user to the card selector. The card selector selects a card which meets the authentication requirement and forwards the card to the corresponding identity provider to ask a security token(e.g., X.509 certificate). If the security token delivered to the service provider is satisfied, the service access will be then allowed by the service provider. SAML was mainly developed by Liberty Alliance[16] and standardized by OASIS[17]. SAML-based identity authentication sharing is basically assumed to be done within a CoT(Circle of Trust) whose identity providers and service providers trust each other through pre-established agreements[18]. Therefore, in SAML-based identity authentication sharing, member service providers always trust the assertions of identity authentication issued by member identity providers. When a user visits a member service provider, the service provider suggests a list of its trusted identity providers. If user selects an identity provider from the list, it authenticates the user with the authentication context requested by the service provider and returns the authentication assertion to the service provider.

2.2   Interoperability Status

Existing identity authentication sharing protocols were originally developed on the basis of their own representation methods for authentication requirements and results. Recently, however, they are trying to adopt the LoA(Level of Assurance for identity authentication)s defined by US OMB[19] and NIST[20] and standardized by ITU-T[21] as a representation method for the identity authentication requirement and result. The LoA is defined as the degree of confidence associated with an identity assertion. ITU-T(same in US OMB/NIST) defines four LoAs, where LoA 4 assures highest authentication level requiring very high confidence in an asserted identity. In November 2009, US ICAM(Identity, Credential, and Access Management) committee[22] announced OpenID 2.0 protocol profile to support LoA 1, and IMI 1.0 and SAML 2.0 protocol profiles to support LoA 1, 2, and 3. While the LoA-based representation for authentication requirements and results is becoming applicable to the major identity authentication sharing protocols such as OpenID, IMI, and SAML, the interoperability among the protocols still remains as a challenging issue. The 1:1 protocol conversion approach for the interoperability suggested in [7] is not realistic in future Internet environment, because it will highly increase the system complexity as new technologies and protocols are emerging.

3   Trust Framework Status for Identity Authentication Sharing

In order for the identity authentication sharing to be widely deployed, the trust infrastructure providing trust services for the participating entities(e.g., identity providers, service providers, and users) is necessarily required. Until now, various frameworks for the trust infrastructure have been proposed in many trials. Existing trust frameworks can be categorized into three types such as centralized trust framework, closed and distributed trust framework, and open and distributed trust framework.

3.1   Trust Frameworks

The centralized trust framework was adopted by the Passport/LiveID identity authentication sharing system developed by Microsoft. In the Passport/LiveID system, Microsoft operating the central Passport server sets the policy for identity authentication sharing, makes agreements with service providers, and provides the identity authentication services for the service providers based on the agreements. The users and service providers who agreed on the trust framework of the Passport/LiveID system entirely trust the central Passport server. The closed and distributed trust framework, mainly adopted by Liberty Alliance to support the SAML-based identity authentication sharing services, relies on the closed trust group called CoT(Circle of Trust). The service providers and identity providers of a CoT trust one another on the basis of pre-established mutual agreements or other business relations. The coordinating organization of a CoT may certificate several identity servers according to its own trust framework for the identity authentication sharing, and they are well-known and trusted by the users and service providers of the CoT.   The open and distributed trust framework was introduced by US ICAM committee with aid of OIX(Open Identity Exchange)[23] in 2010[24,25]. Most important characteristic of the open and distributed trust framework is that the trust framework is published by the corresponding policy maker(e.g., government users group, an association of banks, and an association of universities). Any organization which has been proved to be able to provide trust services according to the trust framework for identity providers, service providers, and users can be selected as a TFP(Trust Framework Provider). The trust framework provider can certificate identity providers for their levels of assurance for identity authentication, and list the certified identity providers for the service providers and user agents. OIX, InCommon, and Kantara Initiative are the trust framework providers selected by US ICAM committee at present time of 2012[22].

3.2   Comparative Analysis

The centralized trust framework is very simple, because there is only one sufficiently well-known and trustworthy identity server, so as to be easily implemented and conveniently used. Since, however, all user activities to access service providers are revealed to the central server, it may cause privacy problems. And, high burden and dependency on the central server may lower the system scalability and flexibility. Thus, the centralized trust framework is not applicable to open environments. The closed and distributed trust framework is well-applicable to a closed group whose members require similar level of assurance for identity authentication and trust one another on the basis of pre-established agreements. However, it is difficult for the closed and distributed framework to be applicable to open environments where there are no pre-established trust-relationships among the participating entities. The open and distributed trust framework is a static trust framework from the viewpoint that the information about certified identity providers is accessed from trust framework providers on the basis of manual downloads, which eventually makes the service providers and user agents difficult to timely access the information about many identity providers certified by various trust framework providers.

4   Next-Generation Identity Authentication Sharing Architecture

4.1   Open and Dynamic Trust Framework

In order for the existing open and distributed trust framework to support global Internet well, its static characteristics needs to be eliminated and provide the trust services more dynamically, instead of providing download-based services.

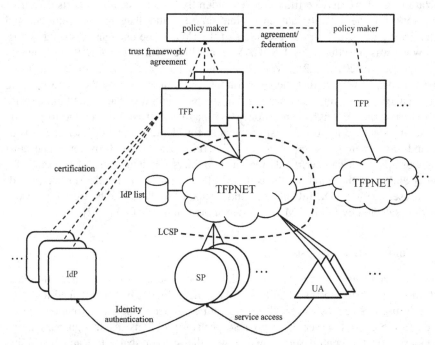

Fig. 1. Proposed Open and Dynamic Trust Framework

Fig. 1 shows the open and dynamic trust framework model of the proposed next-generation identity authentication sharing architecture. In the open and dynamic trust framework, the trust framework providers selected by a policy maker to execute the published trust framework form a TFPNET(Trust Framework Provider NETwork), through which the trust framework providers share the information about the certified identity provider(IdP)s one another. How to share the information within a FTPNET is a matter of implementation of corresponding TFPNET. Several policy makers may agree with one another to federate their trust frameworks. In this case of federated trust framework, their FTPNETs are interconnected so that their trust services can be shared. In the open and dynamic trust framework, the trust services provided by a TFPNET can be dynamically accessed through the LCSP(LoA Certified Status Protocol). That is, by using the LCSP, user agent(UA)s and service provider(SP)s can access, at any time, the list of identity providers certified for LoAs by the TFPNET, and check the certification status of an identity provider. Since, furthermore, the trust framework providers of different but federated TFPNETs exchange their trust services via the LCSP, the LCSP is a crucial means to realize the interoperability among the TFPNETs. There can be many TFPNETs including federated TFPNETs in the global Internet environment according to the corresponding policy makers, and they are selected by users and service providers according to their QoS(Quality of Service)s. More competitive TFPNETs will eventually survive in the global Internet environment.

4.2   Interoperability Support

The proposed open and dynamic trust framework provides the trust services about identity providers on the basis of standard LoAs through LCSP. The next-generation identity authentication sharing architecture proposed in this paper defines another

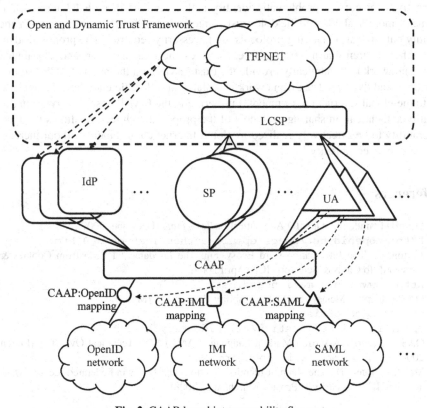

Fig. 2. CAAP-based interoperability Support

protocol called CAAP(Common Authentication Access Protocol) for the interopera-bility support among the identity authentication sharing protocols, as shown in Fig. 2. The CAAP provides the LoA-based standardized access interfaces for the identity providers, service providers, and user agents among which the LoAs are commonly understood, thanks to the open and dynamic trust framework. The CAAP allows a service provider(SP) to request authentications and receive responses to and from user agent(UA)s based on the standard LoAs. The CAAP is working independently from the underlying identity authentication sharing protocols, and the user agent performs the mapping functionality between the CAAP and its own identity authentication sharing protocol(s). Since, like this, this CAAP-based interoperability support model requires just the mapping between the CAAP and its own identity authentication shar-ing protocol(s), the model will be well applicable to next-generation global Internet, without increasing the system complexity, where various identity authentication shar-ing protocols may emerge.

5   Conclusion

In order for the identity authentication sharing technologies to become the realistic alternatives for current problematic identity authentications in global Internet envi-ronment, more scalable and flexible trust framework and interoperability among the identity authentication sharing protocols are necessarily required. The proposed iden-tity authentication sharing architecture enhances the existing open and distributed trust framework to dynamically provide the trust services on the basis of LCSP so that new open and dynamic trust framework is scalable and flexible enough to be applica-ble to the global Internet environment. Furthermore, the CAAP-based interworking of identity authentication sharing protocols of the proposed architecture allows the inte-roperability to be effectively realized in global Internet environment without increas-ing the system complexity.

References

1. OpenID Foundation: OpenID Authentication 2.0 – Final (December 2007),
   http://openid.net/specs/openid-authentication-2_0.html
2. Burton, C.: The Information Card Ecosystem: The Fundamental Leap from Cookies & Passwords to Cards & Selectors. ICF (April 2009),
   http://www.informationcard.net
3. OASIS: Identity Metasystem Interoperability Version 1.0. (May 2009),
   http://docs.oasis-open.org/imi/ns/identity/v1.0/identity.html
4. OASIS: Security Assertion Markup Language(SAML) V2.0 Technical Overview (March 2008), http://www.oasis-open.org
5. Maler, E., Reed, D.: The Venn of Identity - Options and Issues in Federated Identity Man-agement. IEEE Security & Privacy(March/April 2008)

6. Maliki, T.E., Seigneur, J.-M.: A Survey of User-centric Identity Management Technologies. In: Proc. of Int'l Conference on Emerging Security Information, Systems and Technologies, pp. 12–17 (2007)
7. Madsen, P., Itoh, H.: Challenges to Supporting Federated Assurance. IEEE Computer (May 2009)
8. Thibeau, D., Reed, D.: Open Trust Frameworks for Open Government: Enabling Citizen Involvement through Open Identity Technologies (August 2009), http://openid.net/
9. Korman, D.P., Rubin, A.D.: Risks of the Passport Single Signon Protocol. IEEE Computer Networks (July 2000)
10. http://en.wikipedia.org/wiki/Windows_Live_ID
11. Chadwick, D., Shaw, S.: Review of OpenID, JISC Final Report (December 2008), http://www.jisc.ac.uk/whatwedo/programmes/einfrastructure/reviewofopenid.aspx
12. OpenID Foundation: OpenID Authentication 2.0 – Final (December 2007), http://openid.net/specs/openid-authentication-2_0.html
13. OASIS: Identity Metasystem Interoperability Version 1.0. (May 2009), http://docs.oasis-open.org/imi/ns/identity/v1.0/identity.html
14. http://www.oasis-open.org/committees/security/
15. http://www.informationcard.net
16. http://www.projectliberty.org/
17. OASIS: Security Assertion Markup Language(SAML) V2.0 Technical Overview (March 2008), http://www.oasis-open.org
18. Dwiputera, A.F.: Single Sign-On Architectures in Public Networks (Liberty Alliance). INFOTECH Seminar Communication Services (2005)
19. US OMB M-04-04 : The E-Authentication Guidance for Federal Agencies (December 2003), http://www.whitehouse.gov/omb/memoranda/fy04/m04-04.pdf
20. NIST SP 800-63: Electronic Authentication Guideline (April 2006)
21. ITU-T X.1254 : Entity Authentication Assurance Framework(March 2012)
22. http://idmanagement.gov/
23. http://openidentityexchange.org/
24. Thibeau, D., Reed, D.: Open Trust Frameworks for Open Government: Enabling Citizen Involvement through Open Identity Technologies. (August 2009), http://openid.net/
25. Rundle, M., et al.: The Open Identity Trust Framework(OITF) Model (March 2010), http://openidentityexchange/

Model-Based Evaluation Approach
for Quality of Web Service

Yan Gong[1], Lin Huang[1,2], Zhiyong Shu[1], and Ke Han[1]

[1] Chinese Electronic Equipment System Engineering Corporation, Beijing, China
[2] State Key Laboratory of Networking and Switching Technology,
Beijing University of Posts and Telecommunications, Beijing, China
gongyan@bupt.edu.cn, huanglin1204@gmail.com, 7086s@163.com,
kehan@yahoo.com.cn

Abstract. With the increasing number of web services that provide similar functionality, it is important to find the best web service that meets the user's needs. In this sense, it is essential to use metrics to evaluate the quality characteristics of web services. This paper proposes a pentagram model for evaluating Quality of Web Service (QoWS). The model consists of five factors, including price, latency, accessibility, accuracy, and reputation. The experimental results demonstrate that our approach can effectively obtain accurate quality of service evaluation for web services.

Keywords: Web Service, Quality of Web Service (QoWS).

1 Introduction

With the rapid development of the service-oriented software architecture, the web service technology based on XML has been widely applied as a good implementation technique for Service-Oriented Architecture (SOA). On the other hand, the increasing number of web services available within an organization or on the web, raises a problem of searching them and highlights the important demand to find the best web service that meets certain requirements of the requester. Thus, the web service needs to be evaluated for its quality of the service by the web service evaluation technology, which calculates the Quality of Web Service (QoWS) through a set of evaluation criteria [1]. According to the W3C's definition, QoWS refers to a kind of ability that can respond to the expected request and complete the related tasks with a certain quality of service that meets the expectations of both the service provider and the customer.

The acquisition of service quality indicator data consists of three channels: firstly, information given by service providers when issuing the services, such as the price of services. Secondly, feedback gained by monitoring the service execution process. Finally, the tests conducted by the third-party on the issued services. Web services quality data are not static, especially for indicators related to performance (such as latency) which will be affected by a variety of factors such as server load and network environment. Thus frequent updates should be conducted to reflect the latest changes.

T.-h. Kim et al. (Eds.): FGCN/DCA 2012, CCIS 350, pp. 64–71, 2012.
© Springer-Verlag Berlin Heidelberg 2012

This paper is based on our previous work on a framework for monitoring the QoWS [2-3]. Our approach presented in this paper is to define a model of web service, taking price, latency, accessibility, accuracy, and reputation factors into account for quality evaluation. We have used the model to measure QoWS.

The remainder of this paper is organized as follows. Section 2 briefly surveys the current literature on the subject. The model is given in Section 3. Section 4 describes the algorithm for each factor. In Section 5 we give some results with measuring QoWS of the proposed model. Finally we give certain conclusions in Section 6.

2   Related Work

At present QoWS evaluation has gained much attention in recent years due to the growth of online transactions and e-business activities in service-oriented environment. The authors of [4] stressed that the quality of service issues should be considered while accessing web services and they proposed the concept of Service Level Agreement (SLA). The authors of [5] proposed the concepts such as web services reputation and gave a quantitative method of calculating based on SLA. The authors of [6] clearly defined QoWS, which has won recognition from the academia and industries as a metric to assess the performance of web services.

References [7-9] instructively gave the factors that should be included in the service quality model, such as price and latency. These models are for QoWS in the monitoring, forecasting and analysis process instead of service evaluation. The relevant studies mentioned above considered the QoWS from a single perspective and failed to make the overall assessment of the web service quality.

3   Modeling QoWS

The purpose of our model is to be able to design quantifiable metrics for quality evaluations by measuring the QoWS of a given web service.

3.1   The Summary of Pentagram

QoWS is presented in Table 1. It shows key attribute indicator and most important measures of the QoWS. Each web service has unique Key Attribute Indicators (KAIs) that need to be identified. Various studies have been conducted on this subject and different standardization bodies have defined these KAIs in their own ways as general guidelines. These guidelines can be used as a basis to find KAIs for each web service.

As shown in Fig.1, QoWS is measured and presented using a pentagram diagram based on the measurement of its five factors in the proposed QoWS model. Each factor is measured based on the results of their refined factors during QoWS measure process.

Let's assume the measurement result of each factor is a value from 0 to 1. The value "1" indicates the maximum value for each factor, and "0" indicates the minimum value. The area of the pentagram is used as the measurement of QoWS. Clearly, the smallest value of this pentagram area is 0, and the maximum value is approximately 2.4. Since the pentagram consists of five triangles. The area of each triangle can be computed $0.5 \times l_1 \times l_2 \times \sin \lambda$ as: where l_1, l_2 represent the sides of the triangle, and λ represents the 72-degree angle between the two sides. The letters a, b, c, d, and e in Fig.1 are used to represent the five factors of QoWS respectively. When each factor is measured, then, QoWS can be computed below:

$$QoWS = \frac{1}{2}\sin 72° \, (ab + bc + cd + de + ea)$$

$$\cong \frac{1}{2} \times 0.9511 \times (ab + bc + cd + de + ea) \qquad (1)$$

$$\cong 0.48 \times (ab + bc + cd + de + ea)$$

Table 1. Factors That Influence QoWS and Most Important Measures

Key Attribute Indicator	Most Important Measures	Symbol
Price	Price represents the amount of money paid for each web service using.	a
Latency	Latency time between starting the request for a service and addressing the requirement.	b
Accessibility	Accessibility represents the frenquency of the service provider answering the request when the client asks for web service.	c
Accuracy	Accuracy represents the probability of the request being responded correctly while providers answering the client's requests.	d
Reputation	Reputation is the credibility of the web service.	e

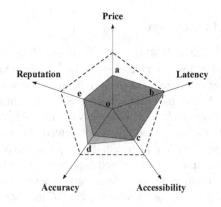

Fig. 1. Quality of web service pentagram model

3.2   The Advantages of the Area Calculation

There are three advantages of the area calculation: firstly, in the pentagram model, every estimate is equal and independent, because the weight leaning to any side will weaken the effect of the omni directional estimation. The sum account adopts the same weight in order to show the coequal recognition on the every estimation index. Secondly, it adopts subjectively and objectively integrative estimation. Finally, it's easy to show the difference of the sum. If one dimension has a lesser change, and the other four have no change, the area calculation method with the influence on total scores is more than weighted average computing (as the light shadow is shown in Fig.1). For example, if each edge score equals to 0.8, and weight equals to 0.2, when d change to 1.0, $\Delta QoWS$=1.67-1.52=0.15 , $\Delta QoWS'$=0.84-0.8=0.04 . The change of scores is obviously, and $\Delta QoWS$ is more than $\Delta QoWS'$. Therefore, the method impels service providers to improve their total qualities of service, giving more attentions to the accuracy but not just to the price.

4   Algorithm

4.1   Price

While providing operation O for service S, the price of its service $q_{pri}(s,o)$ is the expenses that must be paid while accessing the service. And it is generally given directly by the service provider.

4.2   Latency

While providing operation O for service S, its service lag time $q_{lat}(s,o)$ includes the time from clients turning in service request to receiving respond. To describe it specifically in formula:

$$q_{lat}(s,o) = T_{process}(s,o) + T_{trans}(s,o) \qquad (2)$$

In this formula, $T_{process}(s,o)$ represents the service processing time, usually given directly by the service provider; $T_{trans}(s,o)$ represents the required transmission time , which can be calculated with the following formula based on the statistical data of the past service operation.

$$T_{trans}(s,o) = \frac{\sum_{i=1}^{n} T_i(s,o)}{n} \qquad (3)$$

In it, $T_i(s,o)$ is the transmission time obtained through measuring the past experience of providing the service; n is the number of times of measuring the operations.

4.3   Accessibility

The accessibility of the service S refers to the probability of the service that can be accessed, and its quantitative formula is:

$$q_{acce}(s) = \frac{T(s)}{n} \qquad (4)$$

In this formula, $T(s)$ stands for the total time that S can be accessed in recent consecutive time T (usually calculated in seconds). The selection of the T's value is associated with the particular environment. For instance, for a service that has frequent visits, its T should be of a relatively small value. For services that are not frequently accessed, T's value can be bigger. The web services we assumed here can send message to the system to inform their status (accessible and inaccessible).

4.4   Accuracy

The accuracy $q_{accu}(s)$ of the service S refers to the probability of provider correctly providing service S to the service requestor after being requested. The quantization formula is as follows:

$$q_{accu}(s) = \frac{C(s)}{n} \qquad (5)$$

In this formula, $C(s)$ represents the number of times that service S is correctly executed and n represents the total number of executions of the service S.

4.5   Reputation

The service S's credibility $q_{rep}(s)$ is the measure the service requestors use to measure the reliability of the services. Mainly influenced by the user experience, different service requestors might be inconsistent with their views on the same web service. It is can be calculated by the following formula:

$$q_{rep}(s) = \frac{\sum_{i=1}^{n} R_i(s)}{n} \qquad (6)$$

In it, $R_i(s)$ is the service requestor's comment on the credibility of the service. n is the number of times that S is being commented. Under normal circumstances, the service provider will set up an evaluation range to let the service requestors choose.

4.6   Normalization

Each QoWS attribute of web services has different units of measure and value range. In order to ensure the comparability of QoWS calculation, the QoWS evaluation attribute should be normalized and all the QoWS evaluation attributes can be reflected in the same value range. The QoWS attribute's measurement factors is:

$$G =< name, direction, valueRange, unit, location >$$

In it, *name* is the title of the measurement factor, and *direction* is its value reading direction. In this direction, the target object will get better and better evaluation results by the measurement factor. Value reading direction is divided into two kinds—the positive and the negative. For instance, as the smaller the price the better, the value reading direction of the price should be negative. And for reputation which is bigger the better, its direction should be positive. *ValueRange* is the value reading range of the measurement factor, and *valueRange* = *(min, max)*. The measurement index data outside the *valueRange* can be regarded as *min* or *max* according to its location. In the model, all the value readings are numerical form. *Unit* represents a unit of data used when reading the measurement factor in order to avoid the ambiguous explanation and different measure index value range caused by different units. *Location* represents whether the measure data given by living example is from the client side or service side.

As the evaluation effect and *valueRange* of most QoWS evaluation attributes have a linear relationship, this paper also adopted the linear normalization method to standardize the QoWS attribute data. Make linear transformation from the original measure data of its former range *valueRange* = *(min, max)* into the interval [0, 1] and unify the value reading direction of each measurement factor at the same time.

We assume that *G*'s value range is *valueRange* = *(min, max)* and the original measure date of a certain QoWS' evaluation attribute is v_i. If the value reading direction of the measurement factor is positive, then the bigger value suggests better QoWS. It can be normalized as following:

$$v' = \begin{cases} \dfrac{v_i - min}{max - min} & min \leq v \leq max \\ 1 & v_i \geq min \\ 0 & v_i \leq max \end{cases} \tag{7}$$

If the value reading direction is negative, then smaller the value, better the QoWS. It can be normalized as following:

$$v' = \begin{cases} \dfrac{max - v_i}{max - min} & min \leq v \leq max \\ 1 & v_i \leq min \\ 0 & v_i \geq max \end{cases} \tag{8}$$

After the preprocessing of normalization, all the measure data will fall in the interval [0,1] and their value reading directions are all positive. This paper introduced the five-star model to calculate the overall level of QoWS of the target object.

5   Experiment and Analysis

The experimental subjects are two types of professional weather services provided by the China Meteorological Administration. The collected results are listed in the following table.

Table 2. Results[1]

	D_a	D_b	D_c	D_d	D_e
1	0.74	0.48	0.69	0.45	1.0
2	1.0	0.94	0.76	0.88	1.0

Applying QoWS pentagram model for the five factors, we have the followings results:

$QoWS(S_1) =$
$0.48 \times [(0.74 \times 0.48) + (0.48 \times 0.69) + (0.69 \times 0.45) + (0.45 \times 1.0) + (1.0 \times 0.74)] = 1.04$

$QoWS(S_2) =$
$0.48 \times [(1.0 \times 0.94) + (0.94 \times 0.76) + (0.\ 76 \times 0.88) + (0.88 \times 1.\ 0) + (1.0 \times 1.0)] = 2.02$

Based on the QoWS verification, the measurement results of QoWS for both tests are shown in Fig.2. It is clear that the QoWS of Fig. 2(b) is higher than the QoWS of Fig. 2(a).

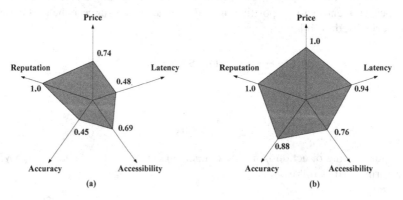

Fig. 2. Comparison

6   Conclusion

In this paper, we proposed a model-based evaluation approach to evaluate the QoWS, discussed the concept and the quantitative methods of web service quality attributes

---

[1] D_a, D_b, D_c, D_d, and D_e respectively represents the price, latency, accessibility, accuracy, and reputation metric of its requirements measurement.

(price, latency, accessibility, accuracy, and reputation) and conduct comprehensive evaluation towards the selected web service based on the evaluation model. Experimental results indicate that our approach is effective. Moreover, it significantly improves web service selection process. We will futher research on how to effectively improve the QoWS from perspective of the quality assessment algorithm in practical applications.

Acknowledgments. This work is supported by the National Basic Research Program of China (No.2009CB320504); the Foundation for Innovative Research Groups of the National Natural Science Foundation of China (No.60821001).

References

1. Qi, Y., Bouguettaya, A.: Computing Service Skyline from Uncertain QoWS. IEEE Transactions on Services Computing 3, 16–29 (2010)
2. Li, F., Yang, F., Shuang, K., Su, S.: A Policy-Driven Distributed Framework for Monitoring Quality of Web Services. In: IEEE International Conference on Web Services, pp. 708–715 (2008)
3. Su, S., Li, F., Yang, F.C.: Iterative selection algorithm for service composition in distributed environments. Science in China Series F-Information Sciences 51, 1841–1856 (2008)
4. Le-Hung, V., Aberer, K.: Towards Probabilistic Estimation of Quality of Online Services. In: IEEE International Conference on Web Services, pp. 99–106 (2009)
5. Nepal, S., Malik, Z., Bouguttaya, A.: Reputation Propagation in Composite Services. In: 7th International Conference on Web Service, pp. 295–302 (2009)
6. Ouzzani, M., Bouguettaya, A.: Efficient access to web services. IEEE Internet Comput. 8(2), 34–44 (2004)
7. Skoutas, D., Sacharidis, D., Simitsis, A., Sellis, T.: Ranking and Clustering Web Services Using Multicriteria Dominance Relationships. IEEE Transactions on Service Computing 3, 163–177 (2010)
8. Zheng, Z., Zhang, Y., Lyu, M.R.: Distributed QoS Evaluation for Real-World Web Services. In: 8th International Conference on Web Service, pp. 83–90 (2010)
9. Ivanovie, D., Carro, M., Hermenegildo, M.: Towards Data-Aware QoS-Driven Adaptation for Service Orchestrations. In: 8th International Conference on Web Service, pp. 107–114 (2010)

Practical Multi-party Versions of Private Set Intersection Protocols with Hardware Tokens

Ju-Sung Kang[1], Ok-Yeon Yi[1], Min-Ku Kim[1], and Ku-Young Chang[2]

[1] Department of Mathematics, Kookmin University
Jeongreung3-Dong, Seongbuk-Gu, Seoul, 136-702, Korea
{jskang,oyyi,kmnine}@kookmin.ac.kr
[2] Information Security Research Division, ETRI
161 Gajeong-Dong, Yuseong-Gu, Daejeon, 305-350, Korea
jang1090@etri.re.kr

Abstract. The objective of the private set intersection (PSI) protocol is that the participants want to compute the intersection based on their private input sets without revealing to another party any additional information about their respective sets. Several protocols for PSI have been proposed. In this paper we focus on the practical symmetric-key based PSI protocols using the hardware tokens, and extend the 2-party PSI protocols of [7] and [5] to the m-party versions where $m > 2$ by adopting the untrusted third party model. Our protocols achieve the same level of security as the original 2-party protocols, and are very efficient compared with the prior general framework.

Keywords: Cryptographic protocol, Private set intersection, Hardware token, Secure multi-party computation.

1 Introduction

The protocol for private set intersection deals with the situation that two or more parties want to compute the intersection based on their private input sets without revealing to another party any additional information about their respective sets except their sizes. Private set intersection (PSI) addresses several realistic privacy issues. PSI can be used directly to enable government agencies to compare their databases of suspects, or allow competing companies to find their common customers.

1.1 Related Work

Several cryptographic protocols for PSI and its variants have been proposed. According to the underlying cryptographic algorithms PSI protocols can be classified into public-key based and symmetric-key based schemes. Most prior works [1,2,6,8,9,10,11,12] for PSI have used expensive public-key algorithms such as homomorphic encryption systems. On the other hand Hazay and Lindell [7] introduced the idea of using standard smartcards for the set intersection problem.

T.-h. Kim et al. (Eds.): FGCN/DCA 2012, CCIS 350, pp. 72–79, 2012.

Their protocol uses only a linear number of symmetric-key computations and the amount of data stored in the smartcard does not depend on the sizes of the sets. Recently Fischlin et al. [5] have revisited the idea of Hazay and Lindell [7], and considered a setting where hardware tokens or smartcards are not necessarily trusted by both participants. It seems that the works of [7] and [5] are truly practical private set intersection protocols especially on the view point of computational efficiency.

1.2   Our Contribution

In this paper we extend the 2-party PSI protocols of [7] and [5] to the m-party versions where $m > 2$. More precisely we propose the m-party versions of [7] and [5] by using the notion of untrusted third party (UTP) model. It is assumed that UTP correctly executes the protocol and doesn't collude with any participating parties to violate privacy. The existence of UTP enables efficient protocols without revealing private information. Vaidya and Clifton [13] have presented a general framework that for associative functions, an efficient protocol for 2-party using UTP can be used to construct an efficient peer-to-peer secure m-party protocol with $m > 2$. However if we straightforwardly adopt the general framework of [13] to the m-party PSI protocols, an information disclosure of the pairwise intersection is inevitable. In our protocols this invasion of privacy does not happen. Moreover by adopting UTP model to our protocols, we take advantage of overall computational efficiency.

2   PSI Problem and Security Model

Assume that there are m parties, $\mathcal{P}^{(1)}, \ldots, \mathcal{P}^{(m)}$, with corresponding lists of private input sets $X^{(1)} = \{x_1^{(1)}, \ldots, x_{n_1}^{(1)}\}, \ldots, X^{(m)} = \{x_1^{(m)}, \ldots, x_{n_m}^{(m)}\}$, where all elements of $X^{(1)}, \ldots, X^{(m)}$ are from the same domain $D = \{0,1\}^n$, that is, $X^{(1)}, \ldots, X^{(m)} \subset D$. The PSI problem is as follows: m parties, $\mathcal{P}^{(1)}, \ldots, \mathcal{P}^{(m)}$, want to collaboratively compute $S = X^{(1)} \cap \cdots \cap X^{(m)}$ without revealing to another party any additional information about their private sets except S and their sizes.

In this work we adopt a computational model using UTP. We show that the existence of UTP enables efficient PSI protocols without revealing private information including even pairwise intersections. Basic assumptions for UTP are as follows:

1. UTP correctly executes the protocol.
2. UTP does not collude with any of the m parties to violate privacy.

UTP is given some information in the form of encrypted data, and performs a computation on the encrypted data. Hence UTP cannot make any sense of the data given to it without the assistance of the participating parties in the protocol. The encrypted computation result of UTP is handed to the local parties who are able to decrypt the result.

3   Two-Party PSI Protocols

In this work we concentrate on the truly practical PSI protocols using hardware tokens which contain proven security mechanisms. Here we introduce Two-party PSI protocols of [7] and [5]. The protocol of [7] achieves full simulation-based security in the presence of malicious adversaries under the assumption that the hardware tokens are tamper-proof and trusted by both participating parties. Meanwhile the protocol of [5] achieve the same level of security as that of [7] where the hardware tokens are not necessarily trusted by both participants.

Let $F_K(\cdot)$ be a pseudorandom permutation (PRP) with domain $D = \{0,1\}^n$ and the key K be chosen uniformly from D, where n is the security parameter. The symmetric-key block cipher AES is a good example of $F_K(\cdot)$ with $n = 128$.

Two-Party PSI Protocol of Hazay and Lindell [7]

- Inputs: Party $\mathcal{P}^{(1)}$ has a set of n_1 elements, $X^{(1)} = \{x_1^{(1)}, \ldots, x_{n_1}^{(1)}\}$, and party $\mathcal{P}^{(2)}$ has a set of n_2 elements, $X^{(2)} = \{x_1^{(2)}, \ldots, x_{n_2}^{(2)}\}$. All elements are taken from the domain $D = \{0,1\}^n$, where n is the security parameter. Both $\mathcal{P}^{(1)}$ and $\mathcal{P}^{(2)}$ are given n_1, n_2, and n.
- Setup of HW token $\mathcal{HT}^{(2)}$: Party $\mathcal{P}^{(1)}$ chooses two keys $CK, MK \leftarrow \{0,1\}^n$ and imports CK into the $\mathcal{HT}^{(2)}$ for usage as a pseudorandom permutation $F_{CK}(\cdot)$. $\mathcal{P}^{(2)}$ sets the usage counter of CK to be n_2 and defines that confirmation to `DeleteObject` is MACed using the key MK. $\mathcal{P}^{(1)}$ sends $\mathcal{HT}^{(2)}$ to $\mathcal{P}^{(2)}$.
- The Protocol:
  1. The first step of $\mathcal{P}^{(2)}$:
     (a) Given the HW token $\mathcal{HT}^{(2)}$, party $\mathcal{P}^{(2)}$ computes the set

     $$F_{CK}(X^{(2)}) = \{F_{CK}(x_1^{(2)}), \ldots, F_{CK}(x_{n_2}^{(2)})\} \ .$$

     (b) $\mathcal{P}^{(2)}$ issues a `DeleteObject` command to $\mathcal{HT}^{(2)}$ to delete CK and receives back the confirmation from $\mathcal{HT}^{(2)}$.
  2. The step of $\mathcal{P}^{(1)}$: $\mathcal{P}^{(1)}$ verifies the MAC-tag of the `DeleteObject` confirmation. If the MAC-tag is correct, then it computes the set

     $$F_{CK}(X^{(1)}) = \{F_{CK}(x_1^{(1)}), \ldots, F_{CK}(x_{n_1}^{(1)})\} \ ,$$

     sends it to $\mathcal{P}^{(2)}$ and halts. Otherwise, $\mathcal{P}^{(1)}$ outputs $\perp$ and halts.
  3. The second step of $\mathcal{P}^{(2)}$: $\mathcal{P}^{(2)}$ outputs the set

     $$S = \{x_j^{(2)} \mid F_{CK}(x_j^{(2)}) \in F_{CK}(X^{(1)})\}_{1 \leq j \leq n_2}$$

     and halts.

It has been proved that the two-party PSI protocol of Hazay and Lindell securely computes $X^{(1)} \cap X^{(2)}$ in the presence of malicious adversaries, where F is a PRP over $\{0,1\}^n$ and only $\mathcal{P}^{(2)}$ receives output. See the proof of Theorem 3 in [7].

Two-party PSI Protocol of Fischlin et al. [5]

- Inputs: Party $\mathcal{P}^{(1)}$ has a set of n_1 elements, $X^{(1)} = \{x_1^{(1)}, \ldots, x_{n_1}^{(1)}\}$, and party $\mathcal{P}^{(2)}$ has a set of n_2 elements, $X^{(2)} = \{x_1^{(2)}, \ldots, x_{n_2}^{(2)}\}$. All elements are taken from the domain $D = \{0,1\}^n$, where n is the security parameter. Both $\mathcal{P}^{(1)}$ and $\mathcal{P}^{(2)}$ are given n_1, n_2, and n.
- Setup of HW token $\mathcal{HT}^{(2)}$: Party $\mathcal{P}^{(1)}$ chooses two keys $CK, RK \leftarrow \{0,1\}^n$ and imports CK and RK into the $\mathcal{HT}^{(2)}$ for usage as a strong pseudorandom permutation (SPRP) $F_{CK}(\cdot)$ and a pseudorandom function (PRF) $f_{RK}(\cdot)$, respectively. $\mathcal{P}^{(1)}$ sets the usage counter of CK to be n_2 and sends $\mathcal{HT}^{(2)}$ to $\mathcal{P}^{(2)}$.
- The Protocol:
  1. $\mathcal{P}^{(1)}$ computes the set $F_{CK}(X^{(1)}) = \{F_{CK}(x_1^{(1)}), \ldots, F_{CK}(x_{n_1}^{(1)})\}$, sends it to $\mathcal{P}^{(2)}$
  2. The first step of $\mathcal{P}^{(2)}$:
     (a) Given the HW token $\mathcal{HT}^{(2)}$, party $\mathcal{P}^{(2)}$ sends $X^{(2)}$ to $\mathcal{HT}^{(2)}$.
     (b) $\mathcal{HT}^{(2)}$ computes the set
     $$Y^{(2)} = \{y_j^{(2)} = F_{CK}(x_j^{(2)}) \oplus f_{RK}(j)\}_{1 \leq j \leq n_2} \, ,$$
     and sends it to $\mathcal{P}^{(2)}$.
  3. The second step of $\mathcal{P}^{(2)}$:
     (a) $\mathcal{P}^{(2)}$ confirms the number of elements in $Y^{(2)}$, and sends the message "done" to $\mathcal{HT}^{(2)}$.
     (b) $\mathcal{HT}^{(2)}$ invalidates CK and sends $\{f_{RK}(j) \mid 1 \leq j \leq n_2\}$ to $\mathcal{P}^{(2)}$.
     (c) $\mathcal{P}^{(2)}$ computes $Z^{(2)} = \{z_j^{(2)} = y_j^{(2)} \oplus f_{RK}(j) \mid 1 \leq j \leq n_2\}$.
     (d) $\mathcal{P}^{(2)}$ outputs the set $S = \{z_j^{(2)} \mid z_j^{(2)} \in F_{CK}(X^{(1)})\}_{1 \leq j \leq n_2}$ and halts.

Fischlin et al. [5] have proved that their two-party PSI protocol securely evaluates $X^{(1)} \cap X^{(2)}$ with respect to a malicious $\mathcal{P}^{(2)}$ that cannot break into $\mathcal{HT}^{(2)}$, and keeps the private input of $\mathcal{P}^{(2)}$ in the indistinguishability sense with respect to a malicious $\mathcal{P}^{(1)}$. See the proof of Theorem 1 of [5].

Two-party PSI protocol of Hazay and Lindell assumes that $\mathcal{HT}^{(2)}$ is fully trusted by both parties. On the contrary Fischlin et al. have extended the protocol of Hazay and Lindell to make it non-interactive and guarantee privacy of $\mathcal{P}^{(2)}$ even if $\mathcal{P}^{(1)}$ and $\mathcal{HT}^{(2)}$ are malicious.

4   Multi-party PSI Protocols

In this section we propose two multi-party PSI protocols which extend the two-party protocols of [7] and [5], respectively, by introducing UTP model. Vaidya and Clifton [13] have presented a general framework that for associative functions, an efficient protocol for 2-party using UTP can be used to construct an efficient peer-to-peer secure m-party protocol with $m > 2$. They pointed out that the UTP is an external party different from all participants of the protocol, and presented an alternative framework without the external party. On the other hand if we straightforwardly adopt the general framework of [13] to multi-party PSI protocols, an information disclosure of the pairwise intersection is inevitable. We would like to remove this invasion of privacy and maintain a practical efficiency of UTP model. We introduce an external untrusted server UTP to design a practically efficient m-party PSI protocol. It is assumed that the UTP correctly executes the protocol and does not collude with any of the internal parties to violate privacy.

- Firstly we assume that:
    - there are m parties, $\mathcal{P}^{(1)}, \ldots, \mathcal{P}^{(m)}$, with corresponding lists of private input sets $X^{(1)} = \{x_1^{(1)}, \ldots, x_{n_1}^{(1)}\}, \ldots, X^{(m)} = \{x_1^{(m)}, \ldots, x_{n_m}^{(m)}\}$,
    - all elements of $X^{(1)}, \ldots, X^{(m)}$ are from the same domain $D = \{0,1\}^n$, that is, $X^{(1)}, \ldots, X^{(m)} \subset D$.
- The objective of m-Party PSI protocols is as follows:
    - m parties, $\mathcal{P}^{(1)}, \ldots, \mathcal{P}^{(m)}$, want to collaboratively compute $S = X^{(1)} \cap \cdots \cap X^{(m)}$ without revealing to another party any additional information about their private sets except S and their sizes,
    - and all parties obtain the result S.

4.1   Multi-party PSI Protocol with Trusted HW Tokens

Let $\mathcal{P}^{(1)}$ be the leader of all participating parties and serve as an issuer for all hardware tokens, $\mathcal{HT}^{(2)}, \ldots, \mathcal{HT}^{(m)}$. Assume that $n_2, \ldots, n_m$ are given to $\mathcal{P}^{(1)}$ at the hardware token initialization step, and the token has PRP and MAC algorithms in its security module. Moreover UTP, the external party, can communicate to all internal parties, $\mathcal{P}^{(1)}, \ldots, \mathcal{P}^{(m)}$.

Initialization of HW Tokens

- For each $2 \leq j \leq m$, the leader $\mathcal{P}^{(1)}$ performs the followings:
    - $\mathcal{P}^{(1)}$ chooses two keys $CK, MK_j \leftarrow \{0,1\}^n$ and imports them into the $\mathcal{HT}^{(j)}$ for usage as a PRP $F_{CK}(\cdot)$ and MAC algorithm $MAC_{MK_j}(\cdot)$, respectively.
    - Also $\mathcal{P}^{(1)}$ sets the usage counter of CK to be n_j and defines that confirmation to DeleteObject is MACed using the key MK_j.
    - $\mathcal{P}^{(1)}$ sends $\mathcal{HT}^{(j)}$ to $\mathcal{P}^{(j)}$.

Protocol 1. (Multi-party PSI Protocol with trusted HW tokens)

1. For $2 \leq j \leq m$, each $\mathcal{P}^{(j)}$ performs the followings:
   (a) Given the HW token $\mathcal{HT}^{(j)}$, party $\mathcal{P}^{(j)}$ computes the set

$$F_{CK}(X^{(j)}) = \{F_{CK}(x_1^{(j)}), \ldots, F_{CK}(x_{n_j}^{(j)})\} .$$

(b) $\mathcal{P}^{(j)}$ issues DeleteObject command to $\mathcal{HT}^{(j)}$ to delete CK and receives back the confirmation $MACtag^{(j)}$ from $\mathcal{HT}^{(j)}$.

(c) $\mathcal{P}^{(j)}$ sends $F_{CK}(X^{(j)})$ and $MACtag^{(j)}$ to UTP.

2. UTP sends $MACtag^{(2)}, \ldots, MACtag^{(m)}$ to $\mathcal{P}^{(1)}$.

3. $\mathcal{P}^{(1)}$ verifies the MAC-tags of DeleteObject confirmation. If all MAC-tags are correct, then it computes the set

$$F_{CK}(X^{(1)}) = \{F_{CK}(x_1^{(1)}), \ldots, F_{CK}(x_{n_1}^{(1)})\},$$

sends it to UTP and halts. Otherwise, $\mathcal{P}^{(1)}$ outputs $\perp$ and halts.

4. UTP evaluates $Y = F_{CK}(X^{(1)}) \cap \cdots \cap F_{CK}(X^{(m)})$ and sends it to all parties $\mathcal{P}^{(1)}, \ldots, \mathcal{P}^{(m)}$.

5. For $1 \leq j \leq m$, each $\mathcal{P}^{(j)}$ outputs the set $S = \{x_l^{(j)} \mid F_{CK}(x_l^{(j)}) \in Y\}_{1 \leq l \leq n_j}$ and halts.

The correctness of $S = X^{(1)} \cap \cdots \cap X^{(m)}$ is guaranteed by the fact that $x = y$ if and only if $F_{CK}(x) = F_{CK}(y)$. Two important operations of the HW token $\mathcal{HT}^{(j)}$, $F_{CK}(\cdot)$ and $MAC_{MK_j}(\cdot)$ can be implemented by using a very efficient symmetric-key block cipher such as AES, and CBC-MAC or HMAC, respectively. The role of CK is to keep the privacy of all parties against UTP. All different $MK_2, \ldots, MK_m$ are served as keys for MAC algorithm that the leader $\mathcal{P}^{(1)}$ can confirm invalidation of CK in all HW tokens $\mathcal{HT}^{(2)}, \ldots, \mathcal{HT}^{(m)}$.

4.2 Multi-party PSI Protocol with Untrusted HW Tokens

Like the just previous subsection, let $\mathcal{P}^{(1)}$ be the leader of all participating parties and serve as an issuer for all hardware tokens, $\mathcal{HT}^{(2)}, \ldots, \mathcal{HT}^{(m)}$. Assume that $n_2, \ldots, n_m$ are given to $\mathcal{P}^{(1)}$ at the hardware token initialization step, and the security module of token includes SPRP and PRF algorithms. We further assume that the external party UTP can communicate to all internal parties, $\mathcal{P}^{(1)}, \ldots, \mathcal{P}^{(m)}$.

Initialization of HW Tokens

- For each $2 \leq j \leq m$, the leader $\mathcal{P}^{(1)}$ performs the followings:
  - $\mathcal{P}^{(1)}$ chooses two keys $CK, RK_j \leftarrow \{0,1\}^n$ and imports CK and RK_j into the $\mathcal{HT}^{(j)}$ for usage as SPRP $F_{CK}(\cdot)$ and PRF $f_{RK_j}(\cdot)$, respectively.
  - Also $\mathcal{P}^{(1)}$ sets the usage counter of CK to be n_j.
  - $\mathcal{P}^{(1)}$ sends $\mathcal{HT}^{(j)}$ to $\mathcal{P}^{(j)}$.

Protocol 2. (Multi-party PSI Protocol with untrusted HW tokens)

1. $\mathcal{P}^{(1)}$ sends $Z^{(1)} = \{z_l^{(1)} = F_{CK}(x_l^{(1)}) \mid 1 \leq l \leq n_1\}$ to UTP.

2. For $2 \leq j \leq m$, each $\mathcal{P}^{(j)}$ performs the followings:

   (a) Given the HW token $\mathcal{HT}^{(j)}$, $\mathcal{P}^{(j)}$ computes the set

$$Y^{(j)} = \{y_l^{(j)} = F_{CK}(x_l^{(j)}) \oplus f_{RK_j}(l) \mid 1 \leq l \leq n_j\}.$$

(b) $\mathcal{P}^{(j)}$ confirms the number of elements in $Y^{(j)}$, and sends the message "done" to $\mathcal{HT}^{(j)}$.

(c) $\mathcal{HT}^{(j)}$ invalidates CK and sends $\{p_l^{(j)} = f_{RK_j}(l) \mid 1 \le l \le n_j\}$ to $\mathcal{P}^{(j)}$.

(d) $\mathcal{P}^{(j)}$ evaluates the set $Z^{(j)} = \{z_l^{(j)} = y_l^{(j)} \oplus p_l^{(j)} \mid 1 \le l \le n_j\}$.

(e) $\mathcal{P}^{(j)}$ sends $Z^{(j)}$ to UTP.

3. UTP evaluates $W = Z^{(1)} \cap Z^{(2)} \cap \cdots \cap Z^{(m)}$, and sends W to all parties.

4. For $1 \le j \le m$, each $\mathcal{P}^{(j)}$ outputs the set

$$S = \{x_l^{(j)} \mid F_{CK}(x_l^{(j)}) \in W\}_{1 \le l \le n_j}$$

and halts.

The correctness of $S = X^{(1)} \cap \cdots \cap X^{(m)}$ is guaranteed by the fact that $z_l^{(j)} = y_l^{(j)} \oplus p_l^{(j)} = F_{CK}(x_l^{(j)})$, and $x = y$ if and only if $F_{CK}(x) = F_{CK}(y)$. Two operations of the HW token $\mathcal{HT}^{(j)}$, SPRP $F_{CK}(\cdot)$ and PRF $f_{RK_j}(\cdot)$ can be implemented by using a very efficient symmetric-key block cipher and CBC-MAC or HMAC algorithm, respectively. The encryption key CK is to keep the privacy of all parties against UTP. All different $RK_2, \ldots, RK_m$ are served as keys for PRF algorithm that the leader $\mathcal{P}^{(1)}$ and UTP can confirm invalidation of CK in all HW tokens $\mathcal{HT}^{(2)}, \ldots, \mathcal{HT}^{(m)}$.

4.3   Analysis of Privacy and Efficiency

In the general framework of [13], so many peer-to-peer 2-party computations are iterated with regarding another internal party as UTP under the hierarchy of about $\log_2 m/2$ stages. However in our protocols, there is no peer-to-peer 2-party computation and each party is required only one-time communication to UTP. Each $\mathcal{P}^{(j)}(2 \le j \le m)$ who has hardware token $\mathcal{HT}^{(j)}$ locally performs two-times communications to its token in both Protocol 1 and 2.

If we adopt the general framework of [13] to multi-party PSI protocols, an information disclosure of each pairwise intersection $X^{(i)} \cap X^{(j)}$ is inevitable. Since there is no peer-to-peer 2-party computation in Protocol 1 and 2, any disclosure of pairwise intersections cannot be occurred. Under the basic assumption that UTP doesn't collude with any of the internal parties, we can show that Protocol 1 and 2 achieve the same level of security as the original two-party protocols of [7] and [5], respectively, where we regard each party $\mathcal{P}^{(j)}(2 \le j \le m)$ of Protocol 1 and 2 as $\mathcal{P}^{(2)}$ of two-party protocols.

5   Conclusion

In this paper we have focused on the practical symmetric-key based PSI protocols using the hardware tokens, and extended the 2-party PSI protocols of [7] and [5] to the m-party versions where $m > 2$. We have proposed the multi-party versions by using the notion of UTP model. Under the assumption that UTP doesn't collude with any of the internal parties, our protocols achieve the same level of security as the original two-party protocols. Moreover our protocols are very efficient compared with the general framework of [13].

Acknowledgements. This research was partially supported by research program 2012 of Kookmin Uninersity in Korea and Next-Generation Information Computing Development Program through the National Research Foundation of Korea(NRF) funded by the Ministry of Education, Science and Technology (Grant No. 2012-0006493).

References

1. Camenisch, J., Zaverucha, G.M.: Private Intersection of Certified Sets. In: Dingledine, R., Golle, P. (eds.) FC 2009. LNCS, vol. 5628, pp. 108–127. Springer, Heidelberg (2009)
2. Dachman-Soled, D., Malkin, T., Raykova, M., Yung, M.: Efficient Robust Private Set Intersection. In: Abdalla, M., Pointcheval, D., Fouque, P.-A., Vergnaud, D. (eds.) ACNS 2009. LNCS, vol. 5536, pp. 125–142. Springer, Heidelberg (2009)
3. De Cristofaro, E., Kim, J., Tsudik, G.: Linear-Complexity Private Set Intersection Protocols Secure in Malicious Model. In: Abe, M. (ed.) ASIACRYPT 2010. LNCS, vol. 6477, pp. 213–231. Springer, Heidelberg (2010)
4. De Cristofaro, E., Tsudik, G.: Practical Private Set Intersection Protocols with Linear Complexity. In: Sion, R. (ed.) FC 2010. LNCS, vol. 6052, pp. 143–159. Springer, Heidelberg (2010)
5. Fischlin, M., Pinkas, B., Sadeghi, A.-R., Schneider, T., Visconti, I.: Secure Set Intersection with Untrusted Hardware Tokens. In: Kiayias, A. (ed.) CT-RSA 2011. LNCS, vol. 6558, pp. 1–16. Springer, Heidelberg (2011)
6. Freedman, M.J., Nissim, K., Pinkas, B.: Efficient Private Matching and Set Intersection. In: Cachin, C., Camenisch, J.L. (eds.) EUROCRYPT 2004. LNCS, vol. 3027, pp. 1–19. Springer, Heidelberg (2004)
7. Hazay, C., Lindell, Y.: Constructions of truly practical secure protocols using standard smartcards. In: CCS 2008, pp. 491–500. ACM (2008)
8. Hazay, C., Lindell, Y.: Efficient Protocols for Set Intersection and Pattern Matching with Security Against Malicious and Covert Adversaries. In: Canetti, R. (ed.) TCC 2008. LNCS, vol. 4948, pp. 155–175. Springer, Heidelberg (2008)
9. Hazay, C., Nissim, K.: Efficient Set Operations in the Presence of Malicious Adversaries. In: Nguyen, P.Q., Pointcheval, D. (eds.) PKC 2010. LNCS, vol. 6056, pp. 312–331. Springer, Heidelberg (2010)
10. Jarecki, S., Liu, X.: Fast Secure Computation of Set Intersection. In: Garay, J.A., De Prisco, R. (eds.) SCN 2010. LNCS, vol. 6280, pp. 418–435. Springer, Heidelberg (2010)
11. Kissner, L., Song, D.: Privacy-Preserving Set Operations. In: Shoup, V. (ed.) CRYPTO 2005. LNCS, vol. 3621, pp. 241–257. Springer, Heidelberg (2005)
12. Sang, Y., Shen, H.: Privacy preserving set intersection protocol secure against malicious behaviors. In: PDCAT 2007, pp. 461–468. IEEE Computer Society (2007)
13. Vaidya, J., Clifton, C.: Leveraging the Multi in Secure Multi-Party Computation. In: WPES 2003, pp. 53–59. ACM (2003)

Design and Implementation of a Signaling Protocol to Transmit UHDTV Contents in the Cable Broadcast Network

Sunsik Roh[1] and Sunghoon Kim[2]

[1] Dept. of Information and Communication, Gwnagju University, Gwangju, Korea
ssroh@gwangju.ac.kr
[2] Broadcasting & Telecommunication Convergence Media Research Dept. ETRI
steve-kim@etri.re.kr

Abstract. ltra high-definition television (UHDTV) is suggested as a next generation television technology beyond high-definition television (HDTV). In this paper, we propose the signaling protocol to transmit large-capacity UHDTV contents in the current cable broadcast network. The signaling protocol based on an in-band signaling is designed to minimize the change of the current cable network architecture. To send the channel bonding information from the headend to STBs, three kinds of 36 bits signaling message are designed. We describe procedures of the headend and the STB to serve UHDTV contents. In order to evaluate the performance of proposed signaling protocol, we implement a testbed system, which consists of a frame classifier, a frame merger, 1024-QAM transmitter/receiver, MPEG-2 TS Generator, and monitoring S/Ws. According to the testbed system, we can ascertain that 200Mbps UHDTV contents are successfully transmitted via four bonded channel.

Keywords: UHDTV, Channel bonding, Cable broadcast network, Signaling protocol, In-band signaling.

1   Introduction

The viewers' demand for higher quality video contents and larger TV screen leads to research and develop of ultra high-definition television (UHDTV). The broadcast content produced for UHDTV has 3,840×2160 (4K) or 7,680 × 4,320 (8K) pixel resolution. Therefore, the UHDTV may serve broadcast contents with an ultra high quality that are 4 to 16 times more vivid than standard HDTV provides broadcast contents with 1,920 × 1,080 (2K) pixel resolution[1-3].

In a current cable broadcast network, a video content is modulated by Quadrature Amplitude Modulation (QAM) devices of a headend, and the modulated video broadcast content is transmitted to a receiving part through one transmission channel predetermined for that video broadcast content.. A standard organization for a digital broadcasting cable provides a 256-QAM single carrier wave scheme. Since 2009, 1024-QAM and 4096-QAM have been proposed and developed in order to increase

T.-h. Kim et al. (Eds.): FGCN/DCA 2012, CCIS 350, pp. 80–87, 2012.

the transmission efficiency and to transmit large capacity data [4]. The data rate of 1024-QAM and 4096-QAM are about 50Mbps and 80Mbps, respectively. However, one QAM channel is not sufficient to transfer UHDTV contents because the data rate of UHDTV contents is about 200Mbps. Therefore, in order that UHDTV broadcast services are provided in the cable broadcast network, a new transmission technology that may bond a plurality of transmission channels is desired.

In this paper, we propose a signaling protocol for transporting 8K UHDTV contents in the cable broadcast network. In order to minimize the overhead of changing protocols used in the current cable broadcast network and provide the simplicity of applying, the protocol designed in this paper is based on an in-band signaling. We design the network architecture and signaling messages to support channel bonding process, by which one 8K UHDTV content stream can be transmitted via a set of QAM channels. Also, in order to evaluate the performance of proposed signaling protocol, we implement a testbed system, which consists of a frame classifier, a frame merger, 1024-QAM transmitter/receiver, MPEG-2 TS Generator, and monitoring S/Ws.

The rest of the paper is organized as follows. In Section 2, we propose the transmission strategy of UHDTV contents in the cable broadcast network. We design the network architecture, the signaling protocol, and procedures of a headend and a STB in Section 3. Section 4 describes to implement and analyze the performance of the protocol. In Section 5 we make the conclusion.

2   Strategy for Transmission of UHDTV Contents

In this paper, we apply the principle of channel bonding to transfer UHDTV contents in a cable broadcast network. First of all, we suggest the strategy to provide 8K UHDTV contents by using of channel bonding in a cable broadcast. The strategy is divided up into 3 Phases according to transmitting the control information that includes channel bonding information. The first Phase is the transport plan based on an in-band signaling. The network structure is as same as the existing cable network, which is a one-way distribution network. As a QAM frame at Layer 1 is used to carry control information, additional control channel and heavy control protocol are not necessary. Therefore, Phase 1 has the advantage of being easy to apply to existing cable broadcast network.

In Phase 2, the network architecture is a one-way distribution networks as similar to that in Phase 1. Phase 2 is based on an out-of-band signaling. An additional signaling channel to carry the control information and to be separated from data channels is required. Either OOB (Out-Of-Band) [5,6] protocol or DSG (DOCSIS Set-top Gate) [7] protocol is considerable as a candidate control protocol. At an early stage, to apply OOB protocol is easy because it is being used in existing cable broadcast network, while ,in the long term, DSG-based approach is suitable for Phase 2 protocol in the view that a set-top box is being equipped with a DSG functional module. However, as two protocols transmit control information between control servers and set-top boxes, not between a headend and set-up boxes, the research to upgrade them or to develop a new control protocol is required.

Unlike in Phase 1 and Phase 2, the network architecture in Phase 3 is a bidirectional cable network. Control information is transmitted from a headend to a set-top box and vice versa. As Phase 3 is characterized by the convergence of a cable broadcast network and a cable data network, data traffics and broadcast traffics share transmission channels in the Phase 3 network. The DSG protocol, or the DOCSIS protocol [8] that supports two-way mode of operation can be used as the protocol in Phase 3. If used, they are needed to be enhanced to carry channel bonding information.

3   Design of Signaling Protocol

3.1   Network Architecture

A logical block diagram of the headend and the STB is shown in Fig. 2. The headend receives video streams from a video server, transforms into QAM frames, and sends them to STBs through QAM devices. The headend is composed of a receiver, a bonding controller (BC), a frame classifier (FC), and QAM modulators. The receiver at a headend receives a video broadcast content from a video server. Modulators at a headend and demodulators at a STB have one of various modulation/demodulation schemes, for example 64-QAM, 128-QAM, 256-QAM, 1024-QAM, and 4096-QAM modulation/ demodulation scheme. In this paper we assume that 1024-QAMs are used. As four 1024-QAM channels are required in order to support 200Mbps 8K UHDTV contents, we assume that the maximum number of bonding channels is 4. Therefore, a headend has at most 4 QAM modulators and transmitters to transport a UHDTV content.

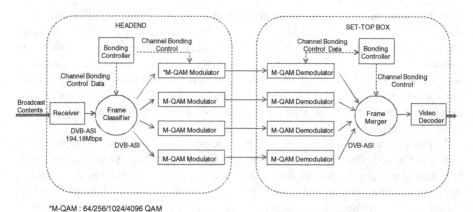

*M-QAM : 64/256/1024/4096 QAM

Fig. 1. Functional diagram of a headend and a STB

The Bonding Controllers (BCs) is a block that performs operations for channel bonding. The BC at a headend determines whether to bond transmission channels based on the definition of the video broadcast content or not, assigns a set of channels bonded to transmit one UHDTV content, and stores it on a channel information table in the storage unit. And then the BC informs BCs at STBs of channel information by using a signaling message. Also, the BC notifies channel information to a Frame Classifier (FC) via an internal interface. The Frame Classifier divides a UHDTV content into as many content segments as the number of bonded channels.

A STB consists of receivers, QAM demodulators, a bonding controller (BC), and a frame merger (FM). For the same reason described earlier, the STB has 4 QAM demodulators and receivers (tuners). The QAM demodulator demodulates received segments and sends them to a FM. The FM reassembles them back into a UHDTV content. The BC at a STB receives the channel bonding information from a headend and notifies it to the FM. The BC assigns each bonded channel contained in the channel bonding information to each individual QAM demodulator/tuner.

3.2   Signaling Message Format

As this paper focuses on minimizing the change of current cable broadcast network structure or protocol, we design signaling messages that are transmitted within QAM frames. Signaling information is recorded on a frame synchronization trailer field of a QAM frame. Fig. 2 depicts the signaling message format that has 36bits. As a 64-QAM frame, a 256-QAM frame, and a 1024-QAM frame have 42 bits, 40bits, and 48bits frame synchronization trailer field respectively, the designed signaling message is suitable for all of them.

The *Message Type (MT)* field is the first 2bits and uniquely identifies the specific function of the message. The *INIT* message indicates that a headend is reactivated or a cable broadcast network is initialized. The *ACT* message notifies that a video broadcast content is being transmitted through transmission channels assigned previously. Additionally, the *BC* message indicates that transmission channels for transporting a video broadcast content or broadcast services are changed.

The *Transmission Control (TC)* field is broken down into the *Bonding Type* sub-field, the *UHD mode* sub-field, and the *QAM Type* sub-field. The *Bonding Type* sub-field includes the two MSBs of the *TC* field. These bits are interpreted by a headend and a STB in the same manner to indicate the number of bonding channels. The first type, "Not-Bonding (00)", uses one transmission channel, and indicates that a broadcast content is transmitted in the same manner as current cable broadcast network. Others notify that 2, 3, and 4 transmission channels are combined and used respectively. Two bits following the *Bonding Type* sub-field is the *UHD mode* sub-field. The use of these bits is dependent on the resolution of the broadcast video content. Two LSBs of the *TC* field is the *QAM Type* sub-field that represents the modulation/demodulation scheme. The *Bonding Channel List* field includes channel IDs of bonded channels. The maximum number of channel IDs contained in this field is four. Each channel ID has 7 bits. The first channel, Channel ID1 is set as a primary transmission channel, and the second through the fourth channels are set as secondary transmission channels.

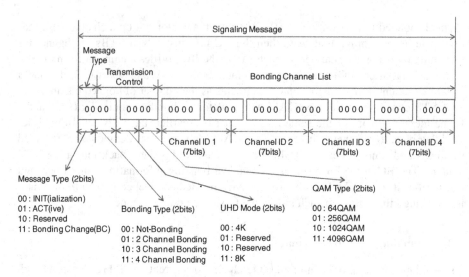

Fig. 2. Signaling message format

3.3   Procedures of a Headend and a STB

Fig. 3 illustrates a procedure of a headend for providing channel bonding technique. There are two cases. One is that a cable network is initialized or the headend is reset or turned on. Another is that the headend normally transmits a broadcast content or updates a transmission information table. In the former case, the headend checks the transmission information table containing assigned channel information, and generates an INIT message for every transmission channel. The headend normally starts to serve transmission of a broadcast content after the processing of initialization is completed. To determine generating either an ACT message or a BC message, the headend checks whether bonded channel IDs is updated. If bonded channel IDs is not changed, an ACT message is generated. Otherwise, a BC message is made.

Fig. 4 shows a procedure of a STB. After receiving a QAM frame through a bonded transmission channel, the STB demodulates the broadcast content segment and gets a signaling message in the frame synchronization trailer field of the QAM frame. In the case of an INIT message, the STB checks whether the message is transmitted through the primary channel. If the primary channel is used, the STB updates a transmission information table, and then assigns a bonded transmission channel to each receiver/tuner.

In the case of an ACT message, the STB stores the demodulated broadcast content segment at a buffer. If the number of buffered segments is equal of the number of bonded channels, the STB reassembles buffered segments into a broadcast content, and then sends it to a subscriber's device.

When the BC message is received, the STB checks whether the message is transmitted through the primary channel. If the message is received through the primary channel, the STB updates the transmission information table and assigns updated channels to corresponding receivers/tuners.

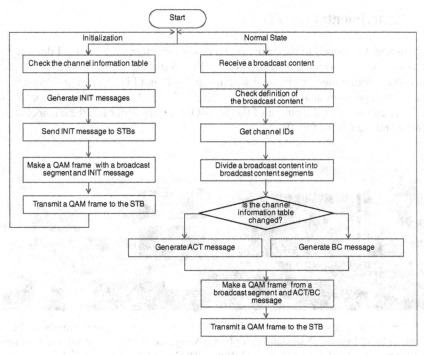

Fig. 3. Procedure of the headend

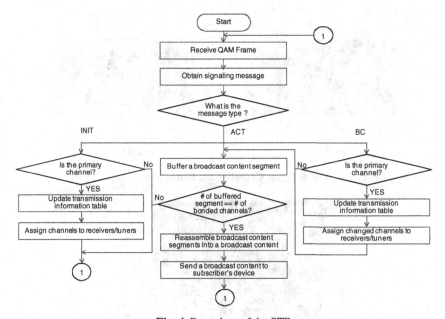

Fig. 4. Procedure of the STB

4   Experimental Results

We implement a testbed to ascertain the process of the signaling protocol designed in this paper. Fig. 5 shows the testbed systems. Fig. 6 depicts the frame classifier platform and the frame merger platform within Fig. 5-(d) and Fig. 5-(c). Fig. 7 depicts the result of the spectrum analyzer (Fig. 5-(f)) for 1024-QAM transmitter. According to Fig. 7, we can see that the output of the 1024-QAM transmitter has the channel space of 6Mhz and the CNR of 55dB.

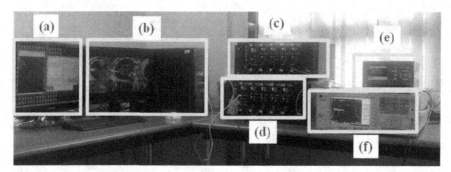

Fig. 5. Testbed Systems for transmission UHDTV contents: (a) Control S/W(Signaling Monitor), (b) MPEG-2 Demux/ Demodulator, (c) Frame Merger & 1024-QAM Receivers, (d) Frame Classifier & 1024-QAM Transmitters, (e) MEPG-2 TS Generator, (f) Spectrum Analyzer

(a) Frame Classifier   (b) Frame Merger

Fig. 6. Frame Classifier and Frame Merger

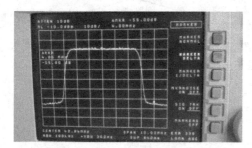

Fig. 7. Output signal spectrum of the 1024-QAM transmitter

According to the results of decoding in Fig. 5-(b), we can know that the proposed signaling protocol provide seamless play out of 200Mbps UHDTV contents. As a result, we can ascertain that the sender and the receiver correctly share the control information about bonded channels and 200Mbps UHDTV contents are successfully transported through bonded channels from a sender to a receiver by using the proposed signaling protocol.

5   Conclusion

In this paper we designed a signaling protocol based on in-band signaling, which uses the channel bonding mechanism in order to offer significant increase in the peak data rate. The design objectives are to minimize the overhead of changing current protocols, provide the simplicity of applying, and transmit a UHDTV content through a set of QAM channels. By implementing a testbed system, we could know that the protocol successfully serves transmission of a 8K UHDTV content.

Acknowledgement. The work was conducted by research funds from Gwangju University in 2012 and the IT R&D program (2008-F-011, Development of Next Generation DTV Core Technology) of KEIT&KCC&MKE.

References

1. Sugawara, M.: Super HI-Vision – research on a future ultra-HDTV system. EBU Technical Review (2008)
2. Oyamada, K., Nakatogawa, T., Nakamura, M.: Ultra-High-Definition Television and Its Optical Transmission. IEICE Transactions on Communications E94-B(4), 876–883 (2011)
3. Cho, C., Heo, J., Kim, J.: An extension of J.83 annex B transmission systems for ultra-high definition (UD) TV broadcasting. IEEE Transactions on Consumer Electronics 55(1), 63–68 (2011)
4. Hasse, P., Jaeger, D., Robert, J.: Boost of cable capacity by DVB-C2 considering realistic channel conditions. In: International Conference on Consumer Electronics (ICCE), pp. 19–20 (2010)
5. CableLabs: Out-of-Band Transfer Interface Specification, OC-SP -OOB-I01-05118 (2005)
6. SCTE: Digital Broadband Delivery System: Out of Band Transport Part 1: Mode A, ANSI/SCTE 55-1 (2009)
7. CableLabs: DOCSIS Set-top Gateway (DSG) Interface Specification, CM-SP-DSG- I15-100611 (2010)
8. CableLabs: DOCSIS 3.0 MAC and Upper Layer Protocols Interface Specification, CM-SP-MULPIv3.0-I16-110623 (2011)

A New Group Key Rekeying
with Homomorphic Encryption

Heeyoul Kim

Department of Computer Science,
Kyonggi University
Suwon, Republic of Korea
heeyoul.kim@kgu.ac.kr

Abstract. Secure group communication enables only authorized group members to communicate securely with each other by means of group key. Because group membership can be changed frequently due to joining or leaving of members, a scalable group key rekeying is essential to preserve security. In this paper we present a new group key scheme based on homomorphic encryption. Compared with the previous schemes, our scheme improves scalability by reducing the number of multicasted keys for rekeying. The abstract should summarize the contents of the paper.

Keywords: secure group communication, group key, homomorphic encryption.

1 Introduction

With the growth of many-to-many interactive systems such as video conference, broadcasting and cloud computing, the importance of group communication has also increased. Group communication enables a group member to communicate with other members simultaneously via multicast to transmit data with relatively little cost, rather than unicast.

From the security aspects, a naive method to transmit data to only authorized group members is to extend one-to-one secure protocol using shared secret keys. However it is not scalable to a large group because it requires too many secret keys. Instead a group key which is a secret key known to only group members has been employed. Since the transmitted data are encrypted with the group key, only group members can access the data.

The major issue of group key management is to preserve security even though the group membership is dynamically changed. When a new member joins the group, rekeying the group key prevents him from discovering messages in the past even if he overheard the encrypted messages. Also, when an existing member leaves the group, rekeying the group key prevents him from discovering messages in the future. However rekeying is very consumptive although it is frequently performed due to the characteristics of group communication. Thus the way to reduce overheads and increase scalability has been researched in the literature.

T.-h. Kim et al. (Eds.): FGCN/DCA 2012, CCIS 350, pp. 88–94, 2012.
© Springer-Verlag Berlin Heidelberg 2012

Scalability estimation is measured by three kinds of costs: storage cost, computation cost and communication cost. Among them the dominant cost in group-based systems is rather communication cost than computation cost [1,2]. Especially multicasting to all group members is very costly because not only group members but also routers or other entities connected by the network must forward the message.

The most widely used approach for scalability is using a logical key tree structure. Wong et al. [3] proposed Logical Key Hierarchy (LKH) scheme where each node in the tree represents a key and each member knows the keys of the nodes along the path from its corresponding leaf node to the root. LKH+ [4] scheme improved rekeying for member join. McGrew and Sherman [5] presented OFT scheme which is a variant of LKH using one-way functions. Canetti et al. [6] presented OFCT scheme using pseudo random generator. Other variants of LKH for optimization have been presented [7,8]. Using a logical key tree reduces communication cost significantly compared with the nave method. However group key rekeying requires at least $O(\log n)$ keys to be multicasted, which is still not sufficient for a large group especially where group membership is changed frequently.

In this paper we present a new group key scheme with low communication cost for rekeying. It utilizes the logical key tree structure but the way that keys are shared by group members is contrary to other schemes. For efficient key derivation and rekeying it utilizes homomorphic encryption which is recently highlighted in the literature. As a result, our scheme requires only two keys to be multicasted for rekeying, which is significant improvement from previous schemes.

2   Homomorphic Encryption

Homomorphic encryption enables computing with encrypted data and is hence a useful tool for secure protocols [9]. Let $E(PK, x)$ be a homomorphic encryption function of message x with a public key PK. Then it has the following homomorphic property: $E(PK, x_1) * E(PK, x_2) = E(PK, x_1 \cdot x_2)$ where $*$ denotes an operation in ciphertexts and $\cdot$ denotes an operation in plaintexts.

After the concept was introduced by Rivest, Adleman and Dertouzos [10], several schemes have been presented. For instance, basic RSA is a multiplicatively homomorphic encryption scheme: given two ciphertexts, one can efficiently compute a ciphertext that encrypts the product of the original plaintexts. ElGamal [11] is also a multiplicatively homomorphic encryption scheme, and [12,13] are additively homomorphic encryption schemes. Above schemes allows homomorphic computation of only one operation (multiplication or addition). After Gentry [14] proposed the first fully homomorphic encryption scheme using ideal lattice, many researches on this area have been in progress.

The major merit of homomorphic encryption is that one can process encrypted data without the decryption key. It has many applications such as secure voting protocols, private information retrieval schemes, and secure data process in cloud computing. In this paper, it is utilized to derive and update subkeys for group key rekeying as described in Section 3.

3   Proposed Scheme

3.1   Setup

Like other centralized group key schemes, our scheme assumes that there is a trusted Key Distribution Center (KDC) that distributes keys and manages group membership. Initially the KDC establishes a new group communication with initial n members as follows. The KDC chooses a homomorphic encryption function $E()$ and generates two public keys PK_L and PK_R. It also chooses a secure hash function $H()$. These are publicly opened to group members. The KDC then randomly generates a group key GK which will be shared between group members securely.

The KDC constructs a logical binary key tree where each group member is assigned to each leaf node (see Fig. 1). Now we define a subkey SK_i of a node n_i as, in contrast to most other schemes, a secret key shared with all group members except for the members assigned in the subtree rooted at the node n_i. The KDC randomly generates SK_1 and it derives other subkeys from the following equation:

$$SK_{2i} = E(PK_L, SK_i), \quad SK_{2i+1} = E(PK_R, SK_i) \tag{1}$$

We define $SKSet_i$ as a set of subkeys of sibling nodes of the nodes along the path from root to n_i. For each member, the KDC securely sends GK and $SKSet_i$ to the member assigned to n_i. With the keys in $SKSet_i$ the member can derive any subkeys except for the subkeys of the nodes along the path from root to n_i by equation (1). For instance, a member u_2 in Fig. 1 receives GK and $SKSet_9 = \{SK_3, SK_5, SK_8\}$. With them it can derive $SK_3 \sim SK_{14}$ except for SK_1, SK_2, SK_4 and SK_9.

Now group members are prepare to communicate with each other securely by encrypting messages with GK.

3.2   Rekeying for Member Join

Suppose a new user u wants to join the group. Before it joins, current group key GK should be rekeyed to prevent it from discovering the messages in the past. The rekeying process for join is as follows and it is relatively simple compared with the rekeying process for leave.

The KDC notifies all group members that a new member will join. Then both the KDC and each member rekey their group key: $GK' = H(GK)$. The KDC finds a proper leaf node n_i not assigned to other members in the tree, and then it securely sends GK' and $SKSet_i$ to u.

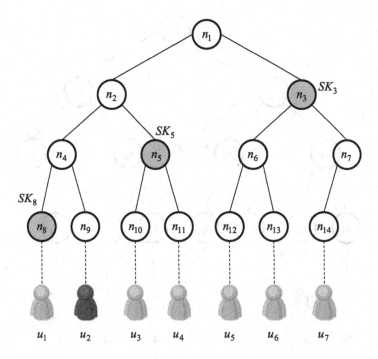

Fig. 1. A logical key tree and $SKSet_9$ of a member u_2

3.3   Rekeying for Member Leave

Suppose an existing member u assigned to a node n_i wants to leave the group. After it leaves, current group key should be rekeyed to prevent it from discovering the messages in the future. Also the subkeys should be rekeyed because it knows some subset of them. The rekeying process is as follows.

The KDC randomly generates a new group key GK' and an update key U_1. These are encrypted with SK_i and multicasted to group members. After deriving SK_i from its $SKSet$ as explained in Section 3.1, each member gets GK' and U_1 by decrypting the message with SK_i.

Now it is time for the member to rekey its $SKSet$ with U_1. For each SK_k in $SKSet$, U_k is derived from U_1 via the following equation similarly to subkey derivation:

$$U_{2i} = E(PK_L, U_i), \quad U_{2i+1} = E(PK_R, U_i). \tag{2}$$

Then SK_k is rekeyed to $SK'_k = SK_k * U_k$. For instance, in Fig. 2 the member u_2s subkeys are rekeyed as

$$SK'_3 = SK_3 * U_3, \quad SK'_5 = SK_5 * U_5, \quad SK'_8 = SK_8 * U_8. \tag{3}$$

By the homomorphic property of $E()$, rekeyed subkeys also preserve the relation of Equation (1) and the key derivation in Section 3.1 is kept valid.

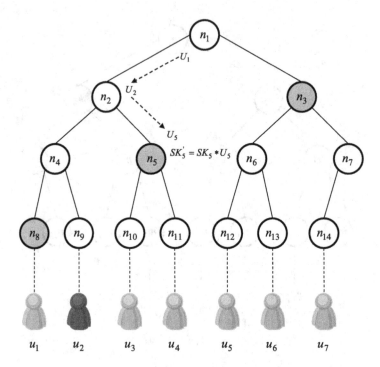

Fig. 2. Rekeying of SK_5 by a member u_2

The advantage of this approach is that subkeys are rekeyed from an update key U_1 instead of distributing a set of new subkeys from the KDC. It significantly reduces communication cost since the previous schemes such as LKH requires $\log n$ keys transmitted at least for n group members.

4   Analysis

Our scheme focuses on reducing communication cost which is the dominant bottleneck in deploying group-based systems. Especially, only two keys are multicasted to group members for rekeying whereas at least $O(\log n)$ keys (for n members) are multicasted in other tree-based schemes. This advantage provides high scalability even if the group is very large and membership is changed rapidly.

Furthermore the KDC needs not to store all subkeys. It just keeps current root subkey SK_1 and it can get any other subkeys by roughly $\log n$ subkey derivation operations whenever necessary. This helps the KDC to manage very large group efficiently.

From the viewpoint of group members, each member just stores its $SKSet$ consisting of roughly $\log n$ subkeys. For subkey rekeying roughly $2 \log n$ update key derivations and $*$ operations are performed. Thus the computation cost is comparable to other schemes.

Here we briefly analyze our scheme with three security properties encountered in group communication [15,16]. The adversary is assumed to be outside the group even though he might belong to the group in the past. The essential point in our scheme is that a member cannot guess the subkeys of the nodes in the path from its leaf node to root although it knows the subkeys in its $SKSet$, and this point is guaranteed unless used homomorphic encryption is broken.

Group key secrecy means that any adversary cannot guess current group key. Our scheme guarantees it because initial group key is securely distributed to only group members and the key is rekeyed by legitimate members whenever membership is changed. Forward secrecy means that any adversary who gets some previous keys cannot guess current keys. Our scheme guarantees it because after the adversary leaves the group the keys known to him are rekeyed and he cannot decrypt the rekeying message. Backward secrecy means that any adversary who knows current keys cannot guess previous keys. Our scheme guarantees it because before the adversary joins the group the group key is rekeyed with a hash function having one-wayness property.

5 Conclusion

In this paper we presented a new group key scheme where homomorphic encryption is utilized by key derivation and rekeying. As a result the number of keys to be multicasted for rekeying is much smaller than the previous schemes. Therefore our scheme improves scalability of secure group communication especially where the group is very large and membership is changed frequently.

Acknowledgments. This research was supported by Basic Science Research Program through the National Research Foundation of Korea(NRF) funded by the Ministry of Education, Science and Technology (No. 2011-0013757).

References

1. Amir, Y., Kim, Y., Nita-Rotaru, C., Tsudik, G.: On the performance of group key agreement protocols. In: 22nd IEEE Conference on Distributed Computing Systems, pp. 463–464 (2002)
2. Kim, Y., Perrig, A., Tsudik, G.: Communication-efficient group key agreement. In: 16th International Conference on Information Security, pp. 229–244 (2001)
3. Wong, C.K., Gouda, M., Lam, S.S.: Secure group communications using key graphs. In: ACM SIGCOMM 1998, pp. 68–79 (1998)
4. Waldvogel, M., Caronni, G., Sun, D., Weiler, N., Plattner, B.: The versakey framework:Versatile group key management. IEEE J. Selected Areas in Communications 17, 1614–1631 (1999)
5. McGrew, D.A., Sherman, A.T.: Key establishment in large dynamic groups using oneway function trees. Technical report (1998)
6. Canetti, R., Garay, J., Itkis, G., Micciancio, D., Naor, M., Pinkas, B.: Multicast security:a taxonomy and some efficient constructions. In: IEEE INFOCOM, pp. 708–716 (1999)

7. Selcuk, A.A., Sidhu, D.P.: Probabilistic methods in multicast key management. In: 3rd International Workshop on Information Security, pp. 179–193 (2000)
8. Pais, A.R., Joshi, S.: A new probabilistic rekeying method for secure multicast groups. Int. J. Inf. Sec., 275–286 (2010)
9. Boneh, D., Goh, E.-J., Nissim, K.: Evaluating 2-DNF Formulas on Ciphertexts. In: Kilian, J. (ed.) TCC 2005. LNCS, vol. 3378, pp. 325–341. Springer, Heidelberg (2005)
10. Rivest, R., Adleman, L., Mertouzos, M.: On data banks and privacy homomorphisms. Foundations of Secure Computation, pp. 169–180 (1978)
11. El Gamal, T.: A Public Key Cryptosystem and a Signature Scheme Based on Discrete Logarithms. In: Blakely, G.R., Chaum, D. (eds.) CRYPTO 1984. LNCS, vol. 196, pp. 10–18. Springer, Heidelberg (1985)
12. Naccache, D., Stern, J.: A new public key cryptosystem based on higher residues. In: ACM CCS 1998, pp. 59–66 (1998)
13. Damgard, I., Jurik, M.: A Length-Flexible Threshold Cryptosystem with Applications. In: Safavi-Naini, R., Seberry, J. (eds.) ACISP 2003. LNCS, vol. 2727, pp. 350–356. Springer, Heidelberg (2003)
14. Gentry, C.: Fully homomorphic encryption using ideal lattices. In: 41st ACM STOC, pp. 169–178 (2009)
15. Kim, Y., Perrig, A., Tsudik, G.: Tree-based group key agreement. ACM T. Inf. Sys. Sec. 7, 60–96 (2004)
16. Steiner, M., Tsudik, G., Waidner, M.: Key agreement in dynamic peer groups. IEEE T. Par. Dis. Sys. 11, 769–780 (2000)

Spatially Smoothed Second Order DOA Estimator for Correlated Signals in the Presence of Correlated Antenna Noises

Ill-Keun Rhee, Hee-Soo Kim, and Hun-Jong Lee

Department of Electronic Engineering,
Hannam University, 133 Ojung-dong, Daedeok-gu, Daejeon, Korea
ikrhee@hnu.kr

Abstract. An array signal processing methodologies can provide the high resolution of a signal direction of arrival (DOA) estimation, thanks to their conceptual increase of signal-to-noise ratio (S/N). Exploring the eigen-structure based algorithms such as MUSIC, Root MUSIC, etc, gives efficient DOA results when the multiple signals are incoherent. A class of Spatial Smoothing (SS) algorithms spatially break the correlation of coherent signals using spatially distributed overlapping sub-arrays. On the other hand, Second Order (SO) algorithm has been proven to de-correlate correlated antenna noises with known or estimated noise correlation coefficients. In this paper, Spatially SmoothedSecond Order (SS-SO) algorithm, which is made by combining SS algorithm with SO technique, is proposed to resolve efficiently correlated multiple signals in the environment of correlated noise fields. Furthermore, the simulations are performed and analyzed to show that the proposed algorithm gives robust DOA results in several aspects.

Keywords: Array Signal Processing, DOA, Eigen-structure based Algorithms, MUSIC, Spatial Smoothing Algorithm, Second Order Algorithm, Spatially Smoothed Second Order Algorithm.

1 Introduction

Array signal processing can be defined as a field of analyzing and processing scheme of received data from a spatially distributed antenna array in the presence of noise. A signal direction of arrival (DOA) estimation using array signal processing has been very important research topics in radar, sonar, and mobile communication areas [1], [2], [3]. The Multiple Signal Classification (MUSIC), considered as a benchmark for the subsequently developing DOA estimation methods using array signal processing, based on the eigen-structure algorithm gives better resolution with less complexity of DOA estimation [4], [5], compared with spectral estimation methodologies [6], [7]. However, MUSIC has some critical restrictions for practical applications in real situations. When the multiple signals are correlated each other or additive antenna noises are correlated, MUSIC significantly deteriorates its DOA estimation

T.-h. Kim et al. (Eds.): FGCN/DCA 2012, CCIS 350, pp. 95–101, 2012.

performance. For DOA estimation of the coherent or partially correlated signals, a spatial smoothing preprocessing scheme has been suggested [8]. This scheme is based on the idea that processing of the coherent signals using spatially distributed overlapping sub-arrays can break the coherence between the signals. Most of the DOA estimation algorithms, including MUSIC and Spatial Smoothing (SS), assume that array antenna noises are normally uncorrelated each other. If those algorithms are used for DOA estimation in the environment that array antenna noises are correlated one another, it is obvious that poor DOA results would be obtained.

The authors in [9] have proposed an algorithm which can de-correlate correlated antenna noises with known or estimated noise correlation coefficients. That algorithm, called "Second Order (SO)" algorithm, makes and uses new sample data gathered by auto-convolution operation on original data from received array of antenna, in which original data is composed of the multiple signals arriving at given antenna and antenna noise. Since those new auto-convolved data can retain information on all the other data points with a constant lag, SO algorithm provides improved resolution for DOA estimation in particularly low S/N, in correlated noise fields, etc.

In practical point of view, while DOA estimation, we may encounter the situation where the multiple signals impinging to antenna array are correlated one another and additive noises at array antennas are correlated each other.   In this paper, we propose "Spatially Smoothed Second Order (SS-SO)" algorithm, which is obtained by combining SS algorithm with SO technique, to resolve efficiently the correlated multiple signals arriving at array of antennas having additive correlated noises. Also, through computer simulations, the superiority of the proposed algorithm to other existing algorithms is statistically presented in several situations.

The outline of the paper is as follows. In section 2, SS-SO algorithm for DOA estimation is derived from the signal and noise model as well as some background information. In section 3, computer simulation is performed to evaluate the accuracy level of DOA for the proposed SS-SO algorithm, by calculating rms error in DOA estimation and probability of successful detection of the multiple correlated signals in the presence of correlated noises. In section 4, this paper is concluded with the remarks of the proposed SS-SO algorithm and its application areas.

2   Proposed DOA Algorithm

When the M distant source signals are impinging on a uniform linear array (ULA) with Q antennas, as shown in figure 1, from directions $\{\theta_1, \theta_2, \cdots \theta_M\}$, the signals received at the ith antenna can be expressed as

$$r_i(t) = \sum_{m=1}^{M} s_m(1 - (i - 1)(D/c)\sin\theta_m) + x_i(t), \qquad i = 1, 2, \cdots, Q \qquad (1)$$

where, $s_m(t) = $ the signal emitted by the mth source,
   $D = $ the distance between antennas,
   $c = $ the wave propagation velocity,
   $\theta_m = $ DOA of the mth source,
   $x_i(t) = $ additive noise at the ith antenna.

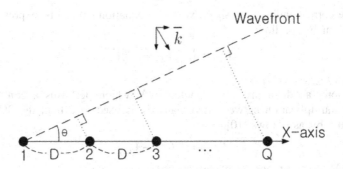

Fig. 1. ULA Antenna Configuration

Using the complex envelope representation applied to the mth narrow-band signal $s_m(t)$ with center frequency f_0[9], the received signal in equation 1 can be obtained as

$$r_i(t) = \sum_{m=1}^{M} s_m(t) \exp[-j\omega_0\tau_{mi}] + x_i(t) \tag{2}$$

where, $\tau_{mi} = (i-1)(D/c)\sin\theta_m$.

The received signals on the Q antennas can be described in the vector form

$$\mathbf{r}(t) = \sum_{m=1}^{M} \mathbf{a}(\theta_m)s_m(t) + \mathbf{x}(t) \tag{3}$$

or

$$\mathbf{r}(t) = \mathbf{A}(\theta)\mathbf{s}(t) + \mathbf{x}(t) \tag{4}$$

where, $\mathbf{r}^T(t) = [r_1(t), r_2(t), \cdots, r_Q(t)]$
$\mathbf{s}^T(t) = [s_1(t), s_2(t), s_M(t)]$
$\mathbf{x}^T(t) = [x_1(t), x_2(t), x_Q(t)]$,

and the columns of the $Q \times M$ steering matrix $\mathbf{A}(\theta)$ are composed of the steering vectors which can be expressed as

$$\mathbf{a}^T(\theta_m) = \left[1, e^{-j\omega_0\tau_{m2}}, e^{-j\omega_0\tau_{m3}}, \cdots, e^{-j\omega_0\tau_{mQ}}\right]. \tag{5}$$

Second Order (SO) algorithm deals with the new signals obtained by auto-convolution operations on the received signals at the ith antenna, as in equation (6).

$$r_{(2)i}(t) = r_i(t) \otimes r_i(t) \tag{6}$$

To derive effectively the spectral density matrix of SO algorithm, it is convenient to use data in frequency domain by taking the Fourier transform of the received data as in equation (2) and (5) [10]. The Fourier transformed received signal vector in equation (4) or (5) has the form of

$$\mathbf{F} = \mathbf{AS} + \mathbf{X} \tag{7}$$

where, $\mathbf{F} = \mathcal{F}[\mathbf{r}]$, $\mathbf{S} = \mathcal{F}[\mathbf{s}]$, $\mathbf{X} = \mathcal{F}[\mathbf{x}]$, and $\mathcal{F}$ denotes the Fourier Transform operator.

Also, the corresponding new signal vector of equation (6) can be expressed in the frequency domain as follows:

$$\mathbf{F}_{(2)}^T = [F_1^2, F_2^2, \cdots, F_Q^2]^T \tag{8}$$

where, $F_1(\omega) = \mathcal{F}[r_1(t)]$.

Furthermore, a "delta product" denoted by Δ, which performs a component to component multiplication between two matrices, is used to extract the SO spectral density matrix by, as follows [10]:

$$\mathbf{L}_{(2)R} = 2\mathbf{L}_{(1)}^{\Delta 2} - \mathbf{L}_{(2)} \tag{9}$$

Where, $\quad \mathbf{L}_{(1)}^{\Delta 2} = E[(\mathbf{FF}^*)^{\Delta 2}] = E[(\mathbf{FF}^*)\Delta(\mathbf{FF}^*)] \tag{10}$

and $\quad \mathbf{L}_{(2)} = E[\mathbf{F}_{(2)}\mathbf{F}_{(2)}^*]. \tag{11}$

SO algorithm is now completed for equation (9) by performing the same orthogonal test as for the MUSIC by squaring each element of the steering vector in equation (5). This doubles the effective aperture of the antenna array and theoretically resolution becomes twice that of the MUSIC, and shows superiority for DOA estimation particularly in low S/N, in correlated noise fields [10]. However, SO still has difficulty in highly resolved DOA estimation when the multiple source signals are correlated.

Applying SO algorithm to SS methodology, consider now a ULA with Q identical antennas divided into $P(=Q-L+1)$ overlapping sub-arrays of size L as shown in figure 2.

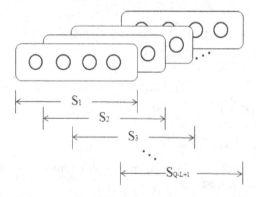

Fig. 2. Configuration of Sub-arrays for Spatial Smoothing

Then, let $\mathbf{r}_{(p)}(\cdot)$ represent the vector of the received signals of the pth sub-array for $p=1,2,\ldots,P$, where $P=Q-L+1$. Adapting the new received antenna signals obtained by auto-convolution operations as in equation (6), the spatial array spectral density matrix of the pth sub-array $(\mathbf{L}_{(2)R})_p$ can be obtained from equation (9).

Define the Spatially Smoothed Second Order (SS-SO) spectral density matrix $\bar{\mathbf{L}}$ as

$$\bar{\mathbf{L}} = \frac{1}{P}\sum_{p=1}^{P}(\mathbf{L}_{(2)R})_p. \tag{12}$$

And the matrix is used for DOA estimation procedure as in SO algorithm.

The following examples demonstrate that when compared to SS, the SS-SO is superior for the correlated signals in the presence of correlated antenna noises.

Two 70 % correlated signals from the directions of 5° and 12°, respectively, are resolved using SS and the proposed SS-SO methods. ULA consisting of 12 antenna elements, divided into 3 overlapping sub-arrays of size 10is considered. Among antennas, 2 antennas have fully correlated antenna noises and the rest of antennas have uncorrelated noises. Resolution capabilities are tested at S/N=5dB and number of sample data N=512, as shown in Figure 3.In this case, only SS-SO method resolves the two peaks without error, and SS method fails to detect the two signal directions.

Next, figure 4 reflects a test performed to determine how well the two DOA estimation methods resolve DOAs when the two 70 % correlated signals are incoming the directions of 5° and 10°, respectively. It is obvious that the proposed method gives accurate results within the tolerance of about 0.25° in this case, too.

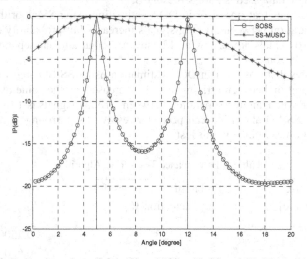

Fig. 3. Estimation of two DOA (5° and 12°) with SS and SS-SO algorithms

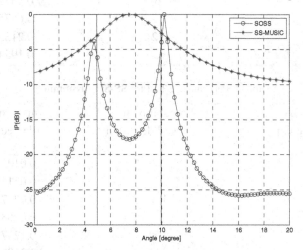

Fig. 4. Estimation of two DOA (5° and 10°) with SS and SS-SO algorithms

For more precise evaluation and comparison of the finding susing SS algorithm and SS-SO algorithm, statistical analysis is performed by examining rms error in DOA estimation and probability of successful detection of the multiple correlated signals in the presence of correlated noises, in the following section.

3   Performance Evaluation of Proposed Algorithm

Comparisons between SS and the proposed SS-SO for resolving the direction angles of closely spaced 70% correlated multiple signals in fully correlated antenna noises are statistically made, where ULA is consisted of 10 antennas, divided into 3 overlapping sub-arrays of size 8, with the distance between the antennas equals half of the wave length. The number of independent experiment performed is 100 and the number of sample data used is 256. S/N is 5 dB.

Table 1 illustrates that rms error in DOA estimation using SS algorithm decreases as angular separation between arriving signals increases but probability of successful detection of two signals are as low as 12% even though angular separation between arriving signals becomes 17°.

Table 2 shows that rms error in DOA estimation using SS-SO algorithm increases as angular separation between arriving signals decreases but the value of error is only about 0.2° even when angular separation between arriving signals is 17°. Also we can easily see that SS-SO algorithm can perfectly resolve two arriving signals with any angular separation examined in this test.

Table 1. Performance Test for SS Algorithm

DOA [degree]	Probability of successful detection[%]	rms error [degree]
$\theta_1 = 5$	3	0.7500
$\theta_2 = 14$		0.6300
$\theta_1 = 5$	6	0.4532
$\theta_2 = 20$		0.6875
$\theta_1 = 5$	12	0.2135
$\theta_2 = 22$		0.1954

Table 2. Performance Test for SS-SO Algorithm

DOA [degree]	Probability of successful detection	rms error [degree]
$\theta_1 = 5$	100	0.0125
$\theta_2 = 14$		0.0514
$\theta_1 = 5$	100	0.0727
$\theta_2 = 10$		0.0968
$\theta_1 = 5$	100	0.1237
$\theta_2 = 8$		0.2104

Overall speaking, from the results in table 1 and 2, SS-SO algorithm can detect thoroughly two correlated signals in fully correlated antenna noise environment with very low rms error. However, SS can poorly resolve two correlated signals in fully correlated antenna noise environment. Therefore, we can declare that SS-SO algorithm gives very robust performance on DOA estimation even both for correlated multiple signals and in correlated antenna noises.

4 Conclusion

In this paper, very reliable DOA estimation methodology called "Spatially Smoothed Second Order (SS-SO)" algorithm is proposed. This algorithm is developed by combining SS algorithm with SO technique, and is verified, using statistical evaluation, to be very effective even when multiple signals impinging to antenna array are correlated each other and in the presence of additive correlated noises.

It is expected that the algorithm proposed in this paper contributes on the development of the direction finding systems with which antenna array equipped might be easily exposed to the environment, such as the airborne, of both correlated signals and correlated antenna noises.

Acknowledgements. This work was supported by the Security Engineering Research Center, granted by the Korea Ministry of Knowledge Economy.

References

1. Manolakis, D.G., et al.: Statistical and Adaptive Signal Processing. Artech House, Inc., Norwood (2005)
2. Zhang, X., et al.: Digital Processing System for Digital Beam Forming Antenna. In: IEEE International Symposium on Microwave, Antenna Propagation and EMC Technologies (2005)
3. Lavate, T.B., et al.: Performance Analysis of MUSIC and ESPIT DOA Estimation Algorithms for Adaptive Array Smart Antenna in Mobile Communication. International Journal of Computer Networks (IJCN) 2(3), 152–158 (2009)
4. Schmidt, R.O.: A Signal Subspace Approach to Multiple Source Location and Spectral Estimation. Ph.D. Dissertation, Stanford University, Stanford (1981)
5. Schmidt, R.O.: Multiple Emitter Location and Signal Parameter Estimation. IEEE Trans. on Antennas and Propagation AP-34, 276–280 (1986)
6. Satorius, E.H., et al.: Maximum Entropy spectral Analysis of Multiple Sinusoids in Noise. Geophysics 43, 1111–1118 (1978)
7. Thorvldsen, T.: Maximum Entropy Spectral analysis in Antenna Spatial Filtering. IEEE Trans. on Antennas and Propagation AP-28, 552–560 (1980)
8. Shan, T., et al.: On Spatial Smoothing for Direction-of-Arrival Estimation of Coherent Signals. IEEE Trans. on Acoust., Speech, and Signal Processing ASSP-33(4), 801–811 (1985)
9. Rhee, I.-K.: Performance Analysis of Highly Effective Proposed Direction Finding Method. The Journal of the Acoustical Society of Korea 14(1E), 88–97 (1995)
10. Rhee, I.-K.: Highly Effective Direction Finding Method under the Particular Circumstances. The Journal of the Korean Institute of Communication Sciences 18(3), 439–448 (1993)

An Analysis of Smartphone Power Dissipation by Use Cases

Min Choi[1] and Namgi Kim[2,*]

[1] Dept. of Information and Communication Engineering
Chungbuk National University,
52 Naesudong-ro, Heungdeok-gu, Cheongju, Chungbuk 361-763, Republic of Korea
mchoi@cbnu.ac.kr
[2] Dept. of Computer Science
Kyonggi University
San 94-6, Iui-dong, Yeongtong-gu, Suwon, Gyeonggi-do, Republic of Korea
ngkim@kyonggi.ac.kr

Abstract. The spreading use of Smartphones stimulates growth of mobile computing. However, mobile computing through smartphones poses challenges due to its intrinsic nature of battery capacity, constraints of wireless networks and device limitation. In this research, we provide the analysis of smartphone power dissipation under two different point of views, usage scenarios and smartphone components. In general, smartphones have various components. We develop a queuing model for power analysis so that we can analyze the power dissipation on different components, and analyze battery lifetime with different usage behaviors.

Keywords: Smartphone Power Consumption, Power Dissipation Analysis.

1   Introduction

Power dissipation occurs when we are not supposed to, and it leads to power leakage. Due to the inherent nature of smartphone in which operating system is working, power consumption continues even on not actively using. Smartphones play various roles that require many foreground and background jobs, whereas traditional feature phones such as conventional cell phones mainly concern call processing. This property of smartphones results in severe power dissipation[2]. The power leakage on smartphones are as follow[3][4]: 1) Applications run as background jobs or services : user can install applications to run as background job periodically such as android service. For instance, once we set up google mail sync, android google mail client try to synchronize the content from Google mail and scheduler. 2) Keeping Wi-Fi, bluetooth, GPS enabled when we are not using explicitly: even though the applications that use those sensors are not working, just turning the sensors on consumes power dissipation. For example, the Wi-Fi protocol periodically communicate with access point(AP) the beacon signals. This results in power consumption even on upper layer of Wi-Fi falling into idle stage.

---

* Corresponding author.

T.-h. Kim et al. (Eds.): FGCN/DCA 2012, CCIS 350, pp. 102–107, 2012.
© Springer-Verlag Berlin Heidelberg 2012

3) Display lightness/contrast: the main concern of power dissipation is due to the LCD brightness. The backlight power minimization can effectively extend battery life for mobile handheld devices [1].

In this research, we provide the analysis of smartphone power dissipation under two different point of views, usage scenarios and smartphone components. Smartphones have various components in general, such as CPU, GSM, LCD, Backlight, GPS, Wi-Fi, Bluetooth, Graphics, and so on. We develop a queueing model for power analysis so that we can analyze the power dissipation on different components, and analyze battery lifetime with different usage behaviors. Thus, we can discuss the significance of power dissipation by various components and various usage behaviors.

The rest of this paper is organized as follows: Section 2 and Section 3 focuses on the details of power dissipation analysis on smartphones. Finally, we conclude our work and present future research directions in Section 4.

2   Analysis of Power Dissipation on Various Components

Prior to running experiments, we established preliminary experiments consisting of two types of workloads : synthesized workload and real workload. The synthesized workload is to check the power consumption of each device (or sensor). Real workloads are to check the power dissipation when popular applications are running. We start measuring with a fully charged battery after charging during the same amount of time. The screens of the smartphones are configured to keep always on. GPS invocation interval is set to 5 seconds. To measure instantaneous battery levels of the phone over several hours, we make use of our battery level monitoring application while running the 2 types of workloads. The battery status monitoring application is based on android service that runs in the background of other current activities. All tests and evaluations were performed with our battery status monitoring application [5] on SAMSUNG Galaxy S [6]. Note that we ran the experiment multiple times, and we always see the same trends in battery-level drops across all runs. The following figures are the preliminary experimental result with synthesized workload.

We first assess the impact of using power-intensive LCD brightness on smartphones as the battery level of the phone during the run. When the brightness of LCD backlight is high, the battery level drops to 65% within two hours, whereas the battery level at the low brightness drops to only up to 90%. The battery lifetime of low brightness is almost twice longer than the lifetime of high brightness. Next, we check the impact of using GPS (Global Positioning System) on smartphones. Figure 2 shows the battery consumption with using GPS navigation application. When GPS is enabled and used, the battery level drops to 63% within one hour. That means smartphone battery level stays around 90% in an hour without GPS, but the battery exhausts up to 60% within an hour in an hour with GPS enabled. This is because GPS is one of the most power consuming sensors or devices in a smartphone. For the Bluetooth, the energy consumption of Blutooth is considerably less than that of GPS.

Our experimental environments are as follows : (a) power supply, (b) digital multimeter (True RMS Multimeter), (c) smartphone (SAMSUNG Galaxy S), (d) laptop computer. The rated input voltage/current range of SAMSUNG Galaxy S is

1500mA at 3.7V. Assuming that the voltage difference is stably supplied with 3.7V without drop of electric pressure, measuring only current change with digital multi-meter is the same as checking power dissipation. After connecting test leads in serial with the smartphone being measured, we log the change of current flow with the laptop computer (d) that is connected by USB with digital multimeter.

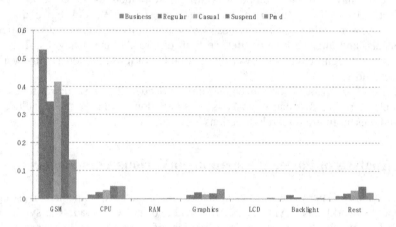

Fig. 1. Mean number of requests in the queue on various components

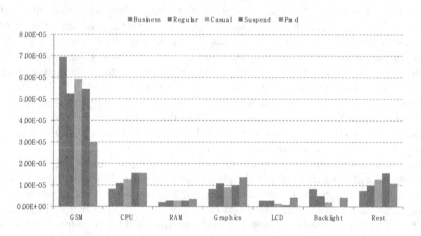

Fig. 2. Mean waiting time on various components

Figure 1 shows the mean number of requests in the queue as various components. It shows the fact that relatively larger numbers of requests are queued on GSM. This is because we mainly make use of smartphones for phone call, so relatively more requests are on the GSM components. Figure 2 represents mean number of requests in the queue depending on various component. Since the GSM and CPU are the two of the most busy components in general smartphones, so they are required more mean waiting time rather than other components.

3   Analysis of Power Dissipation on Various Usage Scenarios

To evaluate the performance, we present a model of queuing network. The model of our REST Open API Web Service architecture is presented in Figure 3. REST Open API Web Service is composed of 3 components comprising: (1) a web server, (2) a REST web server farms, and (3) internet users. As shown in Figure 3, there are a number of components(nodes) that consist of several queues. A request may receive service at one or more queues before exiting from the system. A model in which jobs departing from A arrive at another queue(i.g., the REST Web Server Farm from B1 to B4).

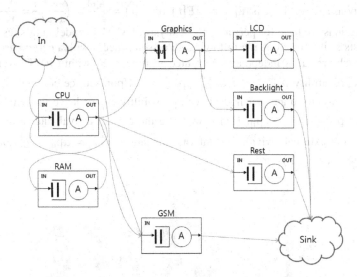

Fig. 3. A queuing model for smartphone power dissipation

Requests arrive at the web server A with frequency "In". The initialization process for the request is done at node A. Then, the request proceeds to the component either "CPU" or "GSM" components depending on the type of the request; if the request is for the call processing, it goes to the GSM components. If the request is for just application processing, then it goes to the CPU components. The requests traverse via the RAM, Graphics, LCD, Backlight and Rest. They are finally collected to the Sink node, represented by the components at the right bottom of Figure 3. Our system model is a sort of open queueing network that has external arrivals and departures. The requests enter the system at "IN" and exit at "OUT". The number of requests in the system varies with time. In analyzing an open system, we assume that the throughput is known (to be equal to the arrival rate), and we also assume that there is no probability of incomplete transfer in this system, so there is no retrial path to go back to node A. Now, the CPU components of recent smartphones can have more than one CPU, known as dual-core or quad-core. However, we assume the simple smartphones with single-core in this research.

At each node, let's consider an M/M/1 queue with a processor sharing service discipline. The interarrival times of requests are according to a Poisson process with rate λ and the service times are exponentially distributed and there is only one server.

There are no buffer or population size limitations and the service discipline is FCFS. The mean number of requests in the system is given by $E[n] = \sum_{n=1}^{\infty} np_n = \sum_{n=1}^{\infty} n(1-\rho)\rho^n = \frac{\rho}{1-\rho}$. The mean number of requests in the queue is given by $E[n_q] = \sum_{n=1}^{\infty}(n-1)p_n = \sum_{n=1}^{\infty}(n-1)(1-\rho)\rho^n = \frac{1}{1-\rho}$. When there are no requests in the system, the server is said to be idle; at all other times the server is busy. The probability of n or more requests in the system is (P $\geq$ requests in system) $= \sum_{n=1}^{\infty} p_{nj} = \sum_{n=1}^{\infty}(1-\rho)\rho^j = \rho^n$. The mean waiting time can be computed using Little's law, which states that mean number in system is arrival rate multiplied by mean response time. That is $E[n] = \lambda E[r]$ or $E[r] = \frac{E[n]}{\lambda} = \left(\frac{\rho}{1-\rho}\right)\frac{1}{\lambda} = \frac{1/\mu}{1-\rho}$. These two expressions are used for performance analysis of M/M/1 model in this research.

Requests arrive from outside following a Poisson process with a certain arrival rate $\lambda > 0$. Each arrival is independently routed to a node B_j within REST web server farm with probability $p_{0Bj} \geq 0$ and $\sum_{j=1}^{j} p_{0Bj} = 1$. Upon service completion at node i, a request may go to another node j with probability p_{ij} or leave the network with probability $p_{i0} = 1 - \sum_{j=1}^{J} p_{ij}$. Hence we have the overall arrival rate to node i, λ_i, including both external arrivals and internal transitions: $\lambda\lambda_i = \alpha p_{0i} + \sum_{j=1}^{J} \lambda_j p_{ji}, i = 1, ..., J$ then $\lambda = (-P)^{-1}a$.

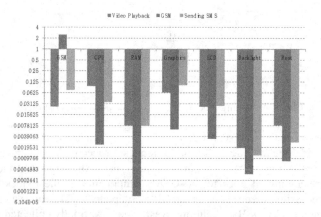

Fig. 4. Mean number of requests in the queue as various use cases

Figure 4 and Figure 5 presents the mean waiting time and mean number of requests in the queue depending on various usage scenarios. We model each component as the M/M/1 queue because we ignore the case of parallel components, such as multi-cores. These figures show the fact that mean number of request and mean waiting time on which components as different components. The reason why the waiting time and queue length on GSM for GSM usage scenario are quite high is that because we frequently utilize the GSM components during the job. For another case, when it comes to sending SMS to someone, the related components for sending SMS such as Graphics, CPU, GSM, LCD are frequentry utilized, so they have higher mean waiting time and mean number of requests during sending SMS use cases.

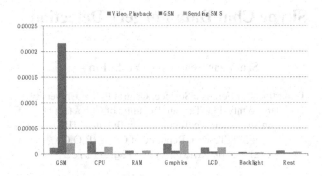

Fig. 5. Mean waiting time as various use cases

4   Conclusion

In this research, we provide the analysis of smartphone power dissipation under two different point of views, usage scenarios and smartphone components. In general, smartphones have various components. We develop a queuing model for power analysis so that we can analyze the power dissipation on different components, and analyze battery lifetime with different usage behaviors.

Acknowledgments. This work is supported by the Basic Science Research Program through the National Research Foundation of Korea (NRF) funded by the Ministry of Education, Science and Technology (2012-0008105). Corresponding author of this paper is Namgi Kim (ngkim@kyonggi.ac.kr).

References

1. Aaron, C., Gernot, H.: An Analysis of Power Consumption in a Smartphone. In: The 2010 USENIX Conference on USENIX Annual Technical Conference (2010)
2. Mahesri, A., Vardhan, V.: Power Consumption Breakdown on a Modern Laptop. In: Falsafi, B., VijayKumar, T.N. (eds.) PACS 2004. LNCS, vol. 3471, pp. 165–180. Springer, Heidelberg (2005)
3. Sagahyroon, A.: Power consumption in handheld computers. In: Proceedings of the International Symposium on Circuits and Systems, pp. 1721–1724 (December 2006)
4. Snowdon, D.C., Le Sueur, E., Petters, S.M., Heiser, G.: Koala: a platform for OS-level power management. In: Proceedings of the 4th ACM European Conference on Computer Systems, Nuremberg, Germany, April 01-03 (2009)

Skype Chat Data Forgery Detection

Szu-Yuan Teng[1,2] and Yu-Li Lin[2,*]

[1] Department of Forensic Science, Central Police University,
Taoyuan County 333, Taiwan, Republic of China (R.O.C.)
[2] Ministry of Justice, Investigation Bureau (MJIB),
Taipei 231, Taiwan, Republic of China (R.O.C.)
{mjib.teng,andrinalin}@gmail.com

Abstract. Internet-based communication technologies are very widespread in recent years. Unfortunately, while the number of technologies such as Skype, Windows Live messenger, Yahoo messenger, QQ implicated in crime activities is relevant and growing, the capability to perform forgery detection of such technologies is limited. Skype is a kind of deployed application by using SQLite. Using SQLite database to store voice data, instant messaging, audio conferencing, and file transfer. Nowadays several GUI editors for SQLite database are developed. The main goal of these editor tools is to allow non-technical users to create, modify and edit SQLite database files. This paper presents an analysis of SQLite database features exploited in order to forge data and a method to detect forgery data using these exploits.

Keywords: Computer forensics, Digital evidence, Skype, Instant messaging, forgery.

1 Introduction

With the development of computer technology and the penetration of network, the P2P applications have become a dominant force in the Internet. Skype is a kind of distributed P2P applications developed by Skype Technologies S.A., which offers VoIP, IM and video communications over the internet. Skype is reliably, simply and convenient way of communication, and provides good voice quality under unstable or resource-constrained networks.

Like its predecessor KaZaA [7], Skype is an overlay P2P network. There are three different components in the Skype network, ordinary Skype clients, super nodes and login servers. The Skype login server is an important entity in the Skype network. This server is used for user authentication and also ensures that Skype login names are unique across the Skype name space. It implied that user names and passwords are stored at the login server. A Skype client is a Skype application that can be used to place voice calls and send text messages. When the Skype client installs Skype application, it gets a list of hard code addresses to which it connects for the first time. Each Skype client holds a list of 200 IPs and Ports of available Skype nodes after successfully connecting for the first time [1]. A super node is ordinary Skype client on

---

* Corresponding author.

T.-h. Kim et al. (Eds.): FGCN/DCA 2012, CCIS 350, pp. 108–114, 2012.

the Skype network. It can become a candidate of a super node while any nodes with a public IP address are having sufficient CPU, memory, and bandwidth. In order to connect to the network, a Skype client must establish a connection to a super node and must authentication itself to the Skype login server for a successful login.

Most researchers on the subject have concentrated on detecting and analyzing peer-to-peer network traffics, such as [2], [3], [4], [5]. For example, Leung and Chan [6] take a forensic approach to formulate a set of socket-based detection and control policies for Skype traffics. The proposed detection method is a hybrid between payload and non-payload inspections. The solution is practicable both inside and outside the NAT firewalls. Dodge R.C. [8] focused on a fingerprint for the Skype application and analyzed profile information on a Windows system that is resident in the Windows registry and the hard disk file system. Simon and Slay [9] focused on the recovery of data from Skype, a common VoIP application. In order to identify and analyze relevant data in physical memory, they defined a set of generic target artifacts. This paper showed that the user's Skype password can be recovered if the physical memory is collected while Skype is still running. Moreover, the results of this paper indicated that it is plausible to recover a user's contacts from the physical memory. This information can be used for social analysis and contact chaining for that user.

This paper will focus on detecting some artifacts of a user's communication content. Due to the sophisticated editing software (for example, phpLiteAdmin, SQLite Database Browser etc.), a user's communication content of Skype application can be easily manipulated and altered without leaving visible clues. It causes a serious problem with regard to how much of user's content can be trusted, whether it is authentic or tampered as a witness. It is important for forensic examiners to understand how the SQLite databases are structured and what additional information can be obtained.

The rest of this paper is sketched as follows. In Section 2, we will review the Skype. In Section 3, we will demonstrate some experiment results. Finally, we give conclusions in Section 4.

2   Skype Overview

Skype is the most popular VoIP application that provides many services to make free of charge including IP phone calls, file transfer, chat service, and audio conference. Skype software uses a number of files to store data. These files relate mainly to historical information, call histories, file transfers, messaging sessions, etc. They also cache user profiles. The interpretation of these log files can yield a significant amount of information about communications that have taken place through the software [10]. Before Windows Skype version 4.0.0.206, Skype log files are stored in a flat-file database format and user data files are stored in the user's Application Data folder under the Skype subfolder [10]. Files are stored with a .dbb extension. Each file name contains a number which indicates the record length, such as chat256.dbb, transfer512.dbb, etc. Table 1 lists the Skype log files and describes what kind of the data is stored in each file. This file format has some characteristics as follows [10].

1. Number items are stored in little-endian format. For example, 1453 is 0x05AD and would appear as two bytes, 0xAD, 0x05.
2. A 4-byte record header is 0x6C, 0x33, 0x33, and 0x6C (ASCII is 1331).

3. The timestamps in records are stored in the standard UNIX format of seconds since 1/1/1970 00:00:00. However the data is not represented as the standard 4 byte unsigned integer as is usually the case, instead using 5 bytes to represent the timestamp. The detailed format description is represented as follows.

For example, we would like to convert hex code "BF CF 8E C1 04" to the timestamp format, we need to invert the sequence.

BF CF 8E C1 04 → 04 C1 8E CF BF
04 C1 8E CF BF → Binary format is as follows.

0000 0100 1100 0001 1000 1110 1100 1111 1011 1111 0000

To remove the "1" at the most signification bit, then the remaining byte generates 32 bits of information.

0100 1000 0010 0011 1010 0111 1011 1111 = (Hex code) 48 23 A7 BF
48 23 A7 BF → Fri, 09 May 2008 01 :24 :15 UTC

Table 1. The Skype log files and potential information [10]

Skype log files	Description	Skype log files
call*.dbb	Call history	call*.dbb
chatmsg*.dbb	Chat history	chatmsg*.dbb
profile*.dbb	Details of user profiles	profile*.dbb
transfer*.dbb	Details of file transfers	transfer*.dbb
chat*.dbb	Chat history	chat*.dbb
contactgroup*.dbb	Unknown	contactgroup*.dbb
user*.dbb	Local user's profile	user*.dbb
voicemail*.dbb	Details of voicemail messages (no contents)	voicemail*.dbb

To simplify the experiments and in order to understand the format of Skype log file, we will parse two of them which we are interested. The call history is composed of the following fields [10]:

Data item indicator	Data item	Format
0xA1 0x01	Time stamp	As described above
0xA4 0x01	Username (remote end)	Null-terminated string
0xA8 0x01	Screen name (remote end)	Null-terminated string
0x04 0x00	Direction	0xA1 = incoming 0xF1 = outgoing
0x85 0x02	Duration of call (seconds)	4-byte unsigned integer. If call failed, record will not exist.
0x80 0x02	PSTN number	Null-terminated string
0x8C 0x02	PSTN status	Null-terminated string

The message history is composed of the following fields [10]:

Data item indicator	Data item	Format
0xFC 0x03	Message content	Null-terminated string
0xE0 0x03	Message ID	Null-terminated string
0xE5 0x03	Time stamp	As described above
0xE8 0x03	User name (sender)	Null-terminated string
0xEC 0x03	Display name (sender)	Null-terminated string

Notes: The message ID is a string which uniquely identifies a chat session. We can group the items with identical message IDs.

After Windows Skype version 4.0.0.206, Skype log files are stored in the SQLite3 format and files are stored with a .db extension. When the user registered and logged into Skype, several database files are created, such as main.db, bistats.db, dc.db, griffin.db, and keyval.db. When considering the experiment below, we focus on the information of two specific tables (Chats table and Messages table) in the "main.db" file.

3   Testing Outline

3.1   SQLite Editor Tools and Skype Forensic Tools

The primary goal of the research presented here is to discuss whether it is possible for a criminal to attempt to negatively affect the existence of evidence by using the SQLite editor. In this subsection, we will show several SQLite editor tools and three forensic tools with designed to work with the Skype database files. All these editor tools are not applicable for each and every file format for database. Table 2 lists the tools and its functions.

Table 2. SQLite editor tools in this study

SQLite editor	Supporting DB file formats	functions
phpLiteAdmin	SQLite2, SQLite3	Add, delete, and edit
SQLite2009 Pro Enterprise Manager	SQLite3	Add, delete, and edit
Database Master 3	MySQL, PostgreSQL, SQLite, ODBC, etc.	Add, delete, and edit
Base (MAC)	SQLite3	Edit
SQLitePlus Database Explorer	SQLite3	Edit
SQLiteman	SQLite3	Edit
SQLite 3 Explorer	SQLite3	Edit
SQLite Studio	SQLite2, SQLite3	Edit
Visual SQLite	SQLite3	Edit
Another SQLite Explorer	SQLite3	Add, delete, and edit
SQLite Database Browser	SQLite3	Add, delete, and edit
SQLite Expert Professional	SQLite3	Add, delete, and edit

The commercial products like EnCase and FTK do not provide for analyzing Skype chat logs, contact lists, SMS messages, etc. In the following, we discuss the tools used in Skype log files forensics, compares an open source tool such as SkypeLogView to two commercial tools such as SkypeAlyzer and Skype Analyzer Pro. Table 3 indicated that the tools work with both the Skype database files such as .db and .dbb. In addition, SkypeAlyzer would analyse more Skype log files than the other ones.

Table 3. Skype forensic tools in this study

Skype forensic tools	Supporting Skype file formats	Analysing the log files
SkypeAlyzer v1.2.20	db, dbb	Accounts, Messages, Contacts, Chats, SMS, Call History
Skype Analyzer Pro v1.04	db, dbb	Message, Chats
SkypeLogView v1.21	db, dbb	Message, Chats, Call History

3.2   Test Environment Overview

The testing was conducted within two computers running windows XP with the latest security patches. These computers were connected to the internet directly, installed the Skype software and registered with three usernames such as forensic001, forensic002, and forensic003. When the user logged on Skype, a number of database files which use to store data are established. We use three accounts to log on both of these computers and simulate the chats each other. For analyzing the chat information, several scripts were created.

In order to detect which type of forgery, the detection framework is given as follow:

(1) Collect SQLite editor/ browser tools and record its version and features.
(2) Check Skype software version which you would like to analyze.
(3) Obtain the *main.db* file and make twelve copies.
(4) Apply forensic software tools, EnCase and WinHex, to examine the contents of *main.db*.
(5) Use the different SQLite editor tools to add, delete, and modify each *main.db* file.
(6) Use WinHex and UltraCompare software to compare the original *main.db* files and the forgery ones.
(7) Repeat (1) to (6), and try to identify the features to each SQLite editor tool.

The first stage in analyzing the counterfeit of Skype database file is to check the default directory and apply EnCase to find *main.db-journal* file. If there is only *main.db* file in the default directory, the investigator can apply the forensic tools to examine the contents directly. Otherwise, if the *main.db-journal* file is found, we can know that Skype database file has been altered or manipulated before. Finally, we focus on 144-byte Header, body_xml, identities, and crc and try to detect such specific artifact or pattern or relation or other strings from these areas.

3.3   Discussion

We use several SQLite editor tools to modify the *main.db* files. In our experiments, three forensic tools are used called SkypeAlyzer, Skype Analyzer Pro, and SkypeLogView for examining the contents. The results of the testing show that main.db-journal file could be generated, when the database files have manipulated or altered such as add, delete, and modify. If the main.db file is often modified, lots of deleted main.db-journal files are generated. A comparison result is listed in Table 4 where several SQLite editor tools have been used to detect specific artifact or pattern or relation or other strings from Skype database file. From Table 4, we can know that the number of specific features is high frequency, the detection accuracy is high.

Table 4. Comparative analysis

Specific features / SQLite editor tool	(1)	(2)	(3)	(4)	(5)
phpLiteAdmin	YES	NO	YES	NO	2
SQLite2009 Pro Enterprise Manager	YES	YES	YES	YES	2
Database Master 3	YES	YES	YES	YES	2
Base (MAC)	YES	NO	YES	NO	2
SQLitePlus Database Explorer	YES	YES	YES	YES	2
SQLiteman	YES	YES	YES	YES	3
SQLite 3 Explorer	YES	YES	YES	YES	3
SQLite Studio	YES	YES	YES	YES	4
Visual SQLite	YES	NO	YES	NO	2
Another SQLite Explorer	YES	YES	YES	YES	2
SQLite Database Browser	YES	YES	YES	YES	2
SQLite Expert Professional	YES	YES	YES	YES	2

(1) Is there any deleted *main.db-journal* file(s)? (2) Are there any changes in 144-byte header?(3) Are there any changes in the data items of Skype log files, such as body_xml, identities, and crc? (4) Are there any fixed strings in some data areas of Skype log files?(5) To summary the total number of feature

Assume that any record in the main.db file is deleted by SQLite editor, we try to use the forensic tools (like SkypeLogView, SkypeAlyzer, and Skype Analyzer Pro) to find the deleted record. In our experiments, we discover that all of these tools cannot detect any deleted records.

4   Conclusions

Nowadays, Skype is playing more and more important role in our daily life. In some criminal investigation, Skype message records could be important evidence. Unfortunately Skype log files can be easily altered by using SQLite editor tools, it causes a serious problem as to how much of their content can be trusted. If Skype log files are manipulated or altered, some features left on the system can present valuable and useful information to an investigator. In this paper, we explore more features of SQLite editor tools when a criminal uses these tools to alter Skype log files. Furthermore, we point out that the deleted record of Skype log file cannot be detected as we want it to be, this is a serious problem that the forensic science in general should be aware. Finally, we hope our study can be some contribution in the area of digital forensics, and we'd like to call up more researchers to work together in this issue.

References

1. Bremler-Barr, A., Dekel, O., Goldschmidt, R., Levy, H.: Controlling p2p applications via address harvesting: the skype story. In: IEEE International Symposium on Parallel and Distributed Processing Workshops and Phd Forum, pp. 1579–1586 (2011)
2. Baset, S.A., Schulzrinne, H.G.: An analysis of the skype peer-to-peer internet telephony protocol. In: Proc. INFOCOM (2006)
3. Guha, G., Daswani, N., Jainn, R.: An experimental study of the skype peer-to-peer voip system. In: 5th Int. Workshop on Peer-to-Peer Systems, pp. 81–91 (2006)
4. Suh, K., Figueiredo, D.R., Kurose, J., Towsley, D.: Characterizing and detecting relayed traffic: A case study using skype. In: IEEE INFOCOM (2006)
5. Wang, X., Chen, S., Jajodia, S.: Tracking anonymous peer-to-peer voip calls on the internet. In: ACM Conference on Computer and Communications Security, pp. 81–91 (2005)
6. Leung, C.M., Chan, Y.Y.: Network forensic on encrypted peer-to-peer voip traffics and the detection, blocking, and prioritization of skype traffics. In: 16th IEEE International Workshops on Enabling Technologies: Infrastructure for Collaborative Enterprises, pp. 401–408 (2007)
7. KaZaA, http://www.kazaa.com
8. Dodge, R.C.: Skype fingerprint. In: Proceedings of the 41st Hawaii International Conference on System Sciences (2008)
9. Simon, M., Slay, J.: Enhancement of Forensic Computing Investigations through Memory Forensic Techniques. In: International Conference on Availability, Reliability and Security (2009)
10. Skype log file analysis, http://cryptocomb.org/Skype%20Log%20File%20Analysis.pdf

Self-synchronized and Energy-Aware Duty Cycle Control Algorithm in Energy-Harvested Wireless Sensor Networks

Sunsik Roh

Dept. of Information and Communication,
Gwnagju University, Gwangju, Korea
ssroh@gwangju.ac.kr

Abstract. The energy harvesting is suggested and studied as the solution for energy constraint in wireless sensor network. In this paper, we propose a new duty cycle control algorithm in wireless sensor network with energy harvesting capability. This algorithm is designed to provide self-synchronization of a sensor and a system as they are concurrently activated during harvesting energy or at upper level of battery, and to guarantee the energy neutral operation of a sensor or a system. In order to achieve this purpose, we propose a neighbor discovery mechanism, a self-synchronization control mechanism and an energy model. We perform simulation with diverse parameters. From the results of simulations, we may ascertain that the proposed algorithm provides self-synchronization and the energy neutral operation regardless of the number of sensor.

Keywords: Duty Cycle Control, Self-Synchronization, Energy Harvesting, Wireless Sensor Network, Energy Management.

1 Introduction

Energy management is the technique that solves the problem of energy conservation in WSNs [1-3]. The primary objective of energy management is to reduce energy consumption for the long lifetime of WSN. The salient algorithm of these protocols is duty cycle control algorithms that manage an active and inactive time of a sensor. However, if energy management only depends on reducing energy consumption without continuous supplement of energy, it is very difficult to ensure continuity of operation of a WSN. Recent researches have proposed an energy harvesting as an alternative method of using non-rechargeable batteries. The energy harvesting is the process by which energy is derived from external sources and stored at energy storage devices such as capacitors, super-capacitors, or EnerChips.

In this paper, we propose a new duty cycle control algorithm in WSN powered by energy harvesting. We assume that the source of energy harvesting is solar power. The primary object of this algorithm is to assure that a system may be activated if one sensor is activated. The characteristic of solar energy is that it is only available during

T.-h. Kim et al. (Eds.): FGCN/DCA 2012, CCIS 350, pp. 115–122, 2012.

day time or office hour. A battery is needed to ensure the sensors to be operated all around the clock. In other word, a sensor needs to be activated during harvesting of energy or when the battery is upper specific value. Furthermore, as sensors in a WSN cooperate with others to pass their data, a WSN need to be activated when sensors are activated. For the purpose of this work, we use the self-synchronization behavior of ant colonies in order to design self-synchronized and energy-aware duty cycle control algorithm in energy harvested wireless sensor networks (EHWSN). The behavior of ant colonies is similar to that of sensors in EHWSN, which this paper focuses on. Firstly, an ant alternatively changes his state between working and resting [4 - 7], whereas a sensor controlled by a duty cycling mechanism does between active and inactive. Secondly, patterns of individual ant's alternate activation also appear in whole colonies, showing synchronized patterns of activity [6, 8, 9]. This is similar to the object of our design that a system or a set of sensors needs to be in active state when a sensor is activated (as mentioned upper). Thirdly, ants' activity patterns are self-synchronized [9, 10]. "Self-synchronization" means that ants are synchronized without external signals for activity synchronization. Therefore, self-synchronized sensor decreases energy consumption due to transmission of synchronization messages. Self-synchronized activation is more effective than random activation because it would maximize the number of simultaneously active neighbors of an active individual [9]. H. Hern´andez researched on self-synchronized duty cycling for static sensor networks [11] and Grid-based mobile sensor network [12].

The secondary object of this algorithm is to provide energy nutrition state to sensors and a system and to keep battery level upper specific value. In order to guarantee incessant operation of a sensor, an amount of energy that a sensor consumes in an active state should be less than an amount of energy that a sensor stores at energy storage during harvesting of energy. A sensor consumes some energy for transporting of control messages and minimum operating even though it is in an inactive state. An amount of energy harvested is different according to a harvesting time and a harvesting area. In order to prevent from energy starvation, sensors may limit an amount of energy consumed in an active state. Therefore, a duty cycle algorithm should ensure that a sensor keeps battery level upper specific value.

The paper is structured as follows. In Section 2, we describe self-synchronization behavior model. In Section 3, we propose a self-synchronized and energy-aware duty cycle control (SEDC) algorithm in energy harvested wireless sensor networks. In section 4, we make a simulation and analyze the results. Section 5 concludes the paper.

2   Self-Synchronization Behavior Model

In order to evaluate the performance of a self-synchronization behavior of ant colonies, Delgado [9, 13] proposed the fluid neural network (FNN), a mathematical model for temporal oscillations. The FNN uses the standard approach of neural networks, introducing a new set of rules which defines local movements and individual activations. The FNN has a set of N automata or neuron-ants that can move on a $L \times L$ two dimensional lattice. A continuous state variable $S_i(t)$ is defined as a state of an automaton $i \in \{1 \ldots n\}$ at a time step $t \in T$. An activity of an automaton that is either active or inactive is defined by the binary variable $a_i(t)$. The value of an activity of an automaton is calculated as follows,

$$a_i(t) = \begin{cases} 1, & if\ S_i(t) \geq \theta_{act} \\ 0, & if\ S_i(t) < \theta_{act} \end{cases} \tag{1}$$

where θ_{act} is the activation threshold. If $a_i(t) = 1$, an automaton is active and may move randomly to one of the eight nearest cells. Otherwise, it is inactive and may return to the active state either with probability p_a or due to the accumulated state of neighbors. The mean activity of ant colonies at time t is calculated as follows,

$$A(t) = \frac{1}{n}\sum_{i=1}^{n} a_i(t) \in [0,1] \tag{2}$$

If N_i is defined as a set of neighbors of an automaton i and $S_j(t)(j \in N_i)$ is given, the state of each automaton is updated as below,

$$S_i(t+1) = tanh\ [g \cdot h_i(t)] \tag{3}$$

where g is a gain parameter and $h_i(t)$ can be defined in diverse ways to obtain different behaviors. As the term $h_i(t)$ includes interactions with the eight nearest neighbors, the authors of [9] defined it as follows,

$$h_i(t) = S_i + \sum_{i \neq j \in N_i} S_j(t) \tag{4}$$

3   SEDC Algorithm

3.1   Neighbor Discovery

The activity of each sensor depends on activities of neighbors (see Eq. 3 and 4). The number of neighbors at each time is very important because the large number of neighbors makes the system to be well self-synchronized even though the density of sensors is same. We use the transmission radius of a sensor as the parameter to choose neighbors. It depends on the battery level and the characteristics of the RF device. In our paper, we define the transmission radius of a sensor i at time $t, r_i(t)$, as follows,

$$r_i(t) = r_0 + r_{max} \times B_i(t)^2 \tag{5}$$

where r_0 is the initial value of the transmission radius and r_{max} is the maximum value of the transmission radius at the full battery level. r_{max} depends on the characteristic of a RF device. A sensor j is a neighbor of a sensor i if $d_{i,j}(t) > r_j(t)$, where $d_{i,j}(t)$ denotes the distance between a sensor i and a sensor j at time t.

3.2   Self-synchronization

A system or a sensor is self-synchronized by interaction of neighbors (see Eq. 3 and 4). In an energy-harvested WSN, they may be differently self-synchronized according to the location or an amount of energy harvested. In order to reduce an amount of energy consumed, sensors that located in an area where energy is not harvested may not be self-synchronized or may reduce an effect of neighbors' interaction. In this paper, we redefine $h_i(t)$ as follows,

$$h_i(t) = S_i + \alpha_i \sum_{i \neq j \in N_i} S_j(t) \tag{6}$$

where $\alpha_i (\in [0,1])$ denotes a parameter that determines the degree of self-synchronization. If $\alpha_i = 0$, a sensor is not self-synchronized. If $\alpha_i = 1$, a sensor is completely self-synchronized.

3.3   Energy Model

A sensor i at a time t harvests a certain amount of energy $e_i^{harv}(t)$. In active state, a sensor i consumes an amount of energy for general active operations $e_i^{awake}(t)$ and for movement $e_i^{move}(t)$. In our work, a sensor that is active may move with a probability p_{move}. A sensor i that is inactive consumes an amount of energy $e_i^{sleep}(t)$. Therefore, an amount of energy consumed by a sensor i at each time t is calculated as follows,

$$e_i^{cons}(t) = e_i^{awake}(t) + e_i^{move}(t) + e_i^{sleep}(t) \tag{7}$$

If a sensor is inactive, $e_i^{awake}(t) = e_i^{move}(t) = 0$. Otherwise, $e_i^{sleep}(t) = 0$. The energy consumption state of a sensor depends on an amount of harvested energy and consumed energy. If $\int e_i^{harv}(t) > \int e_i^{cons}(t)$, a sensor saves a certain amount of energy. If $\int e_i^{harv}(t) = \int e_i^{cons}(t)$, a sensor maintains the level of battery. Otherwise, a sensor losses a certain amount of energy($\int e_i^{cons}(t) - \int e_i^{harv}(t)$). When energy is saved and balanced, a sensor is in energy neutral state. The object of our research is to guarantee that a sensor is always in energy neutral state.

The battery level of a sensor i at a time t is measured as follows,

$$B_i(t) = B_i^0 + \int e_i^{harv}(t) - \int e_i^{cons}(t) \tag{8}$$

In order to provide energy neutral operation, the battery level is maintained as satisfying below constraint,

$$B_i(t) \geq B_{th} \tag{9}$$

where B_{th} is the battery level threshold. If Eq. 9 is true, a sensor i is duty-cycling. Otherwise a sensor i stats at eh inactive state and does not return to the active state although $p < p_a$. As we assume that the source of energy harvesting is solar power and energy neural operation of a sensor is guaranteed, the battery level threshold is calculated as follows,

$$B_{th} \geq \int_t^{t+\Delta t} e_i^{cons}(t)\Delta t \tag{10}$$

where Δt is the time steps when the energy is not harvested.

4   Performance Evaluation

A summary of the value of fixed parameters is shown in Table 1 and a summary of the initial value of variable parameters in shown in Table 2 [9,12].

Table 1. Value of fixed parameters

Parameters	r_0	r_{max}	e_i^{awake}	e_i^{sleep}	e_i^{move}	p_{move}
Value	0.05	0.1	0.001	0.002	0.001	0.01

Table 2. Initial value of variable parameters

Parameters	p_a	θ_{act}	g	α_i	B_{th}	L
Value	0.001	10^{-16}	0.1	1	0.2	25

Fig. 1 shows mean activity and continuous battery level according to the diverse number of sensors. From the results, we may know that mean activity increases with increasing number of sensors because the number of neighbors increases. When the battery level goes below the battery level threshold (B_{th}), all sensors return to the inactive state (see Fig 1-(d)). In other word, we may ascertain that the proposed algorithm provides the energy neutral operation of the sensor.

Fig.2 shows mean activities of the system that is self-synchronized and the system that is not self-synchronized. Averages of mean activity are 0.558 and 0.584, respectively. From Fig.2 we ascertain that the proposed algorithm guarantees self-synchronization of a sensor and a system because the oscillating value of mean activity characterizes self-synchronization behavior. Mean activities of systems with $B_{th} = 0.2$ and $B_{th} = 0.8$ are shown in Fig. 3. Increasing B_{th} introduces decreasing mean activity(the average of mean activity of Fig.3-(a) is 0.558, and that of Figh.3-(b) is 0.415). Mean activity increases with increasing the battery level. Like Fig.1-(d), all sensors return to the inactive state when the battery level goes below the battery level threshold (B_{th}). Also, to set a high value to B_{th} may keep the battery level to be high.

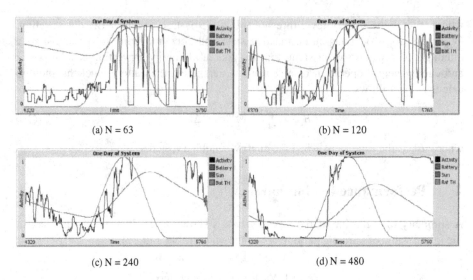

(a) N = 63   (b) N = 120

(c) N = 240   (d) N = 480

Fig. 1. Mean activity according to the number of sensors (average of mean activity: (a) 0.339, (b) 0.587, (c) 0.685, (d) 0.718)

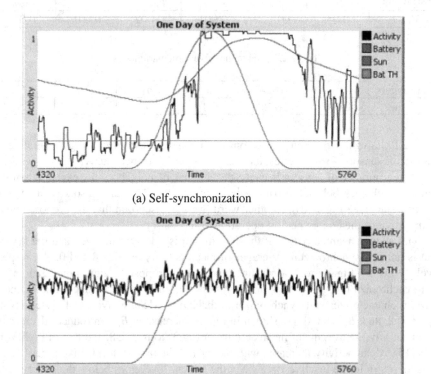

(a) Self-synchronization

(b) non-self-synchronization

Fig. 2. Mean activity according to α_1: (a) $\alpha_1 = 1$, (b) $\alpha_1 = 0$

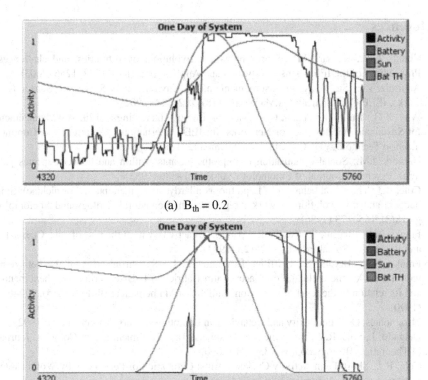

(a) $B_{th} = 0.2$

(b) $B_{th} = 0.8$

Fig. 3. Mean activity according to the B_{th}

5   Conclusion

In recent years, many studies in WSN have interest in the energy harvesting in order to solve the energy constraints. We proposed self-synchronized and energy-aware duty cycle control algorithm in the WSN with energy harvesting capability. The results of simulations show that the proposed algorithm provides self-synchronization to a sensor and a system regardless of the number of sensors, manages the degree of self-synchronization with the parameter α_i, and keeps a system to stay in the energy neutral state.

Further research will include analyzing the proposed algorithm with diverse parameters and designing of algorithms for mobile and wireless sensor network depending on specific application. Also, we plan to design the algorithm with multiple battery level thresholds in WSNs where sensors are widely scattered.

Acknowledgement. The work was conducted by research funds from Gwangju University in 2012.

References

1. Chong, C.Y., Kumar, S.P.: Sensor networks: Evolution, opportunities, and challenges. Proceedings of the IEEE Sensor Networks and Applications 91(8), 1247–1256 (2003)
2. Akyildiz, I.F., Su, W., Sankarasubramaniam, Y., Cayirci, E.: A Survey on Sensor Networks. IEEE Communications Magazine 40(8), 102–114 (2002)
3. Wan, Z.G., Tan, Y.K., Yuen, C.: Review on Energy Harvesting and Energy Management for Sustainale Wireless Sensor Networks. In: IEEE International Conference on Communication Technology (ICCT2011), Jinan, China (2011)
4. Herhers, J.M.: Social organisation in Leptothorax ants: within and between-species patterns. Psyche: A Journal of Entomology 90(4), 361–386 (1983)
5. Cole, B.J.: The social behavior of Leptothorax allardycei (Hymenoptera, Formicidae): time budgets and the evolution of worker reproduction. Behavioral Ecology and Sociobiology 18(3), 165–173 (1986)
6. Franks, N.R., Bryant, S.: Rhythmical patterns of activity within the nest of ants. Chemistry and Biology of Social Insects, 122–123 (1987)
7. Franks, N.R., Bryant, S., Griffiths, R., Hemerik, L.: Synchronization of the behaviour within nests of the antleptothorax acervorum (fabricius)-I. Discovering the phenomenon and its relation to the level of starvation. Bulletin of Mathematical Biology 52(5), 597–612 (1990)
8. Miramontes, O.: Complexity and Behaviour in Leptothorax Ants. Master Thesis (1992)
9. Delgado, J., Solé, R.V.: Self-synchronization and Task Fulfilment in Ant Colonies. Journal of Theoretical Biology 205(3), 433–441 (2000)
10. Cole, B.J.: Short-Term Activity Cycles in Ants: Generation of Periodicity by Worker Interaction. American Naturalist 137(2), 244 (1991)
11. Hernández, H., Blum, C.: Self-synchronized duty-cycling in sensor networks with energy harvesting capabilities: the static network case. In: Rothlauf, F., et al. (eds.) Proc. of GECCO 2009, pp. 33–40. ACM Press (2009)
12. Hernández, H., Blum, C., Middendorf, M., Ramsch, K., Scheidler, A.: Self-synchronized duty cycling for mobile sensor networks with energy harvesting capabilities: A swarm intelligence study. In: Proc. of SIS 2009, pp. 153–159. IEEE Press (2009)
13. Amit, D.J.: Modeling Brain Function: The World of Attractor Neural Networks. Cambridge University Press (1989)
14. Delgado, J., Sole, R.V.: Mean-field theory of fluid neural networks. Physcal Review E 57, 2204–2211 (1998)

Design of PLC NMS Protocol for AMI

Byung Seok Park[1], Cheul Shin Kang[2,*],
Young Hun Lee[2], Hyun Woo Yoo[1], and Kyung Shub Yoon[1]

[1] KEPCO, KEPCO Research Institute, Smartgrid Lab., 305-380 Daejeon, Korea
{blueon,uwill,ksyoon2012}@kepco.co.kr
[2] Dept. of Electronic Eng., Hannam University,
133 Ojeong-dong, Daedeok-gu, Daejon 306-791, Korea
ckang@hnu.kr

Abstract. AMI(Advanced Meter Infrastructure) in electricity collecting real time consumption data of smart meter through communication network is important in supporting to power demand and load of whole electricity system. AMI PLC is a major communication technology at NAN(Neighborhood Area Network) with weak signal radio. In this paper, a PLC NMS protocol was designed and implemented. The PLC NMS protocol supports auto-registration, path construction, remote configuration, and collecting status & statistics at remote slave modems for efficiently operating and constructing NAN.

Keywords: NMS, EMS(Element Management System), AMI, PLC, protocol.

1 Introduction

Recently, devices and technologies related to decreasing energy consumption and introducing of real time electricity pricing for the global warming are developed and researched very intensively. Especially, AMI(Advanced Metering Infrastructure)[1] is a killer application of smart grid. AMI system communicates between customer and utility by exchanging real time power usage information and electricity pricing data.

Generally, AMI system consists of two levels of network. One is wide area network connecting DCU(data Concentration Unit) to AMI server[2]. And the other is NAN used for collecting metering data from smart meter to DCU. Major communication method of AMI NAN is weak signal RF(Radio Frequency) link or PLC(Power line communication). Figure 1 shows architecture of an AMI system.

In Korea, IEC 12139-1 24Mbps High Speed PLC standard is used for AMI NAN. IEC12139-1 specifies PHY and MAC layer for basic communication through power line[3]. In AMI system, NAN requires some kind of management function such as firmware upgrade, remote modem configuration, auto-registration with authentication, mesh or tree-branch repeating and routing path establishment. But IEC12139-1 does not have any management function or protocol for OAM(operation, Administration and Maintenance) of PLC networks.

---

* Corresponding author.

T.-h. Kim et al. (Eds.): FGCN/DCA 2012, CCIS 350, pp. 123–130, 2012.
© Springer-Verlag Berlin Heidelberg 2012

In this paper, a PLC NMS protocol for AMI systems is designed, implemented and tested. DCU can control slave modems or collect previously mentioned modem operation data from slave modems using the proposed PLC NMS protocol.

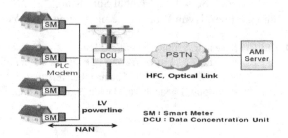

Fig. 1. Architecture of AMI system

2   PLC NMS Protocol

The interface between SNMP agent and PLC modem uses Ethernet protocol for remote management of PLC modem. The PLC NMS protocol provides means to send and receive Modem status information, configuration information, and channel information. The SNMP agent and PLC modems exchange information with $1:N$ polling scheme. When a special situation occurs, or periodically SNMP agent transmits NMS frames to a PLC modem using Ethernet frame scheme such as NMS Request and NMS Command. The PLC modem(station), which received a NMS Request or NMS Command, responds with transmission of the requested information. Or it conducts requested task and changes its state[4].

When the Master station receives MMI frame[3] such as CJR(Cell join request) from any of the slave stations, then it converts the received MMI frame to NMS frame and relays the converted NMS frame to SNMP agent. When the Master Station receives NMS Frame, it just relays to SNMP agent through Ethernet interface. Figure 2 shows frame transmission and conversion between stations.

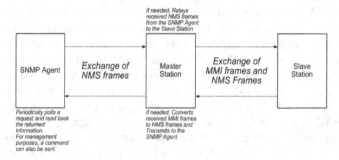

Fig. 2. Frame transmission and conversion between stations

The NMS Ethernet frame address of the stations is used as an IEEE MAC address. And the PLC MAC address is used as the NMS MAC address. NMS data transmission between PLC master and slave modem is based on ISO/IEC 12139-1 standard. Modem registration and link configuration is done automatically by SNMP agent. Manual setting is also possible by setting of related parameters. If configuration method value is *'Manual Configuration'*, then the SNMP agent must keep station registration and link configuration by manual status. If the configuration method of a slave station is set to be *'Automatic Configuration'* and communications are being failed for 15 min, then slave modem registration process is tried again.

The MMI and NMS packets which are used in modem registration process are transmitted using the specified initial GID(Group ID). The NMS packets perform encryption and decryption process using initial encryption key. The successfully registered modem performs packet transmission and encryption/decryption processes using the received GID and encryption key in registration process. The successfully registered modem restrict the transmission of frames applied the initial GID except the MMI and NMS packets used in registration[5]. The system operates two firmware images(image data) in order to support Roll-back function when a problem of firmware image occurs. The *current image* means currently running firmware image. The *reserved image* means the firmware image which is upgraded or will be upgraded. If a firmware update is executed, then the current image is switched to a reserved image. Likewise a reference of firmware image is switched from reserved image to current image.

Station means PLC Master and Slave Modem in a communication flow. Packet is transmitted via a Master modem when SNMP Agent transmits a packet to Slave modem. Figure 3 shows a communication flow according to two types of packets, respectively. Figure 4 shows Ethernet Frame Format for NMS. DA(Destination Address) define to NMS MAC address of destination. If slave modem transmit frame to SNMP agent, DA must be to MAC address of SNMP agent. SA(Source Address) means Ethernet source address. If SNMP agent transmit frame, SA must be to MAC address of SNMP agent likewise.

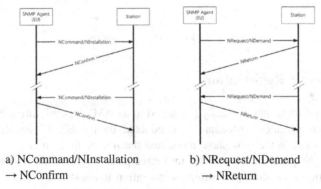

a) NCommand/NInstallation   b) NRequest/NDemend
   → NConfirm   → NReturn

Fig. 3. Flow of NMS frame exchange

DA	SA	EtherType (0x893D)	PFS (0x0001)	NFSB
6bytes	6bytes	2bytes	2bytes	variable

Fig. 4. Ethernet Frame Format for NMS

EtherType is the same as Ethernet protocol type in IEEE 802.3. Ethertype can resolve PLC NMS Ethernet packet from other upper layer protocol Ethernet frame. KEPCO NMS ethertype value, 0x893D is registered to IEEE. PFS(PLC Frame Signature) means the kind of PLC frame. NFSB means NMS information part. It is classified according to NMS frame body. Figure 5 shows a structure of NFSB.

Figure 6 shows NMS frame header Format. NPV field indicates the NMS protocol version. NPI field indicates that the NMS protocol identifier. NFT means type of NMS frame between SNMP agent and PLC modems. The NFT defines NMS frame type, including data request with short format, Modem status control, data installation, and packet acknowledgment. The content of NFVF(NMS Frame Variant Field) is determined by NMS frame type(NFT). NFSN(NMS Frame Sequence Number) is used to detect duplicated responses of received frame from SNMP agent and PLC modem. NFSN value is incremented by one from 0 to 65,535 when SNMP agent and PLC modem respond to NMS frame. NFSN value of Response packets(NReturn and Ninvalid, Nconfirm) is the same as that in request packets.

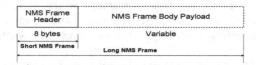

Fig. 5. Structure of NFSB

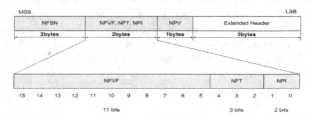

Fig. 6. NMS Frame Header structure

3   Automatic Registration

A new slave modem is automatically registered to an AMI network through the NMS protocol. The registration procedure is conducted by the SNMP agent. The link configuration between the new slave mode and the master modem is also set by the SNMP agent. The procedure is divided into three parts. Figure 7 shows the first part of the registration procedure presenting 'Registration Request' step, also called 'Cell Join Request' step. When a new slave modem in factory mode turns on, it requests registration to neighborhood modems by broadcasting CJR(Cell Join Request) frame. Modems received the frame carry out the collection of channel information between the modems and the new slave modem. It is conducted by switching CIRQ(Channel Information Request) and CIRP(Channel Information Response). The collected information is transmitted to the master modem. If a repeating modem is needed to deliver the collected information to the master modem, CJRL(Cell Join Relay) frame is used. These four frames are implemented in the forms of MMI frames in ISO/IEC 12139-1 standard.

The new modem repeats transmitting MMI/CJR for T_DRT at an interval of T_RT to gather the channel information of various paths. The FBBP format of the MMI/CIRP frame is similarly defined with the MMI/CIRQ frame. It has some additional fields about the device and the link. DCI(Down-Stream Channel Information) represents the down-stream channel throughput measured with PRS of MMI/CIRQ frame in bits per symbol. SN and CJRT fields have the same values as the corresponding MMI/CIRQ frame. The DT(Device Type) and MGWT(Meter Gateway Type) fields contain information for the modem. MID(Meter ID) is the linked meter's 11 bytes length identifier. PM_V presents the program image version of the new modem. However PRS field, which has the same form as the MMI/CIRQ frame, will be used to estimate the channel information of the up-stream channel.

The MMI/CJRL frame is used when the cell join request information is delivered through multi-link path. It contains information about the device and the channel of the passed links. When the collected information about the new modem and the channel is arrived at the master modem, the information is transmitted to the SNMP agent in the forms of NMS frame, NDemand/Cell Join Request.

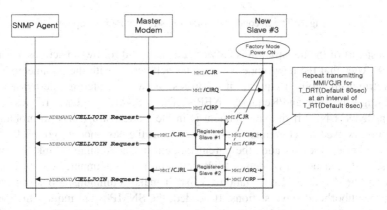

Fig. 7. The first part of the registration; Registration Request

DCI(Down-Stream Channel Information) represents the down-stream channel throughput measured with PRS of MMI/CIRQ frame in bits per symbol. SN and CJRT fields have the same values as the corresponding MMI/CIRQ frame. The DT(Device Type) and MGWT(Meter Gateway Type) fields contain information for the modem. MID(Meter ID) is the linked meter's 11 bytes length identifier. PM_V presents the program image version of the new modem. However PRS field, which has the same form as the MMI/CIRQ frame, will be used to estimate the channel information of the up-stream channel.

The MMI/CJRL frame is used when the cell join request information is delivered through multi-link path. It contains information about the device and the channel of the passed links. When the collected information about the new modem and the channel is arrived at the master modem, the information is transmitted to the SNMP agent in the forms of NMS frame, NDemand/Cell Join Request.

Fig. 8 shows the second part of the registration procedure presenting 'Path Setup' step. The SNMP Agent collects channel information of various paths and determines the best path to communicate. If the best path includes any new repeater, the SNMP agent sets the already registered slave modem to a repeater. After that, the SNMP agent sends the new modem information on the network to be registered with NReturn/Cell Join Request. The frame is transmitted to the parent modem of the new modem and the parent modem broadcasts the received frame to the neighborhood modems.

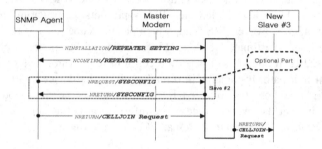

Fig. 8. The Second part of the registration; Path Setup

The last part of the registration is network entering and follow-up actions as shown in Fig. 9. After that the new modem completes self set-up with the parameters given by NRetrun/Cell Join Request, it requests network entering permission by transmitting NCommand/Request NEP. The SNMP agent replies with NRetrun/Request NEP if the new modem is in the white list and has no problem on the parameters used for communications. As soon as the new modem got NEP, it sets link restriction enable and adds the parent modem to the Available Link Station ID list for security reasons. A modem set link restriction can communicate only with the modems in the Available Link Station ID list. It makes communications impossible between neighborhood slave stations. If needed, the SNMP agent inquiry the system configuration of the new modem and modify some parameters need to be changed.

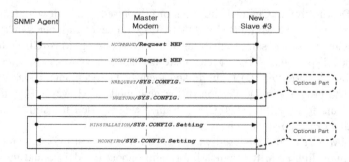

Fig. 9. The last part of the registration; Network Entering and Follow-up Actions

4   Implementation and Experiment

Fig. 10 shows the implemented test modem, in which PLC NMS protocol designed in this paper is built-in, and the SNMP agent emulation program running at windows in PC environment. Experimental set consists of 4 slave modems, 1 master modem, and SNMP agent emulation program. All slave modems are registered to the SNMP agent. And the SNMP collects channel status information and configuration data from them successfully.

a) Captured NMS frame   b) Implemented test modem

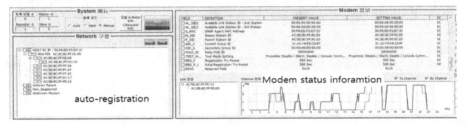

c) Screen displayed modem status information

Fig. 10. The experiment result of the implemented PLC NMS protocol

5   Conclusion

A NMS protocol is required in PLC network in AMI for efficient network installation, operation, and maintenance. In this paper, a PLC NMS protocol is designed for AMI NAN using Ethernet frame and dedicated ethertype number. Through PLC NMS protocol, slave modem can be registered to AMI system and then be controlled or configured by SNMP agent for metering data collecting. The operation of the implemented test-bed shows that the designed PLC NMS protocol functions as intended very well. Performance analysis and measurement of massive installation to real outdoor field are the areas of further study.

Acknowledgments. This research was supported by 2012 Hannam University Research Fund.

References

1. Advanced Metering Infrastructure, http://en.wikipedia.org
2. IEC 12139-1, Powerline communication (PLC) — High speed PLC medium access control (MAC) and physical layer (PHY)-Part 1:General requirements (2009)
3. Kim, M.-S., Ko, Y., Kim, Y., Park, B.: A Simulation Study of the PLC-MAC Performance using Network Simulator-2. In: Proc. of International Symposium on PLC (2008)
4. Choi, I., Park, B., Lee, S., Yoon, J.: Design of Smart Metering Control Protocol based on task_script for Advanced Metering Infrastructure. In: Proc of International Conference of Women Engineers and Scientists (2010)
5. Park, B.-S., Kang, C.-S., Lee, Y.-H.: Design and Implementation of Smart Meter Concentration Protocol for AMI. In: Kim, T.-h., Adeli, H., Fang, W.-c., Vasilakos, T., Stoica, A., Patrikakis, C.Z., Zhao, G., Villalba, J.G., Xiao, Y. (eds.) FGCN 2011, Part I. CCIS, vol. 265, pp. 179–187. Springer, Heidelberg (2011)

A Resistance Deviation-To-Time Interval Converter Using Second Generation Current Conveyors

Han-Seul Kim, Jae-Gyu Shin, Won-Sup Chung[*], and Sang-Hee Son

Department of Semiconductor Engineering, Cheongju University,
Cheongju 360-764, Korea
circuit@cju.ac.kr

Abstract. A resistance deviation-to-time interval converter using second generation current conveyors is designed for connecting resistive bridge sensors with a digital system based on dual-slope integration. Simulation results exhibit that a conversion sensitivity amounts to $15.56\,\mu s/\Omega$ over the resistance deviation range of 0-200 Ω and its linearity error is less than $\pm 0.02\%$. Its temperature stability is less than 220 ppm/℃ in the temperature range of -25-$85\,℃$.

Keywords: Direct digital readout, resistance-to-time converter, second generation current conveyor.

1 Introduction

Due to their high sensitivity, resistive sensor bridges are widely employed in industrial and process control systems and medical instrumentation. In order to interface these sensors with digital systems, an accurate interface circuit converting a small change of resistance into a digital readout is required. Several circuits are available in the literature for realization of such converters [1], [2], [3], [4], [5]. These are usually based on a resistance bridge. In these converters, the resistance deviation of resistive bridge sensors is converted into its corresponding offset voltage via a resistive bridge, this offset in turn is converted into a frequency by various oscillator circuits.

In this paper a new converter based on dual-slope integration using second generation current conveyors (CCIIs) is presented, whereby it is possible to realize a highly linear output/input relation for small resistance deviations with a wide resistance deviation range.

2 Circuit Description and Operation

Fig. 1 shows the circuit diagram of the proposed resistance deviation-to-time interval (RD-to-TI) converter. Here, resistors connected to the terminal Y are half-bridge

---

[*] Corresponding author.

T.-h. Kim et al. (Eds.): FGCN/DCA 2012, CCIS 350, pp. 131–136, 2012.

resistive sensors and R_r connected to the terminal X is the fixed resistor. The converter consists of an integrator implemented with two CCIIs and a capacitor, a comparator, and digital control circuits. The symbol and circuit diagram of the CCII are shown in Fig. 2 [6]. It consists of a unity-gain buffer and two Wilson-current mirrors (or four in CCII−).

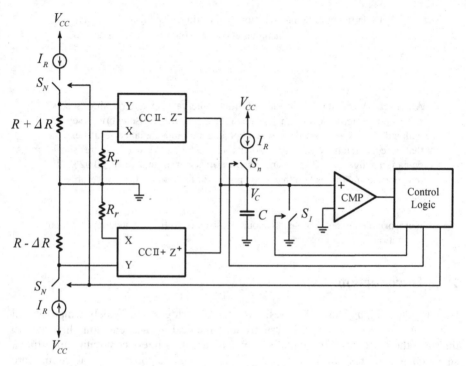

Fig. 1. Circuit diagram of the resistance deviation-to-time interval converter based on dual-slope integrations

The operation of the converter can be divided into three states; "Initialization", "Inverting integration", and "Non-inverting integration", whose sequence and the capacitor voltage waveforms at each state are shown in Fig. 3. The detailed operation in each state will be described in the following.

2.1   Operation in "Initialization" State

In this state, while analog switch S_I is kept "on", analog switches S_N and S_n does not matter. During this state, capacitor C is discharged and its voltage V_C will be kept to zero.

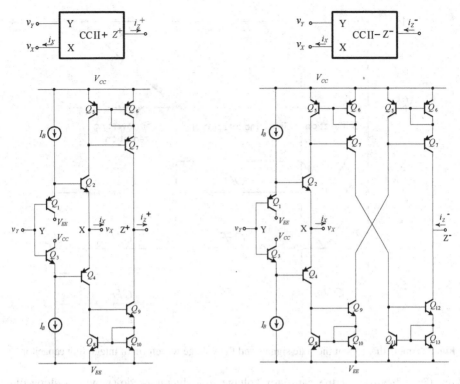

Fig. 2. Symbols and circuit diagrams of CCIIs used for the converter in Fig. 1: (a) CCII+; (b) CCII−

2.2 Operation in "Inverting Integration" State

In this state, S_N is kept "on", while S_n and S_I are kept "off", thereby the analog circuit forms the inverting integrator, which is composed of the half-bridge resistive sensors, the reference current I_R, the fixed resistor R_r, the positive current conveyor CCII+, the negative current conveyor CCII−, and capacitor C. During this state, the current flowing through capacitor C is given by

$$I_c = \frac{2\Delta R}{R_r} I_R \qquad (1)$$

This current charges the capacitor, and thus capacitor voltage $V_c(t)$ may be expressed as follows:

$$V_c(t) = V_c(t_0) - \frac{2\Delta R I_R}{CR_r} \int_0^1 dt \qquad (t_0 < t < t_1) \qquad (2)$$

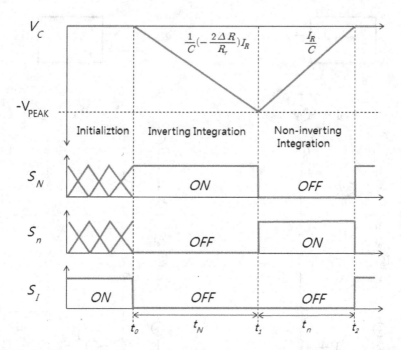

Fig. 3. Timing diagram of the state signals and the voltage waveform of integrating capacitor

Eqn. (2) indicates that the capacitor voltage linearly ramps down with a slope of $-2\Delta RI_R/CR_r$. This inverting integration is carried out for a fixed period of time t_N as shown in Fig. 3. Assuming that the initial voltage $V_C(t_0)$ of the capacitor C is 0 V, the charged voltage of the capacitor at the end of the time period t_N is given by

$$V_C(t_1) = -\frac{2\Delta RI_R}{CR_r}t_N \tag{3}$$

After this integration the circuit turns into the "Non-inverting integration" state.

2.3 Operation in "Non-inverting Integration" State

In this state, S_n is kept "on", while S_N and S_I are kept "off", thereby the analog circuit forms the inverting integrator consisting of I_R and capacitor C. During this state, the current flowing through capacitor C is

$$I_C = I_R \tag{4}$$

Therefore $V_C(t)$ may be expressed as follows:

$$V_C(t) = V_C(t_1) + \frac{I_R}{C}\int_1^2 dt \qquad (t_1 < t < t_2) \tag{5}$$

This shows that the capacitor voltage ramps up with a slope of I_R/C until the ramp reaches back to zero as shown in Fig. 3. The zero crossing of the capacitor voltage will be detected by the comparator, which will then trigger digital control circuits to produce switch control signals for initializing the converter, and the conversion cycle repeats. Let t_n is the time duration of this non-inverting integration state. Then the relation between t_n and ΔR may be expressed as follows:

$$t_n = \frac{2\Delta R}{R_r} t_N$$

(6)

This equation indicates that the output time interval t_n is directly proportional to the resistance deviation ΔR. The digital values of ΔR can be known by counting the number of clock pulses gated into a counter for t_n.

3   Simulation Results

Based on the scheme in Fig. 1, a prototype circuit was built using discrete components. BJTs of 2N2222 and 2N2907 were used for implementing CCIIs. The bias currents I_B of CCII+ and CCII− were set to 200 μA. The comparator used was LM311. All of these devices were biased with ±5 V. The capacitor C was 0.6 μF. The reference current I_R was set to 400 μA. The clock frequency f_c used in control logic circuits was 3.3 MHz. ΔR was increased from 0 Ω to 200 Ω by 20 Ω. Fig. 5 shows experimental results when t_N is 10 ms, which shows time interval versus resistance deviation, its linearity, and temperature stability. It appears that the conversion linearity is less then ±0.02% and the conversion sensitivity is 15.56 μs/Ω. And The temperature stability of the proposed converter measured in the temperature range of −25-85 ℃ is less than 220 ppm/℃.

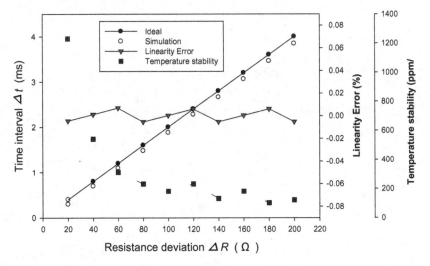

Fig. 4. Simulated time interval versus resistance deviation, its linearity error, and temperature stability measured in the temperature range of −25-85 ℃ when t_N is 10ms

4   Conclusion

A novel RD-to-TI converter based on dual-slope integration using CCIIs has been described. The proposed circuit permits accurate resistance deviation measurement with small device count. Therefore the circuit is particularly suitable for implementing a 'smart sensor', which gives a digital output directly connectable to a microprocessor.

References

1. Weiss, H.J.: Measuring resistance deviations quickly and more accurately. Elec. Eng. (8), 41–43 (1972)
2. Chung, W.-S., Watanabe, K.: A temperature difference-to-frequency converter using resistance temperature detectors. IEEE Trans. Instrum. Meas. 39(4), 676–677 (1990)
3. Mochizuki, K., Watanabe, K.: A high-resolution, linear resistance-to-frequency converter. IEEE Trans. Instrum. Meas. 45(3), 761–764 (1996)
4. Kaliyugavaradan, S.: A linear resistance-to-time converter with high resolution. IEEE Trans. Instrum. Meas. 49(1), 151–153 (2000)
5. Liu, H.Q., Teo, T.H., Zhang, Y.P.: A low-power wide-range interface circuit for nanowire sensor array based on resistance-to-frequency conversion technique. In: ISIC 2009, vol. 2, pp. 13–16 (December 2009)
6. Toumazou, C., Lidgey, F.J., Haigh, D.G.: Anaolog IC design: The current-mode approach, ch. 15. Peter Peregrinus Ltd., London (1990)

Flexible Network Framework for Various Service Components of Network Based Robot

Dong W. Kim[1], Ho-Dong Lee[2],
Jong-Wook Park[3], and Sung-Wook Park[3]

[1] Dept. of Digital Electronics, Inha Technical College,
Incheon, South Korea
[2] Korea Institute of Science and Technology,
Seoul, South Korea
[3] Dept. of Electronics, University of Incheon,
Incheon, South Korea
dwnkim@inhatc.ac.kr, jngw@incheon.ac.kr

Abstract. These days wide variety of platforms and frameworks were researched for network based robot (NBR) but it is difficult to apply those platforms and frameworks to the NBR, because the NBR and its service components keep developed. In other works, the interfaces and execution environments of the NBR and the service components are changed and upgraded very often, and at times, the service components are totally reconstructed. Consequently, a new flexible and reliable network framework that adapts to various service components is necessary. To handle these problems, a solution is suggested in this paper.

Keywords: network based robot (NBR), platform and frameworks for service component.

1 Introduction

The service components are distributed on the network. Thus, the NBRs have to access them easily, and their integration methods have to easy to develop. To develop it, a network core design will be proposed in this paper to easily integrate service components to an NBR using communication interface design based on TCP/IP.

A network core based on TCP/IP organizes service components into a tree structure. Thus, the NBR and the service components can easily access other service components. The network core is implemented as a DLL library to enable the developer of the service components to easily apply them.

TCP/IP(Transmission Control Protocol/Internet Protocol) is a well known and the most popular communications protocol for Internet connection. TCP/IP is a traditional method of integrating components via a network. It is reliable and stable, and it is very easy to develop its components. Various architectures and integration schemes have been researched. In this paper, communications interfaces based on TCP/IP are designed for an NBR.

T.-h. Kim et al. (Eds.): FGCN/DCA 2012, CCIS 350, pp. 137–144, 2012.

2   Communications Interface Design Based on TCP/IP

TCP/IP consists of an IP(Internet protocol), which is an Internet protocol that uses the packet communication method, and a TCP(transmission control protocol). An IP does not guarantee packet forwarding, sending, and receiving. Also, the order of the packets sent and received may vary (unreliable datagram service). The TCP protocol operates over the IP, and the TCP warrants the transfer of the data packet and the order of the data packet. HTTP, FTP, and SMTP, including a large number of IP-based application protocols, run on TCP, which is why we call the protocol TCP/IP.

Fig.1 shows the TCP/IP protocol's stack and related protocols. The hierarchical structure is also shown.

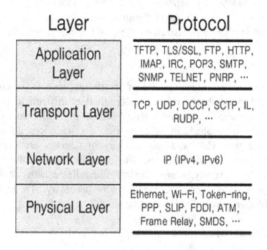

Fig. 1. Internet protocol stack

2.1   Development of a Network Core Using TCP/IP Protocol

Environment data such as video streams and audio streams from an NBR are sent to each resource via the main server. Thus, if the number of service components increases, then the data throughput of the main server is increased. This situation is shown in Fig. 2.

Of course there is the multicast protocol, but it is not suitable for sending large amounts of data reliably. In addition, it is difficult to control each resource based on their role, and it is difficult to adjust each resource based on its usage because it has no structural design. Also, the programming complexity of a main server is increased when the main server manages the resources. To avoid these situations, the main server needs some methods that can classify each service component according to its role.

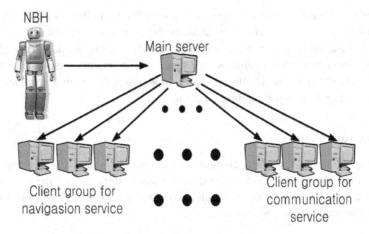

Fig. 2. Case of clients receiving information from the main server

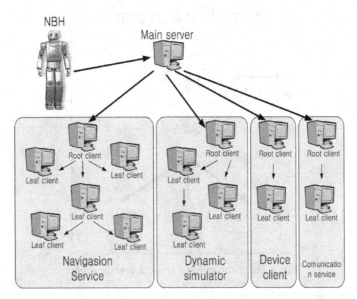

Fig. 3. Example of an NBR system architecture that uses the tree structure

A structural design such as the tree structure is used to solve the aforementioned problems. Each resource is formed as a branch of a tree structure. Only one client, the root of the tree structure, is connected to the main server. Thus, the root client receives the data transmitted from the main server, and then transmits the received data to other clients. In this way, the burden of the main server can be reduced.

Fig. 3 shows an example of an NBR system with the proposed tree structure. The system in Fig. 3 consists of four service groups, an NBR and a main server. For each service group that consists of multiple clients, only the root client is connected to the main server. Other clients are connected to the root client of the service group. Therefore, the main server manages only four root clients. Furthermore, each client in the service group is formed within the tree structure. The client's location and mission are shown clearly and conceptually in Fig. 3. In addition, the main server can control the service group by controlling the root client.

2.2   Network Core

To develop the network framework described previously, a network core that can be configured into the network with a tree structure was designed. Also, the network core serves as a server and a client simultaneously. In Fig. 4, the network core that was designed and implemented is shown.

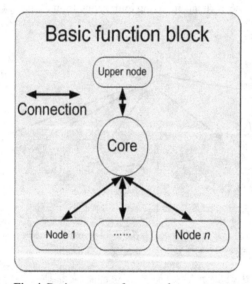

Fig. 4. Basic concept of a network core structure

By default, the network core performs the roles of a server and a client. It can also, relay data from an input to multiple outputs. At this point, the kinds of data being entered are unlimited. With these structures, clients were configured with a tree structure on the network. Fig. 5 shows an extension of a network core. An output of a network core can be an input of other network cores, and the direction of the data movement is bi-directional.

Fig. 6 shows an entire system configuration that uses this network core. As shown in Fig. 6, four network cores are connected to the main server. They are an input from an NBR, a PDA, a client, and a service group that consists of four clients. At this point, the main server transmits an input from the NBR to three clients, and the three clients that comprise the service group receive data from a root client that is connected to the main server. Thus, the root client that receives data from the main server is responsible for realizing the role of the main server with respect to other clients in the service group. Therefore, using the network core that serves as a server and a client simultaneously, each client will be able to organize itself into a tree structure. This reduces the load on the main server.

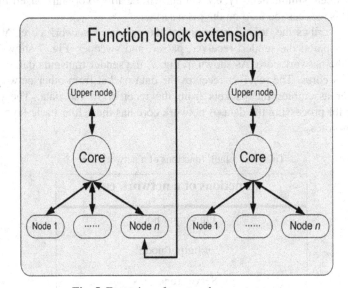

Fig. 5. Extension of a network core structure

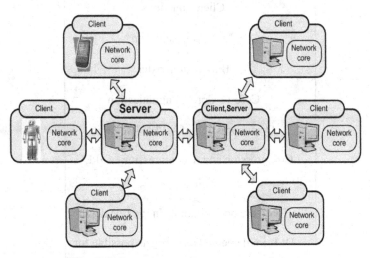

Fig. 6. System structure that uses a network core

As shown in Fig. 6, four network cores are connected to the main server. They are an input from an NBR, a PDA, a client, and a service group that consists of four clients. At this point, the main server transmits an input from the NBR to three clients, and the three clients that comprise the service group receive data from a root client that is connected to the main server. Thus, the root client that receives data from the main server is responsible for realizing the role of the main server with respect to other clients in the service group. Therefore, using the network core that serves as a server and a client simultaneously, each client will be able to organize itself into a tree structure. This reduces the load on the main server.

Table 1 describes the default functions of the proposed network core. A network core has four parts: the sender, receiver, parser, and sweeper. Fig. 7 shows a block diagram of the network core. As shown in Fig. 7, the sender transmits data packets to other network cores. The receiver receives the data packet from other network cores. The sweeper assembles the packets from the receiver to the data. The parser is responsible for processing the data. A network core has these four basic functions and management roles.

Table 1. Default functions of a network core

Functions of a network core
One-input node
n-output node
Server functions
Client functions
Transfer of any data
Bulk data transfer
Core-to-Core communication
Decompression of MPEG4 streams
Compression and decompression of JPEG images
There are no limitations in the tree depth
DLL implemented as easily as possible for use with other applications

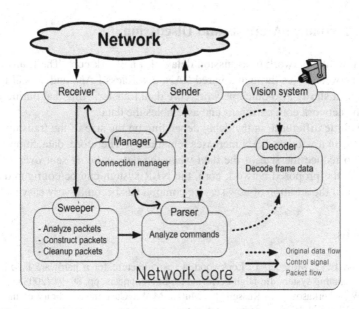

Fig. 7. Block diagram of network core

Table 2. Transfer rate using a network core

Size of transferred data	Send/ Receive ACK	Local machine	Internal machine	Wireless LAN
Command only	**Send completely**	0.194 ms	0.053ms	0.038ms
(28 bytes)	**Receive ACK completely**	2.152ms	2.161ms	2.838ms
1000 bytes data	**Send completely**	0.132ms	0.058ms	0.041ms
with command	**Receive ACK completely**	2.243ms	2.750ms	3.376ms
4000 bytes data	**Send completely**	0.232ms	0.101ms	0.071ms
with command	**Receive ACK completely**	2.218ms	3.209ms	11.166ms
8000 bytes data	**Send completely**	0.639ms	0.134ms	18.764ms
with command	**Receive ACK completely**	1.863ms	3.399ms	76.023ms

3   Performance Analysis and Discussion

Table 2 shows the network transmission delay of a network core. The transfer rate is measured between cores through a wired LAN, a wireless LAN, and a local machine, respectively. it shows also quick network core data transfer. Note that during the data transfer, the network core partitions and assembles the data.

There is little difference in the delay depending on the size of the transmitted data, but the delay in a wireless LAN increases remarkably. Therefore, data compression is necessary to reduce the size of the data when the data is being sent over a wireless LAN. Using the proposed network core, the NBR system can be configured quickly and easily, and the addition of new service components becomes very easy and fast.

References

1. Schuehler, D.V., Moscola, J., Lockwood, J.: Architecture for a hardware based, TCP/IP content scanning system. In: High Performance Interconnects, pp. 89–94 (2003)
2. Tang, W., Cherkasova, L., Russell, L., Mutka, M.W.: Customized library of modules for STREAMS-based TCP/IP implementation to support content-aware request processing for Web applications. In: Advanced Issues of E-Commerce and Web-Based Information Systems, WECWIS 2001, pp. 202–211 (2001)
3. Hansen, J.S., Riech, T., Andersen, B., Jul, E.: Dynamic adaptation of network connections in mobile environments. IEEE Internet Computing 2(1), 39–48 (1998)
4. Lee, K.B., Schneeman, R.D.: Internet-based distributed measurement and control applications. IEEE Instrumentation & Measurement Magazine 2(2), 23–27 (1999)
5. Liao, R.-K., Ji, Y.-F., Li, H.: Optimized Design and Implementation of TCP/IP Software Architecture Based on Embedded System. In: Machine Learning and Cybernetics, pp. 590–594 (2006)

A Study on the Performance Analysis of the File System

Jae-Hwan Lee and Young-Hun Lee*

Dept. of Electronic Eng., Hannam University, 133 Ojeong-dong,
Daedeok-gu, Daejon 306-791, Korea
mcskyzxkk@naver.com, yhlee00@hnu.kr

Abstract. In the current situation requiring high speed saving devices, file system isn't suitable to high speed I/O processing. For that reason, performance needs to be analyzed depending on data processing size of DRAM-SSD and file system. In this paper, It analyzed performance according to block size intended for HDD storage device and DRAM-SSD storage. Case of HDD is not changed performance regardless of the block size changes, Case of DRAM-SSD is improved performance by increasing block size. Therefore, case of using HDD, block size is good to use as Appropriate block size in user environment, but, case of using DRAM-SSD, using maximum block size is good conclusions to maximize the performance.

Keywords: DRAM-SSD, HDD, file system, block size, postmark.

1   Introduction

SSD(Solid State Drive) is a storage technology invented to solve a bottleneck situation of data input and output caused by the difference of velocity between HDD and CPU that HDD velocity increases by only 20 times, while CPU velocity in a computer increases by 500 times[1-3].As a concept appearing in the 1980s, SSD is a device to save information using a semiconductor memory, contrary to a normal hard disk, and it is forming its market in particular fields such as war industry, aviation industry and shipping industry requiring high safety and quick data processing speed . [4].

According to a referencebook[5], it is expected that digital information approaching 1[Zeta Byte] which is six-times bigger than 2006, would be distributed in 2010. This mass storage data needs high-capacity storage device and high storage speed.

In other words, it is difficult to catch up with data's increasing speed using the existing data storage medium, HDD, so there are various researches being performed to solve this problem. Of them, using a DRAM as a storage medium to improve data processing velocity is one of the promising researches[6].

The current File System was developed for a low-speed data I/O processing, based on HDD and thus, isn't suitable for a high-speed I/O processing. That's why analysis of performance depending on data processing scale of DRAM-SSD and File System,

---

* Corresponding author.

T.-h. Kim et al. (Eds.): FGCN/DCA 2012, CCIS 350, pp. 145–148, 2012.
© Springer-Verlag Berlin Heidelberg 2012

is needed. This study, therefore, aims to analyze performance of HDD and DRAM-SSD's storage devices depending on the changes in File System's block size.

2   Test Condition

As shown in Table 1, amongst three test conditions of Postmark(Low, Medium and High), device's performance in 'High' condition was measured. 'Low', 'Medium' and 'High' are classified depending on the number of Subdirectory, File and Transaction. 'Low' condition has the lowest load, whereas 'High' condition has the biggest load. The number of Subdirectory and File refers to the number created by Postmark for a test and the number of Transaction refers to the number of transaction about a file used. In this research, file size was fixed at 327K, and block sizes were set as 4K, 8K, 16K, 32K and 64K, respectively.

Table 1. Experimental condition

Postmark Test Level	Test condition		
	Subdirectory number	File number	Transaction number
Low	10	10,000	50,000
Medium	10	30,000	50,000
High (Measurement)	100	70,000	100,000

3   Experimental Environment

In the experimental environment for this test, The test server is Linux Cent OS 5.3. For the experiment, Postmark installed in the server was designed to perform transaction of DRAM-SSD and HDD, changing file system(EXT2)'s block sizes(4K, 8K, 16K, 32K and 64K) in 'High' condition. For collecting accurate data, each of them was repeated total three times.

4   Experiments

Table 2 shows the results of transaction per second at each of block size of DRAM-SSD. These results demonstrate that when HDD's block sizes were 4K and 64K, both of them were equal in the number of transaction(58) per second, and that there was no significant difference, when they were 16K and 32K that transaction was performed 59 times.

As shown in Figure 1, when HDD's block sizes were 4K, 8K and 64K, transaction was performed 58 times, and when they were 16K and 32k, it was performed 59 times.

Table 2. Performance measurement

Block Size	Test result(trns per sec)		
	HDD	D-SSD	Rate
4K	58	3,449	59.5
8K	58	3,617	62.4
16K	59	3,771	63.9
32K	59	3,838	65.1
64K	58	3,898	67.2

It implies that block size doesn't have a big influence on HDD's performance. However, when DRAM-SSD's block size was 4K, it was performed 3,449 times, and when it was 8K, it was performed 3,617 times that was 100 more than 4K of block size. It shows that contrary to HDD, the number of transaction per second continues to increase, as DRAM-SSD's block size increases. Ultimately, it was observed that the larger the block size gets, the better DRAM-SSD's performance gets, as Figure 2 displays.

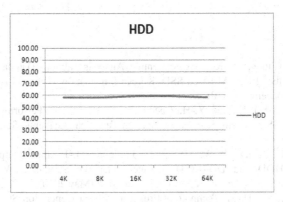

Fig. 1. Performance curve of HDD

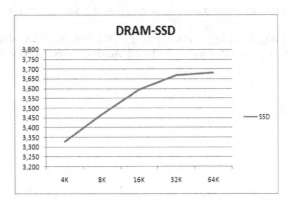

Fig. 2. Performance curve of DRAM-SSD

In conclusion, HDD's block size doesn't influence its performance, but DRAM-SSD's performance gets better, as its block size goes up, as Figure 2 indicates.

5   Conclusion

Currently, high-capacity and quick data storage device is being required due to distribution of mass information, and there are various researches being performed in relation to this. In this paper, HDD and DRAM-SSD storage devices' performance was analyzed, according to their block sizes to observe whether file system's data processing size influences its performance. As the result, it was found that HDD's performance isn't influenced by the changes in its block size, whereas DRAM-SSD's performance is more improved, as its block size increases.

These results mean that user needs to adjust to a proper block size depending on user's environment, when using HDD's storage device, but should maximize a block size to get the best performance, when using DRAM-SSD's storage device.

Acknowledgments.

References

[1] Ko, D.-S., Chung, S.-K.: Experimental Analysis about Database Performance Enhancement using DRAM-based SSD. Korean Information Technical Academic Society Dissertation (December 2010)
[2] Park, K.-H., Choe, J.-K., Lee, Y.-H., Cheong, S.-K., Kim, Y.-S.: Performance Analysis for DRAM-based SSD system. Korean Information Technical Academic Society Dissertation (August 2009)
[3] Cheong, S.-K., Jeong, Y.-W., Jeong, Y.-J., Jeong, J.-J.: Input-Output Performance Analysis of HDD and DDR-SSD Storage under the Streaming Workload. Korean Information Technical Academic Society Dissertation (May 2010)
[4] Cheong, S.-K., Ko, D.-S.: Technology Prospect of Next Generation Storage: Solid State Disk. Korean Information Technical Academic Society Dissertation (May 2008)
[5] The Expanding Digtal Universe: A Forecast of worldwide Information Growth Through (2010)
[6] Park, K.-H., Choe, J.-K., Lee, Y.-H., Cheong, S.-K.: Performance Analysis fo High-speed Data Backup. Korean Information Technical Academic Society Dissertation (February 2009)

The Design and Implementation of the Remote Emergency Control System for an Elevator

Woon-Yong Kim[1] and SoonGohn Kim[2,*]

[1] Department of Computer & Internet Technique, Gangwon Provincial College,
115 Gyohang-ro, Jumunjin-eup, Gangneung-shi, Gangwon-do, 210-804, Korea
wykim@gw.ac.kr
[2] Division of Computer and Game Science, Joongbu University,
101 Daehakro, Chubu-Meon, GumsanGun, Chungnam, 312-702, Korea
sgkim@joongbu.ac.kr

Abstract. An elevator is essential elements that perform a variety of actions, while maintaining the precision of more than 20,000 parts for the building. And also many and unspecified people use publicity as a means of transportation. It required the high stability and reliability and need to build more secure environment to prevent accidents. In this paper, we propose the Remote Emergency Control System for an elevator that support a rapid decision-making in an emergency and make the communications environment that can be connected at any time. And also we suggest the remote system to control the elevator with mobile phone.

Keywords: Remote Control, Elevator, Emergency System, Direct Call, Remote Management System, Smart Phone, Secure System.

1 Introduction

Elevator accident is rising with spread of an elevator. And also it required various service environments for performance and crime enhancements. Recently, compulsory installation provisions of CCTV and direct call device was made for preventing an elevator accidents. And also there are various researches for improving the performance and maintenance environment. So in this paper, we propose the remote emergency control system for coping with emergency situations of the elevator. This remote emergency control system optimizes a variety of communications environments anytime and has connection structure for emergency using mobile and phone line. This system which has the diagnostic capabilities support a field engineer to make decision more quickly for reliable elevator environment to ensure the safety of passengers. Management of the current elevator is difficult to intensive monitoring and inspection because of a decrease in the maintenance of price and operating the hundreds unit per field engineers. Because of these situations, more effective management measures are required. For these problems, in this paper, we suggest the

---

* Corresponding author.

T.-h. Kim et al. (Eds.): FGCN/DCA 2012, CCIS 350, pp. 149–154, 2012.

effective communication environment with interphone and telephone in order to build emergency call. And the field engineer can recognize problem situations quickly and control the elevator remotely and directly.

The remaining parts of the paper are organized as follows, In Section 2, we discuss the related technology for the emergency control service of the elevator system. In Section 3, we propose the system model that is remote emergency control of an elevator. Section 4 presents operation and features of the proposed system and Section 5 concludes this paper.

2   Related Works

2.1   Emergency Control Services of an Elevator System

In the operation of the elevator, the devices of the emergency control service such as CCTV, emergency bell and monitoring system are utilized in the elevator system mainly. The emergency bell is connected to a management office and a guardhouse directly. It can contact the manager when occurring emergency situation by calling [1]. This situation has disadvantage that it takes a lot of time to solve the emergency situation when the manager is not exist. In addition, it is difficult accurate assessment and recognition about the situation of the problem because the caller delivers their situation and location orally [2]. For solving of these problems, a different approach that the caller can connect other manager around any time is required when the manager absence [3]. In addition, the monitoring system has lack of aggressive problem-solving skills because the managers identify the elevator situation manually. An important element of elevator accidents handling is securing safety and faster processing. For this purpose, the emergency control system needs approaches to be diagnosed by the elevator specialists and to solve the problem in the fastest way.

Recently, with expansion of IT convergence technologies, the elevator service environment is rapidly changing. Mainly, the services have evolved to improvement of the user convenience and advancement services [4][5]. And also there are various services such as notice and information service, elevator call and boarding service, elevator diagnostic and checking service so on [6][7].

3   Remote Emergency Control System

3.1   The Proposed Service System Architecture

The remote emergency control system of the elevator includes the ability to deal with various situations through the entire process of emergency among the manager, the field engineer and maintenance company. This system establish communication environment that can be connected at any time and send elevator status at real time to the field engineer to solve the problems. The system architecture of the remote emergency control system is shown in Figure 1.

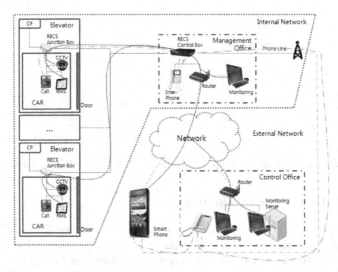

Fig. 1. The system architecture of the remote emergency control system for elevator

The elevator system include of CCTV and interphone and RMS (Remote Management System) and operate with CP(Control Panel) organically. And also the elements are integrated into the RECS Junction Box. The Junction Box operates with RECS Control Box to send and receive data of CCTV and RMS and interphone. And the analogy voice data of interphone will be converted to digital in order to prevent data loss and noise. Management office manages all elevators and is configured to be able to monitor and cope with the emergency situation of the elevator through Control Box. This Control Box copes with the absence of a manager by a call to a pre-designated place through the external phone line. Maintenance Company can manage elevator situation at real time by Control Box in the management office and also support mobile environment for management tool of elevator to a field engineer. Smartphone-based remote emergency control system provides a service that can recognize and respond elevator situation effectively with CCTV and RMS.

3.2   RECS Junction Box Architecture

The RECS Junction Box can control emergency call, CCTV and RMS. The architecture is shown in Figure 2. In the system architecture (left), the system has interphone module, A/D convertor and Codec/Audio service for CCTV, CAN communication module for analysis of the elevator control information, Memory and Connectivity module and Power management module with Process Unit. And also in the software architecture (right), the software is operated based on Linux and Android system [8] and have the various module such as communication and media process module, direct call service module and CCTV module.

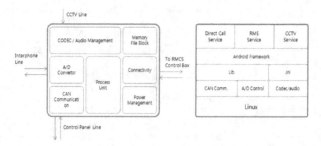

Fig. 2. RECS Junction Box System Architecture (left) and Software Architecture (right)

3.3   RECS Control Box Architecture

The RECS Control Box analysis received data from Junction Box and provides emergency call service, CCTV service and elevator status information for remote control to management office. The hardware and software architecture is shown in Figure 3.

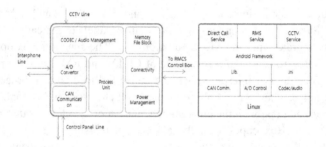

Fig. 3. RECS Control Box System Architecture (left) and Software Architecture (right)

The Control Box include telephone module that control connection management for emergency call with external phone line when the manager is not exist. And also this Control Box send the RMS information to management office and field engineer to control remotely based on the internet.

4   The Operation of the Remote Emergency Control System

4.1   The Flows of the Remote Emergency Control System

The Remote Emergency Control System has purpose to make a more safety environment by providing seamless call services and effective judgment from the situation of an emergency. The flow of each elements and relationship is shown in Figure 4.

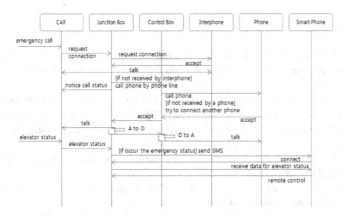

Fig. 4. The flows and relationship of the elements of RECS

The Remote Emergency Control System consists of an elevator control panel, CCTV, interphone, Junction Box, Control Box, external phones and smart phones. And it cooperates with CARs in the elevator, Management office, Maintenance companies. First, Junction Box establishes a unified communications environment for the devices in the CAR and provides the capabilities of the A/D conversion of interphone. And also it collects information of elevator status and then transmits and processes the request for the remote control device devices at real time. Control Box recognizes an interphone call and delivers to the management office. If the manager does not exist, it notifies the situation using announcement and forwards another phone automatically. And also it manages networks and SMS sending and receiving. In this flows of figure 4, First, CAR received emergency call and status information by the elevator control panel and then passed to the Junction Box. The emergency call is delivered through the Control Box on the interphone. If the interphone receives the call, it operates a call service normally. If the call is not answered, Control Box attempts the call with predefined external phone data through the telephone network. The voice of the call is converted digital data to improve voice quality. During an emergency call, the elevator notices the emergency situation by sending their status to a field engineers immediately. It can make immediate response environment. The field engineer determines the cause of the elevator malfunction and can cope with the situation quickly using smart phone remotely.

5   Conclusions

With increasing demand and rapid change of the elevator industry, a variety of requirements is increasing for elevator safety awareness and efficient approach. In this paper, we proposed the Remote Emergency Control System for an elevator that can remain connected status immediately and send the reason of the fault to the field engineer so that the engineer can control the problem of the elevator at real time remotely. The Remote Emergency Control System will be respond to the passenger accidents quickly and will be able to build more reliable and secure environment of elevator maintenance.

References

1. Lee, Y.-H., Kim, H.-G.: A Study on Combined wire-wireless Service System for Emergency Warning Call. In: Korea Information Processing Society Spring Conference, vol. 17(1) (2010)
2. Okazaki, S.: What is SMS advertising and why do multinationals adopt it? Answers from an empirical study in European markets. Journal of Business Research 61(9) (2008)
3. Jotshi, A.: Dispatching and routing of emergency vehicles in disaster mitigation using data fusion. Socioeconomic Planning Sciences 43(24) (2009)
4. Jang, J.: Elevators of the latest technology trends. The Korean Society for Elevator Engineering (December 2004)
5. Jung, J.-H.: A Study on the interface design of elevators in high rise building, Hongik University, Doctoral Dissertation (2007)
6. Seo, H.-G., Kim, K.-H.: Design Methodology of a Real-Time Elevator Monitor and Control System. Journal of the Institute of Industrial Technology 26(2) (December 1998)
7. Choi, Y.-S., Park, B.-T., Choi, Y.-J.: Design and implementation of Location Based Silver Town u-Service System. Journal of Korean Society for Internet Information 11(3) (2010)
8. Google Android, http://www.android.com

An Analysis of Festival Satisfaction Evaluation Using Multiple Regression Model – EXPO 2012 YEOSU KOREA

Bokhee Jung[1] and Soongohn Kim[2,*]

[1] Department of Information Science, JoongbuUniversity,
101 Daehakro, Chubu-meon, Gumsangun, Chungnam, 312-702, Korea
jangel9977@joongbu.ac.kr
[2] Division of Computer and Game Science, Joongbu University,
101 Daehakro, Chubu-Meon, GumsanGun, Chungnam, 312-702, Korea
sgkim@joongbu.ac.kr

Abstract. Expo is a festival held at a national level and it has a great effect on both the economy and the society, while contributing to improving the image of the nation and inducing many visitors. Such mega events as the Olympics, World Cup Games and Expo revitalize the regional tourism industry and have great economic, socio-cultural, and environmental effects on the nation. In particular, it is believed to have a great positive effect on pertinent areas by enhancing regional promotions and improving image at home and abroad.

The paper aims to examine factors influencing the evaluation of satisfaction with festivals centering on visitors of the 2012 Yeosu Expo and to determine which factors lead to higher satisfaction, in order to analyze these effects and make it possible to make a prediction of the satisfaction level of a festival at the time of evaluation.

Keywords: Local Festival, Satisfaction Evaluation, Multiple Regression Model, Festival Evaluation, EXPO 2012 YEOSU KOREA.

1 Introduction

An expo aims to offer resolutions to problems facing mankind while presenting a particular vision. It is a large-scale international event in which a large number of countries and people from across the world take part, with each participating country promoting their development to the world with regard to an export theme through the use of an exhibition hall. It enables visitors and participating countries to widely promote characteristics of their culture, society and economy; such large-scale festivals as Expo, World Cup and the Olympics can be deemed "mega events". These mega events have great economical, social, environmental and political effects on a hosting country or the tourism industry of a hosting region [1]. A country hosting a mega event induces new investments by promoting its own advanced technology and growth potential for the future while increasing exports.

---

* Corresponding author.

T.-h. Kim et al. (Eds.): FGCN/DCA 2012, CCIS 350, pp. 155–160, 2012.

According to a study concluding that the properties of a festival influence visitors' satisfaction, and said satisfaction has a direct effect on loyalty, Yong-gi Lee induced five environmental factors of a festival including "Progress/Contents of an event", "Value of food", "Access/Recognition of regional culture", "Festival products" and "Amenities" [2].

According to a study conducted by Chung-gi Lee, image characteristics of visitors to a festival have an effect on visitors' satisfaction, including "Contents of an event", "Information on promotion of an event", "Prices & products", "Amenities", "Information on an event" and "Tourism in surrounding areas" [3]. In addition, Yoon, Lee, & Lee determined that such environmental clues as "Program", "Souvenir", "Food", and "Facilities" have an effect on visitors' satisfaction and loyalty, while suggesting that promotional factors have nothing to do with visitors' satisfaction [4].

Although many studies on mega events have been conducted on a continual basis, few studies have been conducted on the 2012 Yeosu Expo which is why this large-scale festival was selected.

This paper aims to devise a model based on factors influencing satisfaction with a festival and to determine factors with higher satisfaction based on the 2012 Yeosu Expo. If factors with higher satisfaction are explained thoroughly, such factors can be predicted at a time of evaluating satisfaction with future festivals. The study is focused on generating suggestions that can help thoroughly prepare for and examine a festival in a pre-festival planning stage, as well as in a review stage, based on a factor analysis on satisfaction. Accordingly, the questionnaire survey was conducted based on previous research, and multiple regression analysis was used to analyze effects on evaluation of satisfaction with a festival based on questionnaire data.

2   Design of Study Model

2.1   A Study Model

In order to conduct the paper, the 2012 Yeosu Expo was selected. It aimed to figure out factors influencing evaluation on satisfaction with a festival on the part of visitors to the expo. In order to design a study model, factors influencing evaluation on satisfaction with a festival were divided into dependent variables and independent variables. Eight independent variables ($X_1 \sim X_8$) and one dependent variable (Y) were used.

[Figure 1] shows a basic structure of sample design of a study model.

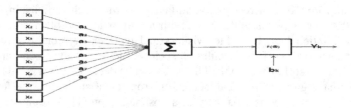

Fig. 1. Design a study model Structure

[Formula 1] indicates an equation based on design structure of a study model.

$$y_k = f\left(\sum_{i=1}^{8} a_i x_i + b_k\right) \tag{1}$$

2.2   Measurement of Variables

Independent input variables influencing evaluation on satisfaction with a festival include gender, residential area, types of reservations, types of tickets, types of entry to an exhibition hall, the time of entry, waiting time, and amenities.

As an output variable, the 5-Point Likert Scale-based on satisfaction with a festival was selected. Input variables and output variables used at the time of evaluation on satisfaction with a festival are shown in [Table 1].

[Y-Satisfaction with a festival, X_1-Gender, X_2-Residential area, X_3-Types of reservation, X_4-Types of tickets, X_5-Types of entry to an exhibition hall, X_6-Time of entry, X_7-Waiting time, X_8-Amenities]

Table 1. Input and Output variables

Types of variables	Name of variable	Characteristics	Definition
	X_1	Gender	Male & female
	X_2	Residential area	Capital area, other regions than capital area
	X_3	Types of reservation	Reservation on the spot, Internet reservation
Input variables	X_4	Types of tickets	Special ticket, ordinary ticket, group ticket
	X_5	Types of entry to an exhibition hall	Entry on the spot, reservation entry
	X_6	Time of entry	Morning, afternoon & evening
	X_7	Waiting time	Within 2hours, 1hour, and 30minutes
	X_8	Amenities	Dissatisfied, average & satisfied
Output variables	Y(Satisfaction with a festival)	Very dissatisfied, Dissatisfied, Average, Satisfied, Very satisfied	

3   Survey Design and Analysis

3.1   Survey Design

The survey was conducted on visitors to the 2012 Yeosu Expo through the use of questionnaires. A questionnaire surveyor explained the purpose of the survey to respondents and conducted the survey through interviews and self-answering questionnaires. Respondents were requested to conduct evaluation through gender, residential areas, types of reservation, types of tickets, types of entry to an exhibition hall, time of entry, waiting time, amenities and satisfaction with the festival. A total of 185 questionnaires were used to conduct analysis, and 150 were used in results analysis, with 35 questionnaires deemed to be inappropriate. The data collected above went through Data Cording to be analyzed with SPSS 18.0.

As for the gender of respondents, males accounted for 40% and females accounted for 60%. For residential areas, the capital area accounted for 40.6% and regions other than the capital area accounted for 59.4%. For the type of reservation, on-the-spot reservations accounted for 44.6%, and Internet reservations accounted for 55.4%. As for types of tickets, ordinary tickets accounted for 53.3%, group tickets accounted for 20.7%, and special tickets accounted for 26%. The rate of ordinary tickets that can be purchased without a discount was higher. As for the types of entry to an exhibition hall, entry on the spot accounted for 80%, and reservation entry accounted for 20%.

For the time of entry, morning accounted for 68%, afternoon accounted for 22%, and evening accounted for 10%. As for waiting time, less than 2 hours accounted for 14.7%, less than 1 hour accounted for 18.0%, and less than 30 minutes accounted for 67.3%. As for amenities, dissatisfaction accounted for 6%, average accounted for 63.3%, and satisfaction accounted for 30.7%. As for satisfaction with the festival, very dissatisfied accounted for 0.7%, dissatisfied accounted for 11.3%, average accounted for 39.3%, satisfied accounted for 28.0%, and very satisfied accounted for 20.7%. [Table 2] indicates general characteristics of samples of respondents to questionnaires.

Table 2. General Characteristics of Samples

	Distinction	Frequency (Persons)	Rate (%)		Distinction	Frequency (Persons)	Rate (%)
Gender	Male	60	40.0	Time of entry	Morning	102	68.0
	Female	90	60.0		Afternoon	33	22.0
Residential area	Capital area	61	40.6		Evening	15	10.0
	Other regions than the Capital area	89	59.4	Waiting time	Less than 2 hours	22	14.7
Types of reservation	Reservation on the spot	67	44.6		Less than 1 hour	27	18.0
	Reservation on the Internet	83	55.4		Less than 30 minutes	101	67.3
Types of tickets	Ordinary ticket	80	53.3	Amenities	Dissatisfied	9	6.0
	Group ticket	31	20.7		Average	95	63.3
	Special ticket	39	26.0		Satisfied	46	30.7
Types of entry to an exhibition hall	Entry on the spot	120	80.0	Satisfaction with a festival	Very dissatisfied	1	0.7
					Dissatisfied	17	11.3
	Reservation entry	30	20.0		Average	59	39.3
					Satisfied	42	28.0
					Very satisfied	31	20.7

3.2   Result of Multiple Regression Analysis

A Multiple regression analysis was conducted to analyze how the eight factors including gender, residential area, types of reservation, types of tickets, types of entry to an exhibition hall, time of entry, waiting time and amenities influence evaluation on satisfaction with a festival.

As a result of multiple regression analysis, coefficient of determination was 0.668, revised coefficient of determination was 0.649 and the rate of explanatory power was 64.9%. It indicates explanatory power of independent variables such as gender, residential area, types of reservation, types of tickets, type of entry to an exhibition hall, time of entry, waiting time and amenities against dependent variables such as satisfaction with a festival. [Table 3] indicates a summarized model.

Table 3. A Summarized Model

Model	R	R square	Revised R square	Standard error of estimated value
1	.817	.668	.649	.572

As for examination on the relationship between satisfaction with a festival and gender, t value .623 and p value was .534. As for residential area, t value 3.939 was 3.939, and p value was .000, which turned out to be significant in the evaluation of satisfaction with a festival. As for types of reservation, t value was -1.079 and p value was .282. For types of tickets, t value was -1.095, and p value was .275. For types of entry to an exhibition hall, t value was -3.509 and p value was .001, which turned out to be significant in the evaluation of satisfaction with a festival. As for the time of entry, t value was .678 and p value was .499. As for waiting time, t value was 3.918 and p value was .000, which turned out to be significant in the evaluation of satisfaction with a festival. As for amenities, t value was 13.333 and p value was .000, which was also significant in the evaluation of satisfaction with a festival.

Accordingly, the most influential factor in terms of satisfaction with a festival was amenities, followed by residential area, waiting time, types of entry to an exhibition hall, types of tickets, types of reservation, time of entry and gender in that order.

[Table 4] indicates the result of coefficient of determination.

Table 4. Effects on Satisfaction with a Festival in Regard to the 2012 Yeosu Expo

Model	B	Standard Error	Beta	t	p
(Constant)	.106	.389		.273	.785
Gender	.086	.138	.044	.623	.534
Residential area	.450	.114	.230	3.939	.000
Types of reservation	-.127	.118	-.066	-1.079	.282
Types of tickets	-.073	.067	-.065	-1.095	.275
Types of entry to an exhibition hall	-.422	.120	-.176	-3.509	.001
Time of entry	.060	.088	.041	.678	.499
Waiting time	.259	.066	.198	3.918	.000
Amenities	1.201	.090	.690	13.333	.000

[Formula 2] indicates the result of multiple regression formula.

$$Y = .086X_1 + .450X_2 - .127X_3 - .073X_4 - .422X_5 + .060X_6 + .259X_7 + 1.201X_7 + .106 \qquad (2)$$

4   Conclusions

This paper adopted multiple regression analysis to predict factors to be applied to evaluation on satisfaction with a future festival by examining factors influencing the evaluation of satisfaction with a festival based on the 2012 Yeosu Expo and determining which factors influence higher satisfaction.

As a result of analysis on the 2012 Yeosu Expo, the factor influencing satisfaction with a festival the most turned out to be amenities, followed by residential area, waiting time and type of entry to an exhibition hall. The analytical results are expected to help maximize marketing effects at the time of holding other festivals and play an important role in improving visitors' satisfaction by selecting independent variables with higher effects according to the scale of a festival in advance.

The paper evaluated satisfaction based on the 2012 Yeosu Expo, but it is possible to conduct evaluation on satisfaction with other festivals. Independent variables influencing evaluation on visitors' satisfaction with a festival could be divided into external environmental factors and internal environmental factors to determine satisfaction factors. As for annual festivals, if variables are generalized in evaluation on re-visitation to be applied recognition is expected to improve on the part of visitors to a festival.

References

[1] Xu, H.: The Effect of Shanghai EXPO Environment Cues on Satisfaction (2011)
[2] Lee, Y.-K., Lee, D.-W., Lee, C.-K.: The Impact of Perceived Festival Environmental Cues on Visitor's Satisfaction and Loyalty 27(1) (2003)
[3] Lee, C.-K., Jeoung, W.B., Ko, H.S.: The Effect of the 2003 Bucheon Luminarie. Festival Image on Visitors' Satisfaction, Revisit Intention, and Recommendation 14(2), 1–20 (2005)
[4] Yoon, Y.S., Lee, J.S., Lee, C.K.: Measuring festival quality and value affecting visitors' satisfaction and loyalty using a structural approach. International Journal of Hospitality Management 29, 335–342 (2010)
[5] Zhu, M.-H., Li, X.-M., Li, J.: Travel Mode Choice of Residents in Spring Festival based on Neural Network (2010)

Performance Analysis of the Multichannel Wireless Mesh Networks

Kyungjun Kim[1] and Jonghoon Park[2],*

[1] 2f ICT Park(1) Bldg, 2139-12, Daemyeong, Nam-gu,
705-701 Daegu, Korea
kimkj@dip.or.kr
[2] Department of Computer , Joongbu University,
101 Daehakro, Chubu-Meon, GumsanGun, Chungnam, 312-702, Korea
jhpark@joongbu.ac.kr

Abstract. This paper identifies a problem in spreading the trials of channel re-assignment toward neighbors due to the channel interference in a wireless mesh network (WMN), and then newly defines an analytical model that can evaluate the identified problem that does affect the performance in WMNs. The results from simulation demonstrate that the proposed model can exactly evaluate the attempts of channel re-assignment occurred from mesh networks.

Keywords: Mesh network, interference, channel overlapping, ripple effect problem.

1   Introduction

There are two domains for radio resource management that are followed: fixed one and dynamic. The first one manually assigns channels and the second dynamically. A technique of multiple non-overlapping channels assignment, called dynamic channel assignment (DCA), has arisen as one of promising strategies to be applied in wireless systems. The power range overlapping of mesh router (MR) with neighbors in WMNs, referred to as cell, leads to inter or intra-channel interference due to sharing the same channel or path at neighbor MRs, respectively. An adjacent channel interference between neighboring cells that share the bandwidth may reduce a certain quality of service, To consider interference in WMN, methods for assigning channels and minimizing interference have been studied in [1, 2], respectively, where the authors focused on network capacity on cross-layer (i.e. routing and MAC), and modeled traffic and interference which is created by acknowledgement packet. Solutions for joint channel assignment and routing can be found in the literature [3], which does consider traffic loads, but not think over both of intra-flow interference and inter-flow. The performance in WMNs is specifically related to the intra/inter-flow interferences which are caused in the process of channel assignment, and which

---

* Corresponding author.

T.-h. Kim et al. (Eds.): FGCN/DCA 2012, CCIS 350, pp. 161–166, 2012.
© Springer-Verlag Berlin Heidelberg 2012

are mutual problems among MRs. For this reason, interference is extended to the other neighbors from a node since the interferences induced by the repetitive trials of channel re-assignment (referred to as a ripple effect problem hereafter). To measure the performance from the ripple effect problem by influencing collision ratio in the presence of the underlying link interference, this Letter, which is motivated in the literatures which did not consider the channels assigned in the neighbors, measures the performance of WMNs in terms of DCA using Markov chain.

2   Problem Formulation

This paper considers communication between two MRs based on the IEEE 802.11 (e.g. 2.4 Ghz and 5.0 Ghz), and assumes that channel is assigned when data in radio interface is completely received. Each channel is assigned by gateway MR with the on-demand manner, which is connected to the Internet. To cope with this, one channel at a time is assigned to each node but not simultaneously, which is returned when all data received in the node is completely transmitted. In this analysis, Markov chain model in [4] is utilized for calculating the conflict probability between a cell and its neighboring cells. To rethink the interferences, we consider two cells model (i.e. referred to as cell i and j) since the interference always occurs between more than one channels (or near channels) over the same radio, and also assume the interference as the conflict in the specific time period of wireless networks because of the same results [5, 6]. Note that call arrival, block, and departure originated in each state are as request, failure, and return of channel assignment, respectively. These events follow the Poisson distribution with mean arrival rate l and exponential distributions, e.g. the holding time of a channel assigned, with common means 1/m.

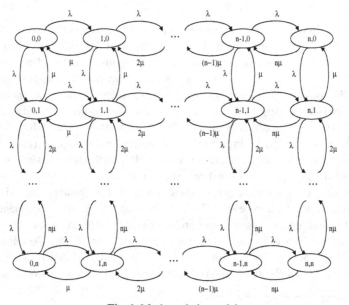

Fig. 1. Markov chain model

In order to estimate the collision probability caused by the ripple effect, the discrete-time Markov chain shown is defined using the bi-dimensional state $\{a_t, b_t\}$ in Fig. 1 . Let $P(i, j)=\lim_{t\to\infty}P\{a_t=i, b_t=j\}$ be the steady state probability of Markov chain, where $i \in [0, n]$ and $j \in [0, n]$, (i.e. the number of occupied channels in two MRs A and B), respectively. Using the Markov chain, we can determine that is the global balance equations for the steady state occupancy probabilities $P(i)$ and $P(j)$ in state i and j for M/M/n/n system. These probability is given by $P(i)$ and $P(j)$ as follows,

$$P(i)=\frac{\dfrac{\rho^i}{i!}}{\displaystyle\sum_{i=0}^{n}\dfrac{\rho^i}{i!}}, \quad P(j)=\frac{\dfrac{\rho^j}{j!}}{\displaystyle\sum_{j=0}^{n}\dfrac{\rho^j}{j!}}, \quad \text{for } i \text{ and } j=0, 1, 2, ..., n, \tag{1}$$

The number of channel occupied in MR A and the number of channel occupied in MR B at the same time instant are independent random variables. A two-cell network has a product-form solution when the joint pmf of the vector of numbers of occupied channels in MRs is equal to the product of the marginal pmf's of the number of occupied channels in the individual MR.

$$P(i, j)= P(i)P(j)=\frac{\dfrac{\rho^i}{i!}\dfrac{\rho^j}{j!}}{\displaystyle\sum_{i=0}^{n}\dfrac{\rho^i}{i!}\sum_{j=0}^{n}\dfrac{\rho^j}{j!}} \quad , for \ i \ and \ j=0, 1, 2, ..., n \tag{2}$$

Let $\alpha(i,j)$ be the collision probability between two cells in state (i, j) of a Markov chain, which can be obtained as follows,

$$\alpha(i,j)=\begin{cases} 0, & \text{for } i = 0 \text{ or } j = 0 \\ 1, & \text{for } n-j < i, \ i>=j \\ 1, & \text{for } n-i < j, \ i<j \\ 1 - {}_{n-j}C_i / {}_nC_i, & \text{for } n-j >= i, \ i>=j \\ 1 - {}_{n-i}C_j / {}_nC_j, & \text{for } n-i >= j, \ i<j \end{cases} \tag{3}$$

Therefore, the collision probability P_c to new requests of channel assignment is given by

$$P_c = \sum_{i=0}^{n}\sum_{j=0}^{n}\alpha(i, j)P(i, j). \tag{4}$$

3   Results

We evaluated the conflict probability Pc and assumed that the channel condition is free of bust errors with a constant link rate, which yields a raw link rate about 5 Mbps.

The model simulated on two MRs in which different number of channels is considered (i.e. 3 and 12). Table 1 shows collision probability against network load depending on the number of channel assignments (n=12) requested for service time, e.g. m=1, respectively. The saturations happened over a flow and inter-flow specifically are due to the failure of channel assignment, referred to as intra-channel interference and inter-channel, respectively. To obtain the offered load available at each node during the simulation, a fixed packet size and arrival rate 1 (0.1~0.9) following a Poisson law is assumed. This means that channel assignment requests have been generated either uniformly with value 1 for each router. The quantity estimations of the conflict probability between MR A and B are shown in Table 1, which is indexed by $\alpha(i, j)$ where it expresses the channels to be assigned in each MR.

Table 1. Blocking probability against network load depending on the number of channel assignments

B \ A	0	1	2	3	4	5	6	7	8	9	10	11	12
0	0	0	0	0	0	0	0	0	0	0	0	0	0
1	0	1/12	11/66	55/220	165/495	330/792	462/924	462/792	330/495	165/220	55/66	11/12	1
2	0	11/66	21/66	100/220	285/495	540/792	714/924	672/792	450/495	210/220	65/66	1	1
3	0	55/220	100/220	136/220	369/495	666/792	840/924	756/792	486/495	219/220	1	1	1
4	0	165/495	285/495	369/495	425/495	736/792	896/924	784/792	494/495	1	1	1	1
5	0	330/792	540/792	666/792	736/792	771/792	917/924	791/792	1	1	1	1	1
6	0	462/924	714/924	840/924	896/924	917/924	923/924	1	1	1	1	1	1
7	0	462/792	672/792	756/792	784/792	791/792	1	1	1	1	1	1	1
8	0	330/495	450/495	486/495	494/495	1	1	1	1	1	1	1	1
9	0	165/220	210/220	219/220	1	1	1	1	1	1	1	1	1
10	0	55/66	65/66	1	1	1	1	1	1	1	1	1	1
11	0	11/12	1	1	1	1	1	1	1	1	1	1	1
12	0	1	1	1	1	1	1	1	1	1	1	1	1

Note that the diagonal result values (not 1) in Table 1 do not occur the ripple effect problem in the process of channel reassignment; however, on the contrary, ripple effect problem can be occurred when the number of assigned channels is equal to n (the total number of assigned channels in MRs involved in the network).

The simulation results is seen more clearly in Fig. 2 (where n is between 3 and 12, which concerned the channels from the IEEE 802.11), which shows the proportional of the collision ratio against the average loads. When 1 increases in steady rate, the collision ratio C is affected by the number of the channels assigned. Basically, for n = 3, C is higher than that for n = 12, which shown the decreased collision probability around 41 to 52%. The proposed analytical model gives great promise in terms of the performance depending on the number of channels and reflects the precision we have not seen in the prior study from [1] because of concerning the variant features of distributed system.

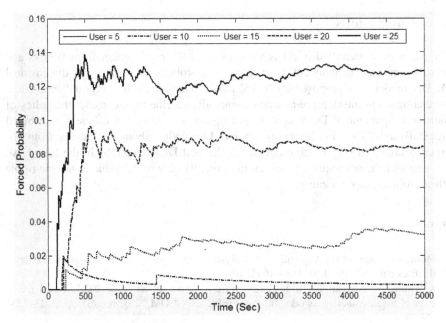

Fig. 2. Forced probability among interference

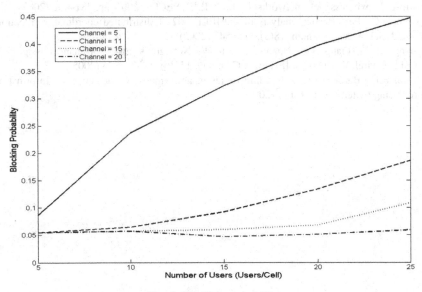

Fig. 3. Blocking probability

The parameter which affects to network performance is a channel blocking. A blocking probability, when increasing the numbers of users and channels, is shown in Fig. 3. The blocking probability rapidly increases in 5 channels. When increasing from 20 to 25 users, on the contrary, the variant of block probability in 5 to 15 channels is slow.

4   Conclusions

The paper have identified interference caused by the ripple effect from WMNs and proposed an analytical model to evaluate this problem using the two dimensional Markov model. The proposed analytical model which takes into account the factual correlation about interference around channel gives a clue to re-consider the policy of channel assignment of DCA as well as to guide the design of efficient distributed protocol on WMNs. Furthermore, a priori knowledge about the results from the experiments helps very much on choosing the best DCA methods. In the future, we will consider the scheduling algorithm to optimally choose the value n that the ripple effect problem does not cause.

References

1. Molle, C., Voge, M.E.: A quantitative analysis of the capacity in wireless mesh networks. IEEE Commun. Lett. 14(5), 438–440 (2010)
2. Raniwala, A., Chiueh, T.: Architecture and algorithms for an IEEE 802.11-based multi-channel wireless mesh networks. In: Proc. IEEE INFOCOM 2005, vol. (3), pp. 2223–2234 (2005)
3. Subramaniana, A.P., Gupta, H., Das, S.: Minimum-interference channel assignment in multi-radio wireless mesh networks. In: Proc. IEEE SECON 2007, pp. 481–490 (2007)
4. Bianchi, G.: Performance analysis of the IEEE 802.11 distributed coordination function. IEEE J. Sel. Areas Commun. 18(3), 535–547 (2000)
5. Cheng, M.X., Huang, S.C., Huang, X., Wu, W.: New graph model for channel assignment in ad hoc wireless networks. IEE Proc. Commun. 152(6), 1039–1046 (2005)
6. Dutra, R.C., Barbosa, V.C.: 'Finding routes in anonymous sensor networks. Information Processing Letters 98, 139–144 (2006)

An Efficient BRS Management System Using OAuth

Jeong-Kyung Moon[1], Hwang-Rae Kim[1,*],
and Jin-Mook Kim[2]

[1] Division of Computer Science and Engineering, Kongju National University,
331717, Cheonan, Korea
[2] Division of Information Technology Education, Sunmoon University,
336708, Asan, Korea
{moonjk1018,plusone}@kongju.ac.kr, calf0425@sunmoon.ac.kr

Abstract. Trend of information is diversified fast by the spread of wireless internet recently. The service of book information search may be available without limitation of time and place in university library, because fast diffusion of electronic publishing is increasing. Therefore, we wishes to propose the convenience to search another college's digital property or display by printer simplifying certification between majority college that is using OAuth. We can propose case and certification formality of the library which is not conferred mutually that is conferred mutually and share island and media search effectively cloud computing and Mobile communication environment.

Keywords: Book Information Search, OAuth, Cloud computing, BRS.

1 Introduction

Cloud computing is activated are growing because efficient practical use of IT resources and request of Green-IT. By Gartner's justice, cloud computing is a concept of service that do up computer resources in that use and make can offer existent computing resources. Google, Microsoft, Amazon and many world main corporations are support this services. And Smart-phone, Mobile internet communication and computer development are going diversification and high-capacity by novel trend of information.

Domestic Smart-phone user's number passed over 30 million in 2012, and the entire world Mobile SNS user's number expects to reach in one billion in 2013. But, cloud computing services have much security threats [1]. And Availability of data is very low, because domestic each college's library possess much data but they are not sharing DB between each other university library. So, it can keep away waste of resources and reduce repetition of data and augment efficiency by sharing to database. Therefore, we wish to propose method that can search other college's data by safe method when user who has mobility searches book data. And, wished to solve various kind security problems such as user authentication, authority, access control for

---

* Corresponding author.

T.-h. Kim et al. (Eds.): FGCN/DCA 2012, CCIS 350, pp. 167–174, 2012.
© Springer-Verlag Berlin Heidelberg 2012

resources that is stored to server, and user trace protection among cloud computing security threat elements.

Composition of this treatise is as following. Our paper has five components. Chapter one is introduction. Chapter two described about connection research about cloud computing and certification. It is a related works. And chapter three described about safe BRS management system using OAuth that was we proposed. Chapter four described about estimation for safe BRS management system. Finally, chapter five is conclusion.

2   Related Works

2.1   Cloud Computing Environments

The cloud computing service is a novel service that can provide to a novel computer function by network infrastructure. Cloud computing service can divide by three categories. It is SaaS, PaaS, and IaaS. Below Table 1 divides cloud computing model by three and described explanation about it.

Table 1. Cloud computing model

	Feature	Examples
SaaS	It is way to lease and uses software that user is necessary in Internet. Against of elder way. User is different from thing which should buy and install direction software in existing when past-time[3],[4],[5].	Salesforce.com MobileMe, Google DOCS[6]
PaaS	It is a Platform that borrows and uses tools that developer is used in development. By this way, software development is easy and fast, and price is cheap.	Google App Engine, Windows Azure, [7][8]
IaaS	It is model that lent a computing infrastructure such as CPU, Memory, and Storage representatively.	Amazon AWS, GoGrid, At&T [9][10][11]

2.2   BRS (Book Research System)

BRS is a system for search a book or digital information in library that runs in KINITI in 1982 in domestic. They choose BRS/SEARCH that is IBM host selects IRS system and executed domestic on-line information service. It is simple and digit of data's field is few against of DBMS. And it is standardization document administration system that base on Full-Text search. This has a renewal method by batch and it is difficulty of repetition prevention and literature information data item has better be less comparatively. So, it will be use in case user's request form is fixed and small.

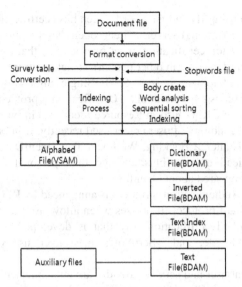

Fig. 1. Procedure of BRS Database Construction

BRS database is not class style that is hierarch architecture. And it can manage by reverse conversion file type and Full text file type. All databases of BRS are managed to search file and assistance file that permit information retrieval. Search file are text file, text index file, inverted file, dictionary file, reversed dictionary file.

2.3   OpenID and OAuth

Usually, certification refers to keep away unlawful taking in and out confirming identification of a person or application program to use network communication network and keep system security. Certification method is various kinds.

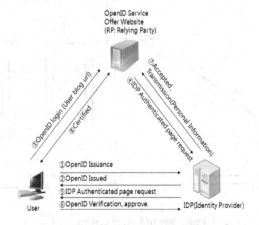

Fig. 2. Procedure of OpenID for certification

Basis certification using ID and Password, token base certification (PIN or Token), client certificate certification (Server, Client open height authentication), duplex certification (2 association certification: That own knows, that own holds, that self), mutually certification (that confirm other person's social position).

Certification method to use most is SSO (Single Sign On), PKI (Public Key Infrastructure), Kerberos certification. Certification protocol that does to discriminates user using URI (Uniform Resource Identifier) in Internet by the breakup style open standard technology of user center used recently. If information of OpenID certification system is altered Hacking, Web-page that OpenID supplies certification server information lead user to Phishing site than personal information can be outpoured. Figure 2 appeared about OpenID.

OAuth 1.0 (Open Authentication) protocol is announced by RFC5849 in 2007. It is an international standard protocol. It utilizes when allow user certification in various applications by standard certification way that is developed by OpenAPI. Daum Tstory, Facebook, Google, and MicroSoft's messenger use OAuth2.0 protocol presently.

OAuth suppose that user and service provider are authenticated, and consumer and service provider are using OAuth protocol. User is keeping data such as document, picture, and animation etc. and he keep the membership between service providers.

In this situation, user wishes to print document that keep to Service Provider. Then user wants to request of print to consumer because he is near consumer server. Step one, he makes temporary token to consumer for consumer's certification. And step 2, consumer certificates to user by access token generation process that consumer request to access token to user. Step 3, consumer checks his identification by access token and makes security card and send to user than user can search and forward to consumer.

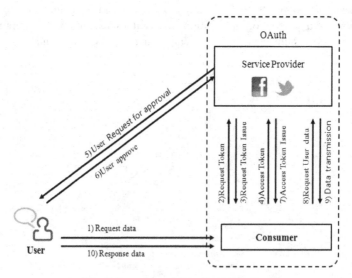

Fig. 3. Procedure of OAuth certification

3   Proposal System

3.1   Structure of Proposal System

We wish to propose to design based on OAuth 1.0 that is the entire world standard. Characteristic of proposal system is that included Delegated administrator as independent element on system component. If we do so, think that may improve efficiency of certification process. Main component of proposal system is four such as user, consumer, delegated administrator, and service provider. Proposal system compares and composed delegated administrator who becomes subject of certification by becomes independent outside module with OAuth 1.0. This is to improve incommodiousness at certification process of existent OAuth 1.0.

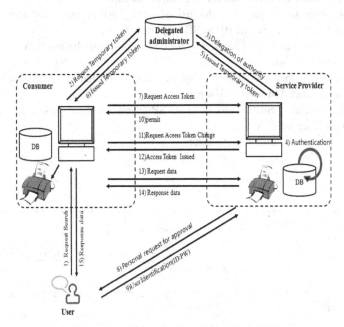

Fig. 4. Structure of Non-mutual authentication BRS system

Figure 4 is expressing process that provides book search service in case consumer and service provider do not authentication mutually in our proposal system. Proposal system has more 2 action mode.

3.2   Procedure of Proposal System

Proposal system has 15 details formality as following in reply.

1) User does data request that is fenced to Consumer.
2) Consumer requests temporary security card to SP. It establishes Consumer's URI and does temporary security card so that can do callback in this time.
3) Delegated administrator foretells Consumer's competence and transmits by SP.

4) SP confirms request and competence in DB.

5, 6) SP issues temporary security cards and transmits to Consumer. In this time, token is used to prove token qualification at next time step security card is not.

7) Consumer demands ratification using temporary security card to gain user's Access approval. In this time, Consumer makes out URI that confirm whether User is resources owner.

8) SP presents Consumer's information to User and verify User's Identification.

9) User permission about Consumer request access using ID/PW access competence approves.

10) SP completes User certification process as that guess creates difficult certification code and delivers to Consumer through User.

11) Consumer sends request URI using oauth_verifier and temporary security card etc. that receive in 10) to SP by parameter.

12) SP verifies validity of request and does response including token and public ownership height.

13) Access is possible in volunteering that Consumer that is issued token security cards is fenced instead of User.

14) While token security card is kept, SP furnishes data. Token security card makes User abolish.

15) Consumer transmits data to User.

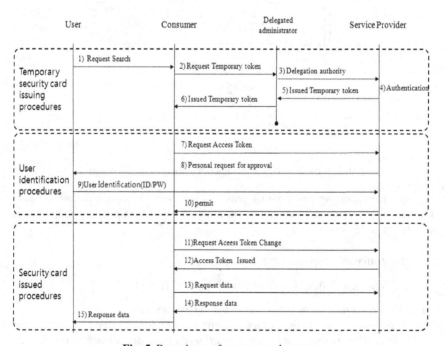

Fig. 5. Procedures of our proposal system

4   Experiment and Analysis

Proposal system action environment has two book search server who load LINUX Operating System. And, each book search server designed to have DBs for 3 books search all. In this time, we applied Hadoop that can achieve book search effectively in cloud computing environment. And each DBMS uses Oracle 10.0g.

In cloud computing environment, our proposal system using OAuth that can support temporary authentication, resources owner authentication, token authentication as that can compose security module as well as security guarantee.

1) Authoritativeness guarantee: Proposal system is doing based on OAuth 1.0. And it can secure authoritativeness applying TLS security mechanism unlike existent system in addition.

2) Confidentiality guarantee: In case consumer's source code or execution file exhibited, attacker can analyze copy of this receiving download for analysis. And it can use included security card inside. But, proposal system can secure confidentiality because quote using together IP address with security card, nonce, TS etc. when SP quotes consumer.

3) Request extent limitation: User and Service provider can limit competence dimension that consumer can have. Therefore, proposal system can offer easily Access control.

4) CSRF (Cross-Site Request Forgery): This is representative attack method based on web. This can be approved resources fenced without user and SP agreement acquiring easily in OAuth callback URI. But, proposal system this user and SP going through communication Finish signal whenever communication is completed prevent.

5) HMAC-SHA1 use: Proposal system can prevent secret sex, integrity, denial of service because use this.

5   Conclusion

We propose and designed to provide certification service about library web service. And experiment and analyzed availability whether act well because embodying relevant system. Our system could solve user certification security service. And showed that suitable certification is available mutually in cloud computing environment hereafter by proposal system uses pinch hitter model.

In future research, we were proposing to an efficient BRS (book research system) using OAuth. So, we wish to examine that can apply in more various cloud service.

References

1. Armbrust, M., Fox, A., Griffith, R., Joseph, A.D., Katz, R., Konwinski, A., Lee, G., Patterson, D., Rabkin, A., Stoica, I., Zaharia, M.: Above the clouds: A Berkeley View of Cloud Computing. Technical Report (February 2009)

2. Shabeeb, H., Jeyanthi, N., Iyengar, N.C.S.N.: A Study on Security Threats in Cloud. International Journal of Cloud Computing and Services Science (IJ-CLOSER) 1(3), 84–88 (2012)
3. Joha, A., Janessen, M.: Design Choices Underlying the Software as a Service (SaaS) Business Model from the User Perspective: Exploring the Fourth Wave of Outsourcing. Journal of Universal Computer Science 18(11) (2012)
4. Lawton, G.: Developing Software Online with Platform-as-a-Service Technology. Computer (June 2008)
5. Amazon: Amazon Web Service: Overview of Security Process white paper (September 2008), http://aws.amazon.com
6. Moon, J.-K., Kim, J.-M., Kim, H.-R.: A Secure Authentication Protocol for Cloud Services. Jaitc 1(2) (2011) (manuscript)
7. Amazon Elastic Compute Cloud (Amazon EC2), http://aws.amazon.com/ec2
8. Amazon Simple Storage Service (Amazon S3), http://aws.amazon.com/s3
9. Kazai, G., Kamps, J., Koolen, M., Milic-Frayling, N.: Crowdsourcing for Book Search Evaluation: Impact of HIT Design on Comparative System Ranking. In: SIGIR 2011, July 24–28 (2011)
10. Jacobs, P.S.: Text-Based Intelligent Systems: Current Research and Practice in Information Extraction and Retrieval (1992), http://acl.ldc.upenn.edu
11. Mostarda, M., Palmisano, D., Zani, F., Tripodi, S.: Towards an OpenID-based solution to the Social Network Interoperability Problem. In: W3C Workshop on the Future (2009), http://w3.org
12. http://openid.net/
13. Paul, R.: Compromising Twitter's OAuth security system (2010), http://immagic.com
14. Al-Sinani, H.S.: Browser Extension-based Interoperation Between OAuth and Information Card-based Systems (2011), http://pure.rhul.ac.uk
15. http://art.tools.ietf.org/html/rfc5849

Software Qualification Approach for Safety-Critical Software of the Embedded System

Jangyeol Kim[1] and Soongohn Kim[2,*]

[1] Instrumentation & Control and Human Factors
Division/Korea Atomic Energy Research Institute(KAERI)
989-111 Daedeok-daero, Yuseong-gu, Daejeon, Republic of Korea 305-353
jykim@kaeri.re.kr
[2] Division of Computer and Game Science, Joongbu University,
101 Daehakro, Chubu-Meon, GumsanGun, Chungnam, 312-702, Korea
sgkim@joongbu.ac.kr

Abstract. Programmable Logic Controller (PLC) is applied to a control system as major components in industrial functional safety facilities. This paper describes the safety-critical software qualification approach which corresponds to the software verification and validation, software safety analysis, software quality assurance and software configuration management etc. Major qualification activities for safety-critical software are a technical evaluation, licensing suitability evaluation, inspection and traceability analysis, formal verification, software safety analysis, software quality assurance and its software configuration management etc. First, the technology evaluation performs a technical review which was based on engineering decision-making by verifiers. Second, the licensing suitability evaluation was performed according to the Code & Standard criteria by analyzing the designed outputs based on the functional characteristics and process characteristics defined in the verification and validation guidelines. Third, the inspection and traceability analysis covers the correctness, consistency, completeness, properties of the inputs and outputs, behavioral entities, interfaces, etc. with a three-folded checklist topology. Fourth, a formal verification perform for the statechart based on the Software Requirement Specification (SRS) and the Software Design Specification (SDS) by a Graphical Back Animation (GBA) and a simulation. Fifth, the software safety analysis use the HAZard Operability (HAZOP) method and it analyze the Failure Mode Effect Analysis (FMEA). Finally, a software configuration management under the software quality assurance estimate for the software documents and the source codes by using Software Configuration Management tool. We believe that we achieve the functionality, performance, reliability and safety that are the software qualification objective goals of the embedded system.

Keywords: Software Qualification, Software Quality Assurance, Software Verification and Validation, Software Safety Analysis, Safety-Critical, Software Configuration Management, Embedded Systems.

---

* Corresponding author.

T.-h. Kim et al. (Eds.): FGCN/DCA 2012, CCIS 350, pp. 175–180, 2012.
© Springer-Verlag Berlin Heidelberg 2012

1   Introduction

In order to qualify for the safety-critical software, defines of responsibility among the assurance organization are very important. The Development team is responsible for producing design output during the software life cycle. The Software Verification & Validation(SVV) and Software Safety Analysis(SSA) are responsible for safety qualification on produced design output by development team. First of all, prior to use Commercially Off-The Shelf (COTS) software tool should be dedicated by quality assurance organization. The Software Configuration Management under Software Quality Assurance is responsible for configuration identification, status accounting, revision control on all of the design output and its verification results respectively. The suggested well-structured organization in this paper is as shown in Figure 1[1].

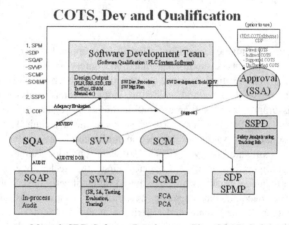

(SPM : Software Program Manual, SDP: Software Development Plan, SQAP: Software Quality Assurance Plan, SVVP: Software Verification and Validation Plan, SCMP : Software Configuration Management Plan, SO&MP : Software Operation and Maintenance Plan, SSPD : Software Safety Plan Description, CDP: Commercial Off the Shelf Dedication Plan, COTS: Commercial Off The Shelf Software, SQA: Software Quality Assurance, SVV: Software Verification and Validation, SCM: Software Configuration Management), SR: Software Review, SA: Safety Analysis, FCA: Functional Configuration Audit, PCA: Physical Configuration Audit)

Fig. 1. Well-structured qualification organization for safety-critical embedded system

2   Approaching of the Software Qualification

2.1   Methods of the Software Qualification

A methods of the software qualification use for review of the licensing suitability, inspection and traceability analysis, formal verification, software testing. Software safety analysis method is HAZOP(HAZard OPerability). Software quality assurance and software configuration management are suggested for software qualification.

2.1.1 Review of the Licensing Suitability

The purpose of the licensing suitability review confirms whether or not the software requirements which coincide with the criteria of the software, performance and safety requirements defined in the embedded system software requirement statement are suitable from a Code & Standard and technological viewpoint. According to the IEEE-Std. and IEC-Std. criteria, they must satisfy all the functionality characteristics and process characteristics such as those in Table 1.

Table 1. Criteria of licensing suitability

Functional Characteristics	Process Characteristics
Safety	Completeness
Robustness	Consistency
Security	Correctness
	Style
	Traceability
	Verifiability

2.1.2 Inspection and Traceability Analysis

Inspection and traceability analysis is performed via the three properties of a completeness, correctness and consistency. Accuracy of a definition, input/output accuracy, accuracy of software behavioral characteristics, and the accuracy of an interface of a software function are very important. Inspection and traceability analyses are classified by basis reviews & comments and the latter details the review criteria as shown in Table 2.

Table 2. Checklist example on the correctness of software behavioral characteristics

Items	Criteria	Detailed review criteria for real time kernel		Status
Correctness of software behavioral	IEEE Std./ IEC Std.	How is the clock tick defined? Is there a definition of interrupt latency, response, return time? Each ISR execution time required. How is the context switching time defined? How is the Task Response time defined?	Is it periodic and stable for real time clock tick? - Interrupt disable time - Interrupt entering time - Context switching time - Dispatching time from Ready Queue to CPU	Open Item

2.1.3 Formal Verification

Formal verification in this paper means the use of verification techniques for the formal logic and discrete mathematics in the specification, design, and implementation of the PLC system and software. There are three types of formal verification techniques which include equivalence checking, theorem proving, and a model checking. Among these formal verification techniques, we use the model checking method. Model checking is a technique for verifying a finite state of a machine. Verification can be performed automatically by the Model Checker/Model Certifier. Specifications for a model checking are usually based on the finite state of a machine which is a model of a system.

2.1.4 Software Testing

Software testing consisted of a component test, an integration test, and a system test. These test execution produce a test plan generation, a test design generation, a test case generation and a test procedure generation according to the software test life cycle as shown in Figure 2. A test plan should be prepared to satisfy the functional requirements and performance requirements of the embedded system[2].

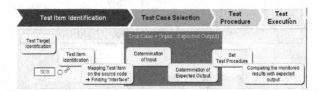

Fig. 2. Testing process by Test Life Cycle

The system test performs on functionality, performance and safety including status of application state, error detection and diagnosis, scan time violation and communication independence etc.

2.2   HAZOP Safety Analysis

At the software requirement specification phase and the software design phase for the software development life cycle, we use the HAZOP to achieve a hazard analysis. HAZOP is a technique that has been used successfully for a hazard analysis in the industry such as a chemical factory. Once we achieved the software hazard analysis for the safety software analysis guidelines and checklist, we took advantage of this HAZOP concept in the hazard analysis of the safety-grade PLC software requirement specifications and the software design specifications. After the hazards and risks had been collected, we used software verification and the hazard analysis in the next step. Level of significance that is imposed on the various software requirements becomes necessary information to determine the resources to medicate in the development, verification, independent tests etc.

3   Software Quality Assurance Measurement

After the system test is completed, an inside peer review was performed in the same way as that of the component test, integration test and system test. The defects, problems and corrective actions list should be submitted to the Software Quality

Assurance (SQA) organization for Anomaly Report (ANR). A review meeting should be held according to the quality assurance procedure. It should focus on an objective quality goal as a quality management in the system test phase. After a review of the system's test results, SQA should inspect and follow-up the test results with a checklist as to whether a system's test will achieve enough of the original objectives. Also, whether the system test level was proper for the physical configuration audit and the performance based audit by the SQA. After comparing the expected value and the resulting value by the SQA, it is required that they take the necessary actions. We have used confirmation of the results of the SQA for the system test results. One can use the software qualification results for the physical configuration audit and the performance based audit by the SQA. Software Quality Assurance activities have been performed during the software life cycle as shown in Table 3.

Table 3. Software Quality Activities under a System QA Program

SWLC	Software Development Baselines	Recommended Software Quality Assurance Activities
Requirements	SQAP, SVVP, SRS	. SRS review . . In-process audit . Software Test Plan Review . Managerial Review
Design	Preliminary Design Description	. Preliminary Design Review . In-process Audit
	Software Design Description	. Detailed Design Review
Implementation	Code Listing, Other Documentation(Code Implementation Specification)	. In-Process Audit
Test	Test Documentation	. Functional Configuration Audit
Installation and Checkout	Deliverable items, Installation Report etc., SVVR	. Physical Configuration Audit . Performance-based Audit
	User Documentation	. User Documentation Review

Notes : SWLC : Software Development Life Cycle, SVVR : Software Verification and Validation Report.

The division of responsibilities among the System Quality Assurance and Software Quality Assurance (SQA) are that the former primarily focuses on quality assurance criteria and quality assurance procedure in upper level whereas the latter implements review and audit from the technical perspective in lower level. The classification in audit consists of Functional Configuration Audit, Physical Configuration Audit and In-Process Audit. Functional Configuration Audit compiles PLC system software whether it meets the requirements in testing level from functional entities (logical viewpoint). Although In-Process Audit is largely applicable in all software life cycle, it is applied in design and implementation phases respectively. Physical Configuration Audit and Performance-based Audit are planned to be applied in the release phase (final phase). Review performed requirement phase, design phase, and user documentation to ensure quality assurance criteria and quality assurance procedure.

3.1   Software Configuration Management

Software Configuration Management (SCM) under a software quality assurance policy perform during the whole software life cycle[3]. Inconsistencies among the software configuration items were found to be the date and revision number of software documents and source codes. Some of the reported anomalies have been resolved throughout the software configuration management process.

4   Conclusions

Applied software qualification approach for an embedded system used the methodologies, tools and techniques. Our software qualification approach through the collaboration works was well established. The toolset used was a self-developed one and a commercially available one. The technique took advantage of the qualification techniques that used a formal verification technique. We have investigated software qualification processes which were the requirements, design, implementation and test phase by using the proposed qualification approach methodologies. Our major qualification techniques are the licensing suitability evaluation, inspection and traceability analysis, formal verification, hazard analysis, testing techniques including a component test, integration test and system test. The applied qualification methodology satisfies the IEEE-Std. and IEC-Std. criteria about industrial functional safety area of the safety-critical software in embedded system. The qualification methodology and our experience are going to be continued to upgrade the upcoming new projects.

References

[1] Kim, J.Y., Kwon, K.-C.: The Commercial Off The Shelf (COTS) Dedication of QNX Real Time Operating System (RTOS). In: International Conference on Reliability, Safety and Hazard 2010, Mumbai, India, December 14–16 (2010)
[2] Kim, J.Y., Cheon, S.W., Lee, J.S., Lee, Y.J., Cha, K.H., Kwon, K.-C.: Software V&V Methods for a Safety Grade Programmable Logic Controller. In: International Conference on Reliability, Safety and Hazard 2005, Mumbai, India, pp. 1–3 (December 2005)
[3] Cha, K.H., Kim, J.Y., Cheon, S.W., Lee, J.S., Lee, Y.J., Kwon, K.-C.: Software Qualificaiton of a Programmable Logic Controller for Nuclear Instrumentation and Control Applications. In: 2006 WSEAS International Conferences, ISCGAV 2006, Crete (August 2006)

Defense–in–Depth Strategy for Smart Service Sever Cyber Security

Hanseong Son[1] and Soongohn Kim[2,*]

[1] Department of Game Engineering, Joongbu University,
101 Daehakro, Chubu-Meon, GumsanGun, Chungnam, 312-702, Korea
hsson@joongbu.ac.kr
[2] Department of Computer Science, Joongbu University,
101 Daehakro, Chubu-Meon, GumsanGun, Chungnam, 312-702, Korea
sgkim@joongbu.ac.kr

Abstract. Defense-in-Depth (DID) is a crucial concept for the cyber security of computer systems. The strategies for DID have been suggested in many researches. In this work, a DID strategy is proposed for smart service servers in more concrete manner. We tried to find out the special features in applying DID concept to nuclear industry cyber security. To do this, we assigned cyber security levels to a typical digital I&C system using the DID concept in nuclear industry cyber security. Based on the lessons learned from the security level assignment case study, we could set up a DID strategy for smart service servers. The main strategy for smart service server security is an n-tier and 'thin' server architecture which is based on the DID concept. This work is expected to be very useful in applying the concept of DID to smart service industry with respect to cyber security.

Keywords: Defense-in-Depth, cyber security, security level assignment, thin server.

1   Introduction

In assuring the quality of smart services, the cyber security of service systems is a crucial factor. The cyber security of service systems can be assured by the integrated consideration of methods, techniques, tools, people and processes required to protect information. This is because there is no single measure or single technology that will make information safe and secure from all external and internal threats.

An IBM researcher has been successful in controlling the software by penetrating a nuclear power plant network in U.S. on July 2008 and acquiring the control right of nuclear facilities after one week. Moreover, the malignant code called "stuxnet" impaired the nearly 1,000 centrifugal separators in Iran according to an IAEA report. The problem of cyber attacks highlights the important of cyber security, which should be emphasized in various industry fields as well as in service industry.

In this context, we have paid our attention to the fact that Defense–in–Depth (DID), which is a design concept, originally coined in a military context and crucially

---

* Corresponding author.

T.-h. Kim et al. (Eds.): FGCN/DCA 2012, CCIS 350, pp. 181–188, 2012.
© Springer-Verlag Berlin Heidelberg 2012

used in nuclear industry, can be a significant concept for the smart service cyber security to work properly. In this work, we tried to find out the special features in applying DID concept to nuclear industry cyber security, which are described in Section 2. To do this, we assigned cyber security levels to a typical digital I&C system using the DID concept in nuclear industry cyber security. Based on the lessons learned from the security level assignment case study, which are described in Section 3, we could set up a DID strategy for smart service servers. The strategy is described in Section 4. This work is expected to be very useful in applying the concept of DID to smart service industry with respect to cyber security.

2   Defense-in-Depth

In this section, the basic concept of DID and the DID concept in nuclear industry cyber security are described.

2.1   Defense–in–Depth Concept

The idea of DID is to add protection at multiple layers rather than relying only on a perimeter firewall. DID requires that relationships between network resources and network users be a controlled, scalable and granular system of permissions and access controls that goes beyond simply dropping firewalls between network segments. In other words, DID is not a product, like a perimeter firewall. Instead, it is a security architecture that calls for the network to be aware and self-protective. According to literatures, the main strategies for DID can be summarized as follows:

- Strategy 1: Authenticate and authorize all network users
- Strategy 2: Deploy the systems like VLANs for traffic separation and coarse-grained security
- Strategy 3: Use state-of-the art firewall technology at the port level for fine-grained security
- Strategy 4: Place encryption throughout the network to ensure privacy
- Strategy 5: Detect threats to the integrity of the network and remediate them
- Strategy 6: Include end-point security in policy-based enforcement

The above strategies shall be more concrete when they are applied to the development and operation of actual service systems. For example, as for the authentication and authorization, it is critical that a user's privileges on the network vary not just based on their identity but also based on other intelligence about the user such as machine identity, security level of the machine, location of the user, time of day, and authentication method. This work suggests a strategy to make these high level strategies more concrete.

2.2   Defense–in–Depth Concept in Nuclear Industry Cyber Security

DID is a protective strategy that when one site is penetrated by some cyber attacks, the other site can be maintained safely without these cyber attacks. Cyber security programs must be designed, applied, and maintained by using DID protective strategies to ensure the capability to detect, prevent, respond to, mitigate, and recover about critical digital asset (CDA) against cyber attacks. Originally, DID is a basic concept for safety design of nuclear facilities. The DID concept provides enough margin with the design for nuclear facilities by priority. And it maintains the safe state of a system sustainably when it has some problem with its safety. The multi-barriers and multiple levels of protection concept are used in nuclear power plants for DID design [1]. The DID concept is applied for the design of digital I&C system architecture for nuclear power plants and research reactors.

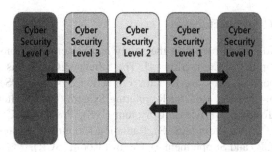

Fig. 1. The architecture of defense–in–depth concept in cyber security

DID is also an approach in which multiple levels of security and methods are deployed to guard against failure of one component or levels in terms of cyber security. The architecture of DID for cyber security is presented in Figure 1. This defensive architecture includes the five concentric cyber security defensive levels separated by security boundaries. The systems requiring the greater degree of security are located within a greater number of boundaries. Figure 1 shown above does not always correspond directly to the physical location.

The rule of this architecture is as follows. The CDAs associated with safety, important to safety and security functions, as well as support systems and equipments which, if compromised, would adversely impact safety, important to safety and security functions, are allocated to Level 4 and are protected from all lower. And only one-way data flow is allowed from level 4 to level 3 and from level 3 to level 2. Here, the initiation of communications from digital assets at lower security levels to digital assets at higher security levels is prohibited. Data only flows from one level to other levels through a device or devices that enforce security policy between each level, by maintaining the capability to detect, prevent, delay, mitigate, and recover from cyber attacks [2].

3   Case Study for Security Level Assignment

In this section, a digital I&C architecture of a nuclear reactor is described. Furthermore, the level assignment of a digital I&C architecture using DID concept and the lessons learned from this are included. Due to recent aging of the analog instrumentation of many nuclear power plants and nuclear research reactors, the system reliability decreases while maintenance and testing costs increase. In addition, it is difficult to find the substitutable analog equipments due to obsolescence. Therefore, the instrumentation and control (I&C) systems have changed from analog system to digital system due to these facts [3]. With the introduction of digital systems, nuclear research reactors are forced to care for the problem of cyber attacks because I&C systems have been digitalized using networks or communication systems. Especially, it is more issued at research reactors due to the accessibility of human resources.

3.1   Digital I&C Architecture

I&C systems are identified based on the safety and system functions for protecting, controlling and monitoring the facility [4]. The salient I&C systems are presented in the Figure 2.   These systems are Reactor Protection System (RPS), Post-Accident Monitoring System (PAMS), Reactor Regulating System (RRS), Alternate Protection System (APS), Information Processing System (IPS), Process I&C System (PICS), Automatic Seismic Trip System (ASTS), Radiation Monitoring System (RMS), Main Control Room (MCR) and Supplementary Control Room (SCR).

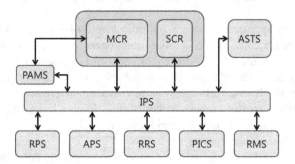

Fig. 2. Architecture of a digital I&C system

3.2   Level Assignment of the I&C System

The CDAs that provide safety, important-to-safety, security, or control functions are allocated to defensive Level 4 protection and CDAs that provide data acquisition functions are allocated to at least defensive Level 3 protection according to RG-5.71 [2]. The others can be classified depending on importance and relationship from Level 2 to Level 0. In digital I&C systems, a digitalized safety function which is provided by the RPS causes a reactor trip to protect the core by generating trip signal to insert control rods into the core whenever the trip signal exceed the trip threshold. Moreover, the RPS offers engineered safety features actuation signals to ensure the reactor safety and to prevent a release of radioactive material to the environment. And the APS is designed to trip the reactor in case that the RPS has failed to perform its protective function, which is considered as beyond designed basis accident. It is independent from the RPS. The ASTS has two different functions. One is to shut the reactor down automatically if the earthquake occurring at site is greater than the operating basis earthquake. The second function of the ASTS is to monitor the seismic motion of the site in continuous basis. RPS, APS and ASTS are included in cyber security DID Level 4 due to their trip functions for a reactor in case of emergency. The PICS is placed at DID Level 3 because it is a computer based data processing and control system for the process system. It is connected to the IPS through the communication network for information integration in the MCR. If Level 2 is defined as the information processing level acquired from Level 3, IPS is assigned to Level 2. The IPS is designed to provide plant status information to the MCR / SCR for assisting the plant personnel in operating the plant safely. The plant information is derived from other I&C systems such as RPS, RRS and PICS. Level 1 includes MCR and SCR to control the obtainable information from the IPS. The MCR is the place performed all operational actions related to the control and monitoring of plant process. The SCR is designed very similar to MCR but it is used under situation when the reactor operation in the MCR is not possible. Level 0 is defined as the level to be controlled by Level 1 and give and take the information with Level 1. The PAMS is to provide the necessary information for operators to monitor and take actions, if required, during and after a design basis accident. According to the demands from the operators, this allows the required information at the main control room. The reactor power level is regulated, using control rods, by the RRS which is a computer-based system. The reactor control functions such as the reactor startup and the scheduled shutdown is performed by the RRS. This is achieved by an operator's changing the power levels through keyboard inputs and maintaining the reactor at a steady state. The RMS is designed to measure, indicate and record the presence and level of radiation. The RMS is also designed for informing personnel protection and precluding the spread of radiation hazards. Therefore PAMS, RMS and RRS are assigned to Level 0.

3.3   Lessons Learned

According to RG-5.71, the CDAs of cyber security DID Level 4 and Level 3 are defined clearly, but the others from Level 2 to Level 0 are not classified clearly until now. In order to apply the DID concept to cyber security for nuclear power plants and nuclear research reactors, they have to be defined clearly, though DID levels are assigned by accessibility of operators and safety in this work. Moreover, the digital I&C systems might be regulated with only one cyber security level due to the complexity of them. For example, the RRS can be assigned from Level 4 to Level 0 because it is a CDA related with safety and at the same time it is controlled by MCR. This is because there are no clear boundaries among all levels for DID and the digital I&C systems are classified by large scale. The levels of security barriers according to DID concept shall be defined clearly and explicitly for cyber security of digital I&C systems.

　　Another important lesson is that it is possible to assign Level 4 and Level 3 to the corresponding CDAs like RPS, APS and ASTS because they offer the mechanisms of one-way data flow. As mentioned in Section 2.2, at Level 4 and Level 3, the initiation of communications from digital assets at lower security levels to digital assets at higher security levels is prohibited. Thus, only if systems have the information that can flow one-way and at the same time is important to safety and security, it is possible to fully apply this DID concept.

4   Strategy for Smart Service Server Security

The main strategy for smart service server security proposed in this work is an n-tier server architecture which is based on DID concept. As for the n-tier server architecture, it is effective to make servers distributed properly. Originally, applying distributed servers is for overcoming the problems with central server frameworks like poor distribution of processing, high user response latency, heavy state management on the servers, and reduced opportunity for interoperability [5, 6, 7, 8]. This strategy, however, also works for the security of servers. When a server is centralized, the communications between client and server and among servers are hidden by the framework and the server 'endpoints' are hard or impossible to isolate. This is not helpful in assigning cyber security levels to servers. On the contrary, in distributed servers, we can get clear boundaries among servers as well as between clients and servers by exposing explicit and secure data-interchange interfaces. As we can know from the lessons mentioned in Section 3.3, it is crucial to clearly assign the security levels to subsystems in implementing the DID concept for a system. Therefore, the strategy of making servers distributed is the basis of the DID strategy for smart service server cyber security proposed in this work.

Basically, each server is assigned to a security level with the consideration of the security policy of the operator of the smart service system. In addition, the security level of information shall also be considered. All the information that the service system deals with is broken down and assigned with different security levels from level 0 to level 4. As the criticality of the information increases, the information shall be handled on the server with the higher level. It is convenient to compose a level assigning table to match the information with the server according to the security policy. Table 1 is an exemplary table.

Table 1. Example of Level Assigning Table

	Information Security Level				
	Level 0	Level 1	Level 2	Level 3	Level 4
Server 1			O		
Server 2		O			
Server 3				O	

Figure 3 shows an exemplary 3-tier server architecture of a smart service system. Each distributed server shall be designed as 'thin' as possible so that it can be as easy as possible to encode or protect the information which it handles. Keeping a server as thin as possible, it shall also be considered that when one server is penetrated by some cyber attacks, the other server can be maintained safely without the cyber attacks. This consideration of DID concept is the core of the proposed strategy for smart service server security. Here it is checked if the system deals with the information that can flow one-way from a server to another and is important to security. If it does any, the information should be handled with a dedicated server, which shall be assigned to Level 3 or Level 4.

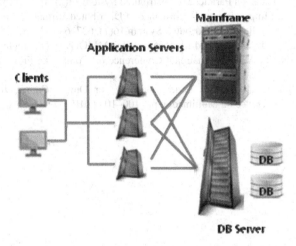

Fig. 3. Example of 3-tier Server Architecture

5   Conclusions

In this work, a DID strategy is proposed for smart service servers in more concrete manner. We tried to find out the special features in applying DID concept to nuclear industry cyber security. To do this, we assigned cyber security levels to a typical digital I&C system using the DID concept in nuclear industry cyber security. Based on the lessons learned from the security level assignment case study, we could set up a DID strategy for smart service servers. The main strategy for smart service server security is an n-tier and 'thin' server architecture which is based on the DID concept. This approach can be applied in future to implement and evaluate the cyber security systematically. The architecture of smart service systems can be designed under this concept.

Acknowledgement. This work was partially supported by Advanced Research Center for Nuclear Excellence (ARCNEX) program funded by the Ministry of Education, Science and Technology (Grant Number: 2011-0031773).

References

[1] Wallance, E.G., Fleming, K.N., Buras, E.M.: Next Generation Nuclear Plant Defense-in-Depth Approach. Idaho National Laboratory (INL) (December 01, 2009)
[2] Regulatory Guide 5.71, Cyber Security Programs for Nuclear Facilities, U.S. Nuclear Regulatory Commission (January 2010)

[3] Gan, B., Brendlen, J.H.: Nuclear power plant digital instrumentation and control modifications. In: IEEE Conference Record Nuclear Science Symp. and Medical Imaging Conf., October 25-31, vol. 2 (1992)

[4] ANSTO Replacement Research Reactor Project Safety Analysis Report Chapter 8 Instrumentation and Control (November 01, 2004)

[5] Lui, J., Chan, M.: An Efficient Partitioning Algorithm for Distributed Virtual Environment Systems. IEEE Trans. on Parallel and Distributed System 13(2), 193–211 (2002)

[6] Morllo, P., et al.: Improving the Performance of Distributed Virtual Environment Systems. IEEE Trans. on Parallel and Distributed System 16(7), 637–649 (2005)

[7] Jordan, H., et al.: Dynamic Load Management for MMOGs in Distributed Environments. In: Proc. of the 7th ACM International Conference on Computing Frontiers, pp. 337–346 (2010)

[8] Rynson, W., Lau, H.: Hybrid Load Balancing for Online Games. In: Proc. of the International Conference on Multimedia, pp. 100–103 (2010)

Dispersion Managed Optical Links with Non-uniform Distribution of Residual Dispersion Per Span

Hwang-Bin Yim[1] and Seong-Real Lee[2,*]

[1] Division of Information Communication Eng., Gangwon Provincial
University, Gangwon, 210-804, Korea
[2] Division of Marine Electronic and Communication Eng., Mokpo National Maritime
University, Joennam, 530-729, Korea
hbinyim7@hanmail.net, reallee@mmu.ac.kr

Abstract. The possibility of implementing non-uniform residual dispersion per span (RDPS) in optical links with net residual dispersion (NRD) controlled by precompensation and postcompensation for 960 Gbps WDM transmissions is studied and discussed. It is confirmed that the optimal NRD is obtained to be one of +10 ps/nm or -10 ps/nm, which depend on the deciding of NRD and the exact RDPS configurations. And, effective NRD ranges resulting eye opening penalty (EOP) below 1 dB are independent of the exact RDPS distribution for relative low launch power.

Keywords: Dispersion management, Optical phase conjugator, Residual dispersion per span (RDPS), Net residual dispersion (NRD), WDM transmission.

1   Introduction

Fiber dispersion and nonlinearity degrade propagating pulses causing communication errors. In long haul communication systems, dispersion management (DM) is used to minimize the pulse broadening [1]. However, the output pulse shape also depends upon the signal power level through nonlinear effects, such as four-wave mixing (FWM), self-phase modulation (SPM) and cross-phase modulation (XPM).

In the presence of fiber group velocity dispersion (GVD) and SPM, the pulse spread is sensitive to dispersion map as well as the values of launch power. Hence for the designing of flexible optical fiber communication links, it is necessary to consider fiber spans having different residual dispersion per span (RDPS) with each other as well as the amount of dispersion compensation at various locations to minimize pulse degradation. However, most of the previous studies on dispersion map were focused on the fixed RDPS for every fiber spans. This means that, if such a dispersion map is used, the length of fiber span including dispersion compensating fiber (DCF) have to be fixed, hence, the implementation of reconfigurable WDM optical mesh networks is very difficult.

Optical phase conjugation is another effective technique to reduce GVD and nonlinear impairment mainly due to SPM [2]. The compensation for signal impairment in

---

* Corresponding author.

T.-h. Kim et al. (Eds.): FGCN/DCA 2012, CCIS 350, pp. 189–192, 2012.
© Springer-Verlag Berlin Heidelberg 2012

this technique is theoretically possible through the use of optical phase conjugator (OPC) in the middle of total transmission length. Authors had shown the implementation possibility of WDM transmission system with good receive performance by applying DM and OPC into optical links through the previous studies [3],[4].

In this paper, a modified periodic dispersion map with non-uniform RDPS for each fiber span, such as ascending-descending RDPS configuration and descending-ascending RDPS configuration, is proposed for 960 Gbps (= 24 channels x 40 Gbps) WDM systems with OPC at mid-way of total transmission length. We will induce optimal net residual dispersion (NRD) in such links, and effective NRD ranges as a function of values of launch power of WDM channels through a numerical study of assessing eye opening penalty (EOP) of worst channel among 24 WDM channels.

2   Configurations of Optical Links for WDM Transmission

WDM system and optical transmission link configuration investigated in this research is shown in Fig. 1. Optical transmission link consists of 12 spans, in which including SMF with 80 km length, i.e., $l_{SMF,n}$ = 80 km (where, n is span number) and DCF with variable length depending on RDPS. SMF was characterized by the attenuation coefficient α_{SMF} = 0.2 dB/km, dispersion coefficient D_{SMF} = 17 ps/nm/km, and the nonlinear coefficient γ_{SMF} = 1.41 $W^{-1}km^{-1}$ at 1,550 nm.

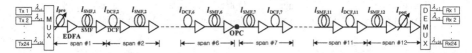

Fig. 1. Configuration of optical links and WDM transmission system

The averaged RDPS are assumed to be equal value of 150 ps/nm in both transmission sections from Tx to OPC and from OPC to Rx, except first fiber span and last fiber span. If RDPS is selected to be the fixed 150 ps/nm, the length of DCF, i.e., $l_{DCF,n}$ (n = 2, 3, 4, ..., 11) has to be 12.1 km at each fiber span, except first and last fiber spans. This case is called to the 'uniform RDPS distribution'. The RDPS for ascending-descending configuration is designed as following; RDPS of second span is to be 50 ps/nm and RDPS of the rest spans up to 6th span are increased by 50 ps/nm than previous span from 100 ps/nm to 250 ps/nm, meanwhile, RDPS of 7th span is to be 250 ps/nm and RDPS of the rest spans up to 11th span are decreased by 50 ps/nm than previous span from 200 ps/nm to 50 ps/nm, under the condition of 150 ps/nm averaged RDPS. And, the RDPS for descending-ascending configuration is designed to be the reverse distribution of ascending-descending configuration. Dispersion coefficient of DCF of every span, D_{DCF} is assumed to be -100 ps/nm/km in all RDPS configurations. DCF was characterized by the attenuation coefficient α_{DCF} = 0.4 dB/km, and the nonlinear coefficient γ_{DCF} = 4.83 $W^{-1}km^{-1}$ at 1,550 nm. The NRD value will be varied by precompensation and postcompensation, which are determined by DCF lengths of first and last fiber section, i.e., l_{pre} and l_{post} plotted in Fig. 1, respectively.

Tx illustrated in Fig. 1 is assumed to be distributed feedback laser diode (DFB-LD). The center wavelength of DFB-LD is assumed to be 1,550~1,568.4 nm by spacing 100 GHz (0.8 nm) based on ITU-T recommendation G.694.1. DFB-LD is externally modulated by an independent 40 Gbps 128($=2^7$) pseudo random bit sequence (PRBS). The modulation format from external optical modulator is assumed to be RZ.

The nonlinear medium of OPC around mid-way of total transmission length is highly nonlinearity-dispersion shifted fiber (HNL-DSF). And, Rx consists of the pre-amplifier of EDFA with 5 dB noise figure, the optical filter of 1 nm bandwidth, PIN diode, pulse shaping filter (Butterworth filter) and the decision circuit. The receiver bandwidth is assumed to be 0.65× bit-rate [5].

3   Simulation Results and Discussion

Fig. 2 illustrates EOPs of worst channel among 24 WDM channels as a function of NRD controlled by precompensation and postcompensation, respectively. It is confirmed that the optimal NRDs are obtained to +10 ps/nm and -10 ps/nm in optical link controlled by precompensation and postcompensation, respectively, for uniform RDPS distribution and descending-ascending RDPS configurations. But, the optimal NRDs are obtained to -10 ps/nm and +10 ps/nm for ascending-descending RDPS configurations.

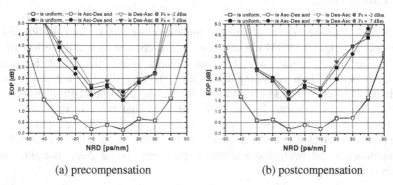

(a) precompensation   (b) postcompensation

Fig. 2. EOP as a function of NRD controlled by precompensation and postcompensation, respectively

Through the analysis the result of Fig. 2, it is also confirmed that the effective NRD inducing EOP below 1 dB at arbitrary launch power is distributed over wide range. These NRD values resulting EOP below 1 dB are defined as the effective NRD range. Fig. 3 illustrates the effective NRD ranges depending on launch power of worst channel in optical links controlled by precompensation and postcompensation, respectively. It is shown that the effective NRD ranges of ascending-descending RDPS configuration and descending-ascending RDPS configuration are similar with that of uniform RDPS distribution for relative low launch power, i.e., -8~1 dBm. And, if wider NRD margin than 60 ps/nm (0±30 ps/nm) is required, launch power is selected to be -5~1 dBm and -6~1 dBm in optical links controlled by precompensation and postcompensation, respectively, which are independence of RDPS distribution. It is also confirmed that the effective NRD range of uniform RDPS distribution is wider than that of ascending-descending RDPS configuration and descending-ascending RDPS configuration for relative high launch power (5~6 dBm), but, in this launch power range, the effecttive NRD range of descending-ascending RDPS configuration is slightly wider than that of ascending-descending RDPS distribution.

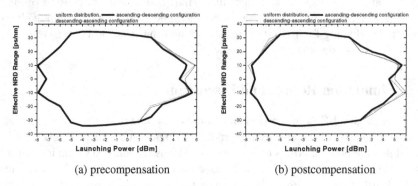

(a) precompensation   (b) postcompensation

Fig. 3. The effective NRD range for launch power

4   Conclusion

This research discussed the possibility of implementing non-uniform RDPS distribution in optical links for WDM transmission. It was confirmed that the effect of non-uniform RDPS distribution on system performance is not significant, because the characteristics of EOP in ascending-descending RDPS configuration and descending-ascending RDPS configuration is similar with that in uniform RDPS distribution for all considered launch power. It was also confirmed that the effective NRD ranges independent on the exact RDPS distribution for relative low launch power, and, if launch power is selected to be -5~1 dBm and -6~1 dBm in optical links controlled by precompensation and postcompensation, respectively, wider NRD margin than 60 ps/nm is obtained.

References

1. Agrawal, G.P.: Fiber-optic Communication Systems, 3rd edn. John Wiley & Sons, New York (2003)
2. Watanabe, S., Shirasaki, M.: Exact compensation for both chromatic dispersion and Kerr effect in a transmission fiber using optical phase conjugation. J. Lightwave Technol. 14, 243–248 (1996)
3. Lee, S.R.: Dispersion Managed Optical Transmission Links with Optimized Optical Phase Conjugator. International Journal of KIMICS 7, 372–376 (2009)
4. Lee, S.R.: Asymmetricity of Optical Phase Conjugation in Optical Transmission Links with Dispersion Management. The Journal of Korea Information and Communications Society 35, 801–809 (2010)
5. Agrawal, G.P.: Nonlinear Fiber Optics, 3rd edn. Academic Press, San Francisco (2001)

A System Architecture for Augmenting Card Playing with a Projector and a Camera

Nozomu Tanaka, Satoshi Murata, and Kaori Fujinami

Department of Computer and Information Sciences,
Tokyo University of Agriculture and Technology, Tokyo, Japan
{umozon.the.world.727,s.murata.irk913}@gmail.com, fujinami@cc.tuat.ac.jp

Abstract. We present a system for augmented playing card with a projector and a camera to add playfulness and communication for a traditional card gaming. The functionalities were specified based on a user survey session with actual play. Cards are recognized by a video camera without any artificial marker with an accuracy of 96%. A player is recognized by the same camera from the direction of the hand appearing over a table. The Pelmanism game was augmented on top of the system as a case study to validate the concept of augmentation and the performance of the recognitions. The results showed the feasibility of the system's performance in an actual environment and the potentials of enhancing playfulness and communication among players.

Keywords: Augmented reality, Projector-camera system, Card games.

1 Introduction

Playing card is popular around the world regardless of age. We can easily converse among players throughout games, which implies that playing card seems to be the most popular toys in many families [1]. Also, as Ono told in her book [7], playing card is effective for child education since card games utilize a wide variety of cards, need skillful finger activity and provide a child with a desire to win. Thus, playing card acts as multipurpose tools with many advantages.

Besides, the popularity and feasibility of recent Augmented Reality (AR) technology has made us determine to augment the playfulness and communication of playing card that has many faces. In this paper, we take an approach of a projector-camera system to realize *Augmented Card Playing*. A video camera is set above the table to recognize the cards and players' hand. A video projector is utilized to project visual effects that aim to add playfulness and provide a player with the state of recognition of cards to improve the accuracy of recognition.

The rest of the paper is organized as follows: we examine related work in Section 2. A user survey is presented in Section 3 to investigate users' requests for augmented playing card and cards recognition algorithm, which leads to the design of a prototype system in Section 4. Section 5 presents the evaluation regarding the cards recognition and the augmentation of playfulness, in which Pelmanism game is developed and tested as a case study. We discuss about these result in Section 6. Finally, Section 7 concludes the paper with future direction.

T.-h. Kim et al. (Eds.): FGCN/DCA 2012, CCIS 350, pp. 193–201, 2012.

2   Related Work

A chemistry experiment support system [8], an augmented "Go" [4], an ancient game in Japan, and a support system for a beginner of billiards [6] have been proposed so far. These studies relate to our study in terms of using traditional tools, focusing original look-and-feel, and projecting on an actual work space. They imply the suitability of a projector-camera system to our system.

Furthermore, studies are found that combine card playing with Information and Communication Technology (ICT). EmoPoker system focuses on playing poker and aims at making players aware of arousal level by providing biofeedback [9]. In order to augment a traditional board game, Surface-Poker, which is a multimodal interface system, takes in physiological inputs and gestures [2]. These study shows possibility that playing card will become superior tool with ICT.

Floerkmeier, et al. proposed a Smart Playing Cards with an RFID system, which advises novice players on strategy and relieves the players of mundane tasks, such as score keeping in playing card games [3]. By contrast, our system takes an input from a video camera as a source of card-related information, which does not need specially manufactured cards, i.e. RFID-embedded cards.

3   Design Background

We conducted a preliminary survey to understand users' requests for augmented card playing. Twelve subjects played four types of games, *Pelmanism, Sevens, Old maid, President*, and expressed their opinions. Typical ones are "Deciding order of players", "Displaying whose turn it is", "Informing players of outcome of their choice", "Giving hints" and "Using visual and auditory effects".

Recognition of the cards' numbers and the suit is required to decide the order of players and to inform players the outcome of their choice. In order to provide hints, it is necessary to recognize cards and players. In addition, many subjects pointed that visual and auditory effects make game more exciting. We specified three features as core functionalities of augmented card playing: 1) recognition of cards, 2) recognition of players, and 3) visual and auditory effects. A wide variety of functions can be realized by utilizing these features, such as keeping score automatically, giving advice to beginners and exciting players by feedbacks.

4   System Design

4.1   Design Decisions

We propose a system architecture for card playing with a projector-camera system to realize the augmentation described in Section 3. The left of Fig. 1 shows an overview of the system. This system recognizes cards on a table by a camera and provides a feedback to players through a projector and a speaker. As described above, studies are found that recognize cards with RFIDs [3,9]; however, the utilization of RFIDs leads three issues: the spatial resolution depends on the density of an RFID reader; the players' smooth operation might be inhibited by an attachment; and relatively expensive. These issues might lose the flavor of traditional card playing and the original entertainment. Meanwhile, recognition of objects with a camera and invisible makers [5] makes it possible to keep the operation of the cards unchanged; however, specialized cards, i.e. painted in retroreflective material, are required. For these reasons, we utilize a camera and directly recognize card playing by image processing. In terms of presentation, we chose a tabletop projection due to case of utilization of existing table and low burden compared to a head mount display.

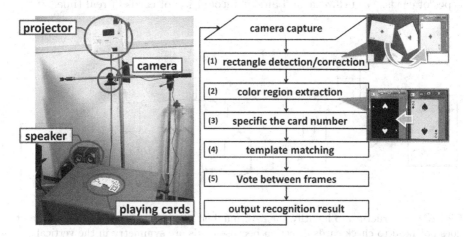

Fig. 1. System architecture (left) and flow of card recognition (right)

4.2   Card Recognition

We also observed the states of cards during the preliminary survey. As a result, we set out the requirements for the recognition of card playing: 1) recognizing all cards at once, 2) handling face-down cards, and 3) handling overlapped cards.

In order to recognize all cards, the system needs a wide field of view to recognize 54 cards (Spades, Clubs, Hearts, Diamonds × 13, Joker × 2). For handling face-down cards, the system records positions of cards when a card is turned over. As for the handling of overlapped cards, however, we put it aside for now. Instead, the system provides the state of recognition to let a player adjust non-overlapped. The flow of processing against a captured image is shown in Fig. 1 and given a brief description below:

(1)   Rectangle Detection / Correction. The whole desktop is captured by a video camera set above the desk, and bounding quadrilaterals to objects in the pictures are drawn. The system extracts the region of a card using length of each side of the quadrilaterals and converts them to rectangles by using the perspective projection in order to compensate for distortion caused by the camera.

(2)   Extraction of Color Regions. To reduce the computational cost of template matching, the system classifies the cards by RGB colors. First, blue regions extraction allows the system to discriminate J, Q and K. Then, by the extraction of red regions, the system extracts 1 to 10 of Hearts and Diamonds with 1 to 10 of Spades, Clubs and Jokers remaining. Finally, J, Q, K, Jokers and 1 of Spade are recognized by template matching.

(3)   Identifying Card Number. We propose a method to generate a tree structure to recognize the number of cards in a computationally cost efficient manner, in which a node corresponds to a certain position of the mark (Fig. 2). The picture of cards and arrangement of marks of each card is common in many types of cards. We utilize it and aim at recognition of cards in real time.

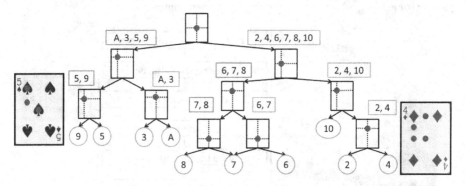

Fig. 2. Tree structure to identify the card number: The system checks red circles and does not need to check cards direction because cards are symmetry in the vertical.

(4)   Template Matching. The system uses template matching to identify 1 to 10 of Spades, Clubs, Hearts and Diamonds. The process (2) and (3) reduces 90% of the amount of calculation.

(5)   Voting between Frames. During a game, a mis-recognition of card is caused due to sudden appearance of obstacles such as players hands. So, we apply voting on the system's decision per frame to eliminate unexpected recognition. The system gives a value (0 to 5) that shows the state of recognition to each card and adds 1 or subtracts 1 depending on a result of step (1) to (4). The system finally marks the card as "recognized" if the value is 3 or more.

4.3   Player Recognition

A player is recognized by the same camera as the recognition of cards. We assume that the position of a player does not change during a game. This allows us to focus on the player's position relative to a table (Fig. 3 left).

(1)   Registration Phase. At the beginning of a game, players are requested to put their hands on a table. The system extracts flesh-colored regions and takes certain amount of areas as hands from captured image. The centroids of hands are recorded by the system as positions of players (G_1–G_4 in Fig. 3-left).

(2)   Identifying Phase. When a hand appears in the photography range, the system compares the position of the hand (G_x in Fig. 3-left) with each player, regards the hand as the nearest player's hand (G_1 in Fig. 3-left) and takes all operation as the action of the player until the hand goes out of the range.

4.4   Visual Effects

Two types of visual effects are provided based on the preliminary survey: 1) Light Frame Effect and 2) Spotlight Effect.

(1)   Light Frame Effect. We expect this effect to make a game gorgeous by turning light around a card (Fig. 3 right). The effect notifies a player of state of card recognition and urges the player not to overlap cards unconsciously.

(2)   Spotlight Effect. Oval light is thrown on a desk. If a card is removed from the table, the system projects a part of a background picture on the desk, and the picture is completed in accordance with the progress of the game. This is realized by recording the vertex of four angles of a card when it is recognizes.

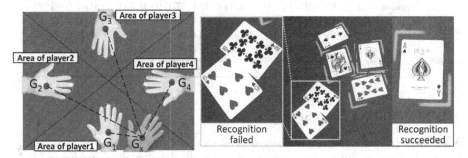

Fig. 3. The way to identify a hand (left) and Light Frame Effect (right)

4.5   Prototype System

Our prototype system is implemented using Microsoft Visual C++ 2010, DX library to develop visual effects and OpenCV2.3 as an image processing library. We chose BICYCLE RIDER BACK as target cards of recognition because they are the most popular one in the world. Our hardware consists of a XGA (1024 × 768) 3000 lm projector, and a Quad-VGA (1280 × 960) camera, both of which are connected to a desktop PC with Intel Core i3 3.07GHz and 4GB RAM.

5   Evaluation

5.1   Fundamental Evaluation: Recognition of Cards

Method. We observed the accuracy and the processing time of basic card recognition algorithm in an ideal environment without the projector light. In the evaluation of recognition accuracy, 54 types of cards were thrown 100 times per card into the photography range at a random position and angle, and a successful recognition ratio is checked. In addition, we displayed 54 cards in one screen, let the system recognize the cards and measured processing time. Also, we evaluated the processing time of J, Q, K, and "8" of Spades. The processing time of J, Q and K were the shortest because they could skip step (3) in Section 4.2, while 8 of Spades was the longest because it needs the step.

Result. In the 5,400 throwing, the system could recognize the cards 5,191 times. 10 of Spades had the lowest recall because the system often mis-recognized it as 8 of spades. The system could recognize the other cards with a recall of more than 90% and in total accuracy of more than 96% (Table 1). As for the processing time per frame, it was 935 milliseconds when the system recognizes 54 kinds of cards at the same time. When only J, Q or K are detected, the system needed 33 milliseconds per frame, and in case of 8 of spades, it took 34 milliseconds.

Table 1. The recall of recognition cards

	A	2	3	4	5	6	7	8	9	10	J	Q	K
Spades	0.99	0.98	0.92	0.97	0.94	0.99	0.99	0.97	0.98	0.76	0.97	0.95	0.96
Clubs	0.97	0.93	0.91	0.94	0.98	0.99	0.97	0.95	0.98	0.99	0.96	0.96	0.97
Hearts	0.97	0.92	0.96	0.95	0.94	1.00	0.96	0.96	0.96	0.95	0.96	0.96	0.95
Diamonds	1.00	0.99	0.98	0.99	0.96	0.95	0.99	0.95	0.98	0.98	0.97	0.98	0.95
Jokers	0.94	0.99											

5.2 Application Case Study

Method. In order to evaluate augmented card playing that is designed to enhance playfulness and mediate communication, we developed an augmented Pelmanism game on the proposed platform, which has 1) a winner determination using cards, 2) player recognition and 3) visual effects. If a player gets a game score or wins, the system performs an auditory effect. Eleven subjects were divided into groups of 4 / 3 / 4 people, played the augmented Pelmanism game and filled in a questionnaire form of eight items with five points (Table 2). Here, 5 is "Strongly agree", 3 is "Neither agree nor disagree" and 1 is "Strongly disagree".

Moreover, we counted the number of times when players turned over cards to see failure of recognition because we considered that the accuracies of recognizing the cards decline according to the light of projector and shadows of players. When the system did not recognize a card, we asked the subjects to put the card again.

We also developed a function, which was actually not included at the time of evaluation, of providing hints. The system gives a winning player hints to miss a chance to get a score and a losing player hints to get a score. We intend to get rid of the difference in the ability in a game and enable to augment the rule.

Result. Fig. 4 shows the mean score of each questionnaire. We could also get their opinions such as "The speed of cards recognition was enough", "The Light Frame Effect was good. But I think the showier, the better", and "Players

Table 2. Questionnaires to evaluate the system

Number	Topics of Question
1	The speed of cards recognition
2	The precision of cards recognition
3	The players recognition
4	The Light Frame Effect
5	The Spotlight Effect
6	The playfulness in comparison with the normal Pelmanism
7	The operability in comparison with the normal Pelmanism
8	The communication in comparison with the normal Pelmanism

recognition is useful". The result showed that the subjects were almost satisfied with the speed and the recall of cards recognition. The questionnaire result also showed that the system improved of playfulness and communication in the game. In the three trials, the number of successful rectangle detection was 348 against 449 attempts. The number of failures in equality decision on a pair of cards was 17. So, at most 34 cards were mis-recognized. We estimate the net recognition accuracy at 70% ((348 - 17 × 2) / 449).

Regarding the new functionality, people often asked us the purpose because of its strangeness. However, once we explained the purpose of the functionality as described above, they seemed to be interested in it.

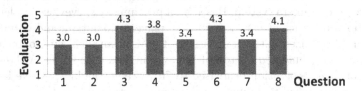

Fig. 4. Mean score of each questionnaire item (N=11)

6   Discussion

6.1   Improvement of Recognition of 10 of Spades

By following the algorithm in Section 4.2, the system made mis-recognition at step (3) when the rectangle detection slipped off, because the space of the design, i.e. the "white" space, is smaller than the other. So, we improved the system so that it can perform template matching with 10 of spades when a card is once identified as 8 of spades. Re-evaluation of the two cards showed that the recall of 8 and 10 of Spades were 95% and 98%, respectively.

6.2   Investigation in Application Case Study

Applicability of the System to an Actual Environment. Through an evaluation in an actual environment, the recognition of cards was obstructed by the light of the projector and the shadows of the players because the card's color was changed considerably. In order to address the issue, we need to investigate a compensation method to estimate the state of a non-projection surface from the one covered with the light and the shadows. We will calculate a relationship between a projection surface and a projection light without prior registration of surface information. Regardless of the issue, the questionnaire survey showed that the subjects were almost satisfied with the speed and the accuracy of the recognition of cards. We consider that the players accepted performance of the system through visual feedback even though the accuracy was not 100%. However, advising to a certain player and automatically keeping a score need complete accuracy. We will continue to improve the accuracy for general purpose augmentation of card games by such as introducing dynamic thresholding and setting a light.

Augmentation Playfulness and Communication. Almost all subjects gave the scores more than 3 for the question 6 and 8. The result of these question showed that the system performed well in improvement of playfulness and communication among players.

7 Conclusion

In this paper, we proposed a system for augmentation of playing card games with a projector-camera system. Based on a preliminary survey, we implemented relevant functions such as card recognition, player recognition, and visual effect. Cards were recognized with an accuracy of 96% in an ideal environment. The Pelmanism was augmented on top of the system as a case study. Although the accuracy of card recognition decreased to 70%, we got highly positive feedback on the improvement of playfulness and communication among the players.

Future work includes the development of functionalities such as the recognition of overlapped cards, audio and visual effects to add playfulness and advising to a novice player to narrow the gap in the experiences, in addition to the improvement of the accuracy of recognition of cards and a player.

References

1. Bandai Co. L.: Bandai children questionnaire report, vol. 125: What is the play by family all together (2006) (in Japanese)
2. Dang, C.T., André, E.: Surface-poker: multimodality in tabletop games. In: ACM International Conference on Interactive Tabletops and Surfaces, ITS 2010, pp. 251–252 (2010)
3. Floerkemeier, C., Mattern, F.: Smart playing cards - enhancing the gaming experience with rfid. In: Third International Workshop on Pervasive Gaming Applications - PerGames 2006 at PERVASIVE 2006, pp. 79–88 (2006)
4. Iwata, T., et al.: Traditional games meet ICT: A case study on go game augmentation. In: Fourth International Conference on Tangible, Embedded and Embodied Interaction (2010)

5. Nota, Y., Kono, Y.: Augmenting real-world objects by detecting "invisible" visual markers. In: Adjunct Proc. of UIST 2008, pp. 39–40 (2009)
6. Ogata, Y., et al.: Shot training system for a beginner of billiards by a projector-camera system. IPSJ SIG Technical Reports (37), 17–23 (2007) (in Japanese)
7. Ono, K.: Cardplaying grows the intelligence of the child steadily. Kodansha Ltd. (2005) (in Japanese)
8. Sokan, A., et al.: A tangible experiment support system with presentation ambiguity for safe and independent chemistry experiments. J. Ambient Intelligence and Humanized Computing 3(2), 125–139 (2012)
9. Yamabe, T., et al.: Biofeedback training with emopoker: Controlling emotional arousalfor better poker play. In: Fun and Games Conference (2010)

Motion Detection Using Horn-Schunck Optical Flow

Wan Nur Azhani W. Samsudin and Kamarul Hawari Ghazali

Vision and Intelligent Research Lab, Universiti Malaysia Pahang, Malaysia
nur.azhani@yahoo.com,
kamarul@ump.edu.my

Abstract. This system is design to detect motion in a crowd using one of the optical flow algorithms, Horn-Schunck method. By performing some appropriate feature extraction techniques, this system allows us to achieve better results in detecting motion and determining the velocity of that motion in order to analyze the human behaviour based on its velocities. This research works able to help human observer to monitor video recorded by closed-circuit television systems (CCTVs) attached in the region of interest (ROI) area.

Keywords: motion detection, optical flow, Horn-Schunck, video surveillance, human behaviour.

1   Introduction

Public security has become the most significant issue in public places such as light rail transit (LRT) stations, market, malls and banks. The increase of crowd occurrence in these public places may increase the probability of criminal cases occurred and unnecessary injuries or fatalities. Over few years, video surveillance systems has been introduced and widely used in the public places. It is said to be useful to human observer, whereby this systems can provide real-time data of crowds in the region of interests to them. However, one common drawback among these systems is their inability to handle high density crowds. The typical large area surveillance system is characterized by a large network of (closed-circuit television) CCTV cameras, which all connected to a control room, where a human operator performs the complicated task to monitor all of them. It is nearly impossible for the human observers to interpret all the data manually for abnormal and emergency events in the high density crowds. Hence, the need for automated system is become crucial. Few years ago, there are some researchers focusing on surveillance system in order to detect the abnormal behaviour in a crowd. They proposed different algorithms in detecting motion in crowd and some of them further the researches in analysing the crowd behaviour. One of the most popular algorithms in motion detection is optical flow.

2   Literature Review

Optical flow is one of the conventional approaches in motion segmentation. From the review [5], they claimed that optical flow-based motion segmentation uses characteristics of flow vectors of moving objects over time to detect moving regions

T.-h. Kim et al. (Eds.): FGCN/DCA 2012, CCIS 350, pp. 202–209, 2012.

in an image sequence. It will compute the velocity of the motion object between two consecutive frames of an image sequence [6] based on brightness and spatial smoothness. The brightness constancy is derived from the observation that surfaces usually persist over time. Hence, the intensity value of a small region remains the same despite its position change. While the spatial smoothness constraint raises out from the observation that neighbouring pixel generally belongs to the same surface and so have nearly the same image motion [1]. Regarding to Jacky Baltes [2], he claimed that motion field cannot be observed directly but we can observe image only and see how the points in the image move. Based on the study, there are a few algorithms can be implemented to compute optical flow but here we only focused on Horn-Schunck method to obtain optical flow.

2.1 Optical Flow Constraint Equation

The optical flow cannot be computed at a point in the image independently of neighbourhood points without introducing additional constraints due to the velocity field at each image point has two components while the change in image brightness at a point in an image plane due to motion yields only one component. From the reviews, researchers assumed that the intensity, I of moving points is constant over a period of time. This assumption is known as brightness constancy assumption.

$$I(x,y,t) = I(x + \delta x, y + \delta y, t + \delta t) \tag{Eq. 1}$$

Thus, the optical flow constraint equation (OFCE) is obtained by using Taylor expansion in (Eq. 1) and dropping its nonlinear terms. Therefore, the OFCE can be expressed in the form as;

$$I_x u + I_y v + I_t = 0 \tag{Eq. 2}$$

Where (u, v) represent the optical flow vectors $(\delta x/\delta t, \delta y/\delta t)$ and (Ix, Iy, It) represent the derivatives of image intensities at coordinate (x, y, t).

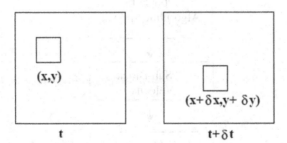

Fig. 1. The image at position (x,y,t) is the same as at $(x + \delta x, y + \delta y, t + \delta t)$

2.2   Horn-Schunck

It is a special approach of using global constraint of smoothness to express a brightness variation in certain areas of the frames in a video sequence [3]. To avoid variations in brightness due to shading effects, objects are assumed to have flat surfaces. The illumination across the surface is assumed to be uniform. Horn and Schunck assumed that reflectance varies smoothly and has no spatial discontinuities. This assures them that the image brightness is differentiable [4].

3   Methodology

Figure 2 illustrated the workflows for this experiment.

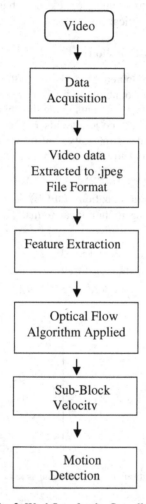

Fig. 2. Workflow for the Overall Process

There are a few processes that involves in this experiment, which are data acquisition, image pre-processing, image processing and classification. The workflow above shows the specific steps performed in the image processing task.

3.1   Data Acquisition

As a data acquisition, CCTVs are attached in the region of interest in the place and the recorded videos are used as a data in this experiment. All the recorded videos are in .avi format with each has its different lengths and should be extracted to make further processing easier. Below are the next processing needs to be done throughout this experiment. As a preliminary experiment, the video dataset is obtained from a website, which contains the normal and abnormal motions.

3.2   Pre-processing

In order to extract the video files, some MATLAB programming is done using m-file. The extracted files are in the .jpeg format since the processing step aims to observe the pixel movement between two sequences of image or frame and so on. Figure 3 below illustrated the pre-processing task which performs by the MATLAB coding created.

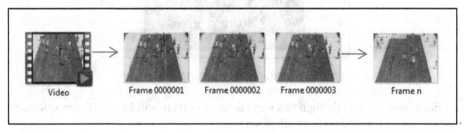

Fig. 3. Video is extracted into *n* frames

3.3   Feature Extraction

When the pre-processing task has been done, the video dataset is extracted into 1454 frames. Bigger size of video data will have a great numbers of frames and will make the processing more complicated without performing feature extraction. Figure 4 shows one of the frames before background subtraction. As can be seen in the figure, there are fifteen people keep walking in their own directions.

Fig. 4. Frame with People Walking

To make easier processing, this experiment only concerned the field area, which is known as region of interest (ROI). It is means that only people in that region will be counted and the result will be used for the further steps. After background subtraction, only thirteen people left in that figure as shown in Figure 5. The people walking outside the ROI will be discarded and can be considered as noise.

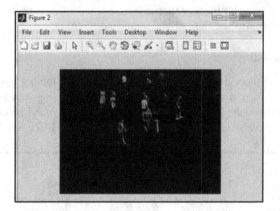

Fig. 5. Frame after Background Subtraction

Each frame will go through this step and each of them will have different velocities values, which is based on its pixel movement.

4   Result Discussion

Figure 6 illustrated the preliminary result when three frames are processed and go through Horn Schunck algorithm. Referring to this figure, it clearly shows the flow vector for each pixel for the frame. The flow vector produced indicates two values, which is u and v, as shown in Figure 7.

Fig. 6. Flow Vector for Three Frames

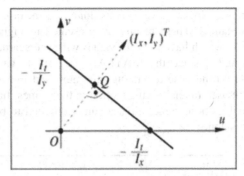

Fig. 7. uv velocity space

These two values will then be used to calculate the velocities and mean velocities as well. The values of u and v are shown in Figure 8 below. The minimum value for u is 3.9520 and this value can reach up to maximum 27.1875. While the minimum value for v is 8.2584 and maximum value is 38.6542.

U	<240x320 double>	3.9520...	27.1875
V	<240x320 double>	8.2584...	38.6542

Fig. 8. uv values

In order to get the good results, the stationary object should be eliminating from the frame so that the remained pixel in the frame is the moving pixel. There are sixteen sub-blocks of velocity is created, whereby it is named as A11,A12,A13, A14,A21,A22,A23,A24 and so on as illustrated in Figure 9.

Fig. 9. Sub-block of Velocity

After the sixteen sub-blocks of velocity is done, the mean of velocity values for each sub-block is obtained. These results are presented in Figure 10. Based on the results, the sub-blocks which have the zero values will be discarded and will make the process not too complex since the MATLAB program is handling thousands of frames to process in a time. The remaining minimum and maximum value of mean velocities are then be used to analyse the motion in the frames. In order to analyse the normal and abnormal motion, some initial assumption need to be created before the pre-processing task is done.

Name ▲	Value	Min	Max
meanA11	0	0	0
meanA12	0.2041	0.2041	0.2041
meanA13	0.3403	0.3403	0.3403
meanA14	0.1485	0.1485	0.1485
meanA21	0	0	0
meanA22	0.1606	0.1606	0.1606
meanA23	0.2510	0.2510	0.2510
meanA24	0.2088	0.2088	0.2088
meanA31	0	0	0
meanA32	0.1751	0.1751	0.1751
meanA33	0.0937	0.0937	0.0937
meanA34	0	0	0
meanA41	0	0	0
meanA42	0	0	0
meanA43	0	0	0
meanA44	0	0	0

Fig. 10. Mean Velocity

5   Conclusion and Future Works

This paper presents the preliminary works towards the motion detection using Horn-Schunck algorithm. From the experiment, it is shown that the motion of people either walking or running can be detected using Horn-Schunck algorithm and good pre-processing task lead to better results. Decision making (whether normal and abnormal motion) can be made when the threshold is defined as an initial assumption. For example, if the velocity is greater than 1, it is indicates that the people is running, whereby leads to abnormal motion. As a future works, this experiment will be continued in determining the behaviour of people in the frame based on its velocity values and other factors, such as panic weight which come out from panic effects in a crowd. Besides, other feature extraction techniques will be used in order to get better results in the end.

References

[1] Sun, D., Roth, S., Lewis, J.P., Black, M.J.: Learning Optical Flow. In: Forsyth, D., Torr, P., Zisserman, A. (eds.) ECCV 2008, Part III. LNCS, vol. 5304, pp. 83–97. Springer, Heidelberg (2008)

[2] Baltes, J.: Optical Flow Algorithms. Lecture Notes, University of Manitoba (October 2003)

[3] Liu, K., Du, Q., Yang, H., Ma, B.: Optical Flow and Principal Component Analysis-Based Motion Detection in Outdoor Videos. EURASIP Journal on Advances in Signal Processing 2010, Article ID 680623, 6 pages (2010)

[4] Liu, S.: Object Trajectory Estimation Using Optical Flow. Utah State University, Bachelor Thesis

[5] Hu, W., Tann, T.: A Survey on Visual Surveillance of Object Motion and Behaviors. IEEE Transactions on Systems, Man, And Cybernetics—Part C: Applications and Reviews 34(3) (August 2004)

[6] Mileva, Y.M.: Invariance with Optic Flow, Mathematical Image Analysis Group, Department of Computer Science, Saarland University. Master Thesis (2009)

Implementation Strategies for ERP Adoption by SMEs

Srimannarayana Grandhi and Ritesh Chugh

Central Queensland University Melbourne, Australia
{s.grandhi1,r.chugh}@cqu.edu.au

Abstract. ERP systems are considered to be mission-critical information systems in the current business environment. The adoption of ERP should not be hindered solely by the size of an organisation. The key aims of this paper are to elucidate the various strategies Enterprise Resource Planning (ERP) vendors have developed to encourage Small to Medium Enterprises (SME) to adopt their products. These strategies focus around solutions such as pre-configured solutions, implementation methodologies and hosting options. In order to meet this aim, this paper utilises two case studies as examples which demonstrate the experiences of companies who have utilised these strategic options. Based on the extant literature, the barriers to implementation of ERP systems in SMEs have also been discussed. Discussion about the implementation barriers is included to explain how organisations can prepare and plan for effective ERP system implementation.

Keywords: ERP, Enterprise Resource Planning, SME, Small to Medium Enterprise, Adoption, Implementation, Strategy.

1   Introduction

Large organisations usually have more than one information system to support their diverse business functions. Often these systems have been built around different functions and business processes that do not pass data to each other [1]. The end result is inefficient business processes, redundant data and additional costs to the firm. Enterprise Resource Planning (ERP) systems were introduced to address this problem by 'providing a single information system for organisation-wide coordination and integration of key business processes' [1, p.56]. ERP systems can be used to replace an assortment of systems that have typically existed in organisations. ERP systems are considered to be a crucial link for enhancing integration between different functional areas in a business whether it is large or small. Traditionally ERP vendors such as SAP, Oracle, Baan, JD Edwards (now Oracle) and IBM focussed on developing and selling software to Fortune 1000 companies. 70% of these Fortune 1000 companies have an ERP system [2]. There has been a shift towards this focus on larger companies and now ERP vendors are focussing upon Small to Medium Enterprises (SME) due to changes in the business environment. Undoubtedly SMEs would want to reap the same benefits that large enterprises have been able to gain through the adoption of ERP.

T.-h. Kim et al. (Eds.): FGCN/DCA 2012, CCIS 350, pp. 210–216, 2012.
© Springer-Verlag Berlin Heidelberg 2012

Due to the saturation of the high end market [2] and as the majority of larger organizations have already adopted ERPs, software vendors have turned their attention to SMEs. ERP vendors are now offering simplified and cheaper products which can help SMEs to take full advantage of ERP with minimal time, effort and manpower [4]. Most of the current studies on ERP systems have focused on large ERP installations with limited focus on SMEs. The escalating trend of ERP adoption by larger organisations was partly driven due to the inherent high costs of ERP and limited products from ERP vendors that catered to the needs of SMEs. In most cases, SMEs have limited resources at their disposal and in comparison to larger companies, their chances of survival are very slim if an ERP implementation fails. Hence it is important to look at some ERP adoption strategies that can be utilised by SMEs when they are confronted with multiple choices. This paper will provide an insight into these strategies. The paper will also delve into the implementation barriers of ERP systems in SMEs as drawn from the literature in this field. This paper has utilised a case study method that involved an interpretive approach, to demonstrate the experiences of two SMEs who have utilised these strategic options and their successful usage of ERP products.

2   A Brief Insight into the State of ERP Systems

Enterprise Resource Planning (ERP) systems can be defined as software infrastructure that helps organisations to manage and improve the efficiency of their business processes and achieve business agility [5]. These systems can also be called integrated systems, because this software allows integration of several business functions to achieve process efficiency and enhance profitability [6].

The goal of ERP is to integrate different business functions across an organization into a single platform that serves the needs of each business function seamlessly [8]. Some of the drivers for implementing ERP systems include replacing legacy systems, simplifying and standardising their existing systems, gaining strategic competitive advantage, improving interactions with both customers and suppliers, and restructuring the organisation [7]. An ERP system can help in lowering inventory levels, reducing production cycle time, decreasing operational costs, and providing a strong back up for enterprise resource integration and business process standardization [9],[10].

There are several vendors in the market offering ERP software with different modules to support businesses. Most of these products include sales order processing, purchasing, production planning, financial accounting, management accounting and human resources modules. Some vendors also include additional modules to aid in customer relationship management, supplier relationship management, corporate performance management, product life cycle management and supply chain management [8]. A survey conducted by Panorama consulting group revealed that SAP, Oracle, Microsoft, Epicor Software, Infor Global Solutions, Sage, Lawson Software, Exact Software, IFS and Open Bravo are the most popular ERP software vendors globally [11]. In 2010, Germany based ERP vendor SAP was ranked first with a market share of 24%, followed by Oracle with 18% and Microsoft Dynamics at 11% [12].

3   Barriers to Implementation of ERP Systems in SMEs

ERP implementations help SMEs to increase their strategic and competitive capabilities [15]; however, there are several barriers too. Despite the many advantages of ERP systems, they do not as yet represent a clear and successful management tool to SMEs or at least they are not easily implementable by SMEs [13]. It is estimated that 50% of all ERP implementations are considered a failure [14]; hence a poorly implemented ERP system can become a heavy liability for SMEs. It is important to delve into the barriers of the implementation of ERP in SMEs so that such costly mistakes can be avoided. Some key barriers to the implementation of ERP in SMEs as gathered from the extant literature follow.

Time and Cost Constraints: Configuring and implementing ERP systems is an expensive task [3]. SMEs either have insufficient resources or are not willing to commit their scarce resources to the lengthy implementation time and high fees associated with ERP implementation [3].

Failure to Redesign Business Process to Fit the Software: Failure to redesign the process to fit the ERP may cause problems in the implementation process [16]. Therefore, it is vital that current business processes are redesigned so that it is close match to the ERP and vice versa. ERP vendors like SAP are offering industry specific or cross industry solutions to assist SMEs. 43% of costs associated with implementing a new ERP system are reengineering costs [6].

Lack of Senior Management Support: Lack of senior management's support would lead to abandonment of the project or unsuccessful implementation of the system. Technical and information services staff would perceive positively, if there is backing of senior management at various levels. For example, if the executive feels implementation of a new system is a high priority, then it is more likely that the subordinates feel the same way too [1].

End User Resistance: People are the main focus when new systems are being implemented. The implementation of new technology can generate fear within employees and lead to a resistance to change. 'Many staff respond with resistance, anger, frustration and confusion' when new systems are being implemented [17]. The best way to deal with this situation is to clearly communicate the change through the entire organisation and keep the users involved in the design process.

Lack of Skilled Staff: The implementation process includes tuning and configuring the system. Failure to recruit ERP professionals and inadequate staffing may become a barrier in the successful implementation of ERP. Solutions could range from recruiting skilled staff, to identifying and training the existing staff [18].

4   Background of the Case Study SMEs

Two case studies (Globe Australia and Italricambi) were chosen from the World Wide Web to demonstrate the experiences of companies who have utilised strategic options for ERP implementations.

Globe Australia is the leading supplier of products and services to the turf maintenance and pest management industries in Australia [19]. Its headquarters are located in Sydney and its 75 staff supply stock nationally through 10 other distribution locations. According to the CEO of Globe Australia, there was a need 'to maximise customer service through effective relationship management, inventory control and real-time reporting' [20]. To achieve this mission, Globe Australia replaced their legacy system with mySAP All-in-One with the help of SAP's implementation partner Extend Technologies [20]. Globe Australia chose mySAP All-in-One because it is a complete ERP solution that is preconfigured and comes with preinstalled tools to manage keys aspects of their business. Their previous system was not preconfigured and needed skilled personnel to tune the system in order to meet the company's day-to-day requirements. SAP's toolset and accelerators including business configuration sets helped them to integrate the old system with the new one and achieve rapid implementation with minimal disruption to the business [20]. As it is necessary to modify the existing business processes prior to the implementation of ERP system to suit the pre-configured system and to improve efficiency [21], some of the existing internal processes had to be modified during the implementation process. Staff training was straight forward because of the user friendly interface [20].

Italricambi is an Italy based manufacturing business founded in 1962 that produces steel parts for earthmoving machinery [22]. Around 90% of the company's sales are abroad. It employs 80 people and its annual revenue is around $16.5 million [22]. Italricambi chose Oracle's ERP system 'JD Edwards Enterprise One' to support existing key business processes and provide transparent interactions with global partners, and more importantly, to reduce delivery times and forecast future demand accurately. Oracle's partner Alfa Sistemi implemented the new ERP system using rapid implementation tools [23]. JD Edwards Enterprise One is an integrated application suite with about 70 application modules, which supports a range of business operations [24]. Rapid Deployment Tools (RDT) such as Oracle Business Accelerators helped Italricambi to implement the new system in 8 weeks. Pre-configured software, services and hardware for mid-size companies can allow rapid deployment of a new system. The new ERP system helped Italricambi to speed up delivery times through improved logistics. The end result was reduced delivery times and costs, improved accuracy of demand forecasts and improved client support [23].

5   Analysis and Findings

The strategies that have been developed by ERP vendors are pre-configured solutions, implementation methodologies and hosting options.

The utilisation of the pre-configured ERP system has worked well for both companies. ERP architecture whose functions are configured to suit the needs of businesses in a specific industry is defined as pre-configured systems. Preconfigured industry specific solutions not only help reduce the total cost of ownership but also enable rapid implementation in as little as 8-12 weeks [27]. Many ERP vendors claim their products are widely configurable and support business processes of any organisation regardless of the products or services they offer [25]. One of the major ERP vendors SAP AG offers preconfigured ERP solutions to meet the business needs and operational needs of mid-sized consumer product companies [26]. Oracle offers JD Edwards Enterprise One, which allows the buyer to choose the databases, operating systems, and hardware to build and expand the customised solutions for rapid deployment to meet business needs [24].

The adoption of the right ERP implementation methodologies includes addressing configuration issues, migrating data from the old system to the new system, building interfaces, implementing reports and pilot testing [7]. Methodology can be defined as proven practices and processes 'followed in planning, defining, analysing, designing, building, testing, and implementing a system' [28]. SMEs may not necessarily have the skills to perform these activities themselves. In order to assist SMEs, ERP vendors like SAP and Oracle, as illustrated in the case examples, offered several implementation tools and methodologies to reduce the implementation cost and time. Although, different companies installed similar ERP software in different ways, there are some common methodologies for implementing ERP systems. These methodologies are rapid implementation, modular implementation and process oriented implementation. All these methodologies offer directives, but may not be very useful for SMEs unless they are backed with the right implementation tools.

The third important strategy that can be utilised by SMEs is ERP hosting or Software-as-a-service, which is gaining popularity. McKay & Marshall [29] define ERP hosting as 'commissioning a third party (or a number of third parties) to manage a client organisation's enterprise resources including IT assets, people, and /or activities to required results' (p.249). Through this approach companies can avoid heavy capital investments on hardware, software, office space, and skilled personnel [30]. Most importantly, this leaves SMEs with more time to focus on core functions of the business. In addition to these benefits, small businesses can achieve steady cash flow, if hosted solutions are purchased from the ERP vendor, because they provide an opportunity to negotiate more favourable terms on the software licenses and/or implementation services [31]. In order to make this option feasible and more attractive, ERP vendors started removing some of the roadblocks to hosted ERP adoption by introducing Service Provider Licensing Agreement (SPLA) options. SPLA would allow solution providers to rent ERP software to small businesses and users would typically pay a per-user, per-month fee depending on the scope of the applications [32].

6   Conclusion

The paper has revealed three strategies (pre-configured solutions, implementation methodologies and hosting options) that were introduced by ERP vendors to assist the needs of SMEs. The case studies clearly demonstrate the experiences of companies who have utilised some of these strategic options. Implementation of pre-configured systems is less risky compared to developing a new system from scratch, because these are developed based on common industry standards and encompass a variety of business processes. Implementation methodologies and tools help in accelerating the implementation process and provide cost benefits too. Hosting is a service offered by some ERP vendors that suits the needs of SMEs who do not want to invest in expensive infrastructure and manage the infrastructure themselves.

Generalisability of the findings is not advised due to the nature of case study methodology. Future research can examine other SMEs in order to perform a deeper analysis and comparison. There is also a possibility of identifying the strategies of larger companies' ERP adoption and comparing them with the adoption strategies identified in this paper.

Moving forward, it can be concluded that the adoption of an ERP system, bundled with cost reduction and operational efficiency, may offer an excellent opportunity for SMEs.

References

1. Laudon, J.P., Laudon, K.C.: Management Information Systems: Managing the Digital Firm, 9th edn. Pearson Education, New Jersey (2006)
2. Yen, D.C., Chou, D.C., Chang, G.D.: A synergic analysis for web-based enterprise resource planning systems. J. Comps. Stds. & Intfs. 24, 337–346 (2002)
3. Dixit, A., Prakash, O.: A study of issues affecting ERP implementation in SMEs. J. of Arts, Sci. & Comm. 2(2), 77–85 (2011)
4. Baki, B., Cakar, K.: Determining the ERP package-selection criteria: The case of Turkish companies. J. Buss. Pro. Mgmt. 11, 75–86 (2005)
5. Turban, E., Volonino, L.: Information Technology for Management: Improving Strategic and Operational Performance, 8th edn. John Wiley & Sons, Inc., USA (2011)
6. O'Brien, J., Marakas, G.: Management Information Systems, 10th edn. McGraw Hill, New York (2011)
7. Sumner, M.: Enterprise Resource Planning. Pearson Education, Inc., New Jersey (2005)
8. Motiwalla, L., Thompson, J.: Ent. Sys. for Mgmt., 2nd edn. Pearson Prentice Hall, New Jersey (2012)
9. Wu, J.H., Wang, Y.M.: Measuring ERP Success: The Ultimate User's View. International J. of Op. and Prdn. Mgmt. 26(8), 882–903 (2006)
10. Liang, H., Saraf, N., Hu, Q., Xue, Y.: Assimilation of Enterprise Systems: The Effect of Institutional Pressures and the Mediating Role of Top Management. J. MIS Quarterly 31(1), 59–87 (2007)
11. Panorama Consulting Group.: 2011 ERP Report (2011a), http://panorama-consulting.com/Documents/2011-ERP-Report.pdf
12. Panorama Consulting Group.: 2011 Guide to ERP Systems and Vendors: An Independent Research Report (2011b), http://panorama-consulting.com/Documents/2011-Guide-to-ERP-Systems-and-Vendors.pdf
13. Huin, S.F.: Managing deployment of ERP systems in SME using multi-agents. Int. J. of Proj. Mgmt. 22(6), 511–517 (2004)
14. Muscatello, J.R., Parente, D.H.: Enterprise Resource Planning (ERP): A Postimplementation Cross-Case Analysis. J. Info. Res. Mgmt. 19, 61–74 (2006)
15. Mareai, B.S., Patil, S.Y.: Taxonomy of Enterprise Resource Planning System. J. Excel J. of Engg. Tech. and Mgmt. Sci. 1(2), 1–12 (2012)
16. Palvia, P., Zhenyu, H.: ERP implementation issues in advanced and developing countries. J. Buss. Pro. Mgmt. 7(3), 276–284 (2001)

17. Anderegg, T.: ERP: A-Z Implementer's Guide for Success. Resource Publishing, USA (2000)
18. Lin, M., Li, S., Chang, I., Huang, S.: Assessing risk in ERP projects: identify and prioritize the factors. J. Industrial Mgmt. & Data Sys. 104(8), 681–688 (2004)
19. Globe Australia.: About Globe Australia (2012), http://www.globeaustralia.com.au/turf/about.htm
20. SAP AG.: SAP Helps Globe Australia raise customer service levels (2004), http://www.sap.com/australia/solutions/customersuccess/sme/businessallinone/globe/index.epx
21. Negahban, S.S., Baecher, G.B., Skibniewski, M.J.: A Decision-making model for adoption of enterprise resource planning tools by small-to-medium size construction organisations. J. of Civil Engg. and Mgmt. 18(2), 253–264 (2012)
22. Italricambi.: Who we are, http://www.italricambi.it/cms/menu/id/17/
23. Oracle.: Italricambi Consolidates International Position With New Technology Platform, Oracle Customer Snapshot (2008), http://www.ebest.hu/UserFiles/File/Snapshots/italricambi-jde-snapshot.pdf
24. Oracle: JD Edwards EnterpriseOne, http://www.oracle.com/au/products/applications/jd-edwards-enterpriseone/index.html
25. Aslan, B., Stevenson, M., Hendry, L.: Enterprise Resource Planning Systems: An assessment of applicability to Make-To-Order companies. J. Comp. in Indst. 63, 692–705 (2012)
26. SAP AG.: Achieve profitable, sustainable growth in a highly dynamic market – with our SME software (2012a), http://www.sap.com/solutions/sme/solutions-overview.epx
27. SAP AG.: Go live in as few as eight weeks – with the SAP Business All-in-One fast-start program (2012b), http://www.sap.com/solutions/sme/erp-business-all-in-one/fast-start.epx
28. Microsoft.: Driving Efficiency and Innovation by Consistently Managing Complexity and Change (2012), http://msdn.microsoft.com/en-us/architecture/ff476941.aspx
29. McKay, J., Marshall, P.: Strategic Management of e Business. John Wiley & Sons Australia Ltd., Australia (2004)
30. Turban, E., McLean, E., Wetherbe, J.: Information Technology for Management, 3rd edn. John Wiley & Sons Inc., USA (2002)
31. Pancucci, D.: ERP Hosting. J. Mfg. Comp. Solns. 17 (2005)
32. Darrow, B.: Microsoft Revises Licenses To Support ERP App Hosting – Enlists partners to counter SaaS plans of Salesforce.com. J. NetSuite 1219, 12 (2006)

Towards a New Order of the Polyhedral Honeycombs: Part I: The New Order Introduced

Robert C. Meurant

Director, Institute of Traditional Studies, 4/11 Shing-Seung Apt, ShinGok-Dong 685 Bungi,
Uijeongbu-Si, Gyeonggi-Do, Republic of Korea 482-863
rmeurant@me.com
http://rmeurant.com/its/home.html

Abstract. The periodic polyhedral honeycombs exhibit an elegant integrity and extraordinary interrelationship, and offer potential for diverse applications, but a satisfactory order that does them full justice appears lacking. Building on my prior order of the regular and semi-regular polyhedra [1, 2], I arrange the honeycombs according to lattice size and expansion/contraction sequences and groups, into an order that comprises three classes of symmetry. Primary polyhedra in all honeycombs are either situated at points of reference cubic arrays, and sometimes generate neutral elements disposed at mid-edges or mid-faces of reference cubic arrays; or they are situated in tetrahedral arrays, with alternating Tetrahedra or Truncated Tetrahedra. Examining lattice size for unit polyhedral edge, together with the disposition of common elements, suggests expansion/contraction groups in two classes, and the regular increase in lattice size at each stage of expansion helps validate the order. Part I provides an overview.

Keywords: polyhedra, honeycomb, tessellation, spatial harmony, form, order.

1   Introduction

The regular and semi-regular honeycombs have attracted attention in the past because of their extraordinary geometric integrity, and are likely in the future to have more interest shown in them, because of their potential applications to such diverse uses as nano-engineering, as 3-D filters (e.g. for carbon sequestration [3]), and for large-scale deployable space structures in Space (e.g. antennae, solar sails) [4], on land (e.g. solar collectors), and in the sea (e.g. marine habitats and reefs). Briefly, there are a very limited number of periodic arrays of the regular and semi-regular polyhedra that properly tile 3-D space. In this paper, we disregard patterns that are based on prismatic developments of 2-D tessellations, as we are only concerned with true 3-D patterns of symmetry. Elsewhere, I have advanced a comprehensive order for the regular and semi-regular polyhedra (together with the regular and semi-regular tessellations of the plane) [1, 2]; this paper shows how the component polyhedra of the honeycombs employ the tetrahedra and truncated tetrahedra of this order of Class I {2,3,3}, and all the elements of Class II {2,3,4} symmetry (except the snub cuboctahedron).

T.-h. Kim et al. (Eds.): FGCN/DCA 2012, CCIS 350, pp. 217–225, 2012.
© Springer-Verlag Berlin Heidelberg 2012

I have long intuited that the polyhedral honeycombs should evince an order that is at least as harmonious and integral as the profound order one encounters in the comprehensive order of individual polyhedra that I previously advanced. But to the best of my knowledge, no such comprehensive order has been provided, notwithstanding sophisticated mathematical treatises on their forms [5, 6]. Typically, arrays are grouped and listed according to symmetry; and truncation sequences are discussed [7]; but I am unaware of an adequate comprehensive pattern being provided that properly accounts for each and every honeycomb in relation to its fellows. I consider it worthwhile to advance my explorations to date, in the hope that they may shed new light on the interrelationships and harmonies of these fascinating forms; and give some insight into the beautiful integral structure of space that accommodates and tolerates them.

This paper is structured as follows: after defining terms and sketching out the new order of honeycombs in section 2, I present the three symmetry cases in section 3, of $\{2,3,4|2,3,4\}$ alternation, $\{2,3,3|2,3,4\}$ alternation of alternations, and $\{2,3,3|2,3,3\}$ four-way alternation or mix and match. I close with a brief summary and outlook.

2   The Great Enablers, Primary Polytopes, and the New Order

Let us commence with what I term the "Great Enablers" (*GEs*), *viz.* the two $\{2,3,3\}$ forms of the Tetrahedron (T) and the Truncated Tetrahedron (D), which occur in either of two orientations (within their reference cube), and which are depicted T^+, T^-, D^+, and D^- (subsequent research will explain their significance). Then, the Primary Polyhedral forms (which may entertain either $\{2,3,3\}$ or $\{2,3,4\}$ symmetry depending on their coloring), are the Octahedron (OH), Cube (CB), Truncated Octahedron (TO), Truncated Cube (TC), Cuboctahedron (CO), Small Rhombic Cuboctahedron (SR) and Great Rhombic Cuboctahedron (GR), to which I add the 0-D Vertex (VT). These give the Primary Elements of 2 Great Enablers and 8 Primary Polytopes, as in Table 1:

$$\text{Great Enablers} = GE = \left\{ T^{+/-} + D^{+/-} \right\} = \{ T^+, T^-, D^+, D^+ \} \qquad (1)$$
$$\text{Primary Polytopes} = PP = \{ VT, TO, SR, GR, OH, CO, CB, TC \} \qquad (2)$$

Finally, secondary Neutral Elements of $\{2,2,4\}$ symmetry are added to these, which develop 4-fold symmetry on just one axis in the honeycombs. Their 3-D forms are the regular Square Prism (SP) and Rotated Square Prism (RP), both identical to the cube; and the regular Octagonal Prism (OP), with square and regular octagonal faces.

$$\text{Neutral Elements (restricted)} = NE_{rst} = \{ SP, RP, OP \} \qquad (3)$$
$$\text{Neutral Elements (expanded)} = NE_{exp} = \{ vt, ae, sq, og, SP, RP, OP \} \qquad (4)$$

where, vt is a vertex, ae an axial edge, ae an axial square, and og an axial regular octagon; depending on the context, these may be denoted in lower or upper case.

Let us then seek to address a new order for the regular and semi-regular honeycombs (or all-space-filling arrays). Begin with a Reference Cubic Lattice RCL_1, which is simply a cubic array of points. Associated with this lattice is a second Reference Cubic Lattice RCL_2, which is the center points of the cubes of RCL_1, and which is identical to RCL_1, except that it is displaced. The center points of the cubes of RCL_2 form the points of RCL_1, and vice versa.

Either reference cubic lattice can subdivide into two equivalent tetrahedral lattices RTL_1, simply by selecting a tetrahedral set of the points of each cube, in alternating orientations. So the points in any one of these lattices form tetrahedra, in alternating orientations that are designated as positive and negative, forming a hit-and-miss pattern of the points of the RCL_1. Without loss of generality, one tetrahedral lattice is denoted as positive, and the other negative. In either case, component tetrahedra alternate in positive and negative, or negative and positive, orientations, respectively, so:

$$RCL_1 = RTL_1^+ + RTL_1^- \tag{5}$$

$$RCL_2 = RTL_2^+ + RTL_2^- \tag{6}$$

Each reference cubic lattice is also associated with a set of points of the mid-edges of that cubic lattice RCL^{ME}, the mid-faces of the other reference cubic lattice RCL^{MF}, so:

$$RCL_1^{ME} = RCL_2^{MF} \tag{7}$$

$$RCL_1^{MF} = RCL_2^{ME} \tag{8}$$

The honeycombs then consist of *primary elements* GE and/or PP, centered either at the points of reference cubic or tetrahedral lattices, (together with neutral elements in some cases). *GEs* show {2,3,3}, and *PPs* {2,3,4} symmetry in the lattice, which makes the first differentiation into classes. The *RTLs* can be shown as: $\begin{vmatrix} RTL_2^- & RTL_1^- \\ RTL_1^+ & RTL_2^+ \end{vmatrix}$; polyhedra located at the points of the tetrahedral lattices are depicted: $\begin{vmatrix} P4 & P3 \\ P1 & P2 \end{vmatrix}$, e.g. $\begin{vmatrix} SR & T^+ \\ T^- & CB \end{vmatrix}$. Reference cubic lattices are simplified to: $[RCL_1\ RCL_2]$, so $[P1\ P2]$, e.g. $[CO\ OH]$.

Table 1. Primary Polyhedral Vertices; Edges, Faces & Areas by Axes & Overall; and Volumes

Polyhedron	Vertices Σ	Edges √1	Edges √2	Edges Σ	3-gon √3	3-gon √3 rot	4-gon √1	4-gon √1 rot	4-gon √2	6-gon √3	8-gon √1	Faces Σ	Area √1	Area √2	Area √3	Area Σ	Volume
T	4	-	6	6	-	4	-	-	-	-	-	8	-	-	4√3	4√2	2√2/3
D	12	-	18	18	4	-	-	-	-	4	-	8	-	-	4√3(1+6)	28√3	46√2/3
OH	6	-	12	12	8	-	-	-	-	-	-	8	-	-	8√3	8√3	8√2/3
TO	24	-	36	36	-	-	6	-	-	8	-	14	24	-	48√3	24(1+2√3)	64√2
CO	12	-	24	24	-	8	-	6	-	-	-	14	24	-	8√3	8√3(1+√3)	40√2/3
TC	24	12	24	36	-	8	-	-	-	-	6	14	48(1+√2)	-	8√3	8(6+6√2+√3)	56(3+2√2)/3
CB	8	12	-	12	-	-	6	-	-	-	-	6	24	-	-	24	8
SR	24	24	24	48	8	-	6	-	12	-	-	26	24	48	8√3	8(9+√3)	16(6+5√2)/3
GR	48	24	48	72	-	-	-	-	12	8	6	26	48(1+√2)	48	48√3	48(2+√2+√3)	16(11+7√2)
SP	8	12	-	12	-	-	6	-	-	-	-	6	24	-	-	24	8
RP	8	8	4	12	-	-	-	2	4	-	-	6	8	16	-	24	8
OP	16	16	8	24	-	-	4	-	4	-	2	10	16(2+√2)	16	-	16(3+√2)	16(1+√2)

For {2,3,4|2,3,4} honeycombs only, secondary neutral elements of {2,2,4} symmetry may appear at the mid-edge/mid-face points of either or both reference cubic lattices. These can be regarded in two senses: of only being required as polyhedral forms in the expanded forms of the arrays, in either one or both of the component *RCLs*; or of always being present, but of sometimes assuming a degenerate form of lower dimension, as axial or transverse regular polygons, edges, or vertices (the difference lies in whether we wish to consider the degenerate forms, or restrict ourselves to the proper polyhedral forms). Neutral forms are centered on the edges of the corresponding *RCL*, and for this symmetry pattern, they are then centered at the midedges of that *RCL*.

So in each honeycomb, primary polyhedra are located at the centers of each of the four reference tetrahedral lattices, counting the Vertex polytope as a polyhedron, and recognizing that the same polyhedron might be disposed at both of the tetrahedral lattices of a reference cubic lattice; in that case, both reference cubic lattices may, or may not, contain the same polyhedron. Alternatively, both positive and negative forms of just one of the *GEs* may occupy either tetrahedral lattice of one of the reference cubic lattices. And in one unique case, positive and negative forms of both *GEs* occupy all four reference tetrahedral lattices.

3   The Three Symmetry Cases of the Honeycombs

There are thus just three symmetry cases, which can be considered as:
- {2,3,4|2,3,4}: an *alternation* of the two reference cubic lattices;
- {2,3,3|2,3,4}: an *alternation of alternations*, which maintains the first alternation of the two reference cubic lattices, but which also invokes alternations of the component regular tetrahedral lattices of both reference cubic lattices, one pair of which is one or other of the Great Enablers (but not both); and
- {2,3,3|2,3,3}: a *four-way alternation* or *mix and match*, a unique case of the four reference tetrahedral lattices alternating with one another using only the *GEs*, but mixing and matching; Reference Cubic Lattices consist of *RTLs* of T and D.

3.1   {2, 3, 4|2, 3, 4}: An Alternation of the Two Reference Cubic Lattices

In the first case, RCL_1 simply alternates with RCL_2, and can be depicted with square brackets: [P1 P2]. Primary Polyhedra of one type $P1$ are centered on RCL_1, and Primary Polyhedra of another type $P2$ are centered on RCL_2; in certain regular cases, both types may be the same i.e. [P1 P1]. Arrays may be contracted, transitional, or expanded, as shown in Fig. 1. For contracted arrays, there are no polyhedral neutral elements; and the polyhedra of one or other of the *RCL* are face-jointed along the $\sqrt{1}$ (XYZ) axes; while the polyhedra of the other *RCL* are connected by vertex or rotated square face, so the honeycomb can be depicted as $[P1\ P2]_{n1}^{n2}$, where $n1$ and $n2$ are the neural elements that separate P1 and P2, respectively. Transitional forms comprise the first step of an expansion, and are formed by separating one of the sets of primary polyhedra by unit length, which as it were brings into being a different primary polyhedron of the other set. The first set of primary polyhedra $P1$ have thus now been separated by either an axial edge *(ae)* or a rotated square prism *(RP)*, while the new second primary set are face-jointed along the $\sqrt{1}$ axes by a square or octagon; and the honeycomb can then be depicted as before (if no polyhedral neural form is invoked), or as $[P1\ P2]_{N1}^{N2}$, where $P1$ is the common Primary Polyhedron of the first expansion, and $N1$ is the polyhedral neutral form, which can only be RP, a rotated square prism (cube). Finally, constituting the second step of the expansion, in the fully expanded forms the second primary set $P2$ is separated by unit length, and a new first set of polyhedra $P3$ is brought into existence; and neutral secondary polyhedra (of two kinds, being either SP or OP) separate elements of the first set, and of the second set, being axially situated on the corresponding $\sqrt{1}$ axes, and centered on the mid-edges of the respective RCL, in other words on $RCL_1^{ME} = RCL_2^{MF}$, and $RCL_1^{MF} = RCL_2^{ME}$, respectively. The honeycomb can then be depicted $[P3\ P2]_{N3}^{N2}$, as both neutral elements are polyhedral. In certain regular cases, $P1 = P2$ and $N1 = N2$, i.e. $[P1\ P1]_{N1}^{N1}$.

This generates four sets of four arrays, and accommodates all the possibilities of reference cubic lattice alternation for one reference cube lattice. Considering either reference cubic lattice, there are therefore a total of 8 sets of 4 arrays, or 32 arrays of {2,3,4|2,3,4} symmetry; deleting the cases where both primary polyhedra are of the same type (see below), there are 28 such arrays; and counting arrays of the same form as one, there are a total of 10 different arrays, including the null array $[VT\ VT]_{vt}^{vt}$.

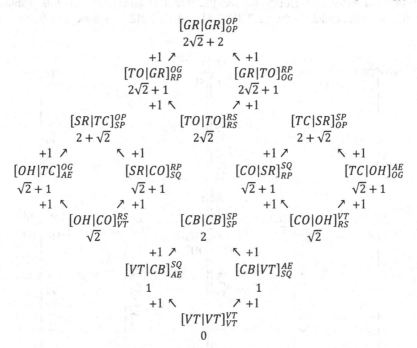

Fig. 1. The {2,3,4|2,3,4} Honeycombs as four groups of 4 contracted, transitional or expanded honeycombs, with lattice dimensions under, and unit expansion distances shown as diagonals

This order is established by assuming the common cubic array as an alternation of cubes and vertices, and recognizing it as a transitional form. The expanded form is then another common cubic array, but of two constituent arrays; each consists of primary cubes CB separated by neutral cubes SP, where the $CB's$ are of two colors, depending on which Reference Cubic Lattice they belong to. Similarly, the neutral cubes belong to one of either Reference Cubic Lattice, (and could be further sub-classified according to their axial orientation along the X, Y or Z axes). We then in-duce the null array, the contracted array $[VT\,VT]_{vt}^{vt}$, whose lattice length is 0, and where all Reference Cubic Lattice points of both *RCLs* coincide in the same dimen-sionless point. This is expanded in the first step of expansion, into the common cubic arrays of $[VT|CB]_{AE}^{SQ}$ or $[CB\,VT]_{sq}^{ae}$, of lattice length 1. The contracted array $[VT\,VT]_{vt}^{vt}$ and its expansion provides a fine metaphor for a decentralized cosmogony, alluding to the circle whose center is everywhere and circumference nowhere, as at-tributed to Timaeus of Locris.

In four cases, both sets of primary polyhedra are the same. These are the contracted $[VT\,VT]_{vt}^{vt}$ and $[TO\,TO]_{rs}^{rs}$; and the expanded $[CB\,CB]_{SP}^{SP}$ and $[GR\,GR]_{OP}^{OP}$, in which the primary polyhedra are separated by *SPs* and *OPs*, respectively.

Figure 2 graphs the lattice sizes for all honeycombs of all three symmetry classes. In later work, I address the striking bilateral symmetry that develops about the vertical axis through the $\sqrt{2}$ co-ordinate, and the nesting correspondence between classes.

Table 2 gives the lattice sizes and volumes for unit polyhedral edge by component polyhedra and expansion groups for the {2,3,4|2,3,4} honeycombs, while Table 3 gives the equivalent data for the {2,3,3|2,3,4} and {2,3,3|2,3,3} honeycombs.

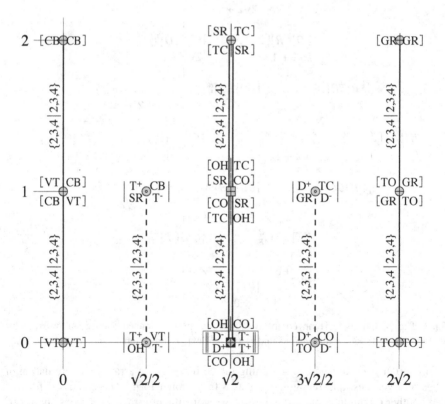

Fig. 2. Graph of Lattice sizes, showing bilateral symmetry and class-to-class correspondence

Table 2. Class $\{2,3,4|2,3,4\}$ Lattice Sizes and Volumes by Component Polyhedra and Group

Lattice	L. size	P1 vol.	P2 vol.	3xN1 vol.	3xN2 vol.	$\sum$ vol.
$[GR\|GR]^{OP}_{OP}$	$2\sqrt{2}+2$	$2(7\sqrt{2}+11)$	$2(7\sqrt{2}+11)$	$6(\sqrt{2}+1)$	$6(\sqrt{2}+1)$	$8(5\sqrt{2}+7)$
$[TO\|GR]^{OG}_{RP}$	$2\sqrt{2}+1$	$2(7\sqrt{2}+11)$	$8\sqrt{2}$	0	3	$22\sqrt{2}+25$
$[TO\|TO]^{RS}_{RS}$	$2\sqrt{2}$	$8\sqrt{2}$	$8\sqrt{2}$	0	0	$16\sqrt{2}$
$[SR\|TC]^{OP}_{SP}$	$\sqrt{2}+2$	$\dfrac{7(2\sqrt{2}+3)}{3}$	$\dfrac{2(5\sqrt{2}+6)}{3}$	$6(\sqrt{2}+1)$	3	$2(7\sqrt{2}+10)$
$[OH\|TC]^{OG}_{AE}$	$\sqrt{2}+1$	$\dfrac{7(2\sqrt{2}+3)}{3}$	$\dfrac{\sqrt{2}}{3}$	0	0	$5\sqrt{2}+7$
$[SR\|CO]^{RP}_{SQ}$	$\sqrt{2}+1$	$\dfrac{5\sqrt{2}}{3}$	$\dfrac{2(5\sqrt{2}+6)}{3}$	3	0	$5\sqrt{2}+7$
$[OH\|CO]^{RS}_{VT}$	$\sqrt{2}$	$\dfrac{5\sqrt{2}}{3}$	$\dfrac{\sqrt{2}}{3}$	0	0	$2\sqrt{2}$
$[CB\|CB]^{SP}_{SP}$	2	1	1	3	3	8
$[VT\|CB]^{SQ}_{AE}$	1	1	0	0	0	1
$[VT\|VT]^{VT}_{VT}$	0	0	0	0	0	0

Lattice volume $\{2,3,4 \mid 2,3,4\} = (P1 + P2 + 3N1 + 3N2)$

3.2 $\{2,3,3|2,3,4\}$: An Alternation of Alternations

This double alternation maintains the first alternation of the two reference cubic lattices, but also invokes alternations of the component regular tetrahedral lattices of both reference cubic lattices, one pair of which is one or other of the GEs. RCL_1 alternates with RCL_2, but within either reference cubic lattice, the two reference tetrahedral lattices alternate with one another, i.e. RTL_1^+ alternates with RTL_1^-, and RTL_2^+ alternates with RTL_2^-. The primary alternation is of RCL_1 with RCL_2; the secondary or subsidiary alternation is of RTL_1^+ with RTL_1^-, and RTL_2^+ with RTL_2^-. In this symmetry situation, one of the RCL is composed of one set of the GEs. This RCL thus consists of alternating T, or of alternating D, in other words, $RTL_1^+ = T^+$ and $RTL_1^- = T^-$; or else, $RTL_1^+ = D^+$ and $RTL_1^- = D^-$. The other primary sets of polyhedra are given by:

$RTL_2^+ = OH$ and $RTL_2^- = VT$ for the constricted form; and by
$RTL_2^+ = SR$ and $RTL_2^- = CB$ for the expanded form, for $RTL_1 = T^{+/-}$; and

by

$RTL_2^+ = TO$ and $RTL_2^- = CO$ for the constricted form; and by
$RTL_2^+ = GR$ and $RTL_2^- = TC$ for the expanded form, for $RTL_1 = D^{+/-}$.

There is no intermediary form; either expansion proceeds in just one step (Fig. 3(a)):

$$\left|\begin{matrix}SR & T^+\\T^- & CB\end{matrix}\right|\left|\begin{matrix}T^- & SR\\CB & T^+\end{matrix}\right| \qquad \left|\begin{matrix}GR & D^+\\D^- & TC\end{matrix}\right|\left|\begin{matrix}D^- & GR\\TC & D^+\end{matrix}\right| \qquad\qquad \left\|\begin{matrix}T^+ & D^+\\T^- & D^-\end{matrix}\right\|$$

$$\sqrt{2}/2 + 1 \qquad\qquad \rightarrow +\sqrt{2}\rightarrow \quad 3\sqrt{2}/2 + 1$$

$$\left|\begin{matrix}T^+ & CB\\SR & T^-\end{matrix}\right|\left|\begin{matrix}CB & T^-\\T^+ & SR\end{matrix}\right| \qquad \left|\begin{matrix}D^+ & TC\\GR & D^-\end{matrix}\right|\left|\begin{matrix}TC & D^-\\D^+ & GR\end{matrix}\right| \qquad \left\|\begin{matrix}D^+ & D^-\\T^+ & T^-\end{matrix}\right\| \quad \left\|\begin{matrix}T^- & T^+\\D^- & D^+\end{matrix}\right\|$$

$$+1 \uparrow \qquad\qquad \{2,3,3|2,3,4\} \qquad \uparrow +1$$

$$\left|\begin{matrix}OH & T^+\\T^- & VT\end{matrix}\right|\left|\begin{matrix}T^- & OH\\VT & T^+\end{matrix}\right| \qquad \left|\begin{matrix}TO & D^+\\D^- & CO\end{matrix}\right|\left|\begin{matrix}D^- & TO\\CO & D^+\end{matrix}\right| \qquad\qquad \left\|\begin{matrix}D^- & T^-\\D^+ & T^+\end{matrix}\right\|$$

$$\sqrt{2}/2 \qquad\qquad \rightarrow +\sqrt{2}\rightarrow \quad 3\sqrt{2}/2 \qquad\qquad \sqrt{2}$$

$$\left|\begin{matrix}T^+ & VT\\OH & T^-\end{matrix}\right|\left|\begin{matrix}VT & T^-\\T^+ & OH\end{matrix}\right| \qquad \left|\begin{matrix}D^+ & CO\\TO & D^-\end{matrix}\right|\left|\begin{matrix}CO & D^-\\D^+ & TO\end{matrix}\right| \qquad\qquad \{2,3,3|2,3,3\}$$

Fig. 3. (a) The Honeycombs of $\{2,3,3|2,3,4\}$ symmetry (left), and (b) $\{2,3,3|2,3,3\}$ (right)

There are four primary cases in two pairs. In the contracted form, pairs consist of edge-jointed positive and negative T's and D's, respectively; in the expanded form, positive and negative T's and D's, respectively, are separated by unit length by square faces, and new forms are brought into existence for the other two primary sets.

3.3 $\{2,3,3|2,3,3\}$: A Four-Way Alternation, or Mix and Match

In the final class, the alternation between RCL_1 and RCL_2 has been overcome by the alternations of RTL_1^+ with RTL_1^-, and RTL_2^- with RTL_2^+, which are of equivalent strength to the alternations between RTL_1^+ and RTL_2^+, and between RTL_1^- and RTL_2^-. This is the most convoluted form of the honeycomb. In this solitary case, only the GEs are involved. Within an RCL, a D^+ alternates with a T^-, while in the other RCL, a T^+ alternates with a D^-, as in Fig. 3(b). That is to say,
$RTL_1^+ = D^+$, $RTL_1^- = T^-$, $RTL_2^+ = T^+$, and $RTL_2^- = D^-$.

Table 3. Classes $\{2,3,3|2,3,4\}$ and $\{2,3,3|2,3,3\}$ Lattice Sizes and Volumes by Polyhedra

$\begin{vmatrix}GE^+ & P2\\P1 & GE^-\end{vmatrix}$	Lattice size	$\dfrac{P1}{2}$	$\dfrac{P2}{2}$	$\dfrac{GE^-}{2}$	$\dfrac{GE^+}{2}$	Σ vol. = lattice size³
$\begin{vmatrix}T^+ & VT\\OH & T^-\end{vmatrix}$	$\dfrac{\sqrt{2}}{2}$	$\dfrac{\sqrt{2}}{6}$	0	$\dfrac{\sqrt{2}}{24}$	$\dfrac{\sqrt{2}}{24}$	$\dfrac{\sqrt{2}}{4}$
$\begin{vmatrix}T^+ & CB\\SR & T^-\end{vmatrix}$	$\sqrt{2}/2 + 1$	$\dfrac{5\sqrt{2}+6}{3}$	$\dfrac{1}{2}$	$\dfrac{\sqrt{2}}{24}$	$\dfrac{\sqrt{2}}{24}$	$\dfrac{7\sqrt{2}+10}{4}$
$\begin{vmatrix}D^+ & CO\\TO & D^-\end{vmatrix}$	$\dfrac{3\sqrt{2}}{2}$	$4\sqrt{2}$	$\dfrac{5\sqrt{2}}{6}$	$\dfrac{23\sqrt{2}}{24}$	$\dfrac{23\sqrt{2}}{24}$	$\dfrac{27\sqrt{2}}{4}$
$\begin{vmatrix}D^+ & TC\\GR & D^-\end{vmatrix}$	$\dfrac{3\sqrt{2}}{2}+1$	$8\sqrt{2}$	$8\sqrt{2}$	$\dfrac{23\sqrt{2}}{24}$	$\dfrac{23\sqrt{2}}{24}$	$\dfrac{45\sqrt{2}+58}{4}$
$\begin{Vmatrix}D^- & T^-\\D^+ & T^+\end{Vmatrix}$	Lattice size	$\dfrac{D^+}{2}$	$\dfrac{T^-}{2}$	$\dfrac{T^+}{2}$	$\dfrac{D^-}{2}$	Σ vol. = lattice size³
$\begin{Vmatrix}D^- & T^-\\D^+ & T^+\end{Vmatrix}$	$\sqrt{2}$	$\dfrac{23\sqrt{2}}{24}$	$\dfrac{\sqrt{2}}{24}$	$\dfrac{\sqrt{2}}{24}$	$\dfrac{23\sqrt{2}}{24}$	$2\sqrt{2}$

$$\text{Lattice vol.}\,\{2,3,3|2,3,4\} = \frac{P1+P2+GE^-+GE^+}{2}\,; \quad \{2,3,3|2,3,3\} = \frac{D^+}{2}+\frac{T^-}{2}+\frac{T^+}{2}+\frac{D^-}{2} = D+T$$

4   Conclusion

This Part I paper determines basic terminology and data, and serves to introduce the outline of a new order for the 3-D honeycombs, according to symmetry, lattice size, and contraction/expansion sequences and groups of arrays. In later parts, I intend to develop this work, by further evincing the elegant comprehensive order they exhibit.

References

1. Meurant, R.C.: A New Order in Space - Aspects of a Three-fold Ordering of the Fundamental Symmetries of Empirical Space, as evidenced in the Platonic and Archimedean Polyhedra. International Journal of Space Structures 6(1), 11–32 (1991), accessible from http://rmeurant.com/its/harmony.html
2. Meurant, R.C.: The Tetraktys of Polyhedra - Their Harmonic Structure According to Traditional Geometric Schema. In: 4th Int. Conf. Space Structures, Guildford, pp. 1138–1147 (1993)
3. Choi, H.S., Park, H.C., Choi, Y.S.: The Effect of Micro-Pore Configuration on the Flow and Thermal Fields of Supercritical CO_2. Environ. Eng. Res. 17(2), 83–88 (2012)
4. Meurant, R.C.: The Individual Integral Space Habitation - Preliminary Sketch Design of an Individual Tensile Space Habitation, Situated within a Large-scale Centralized Tensile Lattice Structured Pneumatic Enclosure, in Microgravitational Space. In: IDEEA2, McGill University, Montreal (1993)
5. Grünbaum, B.: Uniform Tilings of 3-space. Geombinatorics 4, 49–56 (1994)
6. Inchbald, G.: The Archimedean Honeycomb duals. The Mathematical Gazette 81, 213–219 (1997)
7. Critchlow, K.: Order in Space. Thames and Hudson, London (1969)

An On-Body Placement-Aware Heatstroke Alert on a Smartphone

Yuan Xue, Shigeki Hosokawa,
Satoshi Murata, Satoshi Kouchi, and Kaori Fujinami

Department of Computer and Information Sciences,
Tokyo University of Agricalture and Technology
2-24-16 Naka-cho, Koganei,184-8588 Tokyo, Japan
xueyuanhelen@gmail.com,
fujinami@cc.tuat.jp

Abstract. A variety of portable heatstroke risk alert devices are available on the market in Japan; however, an issue in such an environmental measurement device is that the measurement might not be correct if the instrument is not outside, such as in a trousers pocket. We experimentally show the on-body placement-dependency of the measurement. To avoid possible distrust on an over-estimated alert and being at higher risk for heatstroke due to under-estimation, we designed a system that generates an alert message by reflecting the storing position. A prototype system was implemented on a commercial Android-based smartphone, which collects temperature and relative humidity readings from an external device via USB.

Keywords: environmental measurement, heatstroke, WBGT, smartphone, on-body placement-awareness, risk alert.

1 Introduction

In recent years, the number of people suffered from heatstroke is increasing, which is considered due to global high temperatures. Heatstroke occurs due to thermoregulatory dysfunction under heat stress. In Japan, various consumer products for heatstroke risk alert have been available on the market, e.g. [4], which is based on ambient temperature and relative humidity. The device needs to be installed outside, hanging from the neck for instance, since such environmental information has an impact on heat balance of human's body. However, people would not mind if the device is carried in a desirable manner. The measurement might not be correct if the device is not outside, e.g. in the pocket of trousers. As a risk alert device, an over-estimate from the incorrect measurement may lead to a user's distrust due to frequent warning, while the lower-than-actual level of the risk by an under-estimate might make a user careless.

Recent advancement of technologies such as Micro Electro Mechanical Systems (MEMS), high performance and low power computation have allowed a mobile phone to be augmented with various sensors and to extract contextual information of a user, a device and/or environment [2][6]. These sensors are

T.-h. Kim et al. (Eds.): FGCN/DCA 2012, CCIS 350, pp. 226–234, 2012.

utilized not only for explicit usage of mobile phone's functionalities like user authentication [9], display orientation change and backlight intensity control [6], but also for monitoring user's activities, indoor location, and more [8]. So, it is a natural direction that temperature and humidity sensors are embedded or provided as an external module in the near future, which encourages us to investigate a heatstroke risk alert for a smartphone.

The contributions of this paper are that 1) we show the possibility of over (under) estimate of a heatstroke index based on the storing position of a sensor by collected data, and 2) we propose a method of effective communication of a risk level by adapting to a current position of measurement.

The rest of the paper is organized as follows: in Section 2, we introduce Wet-Bulb Globe Temperature (WBGT) as an index of the risk of heatstroke, and show an experiment to prove the on-body placement-dependency of WBGT. Section 3 describes the design of a trustworthy heatstroke alert device that presents under (over) estimation of the calculated WBGT based on a storing position of the device. Section 4 describes about the implementation of the proposed system on an Android-based smartphone terminal. A preliminary evaluation is described in Section 5. Finally, Section 6 concludes the paper.

2   Position Dependency of WBGT

We can imagine that the temperature and humidity sensor readings might have difference among various storing positions on our body, e.g. neck, chest pocket and trousers pocket; however, it is not clear "how" different each other. In this section, an experiment is presented to confirm the difference.

2.1   WBGT and the Risk of Heatstroke

WBGT is considered to be the most informative index for environmental thermal conditions that reflects the probability of heatstroke because it comprises of three important factors: air temperature, air humidity, and radiant heat [3]. However, due to the large form factor of a globe thermometer, a consumer portable device such as [4] is considered to utilize an approximate formula [7] without the term of radiant heat as shown below.

$$WBGT = 0.625 \times Ta + 0.215 \times E(Ta, Rh) + 2.61 \qquad (1)$$
$$E(Ta, Rh) = (Rh/100) \times Es(Ta) \qquad (2)$$
$$Es(Ta) = 6.11 \times (7.5 \times Ta)/(237.3 + Ta) \qquad (3)$$

Here, Ta and Rh represent the air temperature and relative humidity, respectively, that are easily measured in daily life. These formulas imply that we can calculate WBGT by air temperature and relative humidity measured by small sensors such as [12]. Furthermore, for the ease of interpretation of the level of the risk by a user, a WBGT value is interpreted with a level that corresponds to a certain range of WBGT value [1], which is mostly utilized in commercial devices, e.g. [4]. For example, level 4 corresponds to the range of 28 to 31[°C]. Additionally, an advice to avoid heatstroke is provided for each level.

2.2 Placement-Dependency of WBGT

We conducted data collection to understand the dependency of the WBGT value on a storing position. Four positions of a sensor on our body were chosen: front/back pocket of trousers, chest pocket, and around the neck (hanging), which are popular for storing a mobile phone. The data were collected in 20-30 minutes' outside walking from at most six participants who stored sensors in the four positions. The data collection was carried out on August 2011 and July 2012. Tiny data loggers (SHTDL-1/2 [12]) were utilized in the data collection.

The WBGT values were calculated by the formulas (1) to (3). To see the difference between an ideal measurement condition and the others, plots are generated so that the horizontal axis indicates the WBGT values from a sensor hanging from the neck, while the data from the other positions are represented by the vertical axis: from a sensor in a chest pocket (Fig.1 left), a front pocket of trousers (middle) and from a back pocket of trousers (right). The plots on the diagonal line represent that the WBGT values from the neck and the chest pocket (or front/back pocket of trousers) are equal. These figures show that there is a small difference between chest pocket and neck, while the difference is large between trousers pockets and the neck.

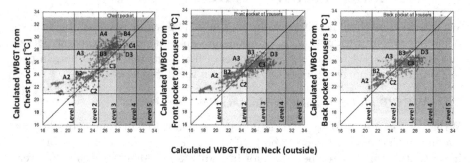

Fig. 1. The difference of WBGT in storing positions. (Left: neck vs. chest pocket. Middle: neck vs. front pocket of trousers. Right: neck vs. back trousers pocket of trousers.)

In Fig. 1, the five levels are overlapped on the surface of the plot. A notable observation was found in the area of D3 of the two cases of trousers pockets (the center and the right). In D3, the level for the neck (outside) is four, while the levels of the corresponding values from trousers pockets are three. A user might miss a "level 4 alert" if he/she puts a device in his/her trousers pocket, which is under-estimate. We consider that this is because the outside temperature is very high and a trousers pocket shaded the sensor from the sun's heat, while, in case of the chest pocket, the heat might not be shaded since a chest pocket is nearly exposed to the air. We also found over-estimate in A4 of the left picture, where the risk level from a device in a chest pocket is higher than actual level. In this case, the WBGT value might be higher than the value from outside due to the effect from the body temperature, clothes, etc.

3   Designing Trustworthy Heatstroke Alert

3.1   Design Goal

An over-estimate might cause a user's distrust due to frequent warning, while an under-estimate would make things worse. A recent study of phone carryingshows that people determine the position of storing a mobile phone based on contextual restrictions [13]. The positional dependency on the calculated WBGT indicates that the positional information of a sensor can be utilized to handle the obtained value correctly, which realizes a trustworthy heatstroke alert. We consider this is an important aspect to respect for the device storing position as users like.

3.2   User Survey on the Preference of Placement-awareness

We carried out a questionnaire survey on appropriate adaptation to a current storing position of a sensor (alert device) with 19 people, in which three types of alerting were compared: 1) a WBGT value from a position other than the neck is corrected to the one from the neck based on a storing position; 2) the storing position and the possibility of over (under) estimation is presented in addition to a WBGT value from a current position; and 3) a device requests a user to put it on a desired position, i.e. hanging from the neck, to measure correctly. Consequently, 16 people chose 1) and 2) as preferable messages. Therefore, our system shows a storing position and the possibility of over (under) estimation as well as a corrected WBGT value.

3.3   Architecture

Fig. 2 illustrates the relationship of relevant components in the proposed system. The proposed system consists of three core functionalities: WBGT calculation, on-body placement detection, and generation of an alert message. The WBGT value is calculated on the terminal side; a message about the potential risk is

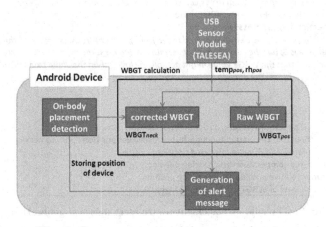

Fig. 2. Core components of the proposed system

determined based on the storing position of a sensor (see the next section). The storing position is tracked by a component developed by the authors [5] that runs as a Service of Android OS. According to the storing position, if there is a warning (from risk level 2 [1]) of heatstroke, the system presents an alert message proposed below. Users can put the device into a trousers pocket or into a shirt's chest pocket as they like since our system generates a self-interpretive message.

3.4   Placement-Aware Alert Message

We have designed an alert message that takes into account the storing position of a device in order to maintain a user's trust on the message. Based on a user survey in Section 3.2, an alert message consists of the name of storing position and the possibility of over- (under-) estimation as well as a corrected WBGT value. Here, the key is the correction of a WBGT value obtained from a position other than the neck into the one that is assumed to be obtained from the neck. The method of correction is described in next section in more detail.

Fig. 3 shows a code snippet of the rule of generating alert messages, in which an alert message is generated for the three cases: over-, equal- and under-estimation. As described in Section 2.2, a WBGT value is discretized into 5 levels of the risk of heatstroke. An over-estimation of a risk level appears when

```
WBGTneck = f(temppos->neck, rhpos->neck);
WBGTpos = f(temppos, rhpos);
if(L(WBGTneck) < L(WBGTpos)){
   //over-estimate alert message
   e.g. "WBGT is 26.2 ℃. The device is located in the front pocket of trousers now. And the risk
        level here is 3, but the corrected risk level into outside is estimated at 2.  Please keep in
        your mind that the WBGT value might actually be higher than the value from outside
        due to the effect from the human's side (body temperature, clothes, etc.)."
}else if(L(WBGTneck) == L(WBGTpos)){
   //alert message
   e.g. "WBGT is 26.2 ℃. The device is located in the front pocket of trousers now. And the risk
        level here is 3, that is equal to the corrected risk level into outside."
}else if(L(WBGTneck) > L(WBGTpos)){
   //under-estimate alert message
   e.g. "WBGT is 26.2 ℃. The device is located in the front pocket of trousers now. And the risk
        level here is 3, but the corrected risk level into outside is estimated at 4. Please keep in
        your mind that the WBGT value might actually be lower than the value from outside due
        to the effect from the outside (air temperature, force of the sunshine,  etc.)."
}
Where
f: a calculation function of WBGT.
pos: chest, front pocket of trousers, back pocket of trousers, etc.
pos->neck: a calibrated calculation function from a particular position "pos" to neck.
WBGTpos: calculated WBGT value of storing position.
temppos: measured temperature from storing position.
rhpos: measured relative humidity from storing position.
L(WBGTpos): risk level of WBGT values (1~5, 5: highest).
```

Fig. 3. The rule of placement-aware alert message generation

a level from a raw (original) WBGT value is higher than the one from a corresponding corrected one. Conversely, an under-estimation is defined as a case in which a risk level from a raw WBGT value is lower than the one from a corrected WBGT. An example message for each case is also shown in Fig. 3. We believe that such interpretive information would allow a user to self-judge the current situation and take an appropriate action to prevent heatstroke in a hot summer day.

4   Implementation

A prototype system has been develped on an Android 4.0-based smartphone (Samsung Galaxy Nexus, Fig. 4 left). We also investigated an external sensing module called TALESEA (Fig. 4 right) since a commercial smartphone terminal at this point does not have environmental sensors in it. As shown on the left of Fig. 4, the user interface consists of two parts: a notification area and a message area. A notification area shows the level of potential risk of heatstroke by a small icon on the top of a display, which is realized by the Android Notification framework. A user can receive a notification while he/she is utilizing other applications. Once a notification is sent, a user can obtain more information by tapping the notification bar downward to show the message area implemented as an "Activity" in the Android programming model. A temperature and relative humidity sensor (Sensirion SHT-71 [11]) is embedded in TALESEA, and a micro-controller (Arduino Pro mini (8MHz)) acquires raw data from the sensor, preprocesses and transmits them to a terminal using Android USB-API.

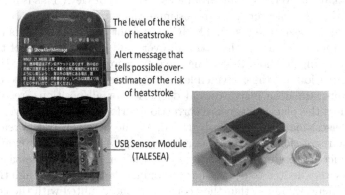

Fig. 4. Implementation of the proposed system. (Left: system overview. Right: TALESEA, a USB-capable external sensing module with temperature and humidity sensor.)

The on-body placement detection is realized by a service of Android developed [5]. The current version detects five storing positions on the body with an accuracy of 72.3% in a strict condition where datasets for a test were obtained from different people whose datasets were utilized for training a classifier.

Regarding the correction of WBGT value, we built linear regression models for temperature and humidity sensors (SHTDL-1/2 [12]) with the data collected in Section 2.2. Then, we obtained another regression model of WBGT using a WBGT sensor SK-150GT [10]. SK-150 can measure the globe temperature value that is difficult to measure using a miniature sensor such as SHTDL-1/2. The estimated WBGT values using formulas (1) to (3) had large error compared with the values measured by SK-150GT. Thus, we determined to obtain a new formula for WBGT estimation. The model was built from dataset of SK-150GT and SHTDL-1/2 collected outside at the same time. Similarly, we got a regression model to convert the sensor readings from TALESEA into the one from SHTDL-1/2, which allows our system to process the most likely WBGT values using temperature and humidity sensors.

5   Preliminary Evaluation

A WBGT value is corrected to the one that is assumed to be obtained from the neck if the storing position is other than the neck, in which the temperature and relative humidity readings are converted into that of neck, and they are utilized to obtain a correct WBGT value as shown in Fig. 3. We evaluated the performance of converting function, i.e. regression model. A metric is the Root Mean Square Error (RMS) that is calculated against corrected WBGT and raw WBGT values, i.e. the one originally obtained from "neck". Additionally, the effect of the correction in terms of the level of the risk (1 to 5) [1] is evaluated. A consumer heatstroke alert device usually shows the level of risk as a user-friendly indicator, e.g. [4]. So, we consider that the accuracy of the level is more important than the WBGT value from a user's point of view. This is assessed by comparing the ratio of over- (under-) estimations with and without correction.

Table 1 summarizes the result. The RMS of front pocket of trousers (FTP) is relatively large, which affect the ratios of over- and under-estimate of the measurement from the position. Regarding the estimation of the risk level, the ratios of equal estimation, i.e. the corrected level is equal to the non-corrected one, and those of over-estimation increases and decreases for all positions, respectively. This indicates the placement-aware correction performed well; however, the ratios of under-estimate are rather degraded. We need to clarify the reason and improve the regression model by a non-linear regression model, for example.

We conducted a preliminary user study on the correction of a message. Three participants were invited to utilize the system in a short time. Through the interviews with them, we found that they concerned and doubted with the corrected value of WBGT. They also concerned about the WBGT value in a position other than the body, e.g. in a bag. Currently, a bag is not supported as a storing position of a mobile phone. We will collect the temperature and humidity data in a bag to find the difference from the neck, and will investigate a correction function as we did in Section 4.

Table 1. Comparison between neck and chest pocket, front/back pocket of trousers. Note that the abbreviations "CP", "FTP" and "BTP" indicate chest pocket, front pocket of trousers and back pocket of trousers, respectively.

	CP	FTP	BTP
Number of samples	939	1158	1158
RMS between raw WBGT and corrected one [°C]	0.6	2.1	1.2
Ratio of equal cases with correction [%]	70.5	63.5	74.9
Ratio of equal cases without correction [%]	56.9	56.5	61.4
Ratio of over-estimated cases with correction [%]	12.0	22.3	27.9
Ratio of over-estimated cases without correction [%]	41.9	64.4	60.4
Ratio of under-estimated cases with correction [%]	17.5	37.6	20.6
Ratio of under-estimated cases without correction [%]	1.3	2.3	1.5

6   Conclusion

In this paper, we experimentally pointed out that there is a possibility of over (under)-estimate of a heat stress index (WBGT) depending on the storing position of a measurement device. To avoid possible distrust on an over-estimated alert and being at higher risk for heatstroke due to under-estimation, we designed a system that generates an alert message by reflecting the storing position. Here, a corrected value of WBGT is presented in addition to an interpretive message about the storing position of a device. A prototype system has been implemented on a commercial Android-based smartphone, which collects temperature and relative humidity readings from an external device via USB.

We will improve the regression model so that an under-estimate of the level of a risk can be reduced. Additionally, we will conduct an experiment to clarify the position-dependency of the perceptibility of an alert, which is intended to let a user notice an alert of heatstroke effectively, i.e. without missing a notification. Furthermore, we will conduct an experiment through daily use.

References

1. Asayama, M.: Guideline for the Prevention of Heat Disorder in Japan. Global Environmental Research 13(1), 19–25 (2009)
2. Blanke, U., Schiele, B.: Sensing Location in the Pocket. In: Adj. Proc. of the 10th International Conference on Ubiquitous Computing (Ubicomp 2008), pp. 2–3 (2008)
3. Yaglou, C.P., Minard, D.: Control of heat casualties at military training centers. Arch. Ind. Hlth. 16(4), 302–305 (1957)
4. Design Factory Inc. Thermal Stress Indicator Series, http://www.necchu-sho.com/en/index.html
5. Fujinami, K., Kouchi, S., Xue, Y.: Design and Implementation of an On-body Placement-Aware Smartphone. In: The 32nd International Conference on Distributed Computing Systems Workshops (ICDCSW), pp. 69–74 (2012)

6. Gellersen, H., Schmidt, A., Beigl, M.: Multi-sensor context-awareness in mobile devices and smart artifacts. Journal on Mobile Networks and Applications (MONET), 341–351 (2002)
7. Design Factory Inc. Portable Environmental Information Measuring Device. Utility Model Register No. 3157604 (2010)
8. Lane, N.D., et al.: A survey of mobile phone sensing. IEEE Communications Magazine 48(9), 140–150 (2010)
9. Okumura, F.: et al. A study on biometric authentication based on arm sweep action with acceleration sensor. In: Proc. of International Symposium on Intelligent Signal Processing and Communications (ISPACS 2006), pp. 219–222 (2006)
10. SATO KEIRYOKI MFG. CO., LTD. WBGT heat stress monitor model SK-150GT, https://www.sksato.co.jp/modules/shop/product_info.php?products_id=862&language=english
11. Sensirion AG, Digital humidity and temperature sensor SHT-71, http://www.sensirion.com/en/products/humidity-temperature/humidity-sensor-sht71/
12. SysCom Co., Ltd. Mini temperature and humidity logger SHTDL-1/2 (2012), http://syscom-corp.jp/doc/product/sensor/hyg_mini-logger.html
13. Cui, Y., Chipchase, J., Ichikawa, F.: A cross culture study on phone carrying and physical personalization. In: Proc. of HCI International, pp. 483–492 (2007)

The Influence of Graphics Effects on Perceiving Depth in Minimized Virtual Environments

Tristan Hartzell, Mark Thompson, and Beomjin Kim

Department of Computer Science
Indiana University-Purdue University
Fort Wayne, IN, U.S.A.
{hartt01,thomma03,kimb}@ipfw.edu

Abstract. Enhancing depth perception accuracy in virtual environments is important and an active ongoing area of study. This research examines the impact of a variety of depth cues on depth perception accuracy in minimized virtual environments. For this study, we developed an application that applies various graphics techniques selectively onto 3D terrain maps. An experimental study was conducted using a one-wall 3D projection system to measure the impact of depth cues and graphical effects on depth perception accuracy. The experimental results showed a tendency of depth overestimation in minimized virtual environments. It also suggests research directions for investigating the influence of depth cues objectively on virtual spaces.

Keywords: Virtual environment, Depth perception, Stereoscopic image.

1 Introduction

The advancement of display technology makes it possible to present users with superior quality images. Higher screen resolution, larger screen size, and faster refresh rate enhance not only the image quality but the amount of information to be rendered on the screen. 3D stereoscopic devices have become increasingly prevalent in the consumer market and benefit users in various ways. They have been utilized in a variety of areas such as simulation, training, entertainment, education, physical sciences, geography, and medicine [1, 2, 3, 4].

Human beings perceive depth by obtaining a different view of the world from each eye and reconstructing a 3D view from it [5]. Stereoscopic 3D devices display two different viewpoints in a similar manner. By seeing two different images from two different perspectives, the user is able to perceive the depth of a rendered environment. Stereoscopic 3D images provide a binocular view point that gives additional depth information not available with monocular viewpoints.

3D stereoscopic environments provide depth perception advantages, but there are known limitations that prevent users from accurately perceiving depth. The lack of natural depth cues and differences between the user's actual convergence in reality and the viewer's convergence on the screen can make depth perception difficult [6]. Researchers have studied methods for enhancing depth perception and reducing visual

T.-h. Kim et al. (Eds.): FGCN/DCA 2012, CCIS 350, pp. 235–242, 2012.

fatigue when using 3D vision technology [7]. Previous experimental studies have produced mixed results, showing a general trend of underestimation in depth perception in 3D environments [1, 8, 9, 10].

The main goal of the research presented in this paper is to examine graphics effects that affect human depth perception accuracy in 3D computer generated stereoscopic environments. We focused upon studying depth perception accuracy in large geographical environments. By systematically studying the role of various depth cues affecting depth perception in minimized 3D virtual environments, this study may provide new insight for improving the depth perception accuracy in virtual reality environments.

2   Method

2.1   Overall Environment

We implemented a stereoscopic viewing system named 3D Stereoscopic Viewer (3DSV). We chose virtual environments that are too large to be displayed on 3D display devices at their original scale. Two different virtual environments were generated, one for the experimental study and one for training before the experiment. We implemented virtual spaces consisting of marker spheres, a reference scale, and a terrain. Marker locations were selected pseudo-randomly. Markers are separated primarily along the axis directed into the screen from the user. Small quantities of distance along the horizontal and vertical axis were incorporated to avoid markers from occluding each other.

The 3DSV system presents terrain models generated from real geological data, including height maps and orthographic aerial pictures. We used the open source 3D graphics software, Blender, to generate the terrain models from the height map and orthographic data [11]. For the training before the experiment, we used a height map and orthographic image of a portion of Fort Wayne that was 4000 feet long and 4000 feet wide. Both images were collected from the Indiana Spatial Data Portal web site [12]. For the experimental test, we utilized terrain data from an area around Denver Colorado. Height and orthographic data for this terrain was retrieved from the USGS National Elevation Dataset and spans an area of 85.25 km by 111.3 km [13]. Unlike the Fort Wayne terrain which has a relatively flat elevation, the data used for the experimental test has a large variation in height that may be more effective in a stereoscopic virtual environment. The aerial image used for the experimental test does not include man made depth cues such as roads and buildings.

A ruler is provided in the scene that establishes the relationship between the scale of the environment and the units of distance to be reported by participants. The ruler is a 3D rectangle that starts from the projection screen and extends beyond the end of the terrain. Figure 1 is a photo of the experimental environment which shows the 3D projection screen rendering one of the images generated by 3DSV system. As shown on the left side of figure 1, the 3D rectangle looks like a traditional ruler showing major and minor ticks on the sides of the 3D rectangles to assist viewers in estimating distances.

Fig. 1. Photo of the 3DSV system rendered on a 3D projection screen showing terrain, markers, reference scale, and gridlines

We utilized an open source cross-platform 3D graphic toolkit called OpenSceneGraph (OSG) for constructing a 3D virtual environment [14]. It provides an object-oriented framework founded on OpenGL that assists software developers to rapidly implement high performance graphics applications.

For the stereoscopic image generation, a pair of images is generated via the asymmetric frustum method. By adjusting projection frustums, this method aligns the viewing plane of each eye to the same location. This approach does not inherently introduce vertical parallax which is a problem in the Toe-in method [5].

2.2   Employed Graphics Techniques

The 3DSV system tested several well-known depth cues to understand their influence upon perceiving depth in virtual environments [7]. Depth cues were applied on an individual basis testing four different categories of depth cues including shading, shadows, magnification, backgrounds and linear perspective.

2.2.1   Typical Scene

The typical scene is the baseline standard for comparing the impacts of adding or removing factors that likely impact depth perception. In the typical scene, lighting is only used for illuminating the distance markers. The markers are illuminated with directional and directionless light components. The 3DSV system did not apply shading to the terrain because it already included lighting components when the orthographic images were generated. The light source that illuminated the markers is located above and behind the camera position. The background is black and other graphics effects are disabled. All scenes other than the magnified scene use the same scale of terrain, ruler, and markers as the typical scene.

2.2.2   Shading and Shadows

In order to understand the correlation between the light related effects and the depth perception, we tested the impacts of shadows and shading. The 3DSV system disabled the directional light components for a set of scenes, making the markers appear flat. This allows us to compare the typical scene to one without diffuse or specular lighting components. The 3DSV also tested a set of scenes where shadows were rendered. The shadows were generated based upon marker locations relative to the light source and terrain. We can compare the scene with shadows to the typical scene for determining the impacts of adding shadows.

2.2.3   Magnification

To understand the influence of magnification of the environment in perceiving depth, the scene was enlarged from the typical scene while the camera frustum remained the same. The magnification of the scene amplifies the details of the environment, such as elevation changes in the terrain. The markers and the ruler were scaled along with the terrain. The eye separation was adjusted to minimize discomfort when viewing the stereoscopic environment.

2.2.4   Background Changes

Three different variations are used to evaluate the impact of background changes in judging the depth including a shade of orange similar to the terrain color, a shade of blue that contrasts with the terrain color, and a textured background that has semi-randomly generated patterns with blue and black components. Unlike the other scenes, the test markers are raised above the ground high enough to be in front of the background so that we can measure the role of background in depth perception more objectively.

2.2.5   Linear Perspective – Gridlines

We tested two different variations of gridlines in the minimized virtual environment. Gridlines were constructed on a plane parallel to the terrain and positioned empirically above the majority of the terrain (see figure 1). The markers were located in close proximity to the gridlines so that the viewer could effectively utilize the gridlines in estimating the distance between the markers.

Two types of gridlines were tested. The first grid pattern is a series of squares on the XZ plane, where each side of every square is five units long relative to the reference scale. In the other variation of gridlines, the angle of the gridlines was changed pointing into the screen so they converged at a distant point away from the user. This grid pattern forces the gridlines to converge before the vanishing point.

3   Experimental Study

3.1   Experimental Procedure and Environment

We conducted experimental tests evaluating how different depth cues affect viewers' depth perception in a minimized virtual space. A total of fifteen Computer Science majors or graduates volunteered for this test. The experiment consisted of depth perception measurement training and tests, and a post-experimental survey.

The experimental test was conducted using a one-wall 3D projection system. The projection system has a screen size of 13.3 feet wide by 7.5 feet tall. Two high definition projectors having a 1920 x 1080 resolution generate two circular polarized images on the rear-projection screen. Each projector displays the image for one of the user's eyes. The users wore passive polarized 3D glasses so they could properly view the scene displayed on the projection system.

Participants sat down in a chair about 6 feet away from the projection screen and centered facing towards the screen. They were asked to verbally estimate the distance of two markers without significant body and head movement. The experimental test started with a training session. The training session consisted of two different scenes with three variations each, showing two markers at pseudo-random locations with a reference scale. Test subjects were asked to judge the distance between the two markers. After participants estimated the distance, we informed them of the actual distance. By informing the user of the actual distance, we expect that the participants should be accustomed to measuring distance in a virtual space before participating in the actual experiment. Participants were allowed to reexamine the training scenes until they were comfortable with measuring distances in the virtual space. Only one participant was tested at a time.

Once participants were familiar with the virtual space, the actual experiment was conducted with a different terrain model. There were 9 different depth cues with three variations tested – typical, shading, shadow, normal grid, altered grid, magnification, and three different backgrounds. Each variation differed only by placement of markers and terrain rotation. Participants estimated the distance between the two markers while utilizing the reference scale with or without other graphics effects. During the experimental tests we did not provide any feedback regarding the accuracy of the provided measurements. Participants were allowed as much time as desired to estimate the distance between the two markers. The elapsed time for individual test subjects varied between 7 to 24 minutes excluding training. After completing experimental tests, participants were asked to provide verbal responses regarding slides comparing monoscopic and stereoscopic views of the same scene. After this, the students were asked to fill out a post-experimental survey.

3.2   Experimental Result

Table 1 presents a summary of the experimental results. It represents a weighted average of the difference between the test subject's response and the actual answer. This weighted average of the difference (W_i) is calculated by $W_i = \Sigma_{j=1..n} ((S_{ij} - A_i) / A_i) / n$

where A_i is the actual answer for measurement item i, S_{ij} is the participant jth answer for measurement item i, n is the total number of participants. A negative W_i corresponds to underestimation and a positive W_i corresponds to overestimation. Table 1 shows the weighted average of the difference and associated standard deviation for all of the measured items. The typical scene was used as a baseline standard for comparison with all of the techniques. The following discussion section describes our post experimental analysis about the possible reasons for producing this kind of result.

Table 1. Experiment results in judging the depth of objects in a minimized virtual environment

Measurement Items	Average Percent Error (Mean $\pm$ SD) %
Typical scene	5.3 ± 17.4
Magnified	-2.3 ± 16.8
Shading off	5.0 ± 10.6
Shadows	5.7 ± 17.5
Normal gridlines	11.0 ± 14.0
Altered gridlines	18.4 ± 26.7
Blue background	6.4 ± 29.0
Orange background	7.7 ± 26.4
Textured background	9.6 ± 26.5

4   Discussion and Future Work

This research was conducted to explore depth perception in an application domain consisting of terrain maps such as a disaster response and a command and control system. The overall results showed that participants slightly overestimated depth when judging depth in the minimized virtual environment. No significant improvement in depth perception accuracy was observed after applying graphics techniques.

As shown in table 1, participants showed good performance when estimating depth in the typical scene. Through the post experimental analysis, it was found that the terrain constructed from geological data included a couple of significant depth cues that assisted participants in judging depth. Natural scenery and prebaked illumination in the terrain map contributed to depth judgment. This result suggests the significance of carefully selecting terrain images that contain implicit depth cues.

Among the graphics techniques evaluated, normal gridlines showed the best performance. Although the typical scene outperformed the normal gridlines with respect to average, the normal gridlines had a better confidence interval than the typical scene. Between the two gridline scenes, the normal gridlines performed almost twice as well as altered gridlines with respect to the average and the confidence interval. Adding shadows to the scene had no significant impact and was comparable to results for the typical scene. When shading was turned off, the test results demonstrated an improved confidence interval compared to the typical scene.

Test subjects demonstrated relatively good performance when measuring distance in the magnified scene. It was the only result showing slight underestimation, which needs further investigation. This trend might occur with other magnified environments. None of the background scenes outperformed the typical scene with respect to average and confidence interval. One possible reason background scenes performed poorly is that markers were positioned higher in the background scenes compared to all the other scenes, including the typical scene.

This study offers several suggestions for improving depth perception accuracy. In our study, some portions of the gridlines were occluded by the terrain. Instead of drawing the gridlines on a 2D plane as was done in this experiment, the gridlines will be enhanced by draping them on the terrain map. It is anticipated this will have a positive effect on gridline usage for depth perception.

Although this study presents important results, two future improvements are planned. Future experiments will use terrain maps that have minimal natural depth cues. This will allow for a more objective evaluation of the impact of graphics effects in a minimized virtual environment. The second improvement will be to increase the total number of participants in an effort to reach more conclusive results.

The exploration of depth perception issues in a magnified environment is expected to be applicable to medical images and areas using microscopic data. Future studies will investigate the tendency of depth perception in two opposite application domains, magnified and minimized, along with the impact of graphics effects. These studies will be valuable endeavors for enhancing the understanding of depth perception issues. Finally, exploring other graphics techniques such as convergence, binocular disparity, and manipulating viewing direction on depth perception is scheduled to be explored in the follow-up study.

5   Conclusion

This paper introduced a study regarding the influence of various depth cues upon depth perception accuracy and precision in 3D virtual environments with minimized scenes. The study compared the impacts of several depth cues when applied individually. The experimental results suggested that, in a minimized virtual space, participants showed a trend of overestimating the depth in all experimental measures except the enlarged environment. This research reiterates the significance of depth cues incorporated into terrain maps in perceiving depth that was used to create virtual landscapes. Conflicting depth cues displayed inconsistently on terrain maps and computer generated objects negatively impacted estimations in depth. Lessons acquired from this study have assisted us in designing a larger scale study for investigating the usage of computer graphics techniques for assisting the estimation of depth in virtually simulated environments.

References

1. Grechkin, T.Y., Nguyen, T.D., Plumert, J.M., Cremer, J.F., Kearney, J.K.: How Does Presentation Method and Measurement Protocol Affect Distance Estimation in Real and Virtual Environments? ACM Transactions on Applied Perception 7(4), article no. 26 (2010)

2. Yang, M., McMullen, D.P., Schwartz-Bloom, R.D., Brady, R.: Dive into alcohol: A biochemical immersive experience. In: IEEE Virtual Reality Conference, pp. 281–282 (2009)
3. Chittaro, L., Ranon, R., Ieronutti, L.: Vu-flow: A visualization tool for analyzing navigation in virtual environments. IEEE Transactions on Visualization and Computer Graphics 12(6), 1475–1485 (2006)
4. Schwartz, R.J., Fleming, G.A.: Real-time aerodynamic flow and data visualization in an interactive virtual environment. In: IEEE Instrumentation and Measurement Technology Conference, vol. 3, pp. 2210–2215 (2005)
5. Zelle, Z.M., Figura, C.: Simple, low-cost stereographics: VR for everyone. In: The 35th SIGSE Technical Symposium on Computer Science Education, pp. 348–352 (2004)
6. Elmqvist, N., Philippas, T.: A Taxonomy of 3D Occlusion Management for Visualization. IEEE Transactions on Visualization and Computer Graphics 14(5), 1095–1109 (2008)
7. Cipiloglu, Z., Bulbul, A., Capin, T.: A framework for enhancing depth perception in computer graphics. In: The 7th Symposium on Applied Perception in Graphics and Visualization, pp. 141–148 (2010)
8. Jones, J.A., Swan II, J.E., Singh, G., Kolstad, E., Ellis, S.R.: The Effects of Virtual Reality, Augmented Reality, and Motion Parallax on Egocentric Depth Perception. In: The 5th Symposium on Applied Perception in Graphics and Visualization, pp. 9–14 (2008)
9. Wartell, Z., Hodges, L.F., Ribarsky, W.: A Geometric Comparison of Algorithms for Fusion Control in Stereoscopic HTDs. IEEE Transactions on Visualization and Computer Graphics 8(2), 129–143 (2002)
10. Livingston, M.A., Zhuming, A., Swan, J.E., Smallman, H.S.: Indoor vs. Outdoor Depth Perception of Mobile Augmented Reality. In: IEEE Virtual Reality Conference, pp. 55–62 (2009)
11. Blender Home Page, http://www.blender.org
12. Indiana Spatial Data Portal, http://gis.iu.edu/datasetInfo/statewide/05nc.php
13. US Geological Survey, http://ned.usgs.gov
14. OpenSceneGraph, http://www.openscenegraph.org/projects/osg

A Token-Based Group Mutual Exclusion Algorithm for MANETs

Ousmane Thiare

University Gaston Berger
Department of Computer Science
UFR S.A.T
BP. 234 Saint-Louis Senegal
ousmane.thiare@ugb.edu.sn

Abstract. A mobile ad hoc network can be defined as a network that is spontaneously deployed and is independent of any static network. The network consist of mobile nodes[1] with wireless interfaces and has an arbitrary dynamic topology. The networks suffers from frequent link formation and disruption due to the mobility of the nodes. In this paper we present a token based algorithm for Group Mutual Exclusion in ad hoc mobile networks. The proposed algorithm is adapted from the RL algorithm in [1]. We utilizes also the concept used in [6] to detect that all the nodes concurrently accessing the same resource have terminated their tasks (*concurrent entering*). The algorithm ensures the mutual exclusion, the bounded delay, and the concurrent entering properties.

Keywords: Critical Section, Mutual Exclusion, Group Mutual Exclusion, Ad Hoc Networks.

1 Introduction

A mobile ad hoc network can be defined as a network that is spontaneously deployed and is independent of any static network. The network consist of mobile nodes with wireless interfaces and has an arbitrary dynamic topology. The mobile nodes can communicate with only nodes in their transmission range and each one of them acts as router in routing data through the network. The networks is characterized by frequent link formation and disruption due ton the mobility of the nodes and hence any assumption about the topology of the networks does not necessary hold.

Wireless links failure occur when nodes move so that they are no longer within transmission range of each other. Likewise, wireless link formation occurs when nodes move so that they are again within transmission range of each other. In [1], an algorithm is proposed to solve the mutual exclusion problem for mobile ad hoc networks. The mutual exclusion problem is concerned with how to control nodes to enter the critical section to access a shared resource in a mutually

---

[1] The terms processes and nodes will be used interchangeably throughout the paper.

T.-h. Kim et al. (Eds.): FGCN/DCA 2012, CCIS 350, pp. 243–250, 2012.

exclusive way. The group mutual exclusion (GME) is a generalization of the mutual exclusion problem. In the GME problem, multiple resources are shared among nodes. Nodes requested to access the same shared resource may do so concurrently. However, if nodes compete to access different resources, only one of them can proceed.

In addition to the paper [1], there are papers proposed to solve mutual exclusion related problems for ad hoc networks. The paper [2] is proposed for solving the k-mutual exclusion problem, [4], for the leader election problem. There are several papers proposed to solve the GME problem for different system models. The papers [7][3][11] are designed for distributed message passing models, the paper [10], for self-stabilizing models. In this paper, we adapt the solution of [1] to solve the GME problem for mobile ad hoc networks. We utilizes also the concept used in [6] to detect that all the nodes concurrently accessing the same resource have terminated their tasks (*concurrent entering*).

The next section discusses the scenario of the algorithm. Section 3 presents our algorithm. We prove the algorithm correctness in section 4. Conclusion and future work are offered in section 5.

2   Scenario of the Algorithm

Now we present the scenario for the GME problem. Consider an ad hoc networks consisting of n nodes and m shared resources. Nodes are assumed to cycle through a non-critical section (*NCS*), an waiting section (*Trying*), and a critical section (*CS*). A node i can access the shared resource only within the critical section. Every time when a node i wishes to access a shared resource S_i, node i moves from its *NCS* to the *Trying*, waiting for entering the *CS*. The GME problem [8] is concerned with how to design an algorithm satisfying the following property:

- **Mutual Exclusion:** If two distinct nodes, say i and j, are in the CS simultaneously, then $S_i = S_j$.
- **Bounded Delay:** If a node enter the Trying protocol, then it eventually enters the CS.
- **Concurrent Entering:** If there are some nodes requesting to access the same resource while no node is accessing a different resource, then all the requesting nodes can enter *CS* concurrently.

Note that this property is a trivial consequence of *Bounded Delay*, unless runs with nonterminating *CS* executions are admissible.

For now let us focus on executions where all request are for the same node. Joung's informal statement of *concurrent entering* was that (in such executions) nodes should be able not only to concurrently occupy the *CS* but to concurrently enter it without "unnecessary synchronization". This means that (in such executions) nodes should not delay one another as they are *trying* to enter the *CS*. Concurrent occupancy ensures that a node i *trying* to enter the *CS* is not delayed by other nodes that have already entered the *CS*. It does not, however, prevent i from being delayed (for arbitrary long) by other nodes that are simultaneously *trying* to enter the CS.

3   Proposed Algorithm

A DAG is maintained on the physical wireless links of the network throughout algorithm execution as the result of a three-tuple, or triple, of integer representing the height of the node, as in [9]. Links are considered to be directed from nodes with higher height toward nodes with lower height, based on lexicographic ordering of the three tuple. A link between two nodes is *outgoing* at the higher height node and *incoming* at the lower height node. A total ordering on the height of nodes in the network is ensured because the last integer in the triple is the unique identifier of the node. For example, if the height at node 1 is $(2, 3, 1)$ and the height at node 2 is $(2, 2, 2)$, then the link between these nodes would be directed from node 1 to node 2. Initially at node 0, height is $(0, 0, 0)$ and, for all $i \neq 0$, i's height is initialized so that the directed links form a DAG in which every non token holder has a directed path to some token holder and every token holder. The lowest node is always the current token holder, making it a sink toward which all request are sent. In this section, we propose a distributed algorithm to solve the GME problem for ad hoc mobile networks.

In this algorithm, we assume that all the nodes concurrently accessing the same resource terminate their tasks. The algorithm is assumed to execute in a system consisting of n nodes and m shared resources. Nodes are labeled as $0, 1, \cdots, n - 1$, and resources are labeled as $0, 1, \cdots, m - 1$. We assume there is a unique token held by node 0 initially. The variable used in the algorithm for node i are listed below.

- *status:* indicates whether node is the *Trying, CS,* or *NCS* section. Initially, *status*=*NCS*.
- *N:* the set of all nodes in direct wireless contact with node i. Initially, N contains all of node i's neighbors.
- *Num:* counts the number of nodes within the critical section.
- *height:* a three-tuple (h_1, h_2, i) representing the height of node i. Links are considered to be directed from nodes with higher height toward nodes with lower height, based on lexicographic ordering. Initially at node 0, $height_0$=(0,0,0) and, for all $i \neq 0$, $height_i$ is initialized so that the directed links from a DAG where each node has a directed path to node 0.
- *Vect:* an array of tuples representing node i's view of *height* of node i, $i \in N$. Initially, $Vect[i]$=*height* of node i. From i's viewpoint, the link between i and j is *incoming* to node i if $Vect[j] > height_i$, and *outgoing* from node i if $Vect[j] < height_i$.
- *Leader:* a flag set to true if node holds the token and set to false otherwise. Initially, *Leader*=true if i=0, and *Leader*=false otherwise.
- *next:* indicates the location of the token from node i's viewpoint. When node i holds the token, *next*=i, otherwise *next* is the node on an *outgoing* link. Initially, *next*=0 if i=0, and *next* is an *outgoing* neighbor otherwise.
- *Q:* a queue which contains request of neighbors. Operations on Q include *Enqueue()*, which enqueues an item only if it is not already on Q, *Dequeue()* with the usual FIFO semantics, and *Delete()*, which removes a specified item from Q, regardless of its location. Initially, $Q = \emptyset$.

• *receivedLI:* boolean array indicating whether the height carrying message *Link-Info* has been received from node j, to which a *Token* message was recently sent. Any height information received at node i from node j for which *receivedLI*[j] is false will not be recorded in *Vect*[j]. Initially, *receivedLI*[j]=true for all $j \in N$.

• *forming*[j]: boolean array set to true when link to node j has been detected as forming and reset to false when first *LinkInfo* message arrives from node j. Initially, *forming*[j]=false for all $j \in N$.

• *formHeight*[j]: an array storing the value of height of node j, $j \in N$, when new link to j is first detected. Initially, *formHeight*[j]=*height* for all $j \in N$.

The messages used in the algorithm are:

• *Request*(): when a node i wishes to enter the *CS* to access the resource S, it sends out *Request*() to the neighbor node indicated by *next*.

• *Okay*(): a message to inform nodes to access the resource S concurrently. There may be several *Okays* in the system simultaneously.

• *Token*(): a message for node to enter the *CS*. The node with Token is called the *Leader*.

• *Rel*(): a message for node i to release the resource S_i, it sends out *Rel*() to one of the neighbor node.

• *LinkInfo*(): a message used for nodes to exchange their height values with neighbors.

Pseudocode of the Algorithm

When node i requests access to the *CS*:
1. *status*← *Trying*
2. *Enqueue*(*Q*,i)
3. If (not *Leader*) then
4.   If ($|Q| = 1$) then *SendRequest*()
5. Else *SendTokenToNext*()

When node i release the *CS*:
1. *status*← NCS
2. If (not *Leader*) then
3.   *SendRel*()
4. Else
5.   If ($|Q| > 0$) then *SendTokenToNext* ()

When *Request*(h) received at node i from node j:
// h denotes j's height when message was sent
1. If (*ReceivedLI*[j]) then
2.   *Vect*[j]← h
3.   If (*height* < *Vect*[j]) then *Enqueue*(*Q*,j)
4.   If (*Leader*) then
5.   If ((*status* = *NCS*) ∧ ($|Q| > 0$)) then
6.   *SendTokenToNext*()

7.   Else
8.   If $(height < Vect[k], \forall k \in N)$ then
9.   RaiseHeight()
10.   Else If $((Q = [j] \vee ((|Q| > 0) \wedge (height < Vect[next])))$
11.   SendRequest()

When $Rel()$ received at node i from node j:
1. If $(Leader)$ then
2.   If $(status = NCS)$ then
3.   SendTokenToNext()
4. Else
5. SendRel()

When $Token(h)$ received at node i from node j:
1. $Leader \leftarrow$ true
2. $Vect[j] \leftarrow h$
3. $height.h_1 \leftarrow h.h_1$
4. $height.h_2 \leftarrow h.h_2 - 1$
5. Send $LinkInfo(h.h_1, h.h_2, i)$ to all $k \in N$
6. If $(|Q| > 0)$ then $SendTokenToNext()$

When $Okay()$ received at node i from node j:
1. Send $Okay(S_j)$ to all $v \in Q$
2. If $((i \in Q) \wedge (Resource = S_j))$ then
3. $Num \leftarrow Num + 1$
4. $status \leftarrow CS$
5. Else If $((Q = [i]) \wedge (Resource \neq S_j))$ then
6. $Resource \leftarrow S_j$
7. $Num \leftarrow 1$
8.   SendRel()
//Resource records the current resource identifier

When $LinkInfo(h)$ received at node i from node j:
1. $N \leftarrow N \cup \{j\}$
2. If $((forming[j]) \wedge (height \neq formHeight[j]))$ then
3.   Send $LinkInfo(height)$ to j
4. $forming[j] \leftarrow$ false
5. If $receivedLI[j]$ then $Vect[j] \leftarrow h$
6. Else If $(Vect[j] = h)$ then $receivedLI[j] = true$
7. If $((j \in Q)$ and $(height > Vect[j]))$ $Delete(Q,j)$
8. If $(Leader)$ then
9. If $((height < Vect[k], \forall k \in N) \wedge$ (not $Leader$)) then
10.   RaiseHeight()
11. Else If $((|Q| > 0) \wedge (height < Vect[next]))$ then
12.   SendRequest()

When failure of link to j detected at node i:
1. $N \leftarrow N - \{j\}$
2. $receivedLI[j] \leftarrow$ true
2. If $(j \in Q)$ $Delete(Q,j)$ then
4. If (not $Leader$) then
5.   If $(height < Vect[j], \forall k \in N)$ then
6. $RaiseHeight()$
7.   Else If $(((|Q| > 0) \wedge (next \notin N))$ then
8. $SendRequest()$

When formation of link to j detected at node i:
1. Send $LinkInfo(height)$ to j
2. $forming[j] \leftarrow$ true
3. $formHeight[j] \leftarrow height$

Procedure $SendRequest()$:
1. $next \leftarrow l \in N : Vect[l] \leq Vect[j] \; \forall j \in N$
2. Send $Request(height)$ to $next$

Procedure $SendTokenToNext()$:
1. $next \leftarrow Dequeue(Q)$
2. If $(next \neq i)$ then
3. $Leader \leftarrow$ false
4. $Vect[next] \leftarrow (height.h_1, height.h_2 - 1, next)$
5. $receivedLI[next] \leftarrow$ false
6.   Send $Token(height)$ to $next$
7.   If $(|Q| > 0)$ then Send $Request(height)$ to $next$
8. Else
9. $status \rightarrow CS$
10. Send $|Q|$ $Okays$ to all $v \in N \cap Q$

Procedure $RaiseHeight()$:
1. $height.h_1 \leftarrow 1 + \min_{k \in N}\{Vect[k].h_1\}$
2. $S \leftarrow \{l \in N : Vect[l].h_1 = height.h_1\}$
3. If $(S \neq \emptyset)$ then $height.h_2 \leftarrow \min_{l \in S}\{Vect[l].h_2\} - 1$
4. Send $linkInfo(height)$ to all $k \in N$
5. For all $k \in N$ such that $height > Vect[k])$ do $Delete(Q,k)$
6. If $(|Q| > 0)$ then $SendRequest()$

Procedure $SendRel()$:
1. If (not $Leader$) then
2.   If $(height < Vect[k], \forall k \in N)$
3. $RaiseHeight()$
4. $next \leftarrow l \in N : Vect[l] \leq Vect[j] \; \forall j \in N$
5. Send $Rel()$ to $next$

4   Proof of the Algorithm

In this section we prove that the algorithm satisfies the three properties: mutual exclusion, the bounded delay, and the concurrent entering.

Theorem 4.1. *The algorithm ensures mutual exclusion.*

Proof 4.1. *A node holding the token can enter the CS and then it informs all its requesting neighbors by sending out Okays messages. When a neighbor node receives the message Okay information, it can enter the CS only if it requests for the same resource as the token holder. Because there is only a unique token, all nodes in the CS must access the same resource. Thus the property of mutual exclusion is satisfied.*

Theorem 4.2. *The algorithm ensures tthe property of concurrent entering.*

Proof 4.2. *A node holding the token can enter the CS and then it informs all its requesting neighbors by sending out Okays messages. When a neighbor node receives the message Okay information, it can enter the CS only if it requests for the same resource as the token holder. Then all nodes can access the same resource as the token holder is currently accessing. Thus, the property of concurrent entering is satisfied.*

Here, we prove that the algorithm satisfies the property of bounded delay by showing that if a node enter the Trying protocol, then it eventually enters the CS i.e., it holds the token. Since the height values of the nodes are totally ordered, the logical direction on links imparted by height values will eventually form a token oriented DAG. Before to prove the bounded delay property, we give the same lemma presented in [1].

Lemma 4.1 *Once link failures cease, the logical direction on links imparted by height values will eventually form a token oriented DAG.*

On the basis of Lemma 1, we prove that a requesting node holds token eventually.

Theorem 4.3. *If link changes cease, then every request is eventually satisfied.*

Proof 4.3. *If a token holder i is in the NCS, it sends the token to the node j whose request is at the head of the queue. Node i then removes j's request from the queue after sending the token. So, every node's request will eventually be at the head of the queue to have the opportunity to hold the token. By Lemma 1, every node's request has a path leading to the token holder. Thus, a requesting node holds the token eventually.*

5   Conclusion and Future Works

We presented a token-based algorithm to solve the group mutual exclusion for mobile ad hoc networks. The algorithm is adapted from the RL algorithm in [1] and utilizes a concept used in [6] to detect that all nodes concurrently accessing the same resource have terminated their tasks. Simulations and message complexity is left as a future task.

References

1. Walter, J., Welch, J., Vaidya, N.: A Mutual Exclusion Algorithm for Ad Hoc Mobile Networks. In: 1998 Dial M for Mobility Workshop, Dallas TX, 15 p. (1998)
2. Walter, J., Cao, G., Mohanty, M.: A k-Mutual Exclusion Algorithm for Ad Hoc Wireless Networks. In: Proceedings of the First Annual Workshop on Principle of Mobile Computing, POMC 2001 (August 2001)
3. Wu, K.-P., Joung, Y.-J.: Asynchronous group mutual exclusion in ring networks. In: 13th International Parallel Processing Symposium and 10th Symposium on Parallel and Distributed Processing (IPPS/SPDP 1999), pp. 539–543 (1999)
4. Malpani, N., Welch, J.L., Vaidya, N.H.: Leader Election Algorithms for Mobile Ad Hoc Networks. In: Proc. Fourth International Workshop on Discrete Algorithms and Methods for Mobile Computing and Communications (PODC 1999), pp. 96–103 (2000)
5. Tseng, Y.-C.: Detectint termination by Weight-Throwing in a Faulty Distributed System. Journal of Parallel and Distributed Computing 25, 7–15 (1995)
6. Keane, P., Moir, M.: A simple local-spin group mutual exclusion algorithm. In: 18th Annual ACM Symposium on Principles of Distributed Computing (PODC 1999), pp. 23–32. ACM Press (1999)
7. Joung, Y.-J.: The Congenial Talking Philosophers Problem in Computer Networks (Extended Abstract). In: Jayanti, P. (ed.) DISC 1999. LNCS, vol. 1693, pp. 195–211. Springer, Heidelberg (1999)
8. Joung, Y.-J.: Asynchronous group mutual exclusion (extended abstract). In: 17th Annual ACM Symposium on Principles of Distributed Computing (PODC), pp. 51–60 (1998)
9. Gafni, E., Bertsekas, D.: Distributed algorithms for generating loop-free in networks with frequently changing topology. IEEE Transactions on Communication C-29(1), 11–18 (1981)
10. Cantarell, S., Petit, F.: Self-Stabilizing Group Mutual Exclusion for Asynchronous Rings. In: 4th International Conference on Principles of Distributed Systems (OPODIS 2000), pp. 71–90 (2000)
11. Cantarell, S., Datta, A.K., Petit, F., Villain, V.: Token based group mutual exclusion for asynchronous rings. In: 21th International Conference on Distributed Computing Systems (ICDCS 2001), pp. 691–694 (2001)
12. Walter, J.E., Kini, S.: Mutual exclusion on multihop wireless networks, Texas A&M Univ., College Station, TX 77843-3112, TR97-014 (December 9, 1997)

Acoustical Analysis of Filled Pause
in Malay Spontaneous Speech

Raseeda Hamzah, Nursuriati Jamil,
and Noraini Seman

Faculty of Computer and Mathematical Sciences,
MARA University of Technology, Shah Alam, 40450 Selangor,
Malaysia
rashamzah82@gmail.com, {liza,aini}@tmsk.uitm.edu.my

Abstract. Filled pause is one of disfluencies types, identified as the often occurred disfluency in spontaneous speech, known to affect Automatic Speech Recognition accuracy. The purpose of this study is to analyze acoustical features of filled pauses in Malay language spontaneous speech as the preliminary step of filled pause detection. The acoustic features that are extracted from the filled pause are formant frequencies and pitch. Two automated segmentation methods which are Zero Crossing Rates and Gaussian Probability Density Function are compared in our study to acquire an exact representation of the filled pause. The results reveal that the pitch and formant frequencies have lower standard deviation when segmented using Gaussian Probability Density Function compared to Zero Crossing Rates. The analysis of Malay filled pause presented in this paper is important as it proved that filled pauses in any language have standard acoustic features such as flat pitch and stable formant frequencies.

Keywords: Malay Filled Pause, Pitch, Formant Frequency, Gaussian Probability Density Function, Zero Crossing Rates.

1   Introduction

Speech recognition is the process to convert a waveform of speech into text. One of the main problems of Automatic Speech Recognition (ASR) for spontaneous speech is the occurrence of disfluencies such as filled pause, repetition and sentence restart. They often interrupt the fluency of conversation and degrade the speech recognition performance. Based on previous researches, filled pause has never been ignored in disfluencies detection in order to improve ASR [1, 2, 3]. The existence of filled pauses in spontaneous speech has been studied from as early as 1992[1]. Filled pause is a verbal device that is usually used by speakers to prevent interruption from others while planning their utterance [4]. In the area of speech recognition, researchers found that filled pause is one of the factors that degrade ASR [2, 3, 5]. In language studies,

T.-h. Kim et al. (Eds.): FGCN/DCA 2012, CCIS 350, pp. 251–259, 2012.

filled pause is an indicator that shows speakers state of thinking [6] and greater rhetorical and emphatic qualities of the spoken utterances [7]. Filled pause is also being used to evaluate prosody and turn-taking in conversation [4].

Filled pause is uttered based on language. An English- standard filled pause is described as /uh/ and /um/ [1], while for other languages as found in Dutch /De/, /Die/ [8], Mandarin /e/, /en/ [2] and Portuguese /uum/, /aaa/, /eee/ [9]. Although filled pause is language dependent, it has the same acoustical features as proven in many researches [5, 6, 10, 11]. The general features that are being studied are pitch (fundamental frequencies), formant frequencies, spectral energy and adjacent silent. Formant frequency is described as vocal tract resonance [10]. As the filled pause is uttered to fill the gap while thinking of the next word, there is minimal articulation effect. The minimal articulations do not change during the filled pause that causes vocal tract resonance to become stable. A flat pitch during filled pause is defined as unvaried vocal cord stress under constant articulator [5]. In English and other languages, filled pause has been widely studied by the research communities [12, 13, 14]. However, for Malay Language, very few language studies are focus on filled pause [4]. Although the work done by [4] is not mainly focus on filled pause phenomena, they have shown that the low pitch of filled pause indicates a possible turn-taking in conversation. Adjacent silent is another feature that has always being studied to locate the filled pause [1, 2, 8]. In the study by [1], 80% of the filled pause is delimited by adjacent silent. Another method of detecting filled pause is by measuring its spectral energy [5, 6, 8]. The results of their analysis on filled pause showed that the spectral energy rises quickly at the start and remains stable in the middle, then falls gradually at the end of the filled pause. As this is only a preliminary study to investigate the Malay filled pause features, only pitch and formant frequencies features are selected. Earlier studies have also shown that pitch and formant frequencies are significant to indicate possible filled pause [2, 3, 5, 8, 9]. A filled pause generally has a stable formant frequency and flat pitch [8, 9] while a normal word has unstable formant frequency and non-flat pitch [5, 10].

The purpose of this study is to analyze and understand acoustical features of filled pauses in Malay language spontaneous speech as the preliminary step of filled pause detection. Filled pause has been constantly detected as normal words and this affect the accuracy of any ASR. In order to discriminate filled pauses from normal words, an accurate standard deviation and mean of formant frequency and pitch of filled pause need to be computed. Standard deviation and mean are used to evaluate the stableness of formant frequency and flatness of pitch in filled pause. A lower standard deviation and mean indicates a more stable formant frequency and flatter pitch of the filled pause. Prior to extracting the formant frequency and pitch, an accurate representation of the filled pause signal has to be acquired. To get the accurate representation of filled pause, a segmentation method needs to be applied. Segmentation of the actual utterance of the filled pause from the background noises is necessary to prevent increase in computation of the non-speech event in the utterance [15, 18]. Furthermore, segmentation can also reduce recognition error of speech and non-speech detection because of incorrect boundaries [15, 18]. In this study, two methods of segmentation are implemented which are Zero Crossing Rates (ZCR) and Gaussian Probability Density Function (GPDF). ZCR is chosen because it is a well-established method and widely used in speech segmentation either for isolated or spontaneous speech recognition [15, 16]. However, research found that GPDF method is simpler to be implemented [17].

1.1   Data Collection

In this experiment, Malaysia Parliamentary Hansard Document (MPHD) is used to get some understanding in language dependency of filled pause occurrence. MPHD that is used in this experiment consists of 9 hours Malay spoken speeches recordings from Malaysia Parliamentary debates which consist of video and text documents [18]. It comprises of 11 topics with 62 speakers including male and female. However, for the purpose of preliminary study the selection of three topics with 10 speakers are used. Thus, the data collection contains 120 filled pauses. The Malay filled pauses that are analyzed in this project are defined as /mhm/, /aaa/ and /eer. Based on the filled pause collection, there are 10 /mhm/, 40 /eer/ and 70 /aaa/.

1.2   Methodology and Implementation

One hundred twenty sentences are extracted from the audio MPHD and the filled pause from each sentence is manually segmented and is known as Manual Datasets (MDs). The segmented FPs are then pre-processed to ensure that the duration of each FP is at least 200ms as recommended by previous work of FP detection in other languages such as Mandarin [2], Dutch [8], and Portuguese [9]. A very short duration utterance can lead to poor frequency resolution and estimation error [21]. Upon close inspection of our MDs, there are 60 FPs having duration of less than 200ms. Therefore, zero-padding is applied to the FPs to modify the speech frame which is a common practice in speech processing work [22]. In the next stage, automated segmentation of all 120 FPs is applied as exact representation of the FPs is crucial before acoustical features are extracted. In this study, Zero Crossing Rates (ZCR) and Gaussian Probability Density Function (GPDF) are tested on each filled pause in MDs. The automated segmented filled pauses are then stored separately in ZCR_FPs and GPDF_FPs, respectively. Formant frequency and pitch features are further extracted from the two collections and evaluated by computing the standard deviation and mean. The summarized methods of this study are illustrated in Fig. 1.

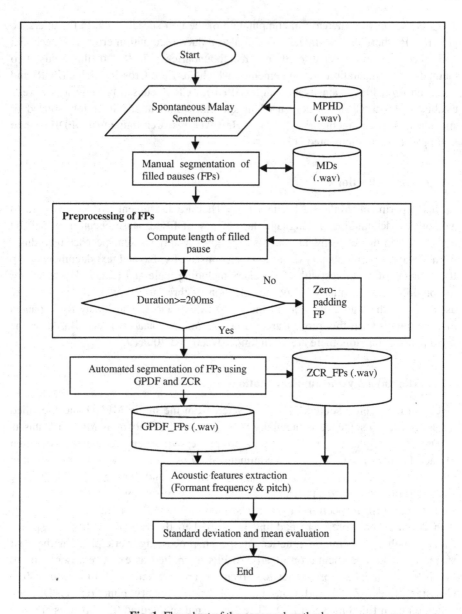

Fig. 1. Flowchart of the proposed methods

1.3 Zero Crossing Rates

Zero Crossing Rates is defined as the mean number of times the sound sequence changes its sign per frame. This method is used to count the frequent of the signal that crosses over the zero axes. It is a useful method to remove the silence part of sound and unvoiced sound [16]. ZCR has been widely used in speech processing for segmentation as can been reviewed in [16]. It was originally developed by Rabiner and Sambur [23]. One of the reasons of its popularity is because the robustness against high energy noises in voice activity detection scenario [24]. ZCR is computed by Eq.1.

$$Zs = \frac{1}{N} \sum_{n=m-N+1}^{m} \left| \frac{\text{sgn}[s(n)] - \text{sgn}[s(n-1)]}{2} \right|$$ (1)

Where:-

$$\text{sgn}(s(n)) = \begin{cases} 1, s(n) \geq 0 \\ -1, s(n) < 0 \end{cases}$$

The detection of filled pause boundaries is important to remove the unvoiced speech and background noise. This is to ensure that the system will only process the voice and eliminated the unvoiced and noise. The unvoiced speech is produced due to excitation of the vocal tract by the noise-like source at a point of construction in the interior of the vocal tract and shows a high zero crossing count [16].

1.4   Gaussian Probability Density Function

The second segmentation method which is Gaussian Probability Density Function (GPDF) is also applied on each filled pause in GPDF_FPs to make comparison between ZCR. Previous study shows that GPDF is simpler and accurate compared to ZCR [17]. Gaussian or Normal PDF has been widely used since its introduction in 1976 [20]. This method in classifying data as unvoiced or voiced and silent has shown its reliability in their result of work [20]. GPDF is used in an assumption that the speech segment is assigned to a particular group based on a minimum distance rule. The minimum distance rules are gained under the assumption that the measured parameters are distributed according to the multidimensional Gaussian probability density function. For normal GPDF, it is defined as in Eq. 2.

$$p(x) = \frac{1}{\sqrt{2\pi\sigma}} e^{\frac{-1}{2}(\frac{x-\mu}{\sigma})^2} .$$ (2)

Central limit theorems stated that under various conditions, the distribution for the sum of independent random variable draws near to the normal distribution [17]. The normal probability density function can be viewed as a 'bell-shaped curve' with x is distributed normally with mean μ and σ^2 as in Fig. 2 by writing $p(x) \sim N(\mu\sigma^2)$ [17]. It is determined by the parameters of mean μ and the variance σ^2. The area below the probability density function to the left of a given value, x, is equal to the probability of the random variable represented on the x-axis being less than the given value x.

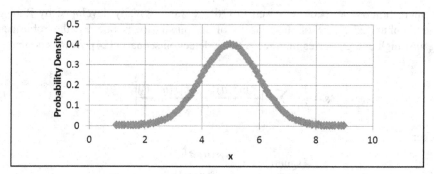

Fig. 2. One-dimensional normal distribution

Since the probability density function represents the entire sample space, the area under the probability density function must equal to one. Since negative probabilities are impossible, the probability density function, $p(x)$, must be positive for all values of x. The empirical rules of GPDF are stated as below:

Approximately 68% of the area under the curve is between μ-σ and μ+σ.

$$pr[|x - \mu|] \le \sigma \approx 0.68. \tag{3}$$

Approximately 95% of the area under the curve is between μ-2σ and μ+2σ.

$$pr[|x - \mu|] \le 2\sigma \approx 0.95. \tag{4}$$

Approximately 99.7% of the area under the curve is between μ-3σ and μ+3σ.

$$pr[|x - \mu|] \le 3\sigma \approx 0.997. \tag{5}$$

2   Evaluation

In order to evaluate the performance of both Gaussian Probability Density Function (GPDF) and Zero Crossing Rates (ZCR), standard deviation and mean of each pitch and formant frequency is computed as these two parameters are common evaluation method employed by previous researches [5,9,10]. As mentioned earlier, the pitch of filled pause is flat and the formant frequencies are stable through the utterance. The standard deviation σ shows the variation that exists from the mean μ of the overall data. A low standard deviation indicates that the data tend to be closer to mean, whereas high standard deviation shows that the data is spread out over large range of value. The standard deviation and mean is computed by using Eq. 6 and Eq. 7.

$$\sigma = \sqrt{\left(\frac{\sum_{i=1}^{n} ai^2}{n-1} - \frac{n}{n-1}\left(\frac{\sum_{i=1}^{n} ai}{n}\right)^2\right)}. \tag{6}$$

$$\mu = \frac{\sum_{i=1}^{n} ai}{n} .$$

(7)

Where:-

    ai =Sample

    N =Number of sample

2.1   Results and Discussion

Two acoustic features, namely pitch and fundamental frequency are extracted from the segmented filled pauses and evaluated using mean and standard deviation. The result shows that GPDF method performed better than ZCR. After applying GPDF on each filled pause, lower standard deviation of pitch is produced. This is comparable with the work done by Veiga [9] with average of 15Hz standard deviation. The lower standard deviation showed that low range of data that is being spread out, thus indicating flat pitch and stable formant frequency.

Each formant frequency corresponds to a resonance in the vocal tract. The formant frequency shows lower value for F1 and changes in F2, F3 and F4 which vary according to the place of the speech articulation. Different formant frequency will be produced while changing the shape and the length of the vocal tract [25]. Stable formant frequency as has been defined previously is unvaried vocal tract resonance produced whenever the speaker tries to fill the gap while thinking of the next word. It therefore causes minimal articulations effect that does not change during the filled pause i.e. stable. A research that is conducted by [10] showed that about 78.7 % of their overall filled pause produced an average of 40Hz formant frequency for the first two formant frequencies (F1 and F2). They compared the filled pause with normal words formant frequencies to show that the formant frequencies of filled pause are more stable than normal words. By comparison, only 19.5% of the normal word formant frequencies are below 40Hz. In this study, result shows that F2 and F4 are more stable with its lower standard deviation compared to F1 and F3. However, there is no standard value of the filled pause formant frequencies standard deviation in the literature. Another work done by [5], also computed the formant frequencies of the filled pause. In their work, the standard deviation of the filled pause formant frequencies is being compared in another voiced segment including normal words. The possible filled pause is detected whenever there is the lowest standard deviation of formant frequencies among the voiced segment. They have proven that the higher formant frequencies F2, F3 and F4 are more robust compared to F1 and F2 only. In our analysis on Malay language filled pause, it shows that F2 and F4 are more robust compared to F1 and F3. In the work done by Wu and Yan [11], each Mandarin filled pause (/ah/,/ung/, /um/, /em/, /hem/) is classified based on its pronunciation and the formant frequencies (F1 and F2) is computed accordingly.

In conclusion, this paper presents the analysis of Malay filled pause features which is pitch (fundamental frequency) and formant frequency. This analysis is important to develop an automatic filled pause detection method. It is shown that although the filled pause is based on different language it has standard features that are flat pitch and stable formant frequencies. It is also observed that an accurate segmentation of filled pause from the unvoiced speech and silence lead to better standard deviation of pitch and formant frequencies. In the future, we hope to implement more robust segmentation of filled pause using fuzzy hybridization method to improve the results of pitch and formant frequency standard deviation.

Table 1. Result of ZCR and GDPF

Methods	Mean of pitch STD
Manual Extraction	44.141Hz
Zero Crossing Rates	14.1340Hz
Gaussian Probability Density Function	12.1320Hz

Table 2. Result of ZCR and GDPF for formant frequencies

Methods	Mean of Formant Frequency4	Mean of Formant Frequency3	Mean of Formant Frequency2	Mean of Formant Frequency 1
Manual Extraction	113.1136Hz	256.9660Hz	337.2911Hz	181.3249Hz
Zero Crossing Rates	31.0741Hz	66.4791Hz	31.4903Hz	84.9441HZ
Gaussian Probability Density Function	27.5134Hz	65.2660Hz	29.3178Hz	84.6819HZ

References

1. O'Shaughnessy, D.: Recognition of hesitations in spontaneous speech. In: Proceedings of the International Conference on Acoustics, Speech, and Signal Processing, pp. 1521–1524. IEEE, New York (1992)
2. Yan-Xiong, L.: A Novel Detection Method of Filled Pause in Mandarin Spontaneous Speech. In: Seventh IEEE/ACIS International Conference of Computer and Information Science (2008)
3. Peters, J.: LM Studies on Filled Pauses in Spontaneous Medical Dictation. In: Proceedings of HLT-NAACL (2003)
4. Zuraidah, M.D., Knowles, G.: Prosody and Turn Taking in Malay Broadcast Interviews. Journal of Pragmatics 38, 490–512 (2006)
5. Kaushik, M.: Automatic detection and removal of disfluencies from spontaneous speech. In: Proc. 13th Australasian Int. Conf. on Speech Science and Technology Melbourne, pp. 98–101 (2010)
6. Garg, G., Ward, N.: Detecting Filled Pauses in Tutorial Dialogs. Report of University of Texas at El Paso, El Paso (2006)
7. O'Connel, D.C., Kowal, S.: Uh and Um Revisited: Are They Interjections for Signaling Delay? Journal of Psycholinguistic Research 34(6) (November 2005)
8. Stouten, F., Martens, J.P.: A Feature-Based Filled Pause Detection System For Dutch. In: IEEE Workshop on Automatic Speech Recognition and Understanding (2003)

9. Veig, A., Candeias, S., Carla, L., Fernando, P.: Characterization of Hesitations Using Acoustic Models. In: ICPhS XVII, Hong Kong (2011)

10. Audhkhasi, K.: Formant-Based Technique For Automatic Filled-Pause Detectio. In: Spontaneous Spoken English. In: IEEE International Conference on Acoustics, Speech and Signal Processing, ICASSP (2009)

11. Wu, C.H., Yan, G.L.: Acoustic Feature Analysis and Discriminative Modeling of Filled Pauses for Spontaneous Speech Recognition. The Journal of VLSI Signal Processing 36(2-3), 91–104 (2004)

12. Bell, A., Jurafsky, D., Fosler-Lussier, E., Girand, C., Gregory, M., Gildea, D.: Effects of Disfluencies, Predictability, and Utterance Position on Word Form Variation in English Conversation. J. Acoust. Soc. Am. 113(2), 1001–1024 (2003)

13. Lee, T.L., He, Y.F., Huang, Y.J., Tseng, S.C., Eklund, R.: Prolongation in Spontaneous Mandarin. In: Interspeech 2004, Jeju Island, Korea, pp. 2181–2184 (2004)

14. Shriberg, E., Stolcke, A.: Prosody Modeling for Automatic Speech Recognition and Understanding. In: Proc. Workshop on Mathematical Foundations of Natural Language Modeling (2002)

15. Ying, G.S., Mitchell, C.D., Jamieson, L.H.: Endpoint Detection of Isolated Utterances Based on A Modified Teager Energy Measurement. In: Proc. IEEE ICASSP 1992, pp. 732–735 (1992)

16. Seman, N., Bakar, N., Bakar, Z.A., Mohamed, H.M., Abdullah, H.,, N.A.: S Ramakrisnan, P. Ahmad: Evaluating Endpoint Detection Algorithms for Isolated Word from Malay Parliamentary Speech. In: 2010 International Conference on Information Retrieval & Knowledge Management, CAMP, March 17-18, pp. 291–296 (2010), doi:10.1109/INFRKM.2010.5466898

17. Saha, G., Chakroborty, I., Senapati, S.: A New Silence Removal And Endpoint Detection Algorithms For Speech And Speaker Recognition Applications. In: Proceedings of NCC, pp. 56–61 (2005)

18. Seman, N., Bakar, N., Bakar, Z.A.: An Evaluation of Endpoint Detection Measures for Malay Speech Recognition of an Isolated Words. In: 2010 International Symposium in Information Technology (ITSim), 15-17, vol. 3, pp. 1628–1635 (2010), doi:10.1109/ITSIM.2010.5561618

19. Sjölander, K., Beskow, J.: Wavesurfer - an Open Source Speech Tool. In: Proceedings of the 6th International Conference on Spoken Language Processing, Beijing, China, October 16-20, pp. 464–467 (2000)

20. Atal, B.S., Rabiner, L.R.: A Pattern Recognition Approach to Voiced—Unvoiced—Silence Classification with Applications to Speech Recognition. IEEE Transactions On Acoustic, Speech, and Signal Processing Assp-24(3) (1976)

21. Havelock, D., Kuwano, S., Vorlander, M.: Acoustic Signal and System. Handbook of Signal processing in Acoustic 1 (2008)

22. Arai, T.: Padding Zero Into Steady-State Portions of Speech as a Preprocess for Improving Intelligibility in Reverberant Environments. Acoustic Sci. & Tech. 26(5) (2005)

23. Rabiner, L.R., Sambur, M.R.: An Algorithm for Determining the Endpoints of Isolated Utterances. Bell Syst. Tech. J. 54, 297–315 (1975)

24. Ramírez, J., Górriz, J.M., Segura, J.C.: Robust Speech Recognition and Understanding, chapter Voice Activity Detection. In: Fundamentals and Speech Recognition System Robustness, pp. 1–22. Academic, New York (2007)

25. Hannu, T., Anna, M.M., Ville, M., Patrick, J.C., Paavo, A.: Disentangling The Effects of Phonation and Articulation: Hemispheric asymmetries in the auditory N1m response of the human brain. Biomed. Central (2005)

Strategically Managing Facility Management Knowledge Sharing via Web 2.0

Donald Henry Ah Pak[1] and Rita Yi Man Li[2]

[1] Xi'an Jiaotong-Liverpool University, 111 Ren'ai Road, Dushu Higher Education Town,
Suzhou, Jiangsu Province, China
donald.pak@xjtlu.edu.cn
[2] Rita Li Yi Man, Hong Kong Shue Yan University, Braemar Hill Road,
North Point, Hong Kong
ritarec1@yahoo.com.hk

Abstract. Transaction costs requires reductions and via knowledge practices and the Web 2.0. This can be significantly curtailed, the study looks at the literature and the success of the social network site, Facebook and draws conclusions thereof.

1 Introduction

Expenditures for facility and real estate represent the largest part of the operating expenses for a company after salary and wages. Any improvement of cost effectiveness in facility management results in a significant saving of total costs. The adoption of information and communication technologies has affected property management over the past years. Computer-aided facility management (CAFM) has provided an efficient information technology tools for the controlling, mapping and evaluation of facility management processes. Many software systems with various systematic functions and approaches have been established on the market. The usage of IT allows control over the enormous complexity of FM processes. Without IT support, the challenging goals of FM cannot be accomplished. Nowadays, IT does not only function as an integrating factor, but also a catalyst in facility management. IT effort becomes a crucial factor in realization of FM [1].

2 Terminology in IT-Aided Facility Management

Previous literature concludes that there is a considerable level of uncertainty in terminology used in IT-FM. Some of them related to IT or IT systems in FM are used synonymously. Other interpretations originate from computer support in early FM. CAFM includes the use of computer-assisted database, drawings and spreadsheets to manage large amount of facility information. Besides, the interpretation of different terminology varies in different parts of the World. For example, the term computerized maintenance management system (CMMS) is usually used for

T.-h. Kim et al. (Eds.): FGCN/DCA 2012, CCIS 350, pp. 260–264, 2012.
© Springer-Verlag Berlin Heidelberg 2012

computer systems that assist in planning, managing, and analyzing maintenance processes in some parts of Scandinavia and Australia. Gartner coined the term integrated workplace management system (IWMS) as an enterprise platform which supports the process of design, planning, and management of an organization's physical asset. And the term "IWMS" is widely used in European FM [1].

3   Facility Management Knowledge Resource

While the relevance of FM is becoming recognized by industry, business and government, FM knowledge is currently at a primitive stage of development. Latest FM knowledge human resource management and facility logistics, property and business, links management and design, business operations and services support together [2]. Its terrain has largely unexplored. There are three source of facility management knowledge: property, general management and facility design and management. The first two are relatively well-developed. And the third one which refers to the interface between facility management knowledge and facility design knowledge at the strategic level is undeveloped [2].

3.1   Strategic Facility Management

The key questions of strategic facility management include what management opportunities are required and the corresponding constraints? What management considerations have to inform the design process? How will facility design affect its management when it is in use? What opportunities and limitations will it impose? Relevant knowledge helps ensure that 1) the facility management objectives go in lie with organizational objectives, 2) facility provisions are aligned with end-user needs, 3) design concepts compatible with property strategy [2].

4   Knowledge Sharing by Web 2.0

The internet revolutionizes the concept of information. While finding information was a lengthy, convoluted process in ten years ago, individuals and computers produce thousands of gigabytes of information a minute nowadays. Furthermore, information is also networked collectively, further increases the amount of information. As information increases, the concept of knowledge also changes. Unlike Web 1.0, which relies on the website owner to provide information, Web 2.0 provides a way to many individuals to create information which consequently becomes knowledge. It is the place where digital information is made through discussion and participation. In other words, knowledge is accessible, decentralized and co-constructed among many different users [3]. The open and participatory nature of Web 2.0 provides a golden opportunity to collaborate, create empowering connections and community between people so that new knowledge can be created. Because there is no one single centralized power controlling the web, it allows us to use and reuse material creatively. Ever since the emergence of blog, the way we produce, store and use information has changed [3]. From this perspective, Web 2.0 is far more than a technology. Web 2.0 envelopes a gravitational core of principles and practices that unite sets of disparate web sites that demonstrate some of these characteristics. The gravitational core refers to the knowledge democratization which promote alteration in expectation and behavior [3].

Of course, there is a technological aspect in Web 2.0. On a basic level, there are three basic recognizable shifts involved from the old web to the new one. The differences are sociological (friends and groups notions); structural (layout and content of the website); technological (script and presentation technologies which are used to run the website);. Combination of these three major shifts allows us to change the way we interact with the web [3].

Therefore, the effects of Web 2.0 are far reaching. It connects us to the new pieces of information, making it relevant and meaningful in a dynamic World. Nevertheless, by viewing Web 2.0 as a state of mind instead of a technology, there are many more possibilities in Web 2.0 [3].

5   Case Study 1: African Facility Management Professional Group in Facebook

African Facility Management Professional Group in Johannesburg, South Africa has set up a new group in Facebook. It is "A group to enhance discussion, knowledge sharing and networking amongst professionals who can have a major impact on profitability, sustainability and environmental friendlyness of any type of facility on a continent where still much can be achieved." Members can post their views and start a discussion there. There are 96 members on 25 January 2011 from different parts of the World [4].

6   Case Study 2: Lückenbach Facility Management in Facebook

Lückenbach Facility Management in Denmark has establish another group in Facebook as well. It has mentioned their core competencies in providing facility management in commercial, office, medical and administrative properties, which include interior design, installation of tiles natural stone and marble etc. Yet, there are 6 members in this group only on 25 January 2011 [5].

7   Case Study 3 Facility in Youtube

Youtube is also another example in spreading and sharing FM knowledge. Youtube allows us to upload and download movie and visual record without fee. All the people can upload video at anytime and at any place. For example, people in India can view video recorded in US easily [6].

8   Mismatch between Strategy and the Structure

Madritsch and May [7] structured their research to focus on the IT issues and to see the performance relatives, while other empirical studies have con concluded that the overall performance and linkages are not contribute to one particular strength, company initiative. A mismatch between strategy and the structure will lead to inefficiency in all cases meaning a less than optimal input/output ratio and therefore affect performance [8, 9]. To date though there remains very few studies available that have focused upon the broader issue of the joint influence of these factors upon organizational performance. It is for this reason that researchers are thus interested in the relationship between strategy and structure in organization. Interestingly, despite the near universal recognition of Chandler's insight and most widely held view that structure follows strategy, there are studies that have also suggested the alternative as true [10, 11]. This gives to the conclusion that strategy, structure and environment are closely linked although their relationship remains complex and iterative which makes the debate continue.

9   Implications for Practice

Organizational architecture can be divided into explicitly mandated formal structures (incentives, information processing structures and authority relationships) and emergent informal structures (culture, social networks and communities) [12]. The above arguments ties up with the structuration theory's and the famous "duality of structure" [13, 14]. Jarzabkowski [15] concludes that top managers may draw upon existing structures in the process of altering them, suggesting a more dynamic structurational process which is continuous and can be either sequential or simultaneously applied.

10   Conclusion

The theoretical framework that underpins strategy, structure and environment has been stringently tested in the past and with the worst of the worst financial crisis finally dissipated. Companies, institutes etc. need to build flexibility in derailing the high transaction costs through sharing knowledge as evident by the social networks available.

References

1. Madritsch, T., May, M.: Successful IT Implementation in Facility Management. Facilities 27(11/12), 429–444 (2009)
2. Nutt, B.: Four Competing Futures for Facility Management. Facilities 18(3/4), 124–132 (2000)

3. Hicks, A., Graber, A.: Shifting Paradigms: Teaching, Learning and Web 2.0. Reference Services Review 38(4), 621–633 (2010)
4. African Facility Management Professionals. African Facility Management Professionals (January 25, 2011),
   http://www.facebook.com/group.php?gid=25943168553
5. Lückenbach Facility Management. Lückenbach Facility Management (January 25, 2011),
   http://www.facebook.com/group.php?gid=25943168553#/pages/
   Luckenbach-Facility-Management/166123626766654?v=info
6. Youtube. Search Results for Youtube (January 25, 2011),
   http://www.youtube.com/results?search_query
   =facility+management&aq=f
7. Madritsch, T., May, M.: Successful IT Implementation in Facility Management. Facilities 27(11/12), 429–444 (2009)
8. Chandler, A.: Strategy and Structure. In: Chapters in History of American Industrial Enterprise, MIT Press, Cambridge (1962)
9. Child, J.: Managerial and Organizational factors associated with Company Performance Part II. Journal of Management Studies 12, 12–27 (1975)
10. Fredrickson, J.W.: The Strategic Decision Process and Organizational Structure. Academy of Management Review 11(2), 280–297 (1986)
11. Hall, D.A., Saias, M.A.: Strategy Follows Structure. Strategic Management Journal 1, 149–163 (1980)
12. Delmas, M.A., Toffel, M.W.: Organizational Response to Environmental Demand: Opening the Black Box. Strategic Management Journal 29, 1027–1055 (2009)
13. Giddens, A.: Central Problems in Social Theory. Macmillan, London (1979)
14. Giddens, A.: The Constitution of Society. Polity Press, Cambridge (1984)
15. Jarzabkowski, P.: Shaping Strategy as a Structuration Process. Academy of Management Journal 51(4), 621–650 (2008)

A Content Analysis in Hong Kong Sustainable Smart Home Knowledge Sharing via World Wide Web

Rita Yi Man Li

Department of Economics and Finance, Hong Kong Shue Yan University,
North Point, Hong Kong
ritarec1@yahoo.com.hk

Abstract. Centuries ago, the major function of residential buildings was to provide a shelter to humans, protecting from wind, rain and dust. Later on, economic development in our society leads us to an increase in requirement on dwellings' quality. Comfortable indoor environment becomes a must in home selection criteria. Nowadays, residential units continue to serve the abovementioned functions. Nevertheless, people has a higher demand. The global warming drives us to looks for ways to minimize the negative environmental impact. With the help of content analysis, this paper studies the Hong Kong sustainable smart home knowledge sharing.

Keywords: content analysis, sustainable development, smart home, knowledge sharing.

1 Sustainable Development

The Brundtland Commission defines sustainable development as development which meets the present generation without depriving the needs of future generations to meet their own aspirations and needs [1]. Sustainable development strives to achieve the goal of environmental protection, economic and social development [2]. Within our building envelops, smart home technology helps us achieve the goal of sustainable development.

Table 1. Elements of sustainability in Agenda 21 [3]

Element	Criteria
Economic sustainability	Growth, development and productivity
Social sustainability	Equity, empowerment, accessibility, participation, sharing, cultural identity and institutional stability
Environmental sustainability	Eco-system integrity, carrying capacity and biodiversity

T.-h. Kim et al. (Eds.): FGCN/DCA 2012, CCIS 350, pp. 265–269, 2012.
© Springer-Verlag Berlin Heidelberg 2012

2   Smart Home

Smart Homes, also known as intelligent buildings, automated homes or integrated home systems are a recent design development [4]. They can be found at every corner of the world [5]. The purpose of the Smart Home Projects is to devise intelligent homes according to the users' needs, providing a better home life experience [6]. The smart home technology, which incorporate electronic devices, was originally used to provide a productive and comfortable environment through automated control systems to control the on and off of HVAC, heating and lighting as well as fire safety system and security through a central computer [4, 7]. Nowadays, it also monitors the activities of the occupant of a home, operates devices in a predefined patterns as the users require [4] and provides solutions to energy saving and reduction. The Advanced Metering Infra-structure (AMI), for example, sends time-varying electricity price messages to smart meters located in residents' houses. Smart meters issue instructions to smart appliances placed in houses based on these message and communicate with the appliances to accomplish the power usage adjustment for the purpose of energy management and improvement in power efficiency [8]. Another smart home technology provider, [9]'s smart home design, consists of control panel for environment, appliance, lighting and security (Figure 1). Apart from energy and power saving, smart home also brings much benefit to those handicapped patients and elderly people. For example, West Lothian Council (WLC) in Scotland creates smart housing to support community care of patients [10], the using.net enables the physician as well as the elderly's relatives to view the status of the elderly by viewing the real-time status and actions performed by the elderly with time and date log. Once the vital data is captured from the elderly remotely, the physician can determine the necessities of transferring the patient to the hospital or subscribing a medicine for him [11]. Other smart homes function both as energy saving tools or tools which aid those who could not otherwise live independently. The Portsmouth smart homes project, for example, identifies appropriate technology to create energy efficient dwelling which supports the disable occupants to achieve an independent life. It also effectively manages the resources with minimum life-time costs [7].

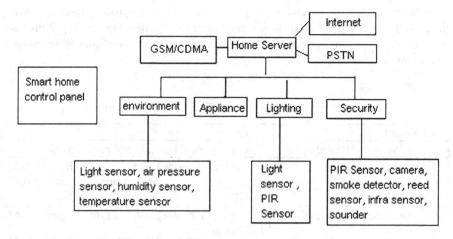

Fig. 1. The use of Smart home control panel [9]

3   Knowledge Sharing

To enhance smart home development, knowledge sharing among the major stake-holders such as smart home technology suppliers and users are important. Knowledge is the basic element and a key strategic resource for firms to acquire intangible capabilities and assets. Some scholars consider it as an important element in firm growth. Knowledge sharing is an indispensable part of organizational activities [12] as growth in knowledge work and knowledge workers requires not only the ability to find and access information and knowledge, but also the ability to share this asynchronously and synchronously in terms of time and location [13]. The process of knowledge sharing bridges the individual and organizational knowledge, improving the absorptive capacity and innovation capacity and thus leading to sustained competitive advantage [12].

4   Research Method and Results

By using the keyword smart home in Hong Kong in Google and HK! Yahoo, the relevant websites for smart home in Hong Kong are located. After that, content analysis will be used as a method of analysis. The first descriptions on content analysis dated from the 1950s and are predominately quantitative but it has been expanded to include interpretations of latent content over time. Qualitative content analysis slowly emerges. In such case, similar information is grouped into similar categories [14]. The results of the data search show that The practitioners view the major merits bring by the smart homes are comfortableness and cost saving. The smart home systems elements usually include the energy saving device such as lighting control system, remote control system for electrical appliance. One company even include home solar system as smart homes systems' equipment.

Table 2. Smart home solutions provided by private companies and merits of smart home

Company	Advantages of smart homes	Smart homes systems elements
Smart Home Automation designer [15]	N/A	CCMS Systems & HVAC System Design, building efficiency & energy management, acoustic Design & Consultant, automation system design & consultant, lighting control system design & consultant
HKC [16]	HKC Home Automation solutions embrace a digital lifestyle which brings us 4C, i.e. care, connectivity, comfort, convenience in an intelligent living.	They include HKC Pro 300+ and HA Express. The HKC Pro300+ is a professional complete Home Automation solution for estate developer and HA Express is a wireless Home Automation Solution to control curtain, lighting, and AV devices for individual end-users.

Table 2. (*Continued*)

E Element [9]	A Smart Home can provide people a safe, comfortable, power-saving and convenient life by enabling intercommunication among all the household appliances which includes TVs, security system, computers, lights, entertainment system and HVAC (air conditioning, heating, ventilation). They can be controlled by a smart home control panel installed at home or through Internet, GSM/CDMA and PSTN networks.	The products include energy harvesting, supervisory control and data, acquisition, solar tracking system, solar installation system, wind turbine pitch control, home solar power system, inverter for Grid-Conn, wind turbine monitoring system, solar micro inverter and smart meter.
Hometouch [17]	The use of intelligent building technology delivers the economies of scale which reduces cost. It improves the ease of use and convenience of the smart home system.	The iPhone and iPad apps allow the user to integrate the iPhone with smart control solution, they can then become remote controllers to control lighting, curtain , LCD etc. Other products include curtain controller and Villa Type Visitor Panel.

5   Conclusions

The global climate change has forced us to reconsider the important elements inside our home. This paper finds that the major advantages of smart home include comfortable housing and cost reduction. Energy saving device is still the major elements in smart homes.

References

1. Chan, E.H.W., Yung, E.H.K.: Is the Development Control Legal Framework Conducive to a Sustainable Dense Development in Hong Kong? Habitat International 28, 409–426 (2004)
2. Li, R.Y.M.: Building Our Sustainable Cities 2011. Common Ground Publishing, Illinois (2011)
3. Basiago, A.D.: Economic, Social and Environmental Sustainability in Development Theory and Urban Planning Practice. The Environmentalist 19(2), 145–160 (1999)

4. Ricquebourg, V., et al.: The Smart Home Concept: Our Immediate Future. In: The 1st IEEE International Conference on E-Learning in Industrial Electronics (2006)
5. Conejero, J.M., et al.: A Model-driven Approach for Reusing Tests in Smart Home Systems. Pers. Ubiquit. Comput. 15, 317–327 (2011)
6. Park, S.H., et al.: Smart home – Digitally Engineered Domestic Life. Personal and Ubiquitous Computing 7(3), 189–196 (2003)
7. Chapman, K., McCartney, K.: Smart Homes for People with Restricted Mobility. Property Management 20(2), 153–166 (2002)
8. Jin, C., Kunz, T.: Smart Home Networking: Lessons from Combining Wireless and Powerline Networking. Smart Grid and Renewable Energy 2, 136–151 (2011)
9. E Element: Sensing Solutions for Smart Home (September 15, 2012), http://hk.element14.com/jsp/bespoke/bespoke7.jsp?bespokepage=e14/common/en/technology-first/applications/sensing/sensing-smart-homes.jsp#
10. Kinder, T.: A Sociotechnical Approach to the Innovation of a Network Technology in the Public Sector - the Introduction of Smart Homes in West Lothian. European Journal of Innovation Management 3(2), 72–90 (2000)
11. Raad, M.W., Yang, L.T.: A Ubiquitous Smart Home for Elderly. Information System Frontier 11, 529–536 (2009)
12. Cao, Y., Xiang, Y.: The Impact of Knowledge Governance on Knowledge Sharing. Management Decision 50(4), 591–610 (2012)
13. Patrick, K., Dotsika, F.: Knowledge Sharing: Developing from Within. The Learning Organization Environment 14(5), 395–406 (2007)
14. Graneheim, U.H., Lundman, B.: Qualitative Content Analysis in Nursing Research: Concepts, Procedures and Measures to Achieve Trustworthiness. Nurse Education Today 24, 105–112 (2004)
15. Smart Home Automation designer. Life Your Home (September 15, 2012), http://smarthome.i-control.com.hk/
16. HKC. Intelligent Systems (September 15, 2012), http://www.hkc.com.hk/BusinessScope_PS_IS.asp
17. Hometouch. Products (September 20, 2012), http://www.hometouch.com.hk

Noise Robustness of Spectrum Delta (SpD) Features in Malay Vowel Recognition

Mohd Yusof Shahrul Azmi[1,*], M. Nor Idayu[1], D. Roshidi[1],
A.R. Yaakob[1], and Sazali Yaacob[2]

[1] College of Arts and Sciences, Universiti Utara Malaysia, Malaysia
{shahrulazmi,noridayu,roshidi,ary32}@uum.edu.my
[2] School of Mechatronics, Universiti Malaysia Perlis, Malaysia
s.yaacob@unimap.edu.my

Abstract. In Malaysia, there is increasing number of speech recognition researchers focusing on developing independent speaker speech recognition systems that uses Malay Language which are noise robust and accurate. The performance of speech recognition application under adverse noisy condition often becomes the topic of interest among speech recognition researchers regardless of the languages in use. This paper present a study of noise robust capability of an improved vowel feature extraction method called Spectrum Delta (SpD). The features are extracted from both original data and noise-added data and classified using three classifiers; (i) Multinomial Logistic Regression (MLR), (ii) K-Nearest Neighbors (k-NN) and (iii) Linear Discriminant Analysis (LDA). Results show that the proposed SpD is robust towards noise and LDA performs the best in overall vowel classification compared to MLR and k-NN in terms of robustness capability especially with signal-to-noise (SNR) above 20dB.

Keywords: Malay Vowel, Spectrum Envelope, Speech Recognition, Noise Robustness.

1 Introduction

Automatic speech recognition (ASR) has made great strides with the development of digital signal processing hardware and software. Currently, despite of all these advances, machines still cannot match the performance of their human counterparts in terms of accuracy and speed, especially in case of speaker independent speech recognition. Today, significant portion of speech recognition research focuses on speaker independent speech recognition problem. The reasons are its wide range of applications, and limitations of available techniques of speech recognition.

Although there are studies on Malay phoneme recognition, but most of them are infancy [1] and use multiple frame analysis. Subsequently, more analyses focusing on the accuracy and processing time when developing speech therapy systems should be done to ensure a worth for value product is produced. Motivated by this necessity, this study is designed to develop Malay speech recognition system in an effort to

---

* Corresponding author.

T.-h. Kim et al. (Eds.): FGCN/DCA 2012, CCIS 350, pp. 270–277, 2012.
© Springer-Verlag Berlin Heidelberg 2012

improve Malay vowel recognition. Applications that use vowel phonemes require high degree of Standard Malay vowel recognition capability. In Malaysia, few studies have been done especially in the study of Malay vowels usage, independent speaker systems, recognition robustness and algorithm speed and accuracy.

When corrupted by low level noise, human listeners are still capable to recognize speech because we can select and follow another speaker's voice [2]. Even at packed football stadium, listeners can select and follow the voice of another speaker as long as the signal-to-noise ratio (SNR) is not too low. In terms of speech recognizers, most of these applications are affected by adverse environmental conditions. According to [3], it is important to suppress additive noise before the feature extraction stage of any speech recogniser [3]. Invariance to background noise, channel conditions and variations of speaker and accent are among the main issues in noise robust applications [4, 5]. Development of signal enhancement techniques as an effort to remove the noise prior to the recognition process is permissible but it may cause some alteration on the speech spectral characteristics. Consequently, the speech signal is not suitable to be used in the designed acoustic models of the recognizer hence deteriorating the performance of the recognizer [6]. This justifies the needs of developing a robust speech recognizer which can be modeled using robust speech features.

This study is an effort to increase Malay vowel recognition capability by using a new speech database that consist of words uttered by Malaysian speakers from the three major races, Malay, Chinese and Indians. This paper will present a robustness study on Spectrum Delta (SpD) method introduced by Shahrul Azmi (2010) [7] which is an improved formant method based on single framed analysis on isolated utterances.

2   Researches in Malay Speech Recognition

In Malaysia, research on speech recognition begins in late 1990s and has grown aggressively. Lim, Woo, Loh and Osman (2000) conducted an experiment on 200 vowel signals using wavelet denoising approach and Probabilistic Neural Network Model [8]. Salam, Mohamad and Salleh (2001) investigated Malay plosives sounds and Malay numbers while Tan and Jantan (2004) investigated Neural Networks to recognized SM digits [9, 10]. Another study includes Ting and Mark (2008) who converted Linear Predictive Coding (LPC) coefficients into cepstral coefficients before being fed into a Multi-layer Perceptron with one hidden layer for training and testing classifications [11]. Yusof (2008) also studied formant difference features in classifying vowels [12]. Most of the recent researchers studied on both dependent and independent speaker systems using mostly multi frame analysis [11, 13-18]. The accuracy obtained was in between 89% to 100% for dependent speaker system and between 70% to 94% for an independent speaker and multi framed analysis system. Ting and Yunus (2004) uses independent and single framed analysis system only obtained an accuracy of only 76.25% [18]. In terms of robustness analysis, Al-Haddad (2009), proposed an algorithm for noise cancellation by using recursive least square (RLS) and pattern recognition by using fusion method of Dynamic Time Warping (DTW) and Hidden Markov Model (HMM) [19]. He collected Malay number speech data from 60 speakers.

3   Vowel Recognition Process

Vowel Recognition process starts with the Data Acquisition process and followed by filtering, pre-processing, frame selection, auto-regressive modelling, and feature extraction process as depictured in Fig. 1. A data collection process was taken from 100 individuals consisting of students and staff of both male and female from Universiti Malaysia Perlis (UniMAP) and Universiti Utara Malaysia (UUM). As Malay language is the official language for Malaysians diverse ethnicities, then the speakers were selected among the main three races Malays, Chinese and Indians.

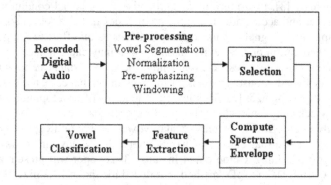

Fig. 1. Vowel recognition process

The recordings were done using a conventional microphone and a laptop computer with a sampling frequency of 8000 Hz. The words "ka", "ke", "ki", "ko", "ku" and "kə" were used to represent six vowels of /a/, /e/, /i/, /o/, /u/ and /ə/ because vowels have more energy than consonants. Different combinations of consonants and vowels were tested but yield similar results in terms of portion of vowel obtained. In this study, a sampling frequency of 8000 Hz was used to sample the vowels and the recordings were done 2 to 4 times per speaker depending on situation convenience.

3.1   SpD Feature Extraction Method

Music has a higher rate of change, and goes through more drastic frame-to-frame changes than speech does; this value is higher for music than for speech. Speech alternates periods of transition between consonant and vowel. Spectral "Flux" (Delta Spectrum Magnitude) is the 2-norm of the frame-to-frame spectral amplitude difference vector, $\|X_i| - |X_{i+1}\|$. This method is somewhat similar to Hawley's method, which attempts to detect harmonic continuity in music [20, 21]. In this new Spectral Delta approach, we use the difference in Band. First, the band where most of the vowel energy is situated is divided into three regions. In this study, the frequency of interest is between 1 to 2350Hz and divided into three equal regions of 780Hz. The steps for SpD feature calculations is as follows:

Determine the number of features, i, to be extracted from the frequency band, BW_{SpD}.

i. Calculate the number of frequency frames, M, within frequency band.

$$M = round(\frac{3}{2}*i) \tag{1}$$

ii. Calculate width, $FrmB$, of a frequency frame M

$$FrmB = \frac{BW_{SpD}}{M} \tag{2}$$

iii. Calculate individual frequency frame mean intensity, K_n, from frequency magnitude J. N is the number of frequency magnitudes within M.

$$K_n = \frac{1}{N}\sum_{f_n=F_{low}}^{f_n=F_{high}} J(f_n) \tag{3}$$

iv. With f_n being the low and high frequency for each frequency frame. F_{delta} is the size of frame shift.

$$F_{delta} = round(\frac{i}{2}) \tag{4}$$

v. Calculate Spectral Delta features, SpD_n

$$SpD_n = K_{n+F_{delta}} - K_n \tag{5}$$

3.2   Vowel Classification Techniques

In this study, two non-linear classifiers namely K-Nearest Neighbours (k-NN) and Multinomial Logistic Regression (MLR), and a linear classifier based on Linear Discriminant Analysis (LDA) are used to classify all the collected features. These classifiers were chosen based on their popularities in speech recognition researches. All the computational works were conducted using *MATLAB* built-in functions for all the three classifiers.

4   Feature Analysis

This method uses features extracted from the intensity of harmonic discontinuity in the form of frequency bands. The characteristics of spectral envelope are unique to each Malay vowel. The features reflect the rate of change between frequency bands. In order to determine the optimum number of features to extract in order to best classify the vowels, an experiment was done using different number of features classified by Neural Network classifier.

Table 1. Anova analysis of spd features

Main Effect	df1	df2	F	Sig. (p)
SpD_1	5	1310	173	<0.001
SpD_2	5	1310	212	<0.001
SpD_3	5	1310	226	<0.001
SpD_4	5	1310	166	<0.001
SpD_5	5	1310	54	<0.001
SpD_6	5	1310	53	<0.001
SpD_7	5	1310	231	<0.001
SpD_8	5	1310	99	<0.001
SpD_9	5	1310	36	<0.001
SpD_{10}	5	1310	39	<0.001
SpD_{11}	5	1310	102	<0.001
SpD_{12}	5	1310	119	<0.001
SpD_{13}	5	1310	38	<0.001
SpD_{14}	5	1310	8	<0.001
SpD_{15}	5	1310	9	<0.001

To determine if the features of the proposed feature extraction methods significantly affect vowel classification an ANOVA analysis was done for all the features using a statistical application called SPSS. Results of this analysis as tabulated in Table 1 show that there are significant main effects from each individual feature of the proposed SpD method at $\alpha=0.01$ (p-value < 0.001). These results indicate that all the represent vowels, i.e. "ka", "ke", "ki", "ko", "ku" and "kə", are significantly different in each of these tested SpD features extraction. Therefore, the proposed extraction approach is able to show the differences of Malay spoken vowels.

4.1   Noise Robust Analysis

A robust analysis was done to study the robustness of the proposed features of SpD and to compare the results with the common single frame Mel-Frequency Cepstrum Coefficients (MFCC). White Gaussian noise was used to proof robustness. Seven signal-to-noise (SNR) levels of 10dB, 15dB, 20dB, 25dB, 30dB, 35dB and 40dB were used in this experiment in addition to the clean signal. These experiments were done on k-NN, MLR and LDA classifiers. For simplifying discussion purposes, the abbreviation "_w" refers to classifier model which was trained with noise and "_wo" refers to classifier model which was trained without noise. The analysis was based on cross validation testing where the original data is split randomly into 70% training set and 30% testing set (unseen input).

Table 2. Comparison of overall spd classification rate by different snr level (tabulated result)

SNR	KNN_w_ noise	KNN_wo _noise	LDA_w _noise	LDA_wo noise	MLR_w _noise	MLR_wo _noise
10dB	19.90	20.03	21.13	14.86	13.81	18.02
15dB	25.96	26.83	54.58	15.93	13.63	24.90
20dB	37.30	38.92	82.80	23.30	19.57	36.37
25dB	58.76	54.56	89.00	37.41	35.41	50.86
30dB	71.90	62.80	89.37	49.19	55.41	58.38
35dB	89.23	70.51	89.70	57.69	78.25	71.15
40dB	95.18	78.44	89.64	78.27	95.94	86.28
Clean	83.82	94.77	89.37	92.41	77.18	95.09

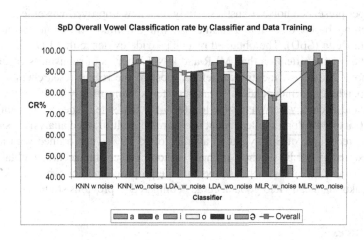

Fig. 2. Overall SpD Classification Rate of Vowels based on Classifiers and Training Conditions using Clean Training Data

Fig. 2 shows the detailed overall classification result of SpD features classified with MLR, LDA and KNN classifiers. It also shows the vowel recognition performance of individual vowels for all classifiers trained either with noisy data or clean data. Table 4 shows MLR_wo_noise performs the best by giving 95.09% overall classification rate for training clean data with vowel /i/ giving the highest result and the rest of the vowel achieving above 91% classification rate. MLR_w_noise gave only 77.18% for testing clean data with /o/ giving the highest classification rate. This difference in vowel recognition performance may be caused by the adaptation of the model to the noisy data. For the model which is trained with noisy data, LDA obtained the highest overall classification rate of 89.37% followed by KNN with 83.82% and KNN with a low classification rate of only 77.18%.

Table 3. Overall classification rate of vowels on spd features using clean training data (tabulated results)

Classifiers	a	e	i	o	u	ə	Overall
KNN w noise	94.37	86.34	92.08	94.38	56.37	79.62	83.82
KNN_wo_noise	97.70	92.62	97.83	89.38	95.11	96.77	94.77
LDA_w_noise	97.69	91.86	78.53	87.84	90.14	90.08	89.37
LDA_wo_noise	94.37	95.29	88.58	84.20	97.90	94.00	92.41
MLR_w_noise	93.11	66.77	78.78	97.21	75.10	45.52	77.18
MLR_wo_noise	95.06	94.85	98.70	91.07	95.36	95.61	95.09

5   Conclusion

This paper presents a noise robustness study on a new improved vowel feature extraction method based on frame-to-frame spectral amplitude difference vector called Spectrum Delta (SpD). The obtained results provide evidence that LDA is the best in overall vowel classification than MLR and k-NN in terms of robustness capability for SNR above 20dB. As mentioned before, most of the recent researchers studied on both dependent and independent speaker systems using mostly multi frame analysis which yield accuracy between 89% to 100% for dependent speaker system and between 70% to 94% for an independent speaker and multi framed analysis system. The proposed technique of SpD yield an average of 95.09% when trained with noise and classified using MLR. When trained without noise, the accuracy obtained was 89.37% using LDA. This result shows that the proposed method which uses independent speaker data can yield good accuracy compared to previous studies.

References

1. Rosdi, F., Ainon, R.: Isolated malay speech recognition using Hidden Markov Models. In: International Conference on Computer and Communication Engineering (ICCCE 2008), Kuala Lumpur, Malaysia, pp. 721–725 (2008)
2. Devore, S., Shinn-Cunningham, B.G.: Perceptual consequences of including reverbera-tion in spatial auditory displays. In: 2003 International Conference on Auditory Display, Boston, MA, USA, pp. 75–78 (2003)
3. Uhl, C., Lieb, M.: Experiments with an extended adaptive SVD enhancement scheme fors-peech recognition in noise. In: IEEE International Conference on Acoustics, Speech, and Signal Processing (ICASSP 2001), Salt Lake City, UT, USA, pp. 281–284 (2001)
4. Al-Haddad, S., Samad, S., Hussain, A., Ishak, K.: Isolated Malay Digit Recognition Using Pattern Recognition Fusion of Dynamic Time Warping and Hidden Markov Mod-els. American Journal of Applied Sciences 5, 714–720 (2008)
5. Huang, X., Acero, A., Hon, H.: Spoken language processing: A guide to theory, algorithm, and system development. Prentice Hall PTR, upper saddle river, NJ (2001)
6. Kyriakou, C., Bakamidis, S., Dologlou, I., Carayannis, G.: Robust Continuous Speech Recognition in the Presence of Coloured Noise. In: Proceedings of 4th European Conference on Noise Control (EURONOISE 2001), Patra, pp. 702–705 (2001)

7. Shahrul Azmi, M.Y.: Feature Extraction and Classification of Malay Speech Vowels," in School of Mechatronics. vol. Ph.D Kangar, Perlis, MALAYSIA: Universiti Malaysia Perlis, UniMAP (2010)
8. Lim, C.P., Woo, S.C., Loh, A.S., Osman, R.: Speech Recognition Using Artificial Neural Networks. In: 1st International Conference on Web Information Systems Engineering (WISE 2000), Hong Kong, China, p. 419 (2000)
9. Salam, M., Mohamad, D., Salleh, S.: Neural network speaker dependent isolated Malay speech recognition system: handcrafted vs genetic algorithm. In: 6th International Symposium on Signal Processing and its Applications (ISSPA 2001), Kuala Lumpur, Malaysia (2001)
10. Tan, C., Jantan, A.: Digit Recognition Using Neural Networks. Malaysian Journal of Computer Science 17, 40–54 (2004)
11. Ting, H.N., Mark, K.M.: Speaker-dependent Malay Vowel Recognition for a Child with Articulation Disorder Using Multi-layer Perceptron. In: 4th Kuala Lumpur Interna-tional Conference on Biomedical Engineering 2008, pp. 238–241 (2008)
12. Yusof, S.A.M., Yaacob, S., Murugesa, P.: Improved Classification of Malaysian Spo-ken Vowels using Formant Differences. Journal of ICT (JICT) 7 (December 2008)
13. Nazari, M., Sayadiyan, A., Valiollahzadeh, S.M.: Speaker-Independent Vowel Recogni-tion in Persian Speech. In: 3rd International Conference on Information and Communica-tion Technologies: From Theory to Applications (ICTTA 2008), Umayyad Palace, Damas-cus, Syria, pp. 1–5 (2008)
14. Carvalho, M., Ferreira, A.: Real-Time Recognition of Isolated Vowels. In: André, E., Dybkjær, L., Minker, W., Neumann, H., Pieraccini, R., Weber, M. (eds.) PIT 2008. LNCS (LNAI), vol. 5078, pp. 156–167. Springer, Heidelberg (2008)
15. Bresolin, A., Neto, A., Alsina, P.: Brazilian Vowels Recognition using a New Hierar-chical Decision Structure with Wavelet Packet and SVM (2007)
16. Muralishankar, R., Kaushik, L.N., Ramakrishnan, A.G.: Time-scaling of speech and music using independent subspace analysis. In: International Conference on Signal Proc-essing and Communications (SPCOM 2004), pp. 310–314 (2004)
17. Merkx, P., Miles, J.: Automatic Vowel Classification in Speech, Department of Mathemat-ics, Duke University, Durham, NC, USA, Final Project for Math
18. Ting, H., Yunus, J.: Speaker-independent Malay vowel recognition of children using mul-ti-layer perceptron. In: IEEE Region 10 Conference, TENCON 2004 (2004)
19. Al-Haddad, S., Samad, S., Hussain, A., Ishak, K., Noor, A.: Robust Speech Recognition Using Fusion Techniques and Adaptive Filtering. American Journal of Applied Sciences 6, 290–295 (2009)
20. Hawley, M.: Structure out of Sound, in School of Architecture and Planning. vol. PhD Massachusetts, USA: Massachusetts Institute of Technology, pp. 185 (1993)
21. Scheirer, E., Slaney, M.: Construction and evaluation of a robust multifeature speech/music discriminator. In: IEEE International Conference on Acoustics, Speech, and Signal Processing (ICASSP 1997), Munich, Germany, pp. 1331–1334 (1997)

Design of Intelligent Controller for Temperature Process

D. Pamela[1,2] and T. Jebarajan[3]

[1] Sathyabama University, Chennai
[2] Karunya University, Coimbatore
mailpamelain@yahoo.co.in
[3] Kings Engineering College, Chennai
drtjebarajan@gmail.com

Abstract. Temperature is one of the most important and significant parameter of control in food processing, pharmaceuticals and in polymerization. The temperature process is highly nonlinear and design of robust controllers for such nonlinear systems is a challenge. This paper proposes a novel method for the control of temperature process. The traditional PI controllers which are in practice produce high overshoot and the design procedure seems complex. The proposed intelligent controller offers better performance in terms of overshoot and settling time and thus increases the robustness of the system. This paper describes the modeling of the temperature process in detail and discusses how the process responds to conventional and intelligent controllers.

Keywords: Fuzzy Controller, PID controller, Peak overshoot, Integral Absolute Error.

1 Introduction

The temperature is an important parameter of control in process control industries. The design of controllers for such nonlinear systems is of great importance in industries. Conventional PI controllers were designed and compared with intelligent controllers like Fuzzy Logic control. Fuzzy logic controllers convert linguistic variables into control signals and because of its ease in design this controllers find lots of application in engineering[1].Conventional non-Linear controllers can yield a satisfactory response if the process is operated close to a normal steady state value or a fairly linear region. But design of intelligent controllers gives a satisfactory response with a reduced overshoot and oscillations time, thus improving the stability of the system [2],[3].

Section 2 deals with the proposed methodology, section 3 describes the process, section 4 explains the system identification, section 5 covers the controller design and section 6 discusses about the results.

2 Proposed Methodology

The conventional PID controller was designed and the controller values were chosen by Ziegler Nichols tuning method. The step response of the system was taken and the process gain and time constant was calculated using step test method. Then the PI

T.-h. Kim et al. (Eds.): FGCN/DCA 2012, CCIS 350, pp. 278–284, 2012.
© Springer-Verlag Berlin Heidelberg 2012

controller settings were tuned using Ziegler Nichols Controller tuning method. This conventional controller response was compared with that of a intelligent Fuzzy logic Controller. The intelligent fuzzy logic controller were designed using fuzzy rules developed by trial and error method. The Design and implementation of the same was done using Matlab.

3   Process Description

The control of temperature process can be done in two ways, in one method the power to the heater alone is controlled keeping the air flow through the blower as constant; in the second method the power to the heater as well the air flow through the blower is controlled. The temperature process uses a K-type thermocouple to measure the temperature. The milli-volt output of the thermocouple is amplified to 0-5V for the temperature change of 0^0C to 100^0C .The desired temperature value and the thermocouple output are compared and the control signal is given to the power control circuitry. The figure below describes the temperature process setup.

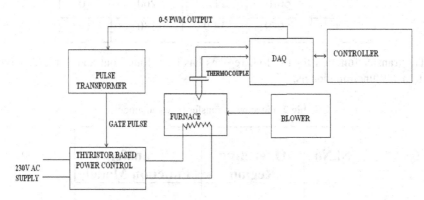

Fig. 1. Block Diagram of the Temperature Process

The two SCRs connected in anti parallel forms the thyristor based power control circuitry. The gate pulse will be generated from the output of the controller. The output from the controller is converted to AC voltage, and passed through a full wave rectifier so that the SCR will receive positive gate pulses. The DC signal with ripples will be converted to ramp signal. This ramp signal is given as the inverting input to the opamp and the non-inverting terminal is grounded. This PWM circuit will produce a square pulse according to the voltages coming on the inverting input of the Opamp. And if this longer duration square pulses are used to trigger the gates of the SCR may raise the device temperature. Pulse transformer is used for isolation.

4   System Identification

The temperature process considered here can be assumed as a first order process with dead time. The system identification can be done mainly in three ways one is the mathematical modeling (Katalin Hangos et al., 2001) and the other is the empirical modeling. The third method make use of some system identification tool box for obtaining the transfer function model of the system. In this work the second method is used. Table 1 shows the experimental result for the step test which includes the time constant, delay time and the process gain.

Table 1. Experimental Data

Input Change (V)	(ΔPV *.632) + I.S.S	Process Gain (°C/V)	Time constant (sec)	Dead Time (sec)
0	-	-	-	-
0-1	31.6	4.1	98	40
1-2	41.34	13.3	231	30
2-3	60.1	21.9	260	20
3-4	77.49	14.9	180	18

The transfer function for the four regions has been found out and Table 2 Shows the transfer function models.

Table 2. Piece wise transfer function model

Sl.No	Operating Region	Transfer Function Model
1	29.2°C-33.3 °C	$G1(s) = \dfrac{4.1e^{-40s}}{98s+1}$
2	33.3°C-46.5 °C	$G2(s) = \dfrac{13.3e^{-30s}}{231s+1}$
3	46.5°C-68.08 °C	$G3(s) = \dfrac{21.9e^{-20s}}{260s+1}$
4	68.08°C-77.49 °C	$G4(s) = \dfrac{18e^{-18s}}{180s+1}$

5   Controller Design

The temperature process was modeled in three different operating region and the controller was designed for the process operating in the region 46°C to 75°C. The desired temperature was achieved using conventional PI controller and intelligent fuzzy logic controller. The design of these controllers are discussed below:

5.1   PID Controller

Conventional PID controllers are characterized with simple structure and simple design procedures. They enable good control performance and are therefore widely applied in industry [3]. The PI controller for the temperature process was designed and the kp, ki and ti values was obtained using Ziegler Nichols tuning method [4]. The design of PI controller was easy but the overshoot offered by PI controller was very high which led to the need for designing intelligent controllers. Hence fuzzy logic controller was designed, which will reduce the overshoot, oscillations and Integral Absolute Error (IAE) [5].

5.2   Fuzzy Logic Controllers

The PID controller values depend basically on the gain and time constant of the controlled system. A different situation exists when the temperature set point is different from the balanced temperature. The farther the set point is from the balanced temperature, the farther the PID constants will be from their optimal values. Just how far depends on how far the set point is from the balanced temperature and whether the current temperature is below or above the set point.[6]. Fuzzy Logic controllers offer a better option for such adaptive mechanism. In reality, any implementation of fuzzy logic or fuzzy control is based on classical numerical processing. The design generally comprises of three steps: fuzzification, applying the fuzzy rules, and defuzzification. Fuzzification aims to convert a single (crisp) input value into corresponding fuzzy-set values. Applying the fuzzy rules, entails processing the "fuzzy" information. The third step, defuzzification, converts the internal fuzzy results back to a crisp output value [7].

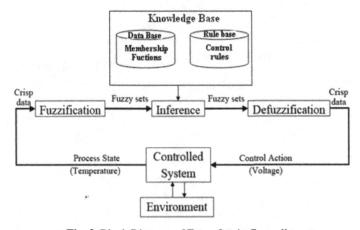

Fig. 2. Block Diagram of Fuzzy Logic Controller

The implementation of the fuzzy logic controller in process control is based on the fuzzy logic based term, output = F [(e (t),) Δ e (t)]. In this the fuzzy sets e(t) and de (t) acts as the input to map F to the output. Associated with the map F is a collection of Linguistic values that represents the term set for the input and output variables of F. For the design of fuzzy logic controller for this process seven linguistic variables are used. Each membership function (MF) is a map from the real line to the interval [-1 +1] for the error and rate of change of error. In this application the MF used is triangular[8].The rules used for the control of this process is given in Table 5.2.1.Here the output of the Fuzzy Logic Controller is the SCR voltage. The range for the membership values of the Gains are chosen depending on the operating region.

Table 3. Piece wise transfer function model

e	de	NB	NM	NS	ZE	PS	PM	PS
NB		PB	PB	PB	PB	PM	ZE	ZE
NM		PB	PB	PB	PB	PM	ZE	ZE
NS		PM	PM	PM	PS	ZE	NS	NS
ZE		PM	PM	PS	ZE	NS	NM	NM
PS		PS	PS	ZE	NS	NM	NM	NM
PM		ZE	ZE	NM	NB	NB	NB	NB
PB		ZE	ZE	NM	NB	NB	NB	NB

6   Results and Discussions

The designed conventional and intelligent controllers were tested on the system and the obtained results are given below.

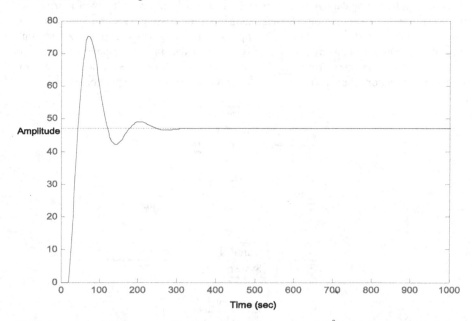

Fig. 3. Response of the Process with PI Controller for setpoint of 47^{0}C simulated with Matlab

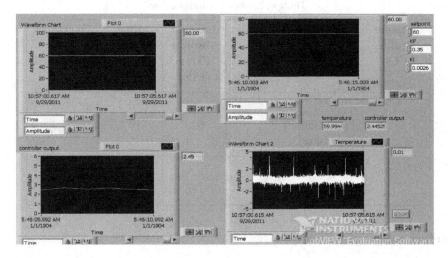

Fig. 4. Response of the Process with PI Controller for setpoint 60°C with LabVIEW

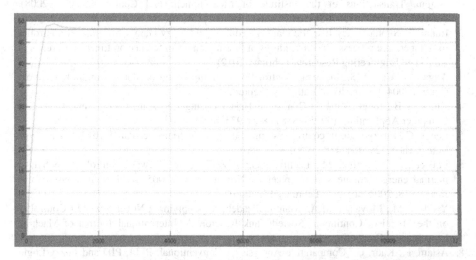

Fig. 5. Response of the Process with Fuzzy Logic Controller for setpoint of 47^{0}C with Matlab

7   Conclusions

The results and discussions shows the output of temperature process for PI controller with large overshoot and IAE and the output of Fuzzy Logic Controller reduces the overshoot and IAE.

Table 4. Perfomance Index Table

Setpoint Profile (°C)	Controller Type	Integral Absolute Error (IAE)	Rise Time (seconds)	Overshoot (°C)
47°C	Fixed Gain PI Controller	624	19.2	27.8°C
	Fuzzy PI Controller	176	98.6	1.3°C

References

1. Huang, S.-J., Wang, C.-C.: Gain-scheduling fuzzy temperature controller for one-way input system. Transactions of the Institute of Measurement and Control 30, 451 (2008), doi:10.1177/0142331207086182
2. Renu, G., Subha Hency Jose, P.: Gain Scheduling and fuzzy Gain scheduling PI controller for temperature process. In: Proceedings of International Conference on Emerging Trends in Advanced Engineering Research (February 2012)
3. Adgar, A., Cox, C.S.: Practical Control Loop Tuning Using A Matlab/Simulink Toolbox. Control 2004, University of Bath, UK (September 2004)
4. Khare, Y.B., Singh, Y.: PID Control of Heat Exchanger System. International Journal of Computer Applications (0975 – 8887) 8(6), 975–8887 (2010)
5. Lee, C.C.: Fuzzy logic in control systems: Fuzzy logic controller-Part I. IEEE Trans. Syst. Man, Cybern. 20, 404–418 (1990)
6. LeBreux, M., Lacroix, M., Lachiver, G.: Fuzzy and feedforward control of an hybrid thermal energy storage system (received November 22, 2005; received in revised form January 18, 2006; accepted February 14, 2006)
7. Yazdani, M., Movahed, M.A., Mahmoudzadeh, S.: Applying a Novel Fuzzy-PI Controller on the Model of Continuous Stirred Tank Reactor, A. International Journal of Machine Learning and Computing 1(2) (June 2011)
8. Aslam, F., Kaur, G.: Comparative Analysis of Conventional, P, PI, PID and Fuzzy Logic ontrollers for the Efficient Control of Concentration in CSTR. International Journal of Computer Applications (0975 – 8887) 17(6) (March 2011)
9. Hangos, K., Cameron, I.: Process Modelling and Model Analysis. Process System Engineering 4, 20–36 (2001)

Modelling of System Configuration
and Reconfiguration for IMS

G. Manoj[1], J. Samson Immmanuel[1], P.S. Divya[1], and A.P. Haran[2]

[1] Eletronics and Communication,
Karunya University, Karunya Nagar,Coimbatore, Tamil Nadu 641114, India
{Manojzcbe,samsonimmanuel566}@gmail.com,
divya_deepam@karunya.edu
[2] Aeronautical Engineering, Park College of Engineering and Technology,
Kaniyur, Coimbatore, Tamil Nadu-641659, India

Abstract. The operation of Discrete Event Systems is represented as a chronological sequence of events. Each event occurs at an instant in time and marks a change of state in the system. A system configuration (SC) of Discrete Event (DE) in linear model has been considered, a formal feature of closed loop structure. To prevent data from getting lost due to noise in the wireless channel, an error-coding scheme is applied. Turbo code is a powerful error coding technique employed nowadays in communication systems. In this paper the image is retained in the receiving end by proper design of the error coding scheme. The images obtained after decoding are found to be suitable for recognition and diagnosis by the doctors. This novel technology will enhance the health care in rural area where the opinion of a specialized doctor is not available. The analyses of system performances for the configured and reconfigured system are done for pre and post layout simulation as per the design methodology. The design methodology used in implementation of 180nm technology, the system instances power, instances and area of the reconfigured system are compared with the configured system. We also infer that the reconfigured system obtain better performance during the run time of the system.

Keywords: Integer Programming, Discrete Event, Institutional Management System, System Configuration.

1 Introduction

Discrete event system of a system is represented as a sequence of events a wide variety of systems such as operating systems, transportation systems, supply chains networks, and communication systems [1]. These systems are dynamic and change their states with the occurrence of discrete events. DES controllers [2] are used to restrict the behavior of DES to a desirable set of behaviors that do not violate the DES control specifications. DES controller consists of two phases namely, controller synthesis and system runtime. During controller synthesis, a DES and its control specifications are used to construct the DES controller. In runtime phase, the

T.-h. Kim et al. (Eds.): FGCN/DCA 2012, CCIS 350, pp. 285–292, 2012.
© Springer-Verlag Berlin Heidelberg 2012

constructed controller interacts with the DES in a closed-loop structure. Different methods are used for DES controller example using Petri-net [3], all the methods are able to synthesize a controller using a suitable model and its control specifications.

A Petri also known as place and transition [4], several mathematical modeling languages for the description of distributed systems. A Petri net is a directed bipartite graph, in which the nodes represent transitions (i.e. events that may occur, signified by bars and places i.e. conditions, signified by circles). A Petri net consists of places, transitions, and arcs [5]. Arcs run from a place to a transition or vice versa, between places or between transitions. The places from which an arc runs to a transition are called the input places of the transition; the places to which arcs run from a transition are called the output places of the transition. Graphically, places in a Petri net may contain a discrete number of marks called tokens. Any distribution of tokens over the places will represent a configuration of the net called a marking [6]. In an abstract sense relating to a Petri net diagram, a transition of a Petri net may fire whenever there are sufficient tokens at the start of all input arcs, when it fires, it consumes these tokens, and places tokens at the end of all output arcs. A firing is atomic, i.e., a single non-interruptible step. Execution of Petri nets is nondeterministic when multiple transitions are enabled at the same time, any one of them may fire. Since firing is nondeterministic, and multiple tokens may be present anywhere in the net, Petri nets are well suited for modeling the concurrent behavior of distributed systems.

2   Related Work

The different types of reconfiguration have been addressed by DES control researchers. A. Giua, F. DiCesare[1], Darabi *et al.* [5] and Liu and Darabi [6] defined a control switching formalism that revises the controller policy when the observation channels fail or are repaired. The DES and its control specifications are modeled by finite automata. A mega-controller monitors changes in the observation channels and selects the proper control logic when changes occur. This is an example of reconfiguration based on observation channel changes.

Lucas *et al.* [2], proposed a reconfiguration approach for a modular plant. They assume one control module for each machine, and other control modules for coordination. When the manufacturing scenario is altered, only the control module called the control plan needs to be reconfigured. The other control modules are not affected. Also, if mechanical modules are added or removed from the system, the appropriate mechanical control modules must also be added or removed.

Badouel and Oliver [3] introduce a class of high-level Petri nets, called reconfigurable nets that can dynamically modify their own structure by rewriting some of their components. The switch from one configuration to another due to a local change in DES behavior is carried out by introducing a new kind of place content that indicates whether place does or does not exist in the current system state. The firing policy of transitions is similar to the case of the Petri net obtained by discarding the nonexistent places. This Petri net is called a configuration of the reconfigurable net. As long as no Structure-modifying rule is fired; the reconfigurable net behaves exactly like this Petri net.

3   Configuration of the IMS System Model

In configuration Scenario to build the Configuration they are two parts they are Control and Plant Configuration. In Control configuration they having the each place is associated with transition. Where as in Plant configuration each place is associated with sub places where as the sub places which having the different types of priority depends on the priority the flow will continue. In the control configuration the institute plant model as shown in the Fig 2.The Patients enters in different conditions and exits after the course of the treatment is over.

Table 1. State Assignment for the Configured System

State	State Assignment	State	State Assignment
S1	Patients Community	S15	Patients being counseled by Doctor
S2	Patients admitted in the course	S16	Patients waiting to GN course change
S3	Patients waiting to be assigned a course in the institution	S17	Patients planning for EM course
S4	Patients waiting to be seen by ER staff	S18	Patients planning for placements
S5	ER GN staff seeing Patients	S19	Patients waiting to EM course change
S6	ER EM staff seeing Patients	S20	Patients planning for EM course change
S7	Patients waiting for GN Course	S21	Patients EM going for higher studies
S8	Patients waiting for EM Course	S22	Patients EM wants placements
S9	GN Course being under taken in various school	S23	ER Patients complete GN course
S11	EM Course being under taken in various school	S24	ER Patients complete EM course
S11	ER GN Patients transferred to dual Treatment	S25	ER Doctor available
TS12	ED EM Patients transferred to dual treatment	S26	ER Assistant Doctor available
S13	ER GN Patients promoted to EM Patients	S27	GN course completed
S14	GN Patients merit to EM Patients	S28	EM Course completed

In the ER (Emergency Resources) where places are denoted as $P_1, P_2, P_3, P_4, ..P_n$ are the places used to model the maximum number of Patients that can be accepted simultaneously in the ED. $v_1, v_2, v_3 ... v_n$ are the vertex of the discrete events. The constraints consist of three condition such as the less than or equal to a ,greater than or equal to the control configuration value. The entire system model for the configuration of the system is done using any of the three condition mention above.

The state transition table is shown above indicates change in the state of the Patients when he or she enters the institute. The two major kinds of Patients who enter the course are GN (Under Graduate) Patients and EM(Emergency) Patients.

In the plant configuration the in each place they are few task will be selected and the emergency situation have one flow, general case no need of admission, for accident case there is one flow of admission, for VIP one type of admission and for breakage of courses one type of admission will be there. After creating the plant configuration every place having the sub places so that for the next stage of plant will be the configuration. In the plant configuration the each place having certain tasks, as like in the control configuration but here more Patients can be placed, courses can be done. For taking the linear constraints for the next step of configuration

The Institute Management System (IMS) works to handle the Patients in various stages of the system. The flexibility of that course makes the Patients to undergo any course as per the interest of the doctor check up procedure. System modeling for IMS is very effective if the system configuration is done in the stable and reliable.

4   Reconfigurations of the IMS

The reconfiguration of the system modeling using the Petri net (also known as a place/transition net or P/T net) is one of several mathematical modeling languages for the description of distributed systems. A Petri net is a ratio directed bipartite graph, in which the nodes represent transitions i.e. events that may occur, signified by bars and places i.e. conditions, signified by circles. The directed arcs describe which places are pre- and/or post conditions for which transitions are signified by arrows. In Fig.1 the modeling of Petri net is shown how token flow and how weight of the token is taken and how the weight of the is added.

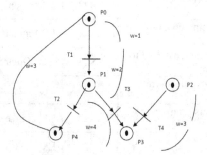

Fig. 1. Petri net Model

In the above model as shown in the figure 2.as the token get activated p0 is initially given as weight w=1 p1 token is enabled when the t1 is enabled   then the p1 token is passed through the p2 so the weight is increased to w=2.So if it passed through the p3 so the w=3.Else if it passed through the   p2 and P4 both the weight at a time increased to w=5. In this reconfiguration procedure, the Petri net concepts are used, in this reconfiguration can be done with respect to the tokens.

When the token get activated the token leave the particular places so the transition will be enabled to pass through the next place so that the token will increases and the weight of the places will increases. The aim of the reconfiguration is to allocate the resources, stability of the system and to optimize the system. For example, there is place followed by p1 and t1 next p2 .if the token is fired so that the transition will enabled   and p2 got the token but token will increases in that particular place and also increased for that particular place. Consider the loop wise structure when the p1 is followed to t2 and t1. T2 will follow the p2 and p3. If p1 is fired so the token is passed to p2 so that weight is increased to one and it passed to p3 so the weight is increased to two but it having the t2 to p3 so weight is increased to three.

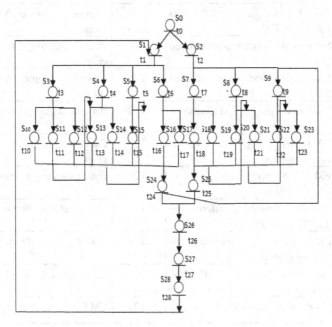

Fig. 2. Institute Management Model of the Reconfigured System

The Institutional managements model (IMS) consists of the various states such as the Patients entry to the course selection, the Patients are then admitted into GN(General) or EM(Emergency). To prevent data from getting lost due to noise in the wireless channel, an error-coding scheme is applied. Turbo code is a powerful error coding technique employed nowadays in communication systems. In this the image is retained in the receiving end by proper design of the error coding scheme. The data which are used for the various for the system has to be passed through various stages and processed to produce the result.

The time transition of the System Model for the reconfigured system is given for each state and its corresponding state is also performed. The images obtained after decoding are found to be suitable for recognition and diagnosis by the doctors. This novel technology will enhance the health care in rural area where the opinion of a specialized doctor is not available.

Table 2. State time transition of system for Reconfigured System

Time	Time Transition	Time	Time Transition
T1	Time required for the Patients enter IMS	T15	Patients being counseled by Doctor
T2	Course assigned to Patients	T16	Patients waiting to GN course change
T3	Courses elected by Patients	T17	Patients planning for EM course
T4	Admitted to be seen by ED Patients in GN	T18	Patients planning for placements
T5	Admitted to be seen by ED Patients in GN	T19	Patients waiting to EM course change
T6	Seen by the Doctor and assigned GN	T20	Patients planning for EM course change
T7	Seen by the Doctor and assigned EM	T21	Patients EM going for higher studies
T8	Patients waiting for EM Course	T22	Patients being counseled by Asst. Doctor
T9	GN Course being under taken in various school	T23	Patients being counseled by Doctor
T10	EM Course being under taken in various school	T24	Patients waiting to crash course
S11	ED GN Patients transferred to dual Treatment	T25	ED Doctor available
S12	ED EM Patients transferred to dual treatment	T26	ED Assistant Doctor available
T13	ED GN Patients promoted to EM Patients	T27	GN course completed
T14	GN Patients merit to EM Patients	T28	EM Course completed

5   Experiment Results

In the configuration scenario the result analysis, the configuration process built by using Finite state automata the pre layout and post layout analysis are done using Cadence Digital Encounter with tsmc 180nm technology and 1.8 Volts. The pre-layout analysis is done for the front end design flow of the system consists of various stages such as the design entry, simulation, synthesis and the net file is created. The net file is analyzed and pre-layout .Here in these number of Instances in pre-layout analysis 548, power of 180uW and Area of 7290um^2.

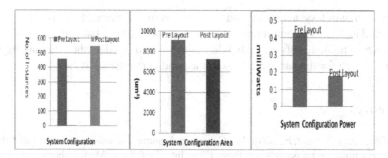

Fig. 3. System Configuration for Instances, Area and Power

Instances in pre layout analysis 458, power of 433uW and area of 9173.4um^2. The comparison of the system performance this done with the reconfigured system.The analysis of the system performance is done with the metric such as the instances, area and the power of the system.

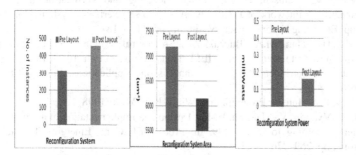

Fig. 4. Reconfiguered System Instances, Area and Power

The layout design of the system reconfiguration is done by using 180nm Technology. The reconfiguration of the system is done and the GDSII(Graphic Data System II Files).The hardware implementation of the system modelling is done for the system model This novel technology will enhance the health care in rural area where the opinion of a specialized doctor is not available. The analyses of system performances for the configured and reconfigured system are done for pre and post layout simulation as per the design methodology.

6   Conclusion

Configuration of the discrete event system is done and reconfiguration is done with Petri net model. The optimization of the resources for the system modeling for the institution management system .The performance of the system modeled is done for configured system. The System configured model is implemented and the parameter such as system instances, power and area of the system are obtained. The reconfiguration of Institution Management System is done and the parameter under analysis has got better performance. In novel applications, the information is mostly sent through wireless networks and the data is more prone to noise. Since very important data has to be communicated, it is necessary to get back the original data in the receiver. The flexibility and reliability of the system model when its running in the real time is high for the hardware is examined and performance is estimated.

References

[1]   Giua, A., DiCesare, F., Silva, M.: Generalized mutual exclusion constraints on nets with uncontrollable transitions. In: Proc. IEEE Int. Conf. Syst. Man, Cybern., pp. 974–979 (1992)

[2]   Lucas, M.R., Endsley, E.W., Tilbury, D.M.: Coordinated logic control for reconfigurable machine tools. In: Proc. Amer. Control Conf., pp. 2107–2113 (1999)

[3]   Badouel, E., Oliver, J.: Reconfigurable nets: A class of high level Petri nets supporting dynamic changes within workflow systems. INRIA Research, Tech. Rep. PI-1163 (1998)

[4]   Vyatkin, V., Hanisch, H.-M.: Formal modeling and verification in the software engineering framework of IEC61499: A way to self verifying systems. In: Proc. IEEE Symp. Emerging Technol. Factory Autom., pp. 113–118 (2001)

[5]   Darabi, H., Jafari, M.A., Buczak, A.L.: A control switching theory for supervisory control of discrete event systems. IEEE Trans. Robot. Autom. 19(1), 131–137 (2003)

[6]   Murata, T.: Petri nets: Properties, analysis and applications. Proc. IEEE, 541–580 (1989)

[7]   Wolsey, L.A.: Integer Programming. Wiley, New York (1998)

[8]   Cai, X., Vyatkin, V., Hanisch, H.-M.: Design and implementation of a prototype control system according to IEC 61499. In: Proc. IEEE Conf. Emerging Technol. Factory Autom., pp. 269–276 (2003)

[9]   Boucher, T.O.: Computer Automation in Manufacturing: An Introduction. Chapman & Hall, London (1996)

[10] Cassandras, G.C., Lafortune, S.: Introduction to Discrete Event Systems. Kluwer, Norwell (1999)

[11] Lin, F., Wonham, W.M.: Supervisory control of timed discrete event systems under partial observation. IEEE Trans. Autom. Control 40(3), 558–562 (1995)

[12] Ramadge, P.J.G., Wonham, W.M.: The control of discrete event system. Proc. IEEE 77(1), 81–98 (1989)

[13] Zhou, M., DiCesare, F., Desrochers, A.A.: A top-down approach to systematic synthesis of Petri net models for manufacturing systems. In: Proc. IEEE Int. Conf. Robot. Autom., pp. 534–539 (1989)

Survey on Effective Audio Mastering

Shajin Prince[1] and K.R. Shankar Kumar[2]

[1] Dept. of ECE, Karunya University, Coimbatore, India
shajinprince@gmail.com
[2] Dept. of ECE, Sri Ramakrishna Engineering College, Coimbatore, India
shanwire@gmail.com

Abstract. Mastering, a form of audio post-production, is the process of preparing and transferring recorded audio from a source containing the final mix to a data storage device (the master); the source from which all copies will be produced (via methods such as pressing, duplication or replication). Recently, the format choice includes using digital masters although analog masters, such as audio tapes, are still being used by the manufacturing industry and by a few engineers who have chosen to specialize in analog mastering. In order to make a deterministic process, mastering requires critical listening; there are software mastering tools available to facilitate this last step, but results still depend upon the accuracy of speaker monitors. In addition, "music mastering" engineers may also need to apply corrective equalization and dynamic enhancement in order to improve upon sound translation on all playback systems. This paper gives an overview of the audio mastering process and the various techniques used in it.

Keywords: Mastering, Critical Listening, dynamic enhancement.

1   Introduction

Historically a mastering engineer was a person who ensured that a musical programme was successfully committed to a musical release medium such as vinyl or cd. This much is true today and yet the mastering engineer's role has changed to some degree to involve a cross over into other areas of audio production. Mastering engineers have had to adapt to the changes in the music industry and the world at large. Mastering audio comprises of a number of processes that predominantly apply to stereo interleaved audio files. Mastering engineers are usually very experienced audio engineers. They should have had tangible practical experience within the music recording and mixing industries so their skill set is wide and varied. This experience filters down to the decisions made when mastering the music and gives the experience required to interpret the sonic information that is produced by using the very finest high resolution audio equipment available. Truly professional audio mastering does not utilize small sized mixing speakers. (bookshelf type near field monitors) A mastering engineer requires accurate and complete sonic information to perform their work. Large scale, full range, highly accurate loudspeakers manufactured by a well respected speaker building company are a pre-requisite for making the correct final decisions on a musicians, producers or record labels musical productions. A mastering

T.-h. Kim et al. (Eds.): FGCN/DCA 2012, CCIS 350, pp. 293–301, 2012.

engineer should take care to preserve his or her hearing and ensure that they are not subjected to potentially damaging sound pressure levels. Every decision made during audio mastering will be based on the engineers hearing acuity. Mastering audio is distinct from mixing because the engineer will predominantly be working with the stereo mixdown that has been provided by the client. This is ideally a .wav or .aiff file at 24 bit resolution.As such it is imperative that the music mix balance is as good as the client can possibly achieve as good mastering will rely on it. Mastering does not usually have the flexibility afforded by multi track recording mix downs and is akin to adding the icing on the cake of a well produced musical mix.

The equipment used in mastering studios will be very high quality analog and digital audio processing equipment. Typically but not exclusively these will be, parametric equalizers, compressors (dynamic range control), limiters and stereo width manipulation tools. There are often 2 goals with this equipment. The first type of equipment is transparent when audio passes through, only influencing the audio when the controls are adjusted intentionally by the mastering engineer. The second is equipment that has a design which adds some specific colouration to the audio even if the equipment parameters remain at zero. The synergy between the equipment choices, monitoring, acoustics and engineering experience should add together to be a subjective improvement of the audio before release.

2   Literature Survey on Audio Mastering Process

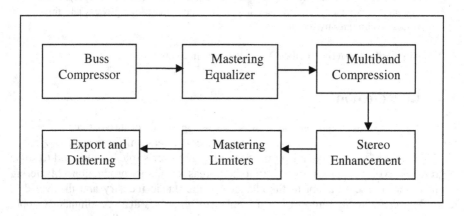

Fig. 1. Block Diagram of Audio Mastering Process

2.1   The Buss Compressor

Essentially buss compression is no different to any other compression treatment. The only real discerning factor here is that buss compression refers to the practice of applying a compressor to a whole group of instruments or even the entire mix. There are a few different types of compressor that are commonly used as buss compressors — single (or full band) and multi-band models. Some consider a true buss compressor to be a traditional single band compressor of a very high quality or with custom components. Technically, any single band compressor in your plug-in list can be put to work as a buss compressor but some would argue that such a critical task deserves a dedicated processor. Some cheaper tracking compressors may introduce unwanted artifacts and dramatically reduce dynamic range. The mastering buss compressor's main job is to reduce the dynamic range of the mix, taming peaks and therefore raising quieter sounds. This will all result in a louder more defined mix but the whole process should occur transparently and be pleasing to the ear.

Compression of Audio Signal Using Gammachirp Wavelet. The main goal of Gammachirp wavelet algorithm in this project is to compress high quality audio signal and maintaining transparent quality at low bit rates. Most psychoacoustic models for coding applications use a uniform spectral decomposition to approximate the frequency selectivity of the human auditory system. However the equal filter properties of the uniform subbands do not match the non uniform characteristics of the cochlear filters. For implementing this algorithm a design of psychoacoustic model was developed following the model used in the standard MPEG-1 audio layer 3. The goal is to identify the best model that can be applied to the audio coders in sub-bands approximating the critical bands and finally to improve the psychoacoustic model. This study shows that the Gammachirp offers a good performance. In fact, it gives the best compression ratio and sound quality in comparison to the FFT and Munich coders.

Digital Audio Compression. Compared to most digital data types, with the exception of digital video, the data rates associated with uncompressed digital audio are substantial. Digital audio compression enables more efficient storage and transmission of audio data. The many forms of audio compression techniques offer a range of encoder and decoder complexity, compressed audio quality, and differing amounts of data compression. The law transformation and ADPCM coder are simple approaches with low complexity, low-compression, and medium audio quality algorithms. The MPEG/audio standard is a high complexity, high-compression, and high audio quality algorithm. These techniques apply to general audio signals and are not specifically tuned for speech signals.

Audio Compression Based on Perceptual Set Partitioning in Hierarchical Trees. The scheme presented is perceptually scalable and also provides for lossless compression. It produces smooth objective scalability, in terms of SegSNR, from lossy to lossless compression. The proposal is built around the introduced perceptual SPIHT algorithm, which is a modification of the SPIHT algorithm. Both objective and subjective results are reported and demonstrate both perceptual and objective measure scalability. The subjective results indicate that the proposed method performs comparably with the MPEG-4 AAC coder at 16, 32 and 64 kbps, yet also achieves a scalable-to-lossless architecture.

2.2   The Mastering Equalizer

When it comes to picking the right EQ for the mastering chain many of you may be looking for a dedicated mastering processor. Although there is hardware and software products that are labelled as such, the truth is any decent EQ plug-in can be used. Obviously sonic integrity is paramount here so the best you can afford is usually a good guideline to stick to. Saying that there are some really excellent equalizers that won't break the bank. Although 'dedicated' mastering EQs can include some very handy features for shaping your final mix, what we are looking for here is a clean interface, pristine signal path and plenty of flexibility. For those of you new to the area of mastering a spectrum analyzer can always be useful as well.

Constant-Q Graphic Equalizers. A new class of graphic equalizers is presented that is characterized by being constant-Q and shown to offer significant advantages over conventional RLC and gyrator based designs. Only constant-Q designs are,in fact, true "graphic" equalizers. Included isan introductory tutorial on the design requirements and trade-offs of constant-Q circuitry, as well as a discussion regarding the combining characteristics of each class of equalizer. Shown is that all equalizers combine equally for the same bandwidths. Constant-Q one-third-octave graphic equalizers have evolved into second-generation models. Future research will result in even better units.

Digital Parametric Equalizer. A new type of second-order digital parametric equalizer was proposed whose frequency response matches closely that of its analog counterpart throughout the Nyquist interval and does not suffer from the prewarping effect of the bilinear transformation near the Nyquist frequency. Closed-form design equations and direct-form and lattice realizations are derived. The method encompasses the conventional design as a special case. For low center frequencies and widths, the new method will be almost identical to the conventional method, because the Nyquist-frequency gain G1 is almost equal to G0. The differences of the two methods are felt only for high frequencies and widths. The method allows various ways of defining the bandwidth in linear- and log-frequency scales and of defining the bandwidth gain GB. Given the wide variety of possibilities in choosing GB, it is perhaps best to leave GB as a free parameter to be chosen by the user.

Equalization for 15 in/s Studio Master Recording. A new equalization and reference fluxivity are proposed: no LF pre-emphasis, reproducing HF equalization +3 dB at 6300 Hz ("25 μs") and reference fluxivity of 250 nWb/m. Measured data and a demonstration compare the NAB and proposed performances. Pre-emphasis at 4 kHz is increased from -2 to +1 dB; at 16 kHz, from +1 to +6.5 dB (NAB was +11 dB in 1950, when developed). Noise and maximum signal at 4 kHz are thus reduced 3 dB, and at 16 kHz, 5.5 dB. Recording response with less than a total of 0.5 dB ripple up to 20 kHz is achieved with one RC recording equalizer. New values of transition frequency F is 0 and 6300 Hz, and reference fluxivity of 250 nWb/m, are proposed. These will give a high frequency noise improvement of 4- to 6-dB, a general signal level increase of 2 dB, and elimination of low-frequency overloading. Change from the present reference fluxivity and the NAB equalization require only a readjustment of presently available gain and equalization controls, and, for some equipment, the removal of one RC circuit.

2.3   Multi – band Compression

Most DAWs now include some kind of multi-band processor (usually a compressor/expander) as standard. Although they may differ in look and layout, they all carry out pretty much the same function. If up until now you have felt that these processors are a little complex in nature it's time to dive in head first, as they can be extremely useful. This frequency dependent compression gives you the ability to home in on specific instruments or areas of your mix and boost or attenuate them in a very accurate fashion. This sort of treatment often gives you a much more transparent result than equalization.

Dynamic Compression Algorithm. One important feature of the implemented compression algorithm is the separate adjustment of the static, linear frequency shaping and the nonlinear dynamic compression. While the former is performed with the maximum frequency resolution of approximately 60 Hz, the latter is performed at a much broader frequency resolution that corresponds to the critical bandwidth of the ear . In addition, the effective frequency resolution for the nonlinear compression can be altered by using different slope values when accounting for upward and downward spread of masking. If these slopes are assumed to be very flat, all frequency channels are synchronized and a broadband compression will effectively result. The values used in this algorithm reflect approximate values for normal listeners in psycho acoustical experiments.

Blind Multiband Signal Reconstruction. The problem of reconstructing a multiband signal from its sub Nyquistpointwise samples, when the band locations are unknown is addressed. This approach assumes an existing multi-coset sampling. To date, recovery methods for this sampling strategy ensure perfect reconstruction either when the band locations are known, or under strict restrictions on the possible spectral supports. In this paper, only the number of bands and their widths are assumed without any other limitations on the sup- port. We describe how to choose the parameters of the multi-coset sampling so that a unique multiband signal matches the given samples. To recover the signal, the continuous reconstruction is replaced by a single finite-dimensional problem without the need for discretization. The resulting problem is studied within the framework of compressed sensing, and thus can be solved efficiently using known tractable algorithms from this emerging area. We also develop a theoretical lower bound on the average sampling rate required for blind signal reconstruction, which is twice the minimal rate of known-spectrum recovery. Our method ensures perfect reconstruction for a wide class of signals sampled at the minimal rate, and provides a first systematic study of com- pressed sensing in a truly analog setting. Numerical experiments are presented demonstrating blind sampling and reconstruction with minimal sampling rate.

Real-Time Multiband Dynamic Compression. A multi-signal-processor set-up is introduced that is used for real-time implementation of digital hearing aid algorithms that operate on stereophonic (i .e .binaural) input signals and perform signal processing in the frequency domain. A multiband dynamic compression algorithm was implemented which operates in 24 critical band filter channels, allows for interaction between frequency bands and stereo channels, and is fitted to the hearing of the individual patient by a loudness scaling method. In addition, a binaural noise reduction algorithm was implemented that amplifies sound emanating from the front and suppresses lateral noise sources as well as reverberation. These algorithms were optimized with respect to their processing parameters and by minimizing the processing artifacts. Different versions of the algorithms were tested in six listeners with sensorineural hearing impairment using both subjective quality assessment methods and speech intelligibility measurements in different acoustical situations. For most subjects, linear frequency shaping was subjectively assessed to be negative, although it improved speech intelligibility in noise. Additional compression was assessed to be positive and did not deteriorate speech intelligibility as long as the processing parameters were fitted carefully. All noise reduction strategies employed here were subjectively assessed to be positive. Although the suppression of reverberation only slightly improved speech intelligibility, a combination of directional filtering and dereverberation provided a substantial improvement in speech intelligibility for most subjects and for a certain range of signal-to-noise ratios. The real-time implementation was very helpful in optimizing and testing the algorithms, and the overall results indicate that carefully designed and fitted binaural hearing aids might be very beneficial for a large number of patients.

2.4   Stereo Enhancement

The main thing that presents a problem when it comes to stereo treatment in mastering is the use of the wrong processor. Many DAWs supply stereo enhancement tools that are perfectly usable in the mix but are not really suited to a mastering environment.

Enhancement of Spatial Stereo Sound Quality. A system for the extraction of uncorrelated reverberation from two-channel (stereo) audio signals is proposed and evaluated. Applications for the new system vary from surround-sound multichannel loudspeaker upmixers for home-theater or automotive audio systems, to headphone-based auralization for enhancing the spatial sound quality of a listening experience. The new system uses the normalized-least-mean-square (NLMS) algorithm to equalize the two input signals with respect to both spectral magnitude and phase before differencing to remove correlated components. A theoretical model of the system based on a stochastic room impulse response model was validated by empirical measurements made in a reverberant hall with a microphone pair, and from a formal subjective evaluation the system is shown to be an effective approach to extracting reverberation from audio recordings. Upmixing two-channel ("stereo") audio recordings to four or five channels allows for reproduction with immersive multichannel loudspeaker systems found in domestic "home theater," automotive audio, and teleconferencing environments. Furthermore, headphone audio systems would benefit from spatial audio enhancement with ambiance auralization processors to reproduce the recorded reverberation in a way that seems more enveloping. These "ambiance extraction" upmixers can reduce the number of channels stored or transmitted, while increasing the spatial sound quality of the recreated sound scene. The model predicts that the level of the extracted reverberation is related to the interchannel signal correlation, which in turn is related to both the correlation between the early-arriving sound to each microphone, and the ratio of the reverberant component of the room impulse response to the early-arriving component.

Omni stereo - Panoramic Stereo Imaging. An Omnistereo panorama consists of a pair of panoramic images, where one panorama is for the left eye and another panorama is for the right eye. The panoramic stereo pair provides a stereo sensation up to a full 360 degrees. Omnistereo panoramas cannot be photographed by two omnidirectional cameras from two viewpoints, but can be constructed by mosaicing together images from a rotating stereo pair. A more convenient approach to generate omnistereo panoramas is by mosaicing images from a single rotating camera. This approach also enables the control of stereo disparity, giving larger baselines for faraway scenes, and a smaller baseline for closer scenes. Capturing panoramic omnistereo images with a rotating camera makes it impossible to capture dynamic scenes at video rates and limits omnistereo imaging to stationary scenes. We, therefore, present two possibilities for capturing omnistereo panoramas using optics without any moving parts. A special mirror is introduced such that viewing the scene through this mirror creates the same rays as those used with the rotating cameras. A lens for omnistereo panorama is also introduced. The designs of the mirror and of the lens are based on curves whose caustic is a circle. Omnistereo panoramas can also be rendered by computer graphics methods to represent virtual environments.

2.5   Mastering Limiters

The first thing to understand about the all important limiting phase of our mastering chain is that even small amounts of the process will increase the perceived level of a track. Simply put this means it may not actually read as louder on your meter but it will sound louder to the human ear. This effect is created by a reduced dynamic response and relies on the fact we as humans judge volume using average levels. So cutting a very long story, very short… compress and limit your track more, reduce it's dynamics and ultimately you will create a signal that sounds louder.

2.6   Export and Dithering

We are now ready to export the master. In most DAWs you will now be presented with a number of options. Some applications will offer more features than others here but there are always a few key things to look out for, one of these is dithering. Pretty much every DAW out there will feature dithering options and it's something my students ask about a lot. Simply put dithering is a process used when moving to lower bitrates. For example if we are working at 24-bit (either at the mixing or mastering stage) we will need to move to 16-bit. This is so our final master is suitable for MP3 conversion and burning to various media.

The move from 24 bits (or higher) requires a fair amount of digital data to be removed. In normal circumstances this would result in a lowering in quality but dithering uses various complex algorithms to ensure that what you hear in your final master is nearly identical to that of your 24-bit premaster. The whole process is pretty clever and there are a number of different algorithms floating about between the various DAWs. You may see Power or Apogee dithering options, or your chosen application may simply have a dithering on or off option. Some applications, such as Cubase, rely on plug-ins that are inserted in your mastering chain to perform their dithering. Whatever the options presented to you its worth knowing a few tricks.

3   Conclusion

The various processes of audio mastering were described in this paper. All the processes told here is very significant in the mastering process. The survey was done for all the process using many references and elaborated. The objective of this survey is to get an idea of the audio mastering process and to develop the same in a software environment. The software will have all the mastering process built in and will reduce the area and cost of the mastering set up.

References

1. Reiss, J.D.: Design of Audio Parametric Equalizer Filters Directly in the Digital Domain. IEEE Transactions on Audio, Speech, and Language Processing 19 (2011)
2. Orfanidis, S.J.: High-order digital parametric equalizer design. J. Audio Eng. Soc. 53, 1026–1046 (2005)
3. Mishali, M., Eldar, Y.C.: Blind Multiband Signal Reconstruction: Compressed Sensing for Analog Signals. IEEE Transactions on Signal Processing 57(3) (March 2009)
4. Holters, M., Zölzer, U.: Graphic Equalizer Design Using Higher-Order Recursive Filters. In: Proc. of the 9th Int. Conference on Digital Audio Effects, Montreal (2006)
5. Orfanidis, S.J.: High-order digital parametric equalizer design. J. Audio Eng. Soc. 53(11), 1026–1046 (2005)
6. Peleg, S., Ben-Ezra, M.: Omnistereo: Panoramic Stereo Imaging. IEEE Transactions on Pattern Analysis and Machine Intelligence 23(3) (March 2001)
7. Barchiesi, D., Reiss, J.: Reverse Engineering of a Mix. J. Audio Eng. Soc. 58(7/8) (2010)
8. Katz, B.: Mastering Audio: The Art and the Science. Focal Press (2002)
9. Breebaart, J., Engdegård, J., Falch, C., Hellmuth, O., Hilpert, J., Hoelzer, A., Koppens, J., Oomen, W., Resch, B., Schuijers, E., Terentiev, L.: Spatial Audio Object Coding (SAOC)-The Upcoming MPEG Standard on Parametric Object Based Audio Coding. Presented at the 124th Convention of the Audio Engineering Society (2008)
10. Simmer, U., Schmidt, D., Bitzer, J.: Parameter Estimation of Dynamic Range Compressors: Models, Procedures, and Test Signals. Presented at the 120th Convention of the Audio Engineering Society, J. AudioEng. Soc. (Abstracts) 54, 736 (2006); Convention Paper 6849
11. Barchiesi, D., Reiss, J.: Automatic Target Mixing Using Least-Squares Optimization of Gain and Equalization Settings. In: Proc. 12th Int. Conf. on Digital Audio Effects (DAFx 2009), vol. 1, pp. 7–14 (September 2009)
12. Zolzer, U.: DAFx: Digital Audio Effects. John Wiley & Sons, Chichester (2002)
13. McNally, G.W.: Dynamic Range Control of Digital Audio Signals. J. Audio Eng. Soc. 32, 316–327 (1984)
14. Bharitkar, S., Kyriakakis, C.: Immersive Audio Signal Processing. Springer, New York

15. Karjalainen, M., et al.: About room response equalization and dereverberation. In: Proc.WASPAA 2005, New Paltz, NY, pp. 183–186 (October 2005)
16. Miyoshi, M., Kaneda, Y.: Inverse filtering of room acoustics. IEEE Trans. Signal Processing 36(2), 145–152 (1988)
17. Hans, M., Schafer, R.W.: Lossless compression of digital audio. IEEE Signal Processing Magazine 18(4), 21–32 (2001)
18. Rad, M., Mertins, A., Bumett, I.: Audio compression using the MLT and SPIHT. In: Proceedings of DSPCS 2002, pp. 128–132 (2002)
19. Irwan, R., Aarts, R.M.: Two-to-five channel sound processing. J. Audio Eng. Soc. 50(11), 914–926 (2002)
20. Faller, C.: Multiple-loudspeaker playback of stereo signals. J. Audio Eng. Soc. 54(11), 1051–1064 (2006)

Multi-algorithm Feature Level Fusion
Using Finger Knuckle Print Biometric

Harbi AlMahafzah[1], Mohammad Imran[2], and H.S. Sheshadri[3]

[1] P.E.T. Foundation Research, University of Mysore, Mandya, India
hmahafzah@hotmail.com
[2] Department of Study in Computer Science, University of Mysore, Mysore, India
emraangi@gmail.com
[3] Department E & C Engg, P.E.S College of Engineering, V.T.U, Mandya, India
hssheshadri@hotmail.com

Abstract. This paper proposed the use of multi-algorithm feature level fusion as a means to improve the performance of Finger Knuckle Print (FKP) verification. LG, LPQ, PCA, and LPP have been used to extract the FKP features. Experiments are performed using the FKP database, which consists of 7,920 images. Results indicate that the multi-algorithm verification approach outperforms higher performance than using any single algorithm. The biometric performance using feature level fusions under different normalization technique as well have been demonstrated in this paper.

Keywords: Feature Level Fusion, Multi-Biometric, Multi-Algorithm, Normalization.

1 Introduction

The need for reliable user authentication techniques has increased in the wake of heightened concerns about security and rapid advancements in networking, communication, and mobility. A wide variety of applications require reliable verification schemes to confirm the identity of an individual requesting their service. Traditional authentication methods using passwords (knowledge-based security) and ID cards (token based security) are commonly used to restrict access to a variety of systems. However these systems are vulnerable to attacked and security can be easily breached. The emergence of biometrics technologies is replacing the traditional methods as it has addressed the problems that plague these systems.

Biometric refers to the automatic recognition of individuals based on their physiological and behavioral characteristics. Biometrics systems are commonly classified into two categories: physiological biometrics and behavioral biometrics. Physiological biometrics (fingerprint, face, iris, etc) use measurements from the human body. Behavioral biometrics (signature, voice, etc) use dynamics measurements based on human actions [1][3]. These systems are based on pattern recognition methodology, which follows the acquisition of the biometric data by building a biometric feature set,

T.-h. Kim et al. (Eds.): FGCN/DCA 2012, CCIS 350, pp. 302–311, 2012.

and comparing versus a pre-stored template pattern. These are unimodal which rely on the evidence of a single source of information for authentication, which have to contend with a variety of problems such as (noise in sensed data, intra-class variations, and inter-class similarities, etc). It is now apparent that a single biometric is not sufficient to meet the variety of requirements imposed by several large scale authentication systems. Possible solutions to compensate for the false classification problem due to intra-class variability and inter-class similarity can be found in the fusion of biometric systems or experts which refers as Multibiometric [8].

The Multibiometric systems can offer substantial improvement in the matching accuracy of a biometric system depending upon the information being combined and the fusion methodology adopted as follows[1]; **Multi sensor**: Multiple sensors can be used to collect the same biometric. **Multi-modal**: Multiple biometric modalities can be collected from the same individual, e.g. fingerprint and face, which requires different sensors. **Multi-sample**: Multiple readings of the same biometric are collected during the enrolment and/or recognition phases, e.g. a number of fingerprint readings are taken from the same finger. **Multiple algorithms**: Multiple algorithms for feature extraction and matching are used on the same biometric sample. **Multi-instance**: Means the use of the same type of raw biometric sample and processing on multiple instances of similar body parts, (such as two fingers, or two irises) also been referred to as multi-unit systems in the literature [2]. The rest of the paper is organized as follows: Section 2 presents related works, proposed methods are given in section 3, normalization techniques in section 4, fusion strategies in section 5, detailed experimental results are given in Section 6, and conclusion is mentioned in Section 7.

2   Related Works

Lin Zhang et al.[4] proposed an effective FKP recognition scheme by extracting and assembling local and global features of FKP images. The experimental results conducted on FKP database demonstrate that the proposed local–global information combination scheme could significantly improve the recognition accuracy obtained by either alone. Xiang QIN et al.[6] introduced a Gabor feature-based PCA approach for apple Physalospora recognition. First, eight orientations and four scales are designed to form a Gabor bank with thirty-two different Gabor filters. PCA reduces the augmented Gabor feature matrix and hence the efficiency improved both in image recognition and classification.

Markus Turtinen et al.[5] have considered of combining Local Binary Pattern (LBP) texture features with a Self-Organizing Map (SOM) classification. It was shown that a log-likelihood distance measure can be successfully used instead of the Euclidean distance normally used with the SOM. According to the authors, unsupervised learning, visualization and high-speed classification capabilities of the SOM combined with the excellent discrimination capability and the computational simplicity of the LBP offer significant potential for new industrial applications.

Karthik Nandakumar et al. [9] have studied the effect of different score normalization techniques in a multimodal biometric system. Min-max, Z-score, and

Tanh normalization techniques followed by a simple sum of scores fusion method result in a higher GAR than all the other normalization and fusion techniques. Xiaoyang Tan and Bill Triggs [10] have investigated the benefits of combining two of the most successful feature sets for robust face recognition under uncontrolled lighting: Gabor wavelets and LBP features. The authors have shown that by combining the two local appearance descriptors, Gabor wavelets and Local Binary Patterns (LBP), gives considerably better performance than either alone. Since both feature sets are high dimensional so PCA used to reduce the dimensionality prior to normalization and integration.

3   Proposed Method

In this paper a hand-based biometric technique, finger-knuckle-print (FKP) have been used, FKP refers to the image pattern of the outer surface around the phalangeal joint of one's finger, which is formed by bending slightly the finger knuckle [4]. The experiments are developed for personal authentication using DZhang FKP database. FKP images were collected from 165 volunteers, including 125 males and 40 females.

3.1   Pre-processing

This section describe the Region of Interest (ROI) extraction, the process involved to extract ROI for each instance is as follows. It is necessary and critical to align FKP images by adaptively constructing a local coordinate system for each image. With such a coordinate system, an ROI can be cropped from the original image using the following steps suggested in [4], as shown in Figure-1.

Fig. 1. a)Image acquisition device is being used to collect FKP samples b)Sample FKP image c)ROI coordinate system, where the rectangle indicates the area d)Extracted ROI

4   Feature Extraction

As this paper concern about multi-algorithm the following feature extraction algorithms have been used to extract the features prior to fuse a different algorithms combination.

4.1   Log-Gabor Filters

Log-Gabor function proposed by Field [11]. Field suggests that natural images are better coded by filters that have Gaussian transfer functions when viewed on the logarithmic frequency scale. On the linear frequency scale the log-Gabor function has a transfer function of the form

$$G(w) = e^{(-log(w/w_0)^2)/(2(log(k/w_0)^2))}$$

where w_0 is the filter's centre frequency. To obtain constant shape ratio filters the term k/w_0 must also be held constant for varying w_0.

4.2   Local Phase Quantization

The local phase quantization (LPQ) method introduced by Ojansivu et al. [12] is based on the blur invariance property of the Fourier phase spectrum. It uses the local phase information extracted using the 2-D DFT computed over a rectangular M-by-M neighborhood N_x at each pixel position x of the image f(x) defined by

$$F(u,x) = \sum_{y \in N_x} f(x-y)\, e^{-j2\pi u^T y} = w_u^T f_x$$

where w_u is the basis vector of the 2-D DFT at frequency u, and f_x is another vector containing all M^2 image samples from N_x [12].

4.3   Principal Component Analysis

Principal component analysis (PCA) was invented in 1901 by Karl Pearson. PCA is a mathematical procedure that uses an orthogonal transformation to convert a set of observations of possibly correlated variables into a set of values of linearly uncorrelated variables called principal components. The number of principal components is less than or equal to the number of original variables.

4.4   Locality Preserving Projections

Locality Preserving Projection (LPP) method introduced by Xiaofei He [13] is a linear projective maps that arise by solving a variation problem that optimally preserves the neighborhood structure of the data set. When the high dimensional data lies on a low dimensional manifold embedded in the ambient space, the Locality Preserving Projections are obtained by finding the optimal linear approximations to the eigen-functions of the Laplace Beltrami operator on the manifold. As a result, LPP shares many of the data representation properties of nonlinear techniques such as Laplacian Eigen-maps or Locally Linear Embedding.

5   Feature Normalization

Normalization refers to changing the location and scale parameters of distributions of the individual features sets into a single feature set or vector. If the features are heterogeneous, then it requires normalization to convert them into a common domain. In a good normalization scheme, the estimates of the location and scale parameters must be robust and efficient. Robustness refers to insensitivity to the presence of outliers. Efficiency refers to the proximity of the obtained estimate to the optimal estimate when the distribution of the data is known [2][3]. There are many normalization techniques among them we have used four well-known normalization methods.

- **Min-Max:** The simplest normalization technique is the *Min-Max* normalization. Min-Max normalization is best suited for the case where the bounds (maximum and minimum values) of the scores produced by a matcher are known. In this case, we can easily transform the minimum and maximum scores to 0 and 1 respectively. Let s_j^i denote the ith match score output by the jth matcher, i = 1,2,..., N; j = 1, 2 , . . . , R (R is the number of matchers and N is the number of match scores available in the training set). The min-max normalized score ns_j^i for the test score s_j^i is given by[2][3]:

$$ns_j^t = \frac{s_j^t - min_{i=1}^N s_j^i}{max_{i=1}^N s_j^i - min_{i=1}^N s_j^i}$$

- **Z-Score:** The most commonly used score normalization technique is the z-score normalization that uses the arithmetic mean and standard deviation of the training data. The z-score normalized score is given by   [2][3]:

$$ns_j^t = \frac{s_j^t - \mu_j}{\sigma_j}$$

Where μ_j is the arithmetic mean and σ_j is the standard deviation for the jth matcher. However, both mean and standard deviation are sensitive to outliers and hence, this method is not robust.

- **Median and Median Absolute Deviation (MAD):** The median and median absolute deviation (MAD) statistics are insensitive to outliers as well as points in the extreme tails of the distribution. Hence, a normalization scheme using median and MAD would be robust and is given by[2][3]:

$$ns_j^t = \frac{s_j^t - med_j}{MAD_j}$$

Where $med_j = median_{i=1}^N s_j^i$ and $MAD = median_{i=1}^N | s_j^i - med_j|$

- **Tanh-Estimator:** The *Tanh-estimators* introduced by Hampel et al., 1986 are robust and highly efficient. The Tanh normalization is given by[2][3]:

$$ns_j^t = 1/2 \left\{ tanh\left(0.01 \left(\frac{s_j^t - \mu_j}{\sigma_j} \right) \right) + 1 \right\}$$

This method is not sensitive to outliers. If many of the points that constitute the tail of the distributions are discarded, the estimate is robust but not efficient (optimal).

6   Biometrics Fusion Strategies

In general a biometric system works in two modes: enrollment and authentication. Verification and identification are the two modes an authentication can be carried out.

Fusion of biometric systems, algorithms and/or traits is a well known solution to improve authentication performance of biometric systems. Researchers have shown that multi-biometrics, i.e., fusion of multiple biometric evidences, enhances the recognition performance.

In biometric systems; fusion can be performs at different levels; *Sensor Level, Feature Level, Score Level, and Decision Level Fusion* [8].

6.1   Levels of Fusion

- **Sensor Level Fusion** entails the consolidation of evidence presented by multiple sources of raw data before they are subjected to feature extraction. Sensor level fusion can benefit multi-sample systems which capture multiple snapshots of the same biometric.
- **Feature Level Fusion** In feature-level fusion, the feature sets originating from multiple biometric algorithms are consolidated into a single feature set by the application of appropriate feature normalization, transformation, and reduction schemes [3][8].
- **Score Level Fusion**, the match scores output by multiple biometric matchers are combined to generate a new match score (a scalar).
- **Decision Level Fusion**, fusion is carried out at the abstract or decision level when only final decisions are available (AND, OR, Majority Voting, etc.).

In all the experiment, the data have been fused at feature   level, using different normalization rules, such as (Min-Max, Median and absolute Median, Z-Score, Tanh) for two and three algorithms combination.

7   Results and Discussion

This section deals with the investigation consequences of combining many biometrics at Feature level fusion to measure the performance of multi-algorithm system. In all the experiments, performance is measured in terms of False Acceptance Rate (FAR in %) and corresponding Genuine Acceptance Rate (GAR in %). First the performance of a single algorithm biometric system is measured; later the results for multi-algorithm biometric system are evaluated. The results obtained from single algorithm biometric system are tabulated in Table-1, and depicted as Receiver Operating Characteristic (ROC) curve in Figure-2.

Table 1. Performance of Single Algorithm

FAR (%)	Finger Knuckle Print			
	GAR (%)			
	LG	LPQ	PCA	LPP
0.01	70.00	59.66	51.00	38.00
0.10	76.33	71.67	61.00	47.67
1.00	86.33	83.00	79.00	58.66

From Table-1 it can be observed that the Log Gabor has the highest score among the four algorithms which have been used to extract the features; whereas LPQ the second highest; whereas LPP comes at lower level score. Next we show the fusion performance results of two, three, and four algorithms, under the *feature level fusion*. The score obtained from fusion two and three algorithms shown in table-2 and table-3 respectively

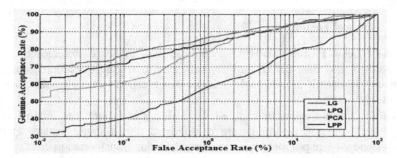

Fig. 2. The ROC Curve Performance of Single Algorithm

Table 2. Performance of two algorithms at Feature level fusion with different normalization techniques

FAR	GAR (%) With Z-Score Normalization					
(%)	LG+LPQ	LG+PCA	LG+LPP	LPQ+PCA	LPQ+LPP	PCA+LPP
0.01	75.33	72.67	73.00	60.67	65.00	49.33
0.10	80.33	79.00	79.00	73.00	81.00	57.33
1.00	93.00	91.67	91.33	88.67	88.00	74.33
	GAR (%) With Tanh Normalization					
0.01	75.33	72.67	73.00	60.67	65.33	49.33
0.10	80.00	79.00	78.33	73.00	81.00	58.33
1.00	93.00	91.67	91.33	88.67	88.33	74.33
	GAR (%) With Median Absolute Normalization					
0.01	70.67	67.33	67.67	51.00	31.00	59.67
0.10	78.67	72.67	79.67	62.33	43.67	65.00
1.00	86.33	86.00	86.00	79.00	58.33	82.67
	GAR (%) With Min-Max Normalization					
0.01	55.67	54.67	52.00	36.00	51.00	35.67
0.10	71.67	73.00	69.33	45.33	59.00	46.00
1.00	83.33	83.67	83.00	66.00	73.00	56.67

From Table-2 it can be observed that the fusion of two algorithms has a significant improve score over a single algorithm with *Z-score* and *tanh-estimators*, but does not have improvement with *Min-Max* and *Median & MAD* which is less or equal the highest performance of the fused algorithms except for fusing PCA+LPP with *Median & MAD* compared with other normalization technique. Figure-3 shows the ROC curve for the performance fusion of two algorithms at Feature level with different normalization techniques.

Table 3. Performance of three algorithms at Feature level fusion with different normalization techniques

FAR (%)	GAR (%) With Z-Score Normalization			
	LG+LPQ+PCA	**LG+LPQ+LPP**	**LG+PCA+LPP**	**LPQ+PCA+LPP**
0.01	75.00	74.67	72.67	72.00
0.10	80.00	79.67	82.33	80.33
1.00	93.00	92.33	93.00	90.00
	GAR (%) With Tanh Normalization			
0.01	74.67	74.33	72.67	72.00
0.10	79.67	79.67	82.33	80.00
1.00	92.67	92.33	93.00	89.33
	GAR (%) With Median Absolute Normalization			
0.01	67.00	71.33	68.33	61.33
0.10	72.67	79.67	73.00	66.00
1.00	86.33	85.67	86.33	82.67
	GAR (%) With Min-Max Normalization			
0.01	57.00	51.00	55.67	48.33
0.10	73.33	71.00	74.67	58.00
1.00	85.33	84.00	87.00	75.00

By looking to Table-3 it can be observed that the fusion of three algorithms does not have any significant score improvement over the fusion of two algorithms; since the best performance among the three algorithms is equal to the best performance of two algorithms. Figure-4 shows the ROC curve for the performance of the fusion of three algorithms at Feature level with different normalization techniques.

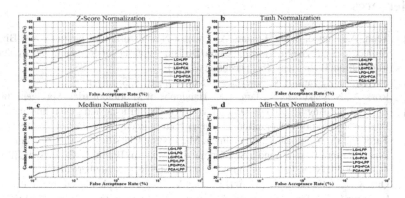

Fig. 3. The ROC curve Feature Level Fusion combination of two algorithms with different Normalization rules, a) Z-Score b) Tanh c) Median d) Min-Max.

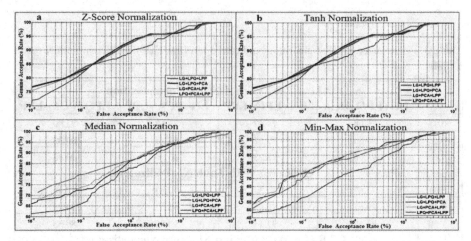

Fig. 4. The ROC curve Feature Level Fusion combination of three algorithms with different Normalization rules, a) Z-Score   b) Tanh c) Median   d) Min-Max.

8   Conclusion

Analyzing the performance of using FKP images as a biometric has been done. Four matching score normalization techniques experimentally evaluated to improve the performance fusions of different algorithm.   The results of evaluation represented by means of system performance (expressed by ROC, FAR vs GAR). From the analysis of experimental results and observations it can be concluded that a multi-algorithm biometric fusion is given better performance than single algorithm. It could also be seen that the fusion performance at feature level depends upon the normalization technique and does not depend on the algorithm performance.

References

[1]   Teoh, A., Samad, S.A., Hussain, A.: Nearest Neighbourhood Classifiers in a Bimodal Biometric Verification System Fusion Decision. Journal of Research and Practice in Information Technology 36(1) (February 2004)

[2]   Stan, J., Li, Z., Jain, A.K.: Encyclopedia of Biometrics. Springer

[3]   Ross, A., Nandakumar, K., Jain, A.K.: Handbook of Multibiometrics. Springer (2006)

[4]   Zhang, L., Zhang, L., Zhang, D., Zhu, H.: Ensemble of local and global information for finger–knuckle-print recognition. Elseveir / Pattern Recognition 44, 1990–1998 (2011)

[5]   Turtinen, M., Mäenpää, T., Pietikäinen, M.: Texture Classification by Combining Local Binary Pattern Features and a Self-Organizing Map. In: Bigun, J., Gustavsson, T. (eds.) SCIA 2003. LNCS, vol. 2749, pp. 1162–1169. Springer, Heidelberg (2003)

[6]   Qin, X., Cai, C., Song, W., Hao, H., Meng, Y., Zhu, J.: Apple Physalospora recognition by using Gabor feature-based PCA. In: Tan, H., Luo, Q. (eds.) Proc. of SPIE. SPIE, vol. 7489, 74890P (2009)

[7]   Kong, A.W.-K., Zhang, D.: Feature-Level Fusion for Effective Palmprint Authentication. In: Zhang, D., Jain, A.K. (eds.) ICBA 2004. LNCS, vol. 3072, pp. 761–767. Springer, Heidelberg (2004)

[8]   AlMahafzah, H., Imran, M., Sheshadri, H.S.: Multibiometric: Feature Level Fusion Using FKP Multi-Instance biometric. IJCSI International Journal of Computer Science Issues 9(4(3)) (July 2012)

[9]   Nandakumar, K., Jain, A.K., Ross, A.A.: Score Normalization in Multimodal Biometric Systems. Elsevier Patteren Recognition (2005)

[10] Tan, X., Triggs, B.: Fusing Gabor and LBP Feature Sets for Kernel-Based Face Recognition. In: Zhou, S.K., Zhao, W., Tang, X., Gong, S. (eds.) AMFG 2007. LNCS, vol. 4778, pp. 235–249. Springer, Heidelberg (2007)

[11] Field, D.J.: Relation between the statistics of natural images and the response properties of cortical cells. J. Opt. Soc. Am. A 4(12), 2379–2394 (1987)

[12] Ojansivu, V., Heikkilä, J.: Blur Insensitive Texture Classification Using Local Phase Quantization. In: Elmoataz, A., Lezoray, O., Nouboud, F., Mammass, D. (eds.) ICISP 2008 2008. LNCS, vol. 5099, pp. 236–243. Springer, Heidelberg (2008)

[13] He, X., Niyogi, P.: Locality Preserving Projections (LPP). In: Advances in Neural Information Processing Systems 16 (NIPS), Vancouver, Canada (2003)

Symbolic Classification of Medical Imaging Modalities

Amir Rajaei, Elham Dallalzadeh, and Lalitha Rangarajan

Department of Studies in Computer Science, University of Mysore,
Mansagangothri, Mysore, 570 006, Karnataka, India
{rajaei80amir,elhamdallalzadeh}@gmail.com,
lali85arun@yahoo.co.in

Abstract. In this paper, we propose a symbolic approach for classification of medical imaging modalities. Texture, appearance, and signal features are extracted from medical images. We propose to represent the extracted features by an interval valued feature vector. Unlike the conventional methods, the interval valued feature vector representation is able to preserve the variations existing among the extracted features of medical images. Based on the proposed symbolic representation, we present a method of classifying medical imaging modalities. The proposed classification method makes use of a symbolic similarity measure for classification. Experimentation is carried out on a benchmark medical imaging modalities database. Our proposed approach achieves classification within negligible time as it is based on a simple matching scheme.

Keywords: Medical imaging modalities, texture features, appearance features, signal features, SVM classifier, KNN classifier, symbolic representation, symbolic classifier.

1 Introduction

Various imaging modalities are playing an important role in disease diagnosis. To have precise and accurate diagnosis, it is required to access specific medical imaging modalities with a particular disease. Recently, Computer Aided Diagnosis (CAD) tool is widely used to assist the physicians and specialists by displaying relevant past cases. Different modalities of medical images such as X-ray, MR, CT, PET, Micro, and Ultrasound are used in CAD.

Automatic categorization of different medical imaging modalities is vastly demanded. In this direction, reliable automatic classification methods are required to deal with large unannotated medical images obtained by clinical centers [1].

Several attempts have been reported in literature for classification of medical imaging modalities. Kitanovski et al. [2] proposed an approach for classification of medical imaging modalities. In their proposed approach, Local Binary Pattern, GLDM, GLRM, and Haralick texture are extracted as features. All the extracted features are concatenated to each other to have a single feature vector representation. They used SVM, KNN and C4.5 classifiers for classification. Malik and Zremic[3] introduced an algorithm based on energy information obtained from the Wavelet transform in order to classify medical images based on modalities and body organ.

T.-h. Kim et al. (Eds.): FGCN/DCA 2012, CCIS 350, pp. 312–323, 2012.

Lookup table is used to identify the image modalities. Different body organs are then classified by extracting and representing the biorthogonal and reversible biorthogonal Wavelet transform.

Florea et al. [4], they proposed to down scaled medical images into the size 256×256. To capture the spatial description of features inside the images, the images are divided into 26 equal blocks. Haralicks coefficients are then extracted from the Gray-Level Co-occurrence Matrix (GLCM) to characterize image texture. The image texture is also described by boxcounted fractal dimension and Gabor wavelet. In addition, they estimated first, second, third, and fourth moments of the obtained features. Finally, K Nearest Neighbor (KNN) classifier is employed for classification. Han and Chen [5] proposed an approach to classify medical imaging modalities by extracting visual features as well as textual features. Visual feature are extracted in terms of global as well as local features. Histogram descriptor of edges, color intensity, and block-based variation are extracted and represented as global features. They used SIFT histogram to represent local features. The binary histogram of some predefined vocabulary words of image caption are extracted and represented as textual features. The extracted features are then concatenated to each other. They applied SVM classifier to classify medical imaging modalities.

Kalpathy and Hersha [6] proposed an approach to classify different modalities of medical images based on concatenation of texture and histogram features. First, each image is resized into 256×256 and then divided into five non overlapping blocks. The Gray Level Co-occurrence Matrix (GLCM) of each block is obtained. From the obtained matrix, a set of texture features such as contrast, correlation, energy, homogeneity, and entropy are extracted. The histogram of each block is also extracted. The gray scale histograms are concatenated with texture features. Neural Network classifier is then applied to classify the medical imaging modalities. Pauly et al.[8] proposed an approach to extract the visual features such as histograms, scale-space, Log-Gabor, and phase congruency of medical images. SVM and Random Forest classifiers are then applied to classify medical images. Florea et al. [16] proposed an approach to categorize medical imaging modalities based on textual annotation interpretation. The textual annotation is interpreted using a set of 96 production rules defined by expert radiologist.

In general, color, texture, and especially textual features are vastly used in classification of medical imaging modalities. Textual features are obtained by the experts interpretation. Hence, different physicians or radiologists may have different interpretation about the medical images with particular diseases. In addition, the resolutions of medical images are very low. Therefore, color features are not robust and also they are with strong noise. Thus, it is necessary to represent medical images by extracting efficient feature without expert intervention.

In this paper, we propose to extract texture, appearance, and signal features of medical imaging modalities. Different medical image modalities are captured with various sources due to their specific purpose. Hence, medical image modalities according to the various classes have different visual features and signal features.

On the other hand, medical images have high intra-class variations as well as low inter-class variations. To capture the variations, we propose to assimilate the extracted features by the concept of symbolic data. The symbolic classifier is then designed to classify medical imaging modalities.

The rest of he paper is organized as follows. The proposed approach for classification of medical imaging modalities are discussed in section 2. The details of the benchmark dataset used in this paper along with the experimental results are presented in section 3. A qualitative comparative analysis of the proposed model with other state-of-the-art models along with their limitations is presented in section 4. The paper is concluded in section 5.

2   Proposed Approach

We propose a symbolic-based approach for classification of medical imaging modalities. We apply 2D adaptive noise removal, median, and 2D order statistics filtering to remove noise as well as to enhance the images. For each image modality, texture, appearance, and signal features are extracted. The extracted features due to all the images of each class of medical imaging modalities are represented symbolically in the form of interval valued. The obtained interval valued features are concatenated and represented as a reference feature vector for a class. We exploit the symbolic similarity measure proposed by Prakash and Guru [9] to classify medical imaging modalities. The stages of the proposed approach for classification of medical imaging modalities are presented in Fig. 1.

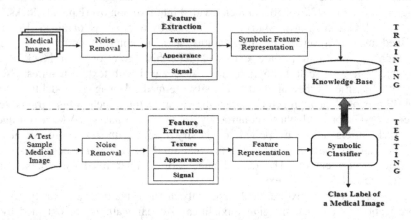

Fig. 1. Block-diagram of the Proposed Classification of Medical Imaging Modalities Approach

2.1   Feature Extraction

The content of medical images are with noise. Further, the resolutions of the images are low. We apply 2D adaptive noise-removal, median, and 2D order-statistic filtering to remove noise as well as to enhance the content of the images. Texture, appearance and signal features are extracted for each of the medical images.

The texture content of medical images are different due to the nature of the devices capturing the images. Hence, texture features are an essential characteristics that can represent the texture content of medical images. It is proposed to extract Local Binary Pattern (LBP) [11], LogGabor [10], Discrete Cosine Transform (DCT) [12], Gray Level Difference Method (GLDM) [13], Gray Level Run-length Method(GLRM)[14], and

Gray Level Co-occurrence Matrix(GLCM) [15] as texture features. LBP is used to describe the gray-scale local texture of the images. LogGabor is a texture feature that localizing the frequency information of the images. DCT is used to represent the transformation of the images in frequency domain. Various local statistical texture properties of medical images can be obtained by applying GLDM. To compute the number of gray level runs of various length of the images, GLRM is applied. GLCM is used to obtain the information about the positions of pixels having similar gray level values in the images. For each of the medical images, texture features are extracted. The extracted texture features are concatenated to each other and represented as a texture feature vector. Hence, medical images of the database are represented by the sets of texture feature vectors, each set represent the texture features of one image. On the other hand, a texture feature matrix, say F_T, is generated that each of its rows represents the texture features of an image.

The appearances of the medical images are different due to the type of the devices capturing the medical images. Hence, appearance features can be considered as other features that can represent different medical imaging modalities. The intensity values of medical images are considered as appearance features to represent the appearance of the images. However, the sizes of the images are large. Instead of storing such huge intensity values, and in order to represent the appearance features of different medical imaging modalities in a uniform format, we apply Principal Component Analysis (PCA) on the medical images. After applying PCA, the medical images are transformed into another space with dimensionality reduction. Hence, the medical images are represented by such transformed appearance features. So a feature matrix, say F_A, is created such that each of its rows represents the appearance features of an image [17].

Signal features refer to the transformation of the input image into a set of representative signal features. We propose to extract Auto Regressive coefficient (AR), Mean Absolute Value (MAV), and Root Mean Square (RMS)as signal features [7]. AR coefficient represents the signal features based on frequency domain. MAV and RMS are extracted as another signal features that represent the signal features based on time domain. So, the extracted signal features are concatenated to each other to represent a medical image. Therefore, a signal feature matrix called as F_S is generated that each of its rows represents the signal features of an image.

2.2 Symbolic Feature Representation

The extracted features of the medical images have high intra-class variations and low inter-class variations. To have an efficient feature representation, we propose to capture the feature variations through feature assimilation by the use of symbolic representation specifically interval valued.

Let $[M_1, M_2, M_3,..., M_n]$ be a set of n sample medical images belonging to a medical imaging modality class, say p, where $p=1,2,..,Q$ (Q denotes the total number of classes) and F_{TP} be the teture feature matrix characterizing the texture features of the class p.

We recommended captuing the variations for each xth column of the feature matrix F_{TP} by the use of interval valued feature vector representation $\left[F_{Tpx}^{-}, F_{Tpx}^{+} \right]$.

i.e,
$$F_{Tpx}^{-} = \mu_{px} - \alpha \sigma_{px} \quad \text{and} \quad F_{Tpx}^{+} = \mu_{px} + \alpha \sigma_{px} \tag{1}$$

Where, the mean of the xth column feature due to all n sample images of the class p is obtained by,

$$\mu_{px} = \frac{1}{n} \sum_{i=1}^{n} F_{TPx}(i) \tag{2}$$

and the standard deviation of the xth feature values due to all n sample images of the class p is calculated by,

$$\sigma_{px} = \left[\frac{1}{n} \sum_{i=1}^{n} (F_{TPx}(i) - \mu_{px})^2 \right]^{\frac{1}{2}} \tag{3}$$

and α is a predefined threshold value used to tuned the interval valued, that is set empirically.

In general, let consider that the texture feature matrix F_{TP} of the class p has m number of column features. The interval valued feature vectors using equation 1 are obtained for each of the columns. Hence, the texture feature matrix F_{TP} is represented as a reference feature vector R_{TP} by concatenating the m number of obtained interval valued feature vectors. Thus, a reference feature vector R_{TP} is represented by,

$$R_{TP} = \left\{ \left[F_{TP1}^{-}, F_{TP1}^{+} \right], \left[F_{TP2}^{-}, F_{TP2}^{+} \right], ..., \left[F_{TPm}^{-}, F_{TPm}^{+} \right] \right\} \tag{4}$$

Similarly, let consider that the appearance feature matrix F_{AP} of the class P has u number of column features 1. A reference feature of the appearance feature matrix F_{AP} is then represented by,

$$R_{AP} = \left\{ \left[F_{AP1}^{-}, F_{AP1}^{+} \right], \left[F_{AP2}^{-}, F_{AP2}^{+} \right], ..., \left[F_{APu}^{-}, F_{APu}^{+} \right] \right\} \tag{5}$$

In the same way, a reference feature vector of the signal feature matrix F_{SP} of the class P with L number of columns features are represented by,

$$R_{SP} = \left\{ \left[F_{SP1}^{-}, F_{SP1}^{+} \right], \left[F_{SP2}^{-}, F_{SP2}^{+} \right], ..., \left[F_{SPL}^{-}, F_{SPL}^{+} \right] \right\} \tag{6}$$

We compute the reference feature vectors R_{PT}, R_{PA}, R_{PS} for all Q number of classes $(p=1,2,...,Q)$.

2.3   Symbolic Classification

Given a medical image as a test sample, it has to be classified. We exploit a symbolic similarity measure proposed by Prakash and Guru [9] for classification. The texture, appearance, and signal features are also extracted and represented as three different feature vectors for a test sample of medical image.

Different combinations of the extracted feature vectors are used for classification. In the first set of combinations, each extracted feature vector, texture, appearance, and signal, are considered individually. In the second set of combinations, any two of the extracted feature vectopors are considered. Combinations of all the extracted feature vectors are considered as the third set of combinations. The combined feature vectors are represented in a feature vector called as F_C.

Similarly, the obtained reference feature vectors of each class are combined with each other in each set of the combinations. The combined reference feature vectors are represented in a reference feature vector, say R_P, for the class p.

The similarity of the xth feature of F_C with respect to the xth interval valued feature vector of R_P, say $\left[F_{px}^-, F_{px}^+\right]$, is calculated using Equation 7. Subsequently, the total similarity of the feature vector F_C with respect to the reference feature vector R_P is computed by Equation 8.

We compute the total similarity with respect to the reference feature vectors of all the Q number of classes. The test sample medical image is then labeled by the class label of the reference feature vector that has the maximum similarity.

$$Sim\left(F_{cx}, \left[F_{px}^-, F_{px}^+\right]\right) \begin{cases} = 1 & \text{if } F_{cx} \geq F_{px}^- \text{ and } F_{cx} \leq F_{px}^+ \\ = \max\left(\dfrac{1}{1+\left|F_{cx}-F_{px}^-\right|}, \dfrac{1}{1+\left|F_{cx}-F_{px}^+\right|}\right) & \text{otherwise} \end{cases} \tag{7}$$

$$Total\_Sim\left(F_c, R_p\right) = \sum_{x=1}^{n} Sim\left(F_{cx}, \left[F_{px}^-, F_{px}^+\right]\right) \tag{8}$$

where n is the total number of features of F_C and R_P respectively.

3   Experimentation

In this section, we present the details of the benchmark database used to evaluate the performance of the proposed classification approach. Further, the experimental results are given.

3.1   Dataset

IMageCLEF2010 is used to evaluate the performance of the proposed classification approach. IMageCLEF2010 contains different medical imaging modalities. In this experimentation, we conducted experiments on classification of medical imaging modalities namely XR, MR, CT, PET, Ultrasound and Micro. Fig. 2 shows examples of different medical imaging modalities samples of IMageCLEF2010 used in this work. The system has been randomly trained by selecting the 40%, 50% and 60% of the image samples of each class of the database. The selected random images have been considered as train samples and the remaining images as test samples. Hence, the system is evaluated in 3 different sets of experiment, i.e., (40:60), (50:50), and (60:40).

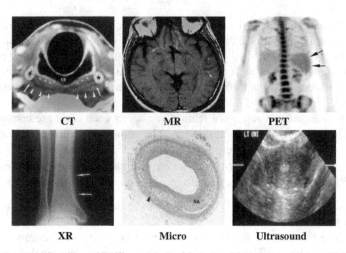

CT   MR   PET

XR   Micro   Ultrasound

Fig. 2. Example Samples of Different Medical Imaging Modalities of IMageCLEF2010

3.2   Experimental Result

In this paper, we have applied 2D adaptive noise removal using neighborhood of size 3 by 3. To remove 'salt and paper' noise, median filtering is used. Each output pixel contains the median value of 9 by 9 neighborhoods surrounding the pixel of the input medical image. To enhance the content of the medical images, 2D order-statistic filtering by the 3rd order element in the sorted set of neighbors of size 3 ×3 is applied. We have studied the performance of our proposed approach using different combinations of the extracted features. The classification accuracy using different combination of the features under different sets of the experiments are tabulated in Table 1 and shown in Fig. 3.

The highest classification accuracy is achieved 93.18% using the combination of texture, appearance and signal features.

Moreover, the precision, recall and FMeasure are computed for each medical imaging modality class using Equations 9, 10 and 11 respectively. Table 2 tabulates the average precision, average recall and average FMeasure for different combination of the features under different sets of experiments.

$$\text{Precision} = \frac{\text{Number of Correctly Classified Images Per Class}}{\text{Total Number of Classified Images Under Class}} \tag{9}$$

$$\text{Recall} = \frac{\text{Number of Correctly Classified Images Per Class}}{\text{Total Number of Expected Images Per Class}} \tag{10}$$

$$\text{FMeasure} = \frac{2 \times \text{Precision} \times \text{Recall}}{\text{Precision} + \text{Recall}} \tag{11}$$

To evaluate the performance of our proposed approach, we have conducted the experiments on other well-known existing classifiers. KNN classifier is used under varying K, K=1, 3, 5, 7. Further, the SVM classifier is exploited by setting the parameters of the classifier appropriately. The classification accuracies of KNN and SVM classifiers using different combination of the features under three sets of experiments are tabulated in Table 3 and Table 4 respectively.

From Table 3 and Table 4, it is observed that the highest classification accuracies are obtained 89.50% and 95.39% using KNN and SVM classifiers respectively.

Table 1. Classification Accuracy in % for Classification of Medical Imaging Modalities under Different Sets of Experiments

	SYMBOLIC CLASSIFIER		
	Experiment Sets		
	Experiment Set 1 (40:60)	Experiment Set 2 (50:50)	Experiment Set 3 (60:40)
Texture	86.18	87.55	87.67
Appearance	42.27	42.50	42.57
Signal	58.31	59.95	60.87
Texture-Signal	88.91	89.04	89.41
Texture-Appearance	88.73	89.08	89.88
Appearance - Signal	63.99	64.11	66.45
Texture-Signal-Appearance	89.21	90.65	**93.18**

Table 2. Average Precision, Average Recall and Average FMeasure for Various Combinations of the Features under Different Sets of Experiments

		Experiment Sets		
		Experiment Set 1 (40:60)	Experiment Set 2 (50:50)	Experiment Set 3 (60:40)
Texture	Precision	0.763	0.780	0.786
	Recall	0.862	0.875	0.876
	F Measure	0.809	0.825	0.828
Appearance	Precision	0.449	0.456	0.457
	Recall	0.422	0.425	0.485
	F Measure	0.435	0.440	0.470
Signal	Precision	0.662	0.680	0.708
	Recall	0.583	0.599	0.609
	F Measure	0.619	0.637	0.654
Texture – Signal	Precision	0.791	0.793	0.796
	Recall	0.746	0.890	0.894
	F Measure	0.769	0.839	0.840
Texture – Appearance	Precision	0.789	0.799	0.807
	Recall	0.887	0.891	0.899
	F Measure	0.835	0.843	0.851
Appearance - Signal	Precision	0.670	0.725	0.793
	Recall	0.641	0.664	0.746
	F Measure	0.669	0.693	0.769
Texture- Signal- Appearance	Precision	0.794	0.802	0.836
	Recall	0.892	0.899	0.933
	F Measure	0.840	0.849	0.881

Table 3. Classification Accuracy in % using KNN Classifier under Different Set of Experiments

	KNN CLASSIFIER											
	Experiment Sets											
	Experiment Set 1 (40:60)				Experiment Set 2 (50:50)				Experiment Set 3 (60:40)			
	K=1	K=3	K=5	K=7	K=1	K=3	K=5	K=7	K=1	K=3	K=5	K=7
Texture	85.9	85.5	85.0	84.5	87.3	85.5	85.2	84.6	87.1	86.9	86.4	84.8
Appearance	88.2	88.1	87.4	87.1	88.9	88.8	88.7	87.1	**89.5**	88.9	88.5	88.4
Signal	78.6	78.4	77.7	77.6	79.5	79.4	78.7	78.5	80.7	80.4	79.5	78.8
Texture - Appearance	87.5	86.4	85.7	84.1	87.1	86.9	86.5	86.1	87.9	87.3	87.0	86.6
Texture - Signal	87.3	85.9	85.8	85.5	87.7	86.6	85.6	85.7	88.9	87.7	85.9	86.7
Appearance - Signal	81.7	81.5	81.1	80.6	82.4	82.2	82.2	81.7	83.7	83.4	82.2	82.0
Texture -Signal-Appearance	86.6	86.2	85.9	85.8	88.9	88.6	88.2	86.2	87.3	87.1	86.3	86.1

Table 4. Classification accuracy in % using SVM Classifier under Different Sets of Experiments

	SVM CLASSIFIER		
	Experiment Sets		
	Experiment Set 1 (40:60)	Experiment Set 2 (50:50)	Experiment Set 3 (60:40)
Texture	93.15	93.82	94.18
Appearance	77.35	77.47	77.85
Signal	76.40	77.42	77.56
Texture - Appearance	94.15	95.38	95.39
Texture - Signal	93.55	94.74	95.05
Appearance - Signal	82.45	83.14	83.27
Texture -Signal-Appearance	94.79	95.33	**95.39**

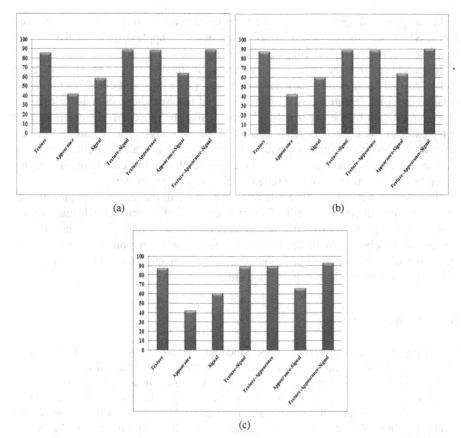

Fig. 3. Accuracy for Classification of Medical Imaging Modalities under Different Sets of Experiments (a) Experiment Set 1 (40:60) (b) Experiment Set 2 (50:50) (c) Experiment Set 3 (60:40)

4   Discussion

In this section, we discuss the state-of-the-arts methods that are similar to our proposed approach for classification of medical imaging modalities. From the literature survey, it is observed that Han and Chen [5] proposed an approach to classify medical imaging modalities. They proposed to extracts visual features as well as textual features for feature representation. They also suggested fussing the extracted features. They applied SVM classifier to classify medical imaging modalities. They conducted the experiments on IMageCLEF2010 database. The highest classification accuracy is obtained 93.89%. Weszka et al [13] proposed an approach to extract the Histograms, LogGabor, and Phase congruency of different medical imaging modalities. They applied the SVM and Random Forest classifiers on the extracted features. They evaluated their method on the IMageCLEF2010 database. They achieved 93.53% classification accuracy.

In our proposed approach, we have used texture, appearance and signal features. KNN, SVM, and the proposed symbolic classifier is applied on IMageCLEF2010 database to classify medical imaging modalities.

It is observed that the contemporary existing methods are used visual features as well as textual features for classification. However, our proposed classification model is based on visual features. Based on the extracted features, the system doesn't require any interpretation by the experts. In addition, it shall be noted that the computational complexity of the classifiers KNN and SVM are very high. The feature vector of a test sample should be compared with the feature vectors of all the training samples. Besides, the SVM classifier is based on the construction of the kernel, and it is highly dependent on selecting the appropriate kernel as well as parameters.

However, in our proposed classification approach, all the training samples of each class are represented by a single feature vector called as reference feature vector. Hence, the feature vector of a test sample is compared with only the reference feature vectors of the classes. With the remarkable reduction in computation and memory space, it can be claimed that our proposed classification approach has better efficiency in classification of medical imaging modalities.

5   Conclusion

In this paper, we extract texture, appearance and signal features of medical images. The extracted features are represented in the form of interval valued feature vectors. Further, symbolic classifier is designed to classify medical imaging modalities.

It can be claimed that our proposed approach being a stand-alone system and first of its kind in literature for classification of medical imaging modalities based on symbolic representation and symbolic classification .It is expected to open up a new dimension for further research in the field of classification by the notions of symbolic data analysis concept.

Acknowledgements. The authors would like to thank TM Lehmann, Department of Medical Informatics, RWTH Aachen, Germany, for making the database available for the experiments.

References

1. Müller, H., Michoux, N., Bandon, D., Geissbuhler, A.: A Review of Content-based Image Retrieval Systems in Medical Applications-Clinical Benefits and Future Directions. International Journal of Medical Informatics 73(1), 1–23 (2004)
2. Kitanovski, I., Trojacanec, K., Dimitrovski, I., Loskovska, S.: Modality Classification Using Texture Features. In: Kocarev, L. (ed.) ICT Innovations 2011. AISC, vol. 150, pp. 189–198. Springer, Heidelberg (2012)
3. Malik, A., Zremic, T.: Classification of Medical Images Using Energy Information Obtained from Wavelet Transform for Medical Image Retrieval. In: 7th International Workshop on Enterprise Networking and Computing in Healthcare Industry, pp. 124–129 (2005)

4. Florea, F., Barbu, E., Rogozan, A., Bensrhair, A., Buzuloiu, V.: Medical Image Categorization using a Texture Based Symbolic Description. In: International Conference on Image Processing, pp. 1489–1492 (2006)
5. Han, X., Chen, Y.: ImageCLEF2010 Modality Classification in Medical Image Retrieval: Multiple Feature Fusion with Normalized Kernel Function. In: Image CLEF 2010 Workshop (2010)
6. Kalpathy, C.J., Hersha, W.: Automatic Image Modality Based Classification and Annotation to Improve Medical Image Retrieval. In: MEDINFO, pp. 1334–1338 (2007)
7. Phinyomark, A., Limsakul, C., Phukpattaranont, P.: A Novel Feature Extraction for Robust EMG Pattern Recognition. Journal of Computing 1(1), 71–80 (2009)
8. Pauly, O., Mateus, D., Navab, N.: ImageCLEF2010 Working Notes on the Modality Classification Subtask. In: Cross Language Image Retrieval Workshop (2010)
9. Prakash, H.N., Guru, D.S.: Geometric Centroids and their Relative Distances for Off-line Signature Verification. In: 10th International Conference on Document Analysis and Recognition, pp. 121–125 (2009)
10. Fischer, S., Sroubek, F., Perrinet, L., Redondo, R., Cristóbal, G.: Self-Invertible 2D Log-Gabor Wavelets. International Journal of Computer Vision 75(2), 231–246 (2007)
11. Ojala, T., Pietikainen, M., Maenpaa, T.: Multiresolution Gray-scale and Rotation Invariant Texture Classification with Local Binary Patterns. IEEE Transaction on Pattern Analysis and Machine Intelligence 24(7), 971–987 (2002)
12. Rajakumar, K., Muttan, S.: Medical Image Retrieval using Modified DCT. In: ICEBT 2010. Procedia Computer Science, vol. 2, pp. 298–302 (2010)
13. Weszka, J.S., Dyer, C.R., Rosenfeld, A.: A Comparative Study of Texture Measures for Terrain Classification. IEEE Trans. Syst. Man, Cybern. SMC 6, 269–285 (1976)
14. Galloway, M.M.: Texture Analysis using Gray Level Run Lengths. Computer Graph and Image Processing 4, 172–179 (1975)
15. Haralick, R.M., Shanmugam, K., Dinstein, I.: Texture Features for Image Classification. IEEE Transaction on System, Man, and Cyberneticists 3(3), 810–821 (1973)
16. Florea, F.I., Rogozan, A., Bensrhair, A., Dacher, J.-N., Darmoni, S.: Modality Categorization by Textual Annotations Interpretation in Medical Imaging. Medical Informatics and BioInformatics, 1270–1274 (2005)
17. Imran, M., Rao, A., Kumar, G.H.: Multibiometric Systems: A Comparative Study of Multi-algorithmic and Multimodal Approaches. In: ICEBT 2010. Procedia Computer Science, vol. 2, pp. 207–212 (2010)

Survey on Information Processing in Visual Cortex: Cortical Feedback and Spiking Neural Network

A. Diana Andrushia[1,*] and R. Thangarajan[2]

[1] Dept of ECE,Karunya University, Coimbatore, India
[2] Dept of CSE,Kongu Engineering College, Erode, India

Abstract. Feedback is the fundamental property of neural circuits in the cerebral cortex. If cortical area A projects to cortical area B, then area B invariably sends feedback connections to area A. Similarly, within a given cortical area, there exists massive recurrent excitatory feedback between pyramidal neurons due to local horizontal connections.In cortical information processing feeback plays vital role. In this paper we reviewed the neural coding strategies and learning methods based on the idea of feedback connections between cortical areas instantiate statistical generative models of cortical inputs.

Keywords: Cerebral cortex, cortical feedback, generative models.

1   Introduction

Our visual world is complex and dynamic. To successfully interpret this world the visual system performs the analysis of various attributes of the visual image and then integrates these attributes into a percept of a visual scene. The most fundamental characteristic of our visual world is that it is not uniform in time and space, and the visual system is well designed to analyze these non-uniformities. Such fundamental dimensions of visual stimuli as spatial and temporal variations in luminance and chromaticity are encoded at the level of the retina, while the encoding of other more complex stimulus features, such as motion, complex form and depth, emerge at the level of visual cortex.

One of the most prominent but least understood neuroanatomical features of the cerebral cortex is feedback.Neurons within a cortical area generally receive massive excitatory feedback from other neurons in the same cortical area. Some of these neurons, particularly those in the superficial and deep layers, send feedback axons [1] to lower cortical areas and receive feedback from higher cortical areas. What is the functional significance of these feedback connections?

It deals with following two hypotheses: (a) feedback connections from a higher to a lower cortical area carry predictions of expected neural activity in the lower area, while the feedforward connections carry the differences between the predictions and the actual neural activity; and (b) recurrent feedback connections between neurons within a cortical area are used to learn, store, and predict temporal sequences of input neural activity. Together, these two types of feedback connections help instantiate a

---

* Corresponding author.

T.-h. Kim et al. (Eds.): FGCN/DCA 2012, CCIS 350, pp. 324–330, 2012.

hierarchical spatiotemporal generative model of cortical inputs. Recent results on synaptic plasticity of recurrent cortical connections indicate a dependence on the temporal order of pre and postsynaptic spikes: synapses that are activated slightly before the postsynaptic cell fires are strengthened whereas those that are activated slightly after are weakened.The hypothesis that such a synaptic learning rule allows local recurrent feedback connections to be used for encoding and predicting temporal sequences. Together with corticocortical feedback, these local feedback connections could allow the implementationof spatiotemporal generative models in recurrent cortical circuits.Feedforward and feedback connections between areas V1 and V2 have similar rapid conduction velocities. It is often assumed that the action of cortical feedback connections is slow and modulatory, whereas feedforward connections carry a rapid drive to their target neurons. Recent results [2] showed a very rapid effect of feedback connections on the visual responses of neurons in lower order areas.To determine whether such rapid action is mediated by fast conducting axons.Using electrical stimulation, the feedback and feedforward connections between V1 and V2 have comparable fast conduction velocities (around 3.5 m/s).

2   Literature Review on Information Processing in Spiking Neurons

Biological neurons communicate by generating and propagating electrical pulses called action potentials or spikes. This feature of real neurons act a central paradigm of a theory of spiking neural models. From the conceptual point of view, all spiking models share the following common properties with their biological counterparts: They process information coming from many inputs and produce single spiking output signals. The probability of firing (generating a spike) is increased by excitatory inputs and decreased by inhibitory inputs and this dynamics is characterized by at least one state variable; when the internal variables of the model reach a certain state, the model is generate one or mores spikes.

Thousands of spikes emitted by sensory neurons are processed by the brain, on each miliseconds, which decides what actions are the most appropriate for the sensed stimuli. Sometimes decisions are made already within tens of milliseconds [4]. It is intriguing, what processes enable such a fast information processing. How the neural signals encode information? What is the temporal resolution of signals required to perform precise computations?

These questions concerning the neural representation of information are often referred to as a problem of the neural code .Various hypotheses on the neural code is suggested and present them in the light of the recent neurophysiological findings on information processing mechanisms in the nervous system in animals. Adrian and Zotterman demonstrated [7] that frog cutaneous receptors responded with more spikes whenever the strength of the external mechanical pressure on the frog skin increased. This finding gave rise to the idea that the neural information is encoded in the firing rate.In neurophysiology the rate code has been a dominant paradigm and artificial neural networks for many years. Recent neurophysiological results, however, suggest that, at least in some neural systems, efficient processing of information is more likely to be based on the precise timing of action potentials rather than on their firing rate.

The primary observation used as an argument against the rate code is that many behavioral responses are completed too quickly for the underlying sensory processes to rely on the estimation of neural firing rates over extended time windows. Evidence for the reproducibility of neural responses to the given stimuli with high precision of the order 0.2–2 ms was found in blowfly's visual cortex,in cat's lateral geniculate nucleus, in the middle temporal area of the macaque or in the rabbit retina.Similar results on the reliable precision (2–3 ms) of single spikes have been reported for spinal neurons in the neonatal rat spinal cord .A population of nerve cells can therefore encode information that would otherwise be outside the limited bandwidth and resolution set by the maximal firing rate and action potential duration in individual neurons.

Many experimental results on the neural code point out particularly to the high importance of each individual spike in the biological neural signals. In humans, precise timing of already first spikes in tactile afferents encodes touch signals at the finger tips [8]. In cats and toads, a few retinal ganglion cells seem to encode information about light stimuli by firing only two or three spikes in about 100 ms under low light conditions. In almost any system where the processing-speed of a neural system is required to be high, the timing of individual spikes carry important information.

To demonstrate the importance of analysis of the neural information processing, both in biological and in artificial systems, with focus on the timing of individual spikes/pulses several neural coding strategies based on spike timing have been investigated. some of these strategies are discussed in below:

Time to first spike - In this model information in the neural systems is encoded in the latency between the beginning of stimulus and the time of the first spike in the neural response.Time to first spike carry enough information e.g. to encode touch signals at the finger tips in the tactile system [8].The first spikes provide more than twice the information about the stimulus shape present in the firing rate during a tactile stimulus discrimination task and similar[9] amount of information about force direction as present in spike counts.Time to first spike scheme enables ultra fast information processing, as a decision on a stimulus can be communicated by the arrival of the first spike already within a few milliseconds. The code is also very simple and can be implemented using just one neuron with inhibitory feedback interactions that prevent emission of all but the first spike. Time to first spike model has been considered for input discrimination.

Rank order coding (ROC) – ROC is one of the simple neural coding scheme. Here information is encoded by the order of spikes in the activity of a neural population. ROC approach has been suggested to explain ultra fast categorization observed in the primate's visual system. Thorpe [10] proposed that the order in which each ganglion cell emits its first spike codes for the visual stimulus. This model assumes that each neuron emits only a single spike during a presentation of the image. This can be easily implemented in a feedforward network with inhibitory feedback connections. Based on these principles,Thorpe [10] and team developed a spiking neural model able to categorize static images with a processing speed comparable to that observed in humans.

Latency code - In this model information is supposed to be contained in the exact timing of a set of spikes relative to each other .The precise timed patterns of spikes have been postulated to play an important role in the nervous system in many functions. Precise relative spike timing is one of the critical parameters that control many forms of synaptic plasticity. Changing the relative timing of presynaptic and postsynaptic spikes in a cortical neuron by as little as 10 ms can determine whether a synapse is potentiated or depressed. In terms of information capacity, latency code is also very efficient timing of just a few spikes can carry a substantial amount of information. Precisely timed sequences of spikes are typically observed in feedforward networks, because noise and inherent dynamics of recurrent networks can easily disrupt spike timing precision [11]. Yet, some attempts to harvest precise spiking timing in recurrent networks have been made for example by exploring the idea [12] of reservoir computation. Resonant burst model – In [13] literature suggested that the frequency of a burst of spikes can determine which downstream neurons are activated. Using the resonance phenomenon it demonstrated that a short burst can elicit strong postsynaptic response if the burst frequency is tuned to the eigen-frequencies of the membrane potential oscillations in the target neurons. The same burst would have a negligible effect on the postsynaptic membrane potential if the burst and eigen-frequencies are not tuned .This phenomenon may provide an effective mechanism for selective communication between neuron.

Coding by synchrony – This model is based on the assumption that neurons that encode different bits of information on the same object fire synchronously. This concept is grounded on several experimental observations. The neurons in the visual cortex tend to synchronize their discharges with a precision in the millisecond range when activated with a single contour, whereas they fail to do so when activated by different contours moving in different directions. It has also been suggested that synchronous firing of neurons in a population can carry information about the global significance of the stimulus for the animal or to organize information together in packets. Neuronal synchronization will serve as a mechanism improving, both information transmission through the network [15] as well as timing precision of spiking events.Synchronization has been investigated in the context of networks with dominant feedforward connections, such as in synfire chain networks, but synchronies events may also dynamically emerge in recurrent networks.Synchronization can be established very rapidly.The simulations demonstrate that networks of reciprocally coupled spiking neurons can undergo very rapid transitions from [16] uncorrelated to synchronized states.

Phase coding – In this model times of emitted spikes are referred to the reference time point in a periodic signal. In this way neuronal spike trains can encode information in the phase of a pulse with respect to the background oscillations. The concept of coding by phases has been suggested in both the models [16,17]. Phase coding has been modled for the olfactory system ,and also other areas of the brain, where oscillations of some global variable are quite common.Spiking networks exploring the phase coding strategy have recently been used in such tasks as [18] odor discrimination or [19] robot navigation.

To analysis the neural information processing, both in biological and in artificial systems, with focus on the timing of individual spikes or pulses several neural coding strategies based on spike timing have been reviewed and it highlights the importance of precise timing of spikes to the neural information transmission and provide strong motivation for investigating computational properties of the systems that compute with precisely timed spikes.

3   Review on Learning Methods for Spiking Neural network

Reinforcement learning mechanism for spiking neural networks is derived for networks of stochastic integrate-and-fire neurons, but it can be also applied to generic spiking neural networks. Learning is achieved by synaptic changes that depend on the firing of pre- and postsynaptic neurons, and that are modulated with a global reinforcement signal.This model recovers a form of neural plasticity experimentally observed in animals, combining spike timing dependent synaptic changes of one sign with non-associative synaptic changes of the opposite sign determined by presynaptic spikes. The model also predicts that the time constant of spike timing [20] dependent synaptic changes is equal to the membrane time constant of the neuron, in agreement with experimental observations in the brain.

Supervised learning was proposed as a successful concept of information processing in artificial neural networks already in the early years of the theory of neural computation. The most documented evidence for this type of learning in the central nervous system comes from studies on the cerebellum and the cerebellar cortex, and thus refers mostly to motor control and motor learning [21].Supervised learning is believed to be utilized by the neural motor centers to form internal representations of the body and the environment or for behavioral simulations and the encapsulation of learned skills. Learning from instructions is supposed also to control information rep-resentation in sensory networks. It is likely that supervised learning also contributes to the establishment of networks that support certain cognitive skills, such as pattern recognition or language acquisition, although there is no strong experimental confirmation of this proposition [22].Instruction signals for supervised learning are thought to have a form of activity templates to be reproduced or error signals to be minimized. There is evidence that, in the nervous system, these signals are provided to learning modules by sensory feedback [23] or by other 'supervisory' neural structures in the brain. Whereas there is a well documented and richly represented group of supervised learning models for rate-based neurons, spike-based coding schemes are still highly uncovered in this regard by the existing approaches. Only recently several concepts have been proposed to explain supervised learning in biologically realistic neuron models operating on the precise timing of particular action potentials [12].

Hebbian learning describes a new computational approach that uses neurogenesis and synaptogenesis to continually learn and grow. Neurons and synapses can be added and removed from the simulation while it runs. The learning is accomplished using a variant of the spike time dependent plasticity method. This Hebbian learning algorithm uses a combination of homeostasis of synapse weights, spike timing, and stochastic forgetting to achieve stable and efficient learning. The approach [24] is not only adaptable, but it is also scalable to very large systems (billions of neurons).

Gradient is a machine learning technique for regression problems, which produces a prediction model in the form of an ensemble of weak prediction models, typically decision trees. It builds the model in a stage wise fashion like other learning methods do, and it generalizes them by allowing optimization of an arbitrary differentiable loss function. Gradient learning method can be also used for classification problems by reducing them to regression with a suitable loss function. In the paper [25] implemented the gradient learning algorithm and performed several preliminary experiments which confirm the method functionality and its reasonable time complexity. In particular, the smoothness of spike creation/deletion process was exhibited. Thus the new gradient learning method can naturally cope with multiple spikes whose number changes in time. Experiments with more complicated temporal training patterns remain for further research.

ReSuMe - a Remote Supervised Method for precise learning of spatiotemporal patterns of spikes in Spiking Neural Networks (SNN). The learning method is dedicated to neuroprostheses control. Neuroprosthetic systems aim at producing functionally useful movements of the paralysed organs by stimulating muscles or nerves with the sequences of short electrical impulses. ReSuMe enables [28] supervised learning while still inheriting interesting properties of unsupervised Hebbian approach, i.e. the locality in time and space, simplicity and the suitability for online processing. On the other hand, ReSuMe avoids drawbacks of the Hebbian and, so called, supervised Hebbian methods. ReSuMe has been successfully applied to feedforward,recurrent and hybrid network architectures.The learning properties of ReSuMe have been investigated in the extensive simulation studies accompanied by the theoretical analysis.In [27] it has been demonstrated that ReSuMe can effectively learn complex temporal and spatio-temporal spike patterns with the desired accuracy and that the method enables imposing on the SNNs the desired input/output properties by learning multiple pairs of input-output patterns.In addition, it has been shown that ReSuMe is able to successfully train the networks consisting of different models of neurons.ReSuMe learning process converged very quickly.

4   Conclusion

In this paper we have reviewed on information processing and learning in spiking neural networks. These concepts are useful for the theoretical models as well as tools for practical applications. Theory of feedback and spiking neural networks can further gain both, from the new algorithms derived within a framework of machine learning, as well as from new discoveries in neurobiology. It is expected that the availability of more efficient learning methods for spiking networks will bring benefit to new areas of applications such as visual pattern recognition, brain machine interface system. Still, more work is needed to further explore necessary technology that would allow for efficient and safe use of spiking neural networks in above tasks.

References

1. Rao, R., Olshausen, B., Lewicki, M.: Predictive Coding, Cortical Feedback, and Spike-Timing Dependent Plasticity. Statistical Theroies of the Brain (2000)
2. Girard, P., Hupe, J., Bullier, J.: Feedforward and Feedback Connections Between Areas V1 and V2 of the Monkey Have Similar Rapid Conduction Velocities. Journal of Neurophysiology (2000)
3. Lee, T.S., Mumford, D.: Hierarchical Bayesian inference in the visual cortex. Journal of Optical Society of America (2003)
4. Ponulak, F., Kasinski, A.: Introduction to spiking neural networks: Information processing, learning and applications. Acta Neurobiology (2011)

5. Pasternak, T., James, W.B., Calkins, D.: Visual Information Processing in the Primate Brain. Biological Psychology 3 (2003)
6. Wysoski, S.G., Benuskova, L., Kasabov, N.: Fast and adaptive network of spiking neurons for multi-view visual pattern recognition. Elsevier Journal of Neurocomputing (2008)
7. Adrian, Zotterman, Y.: The impulses produced by sensory nerve-endings: Part II. The response of a single end-organ. Journal Physiology (1926)
8. Johansson, S., Birznieks, I.: First spikes in ensembles of human tactile afferents code complex spatial fingertip events. National Neuroscience (2004)
9. Saal, H., Vijayakumar, S., Johansson, S.: Information about complex fingertip parameters in individual human tactile afferent neurons. Journal of Neuroscience (2009)
10. Thorpe, S.J., Delorme, A., VanRullen, R.: Spike-based strategies for rapid processing. Neural Networks (2001)
11. Lestienne, R.: Spike timing, synchronization and information processing on the sensory side of the central nervous system. Journal of Neurobiology (2001)
12. Ponulak, F., Kasinski, A.: Supervised learning in spiking neural networks with ReSuMe: sequence learning, classification and spike-shifting. Neural Computing (2010)
13. Izhikevich, E.: Resonance and selective communication via bursts in neurons having subthreshold oscillations. BioSystems (2002)
14. Shin, J., Smith, D., Swiercz, W.: Recognition of partially occluded and rotated images with a network of spiking neurons. IEEE Transcation on Neural Networks (2010)
15. Singer, W.: Neuronal synchrony:a versatile code for the definition of relations. Journal of Neuron (1999)
16. Hopfield, J.: Pattern recognition computation using action potential timing for stimulus Representation. Journal of Nature (1995)
17. Buzsaki, G.: Rhythms of the Brain. Oxford University Press, New York (2006)
18. Chen, H., Bermak, A., Law, M., Martinez, D.: Spike latency coding in a biologically inspired microelectronic nose. IEEE Transaction on Biomedical Circuits Systems (2011)
19. Kiss, T., Orban, G., Erdi, P.: Modeling hippocampal theta oscillation: Applications in neuropharmacology and robot navigation. International Journal of Intelligent Systems (2006)
20. Azvan, R., Florian, V.: A reinforcement learning algorithm for spiking neural networks. In: IEEE Intenational Symbosim on Symbolic and Numeric Algorithms (2005)
21. Mongillo, G., Barak, O., Tsodyks, M.: Synaptic theory of working memory. Science (2008)
22. Ito, M.: Control of mental activities by internal models in the cerebellum. Journal of Nature (2008)
23. Carey, M., Medina, J., Lisberger, S.: Instructive signals for motor learning from visual cortical area MT. Journal of Neuroscience (2005)
24. Long, L.N.: An Adaptive Spiking Neural Network with Hebbian Learning. In: IEEE Workshop on Adaptive Intelligent System (2011)
25. Sima, J.: Gradient Learning in Networks of Smoothly Spiking Neurons. Advances in Neuro Information Processing (2009)
26. Xin, J., Embrechts, M.J.: Supervised learning with spiking neuron networks. In: Proceedings IEEE International Joint Conference on Neural Networks (2001)
27. Kasinski, A., Ponulak, F.: Experimental Demonstration of Learning Properties of a New Supervised Learning Method for the Spiking Neural Network. In: Biological Inspirations, ICANN 2006 (2006)
28. Ponulak, F., Kasinski, A.: ReSuMe learning method for Spiking Neural Networks dedicated to neuroprostheses control. Journal of Neural Computation (2010)

A Tool for Scanning Document-Images
with a Photophone or a Digicam

M. El Rhabi[1], A. Hakim[1], Z. Mahani[2], K. Messou[2], and S. Saoud[2]

[1] Université Cadi Ayyad, Faculté des Sciences et Techniques - Guéliz (FSTG)
Laboratoire de Mathématiques Appliquées et Informatique
Bd. Abdelkrim El Khattabi , B.P. 618 Guéliz, 40000 Marrakech- Maroc
{elrhabi,abdelilah.hakim}@gmail.com
http://www.fstg-marrakech.ac.ma/
[2] Université Ibn Zohr, ESTA, Laboratoire Matriaux,
Systèmes et Technologies de l'information, B.P: 33/S, 80000 Agadir - Maroc
{z.mahani,s.saoud}@uiz.ac.ma
http://www.esta.ac.ma/

Abstract. In this work, we propose a tool to scan a document-image acquired with a photophone or a digicam. Firstly, we try to reduce the noise in the document-image. Then we build a new image by cropping or by rectifying perspective the denoised one. From this step, we can expect the document to a real quadrangle. The new document is analyzed and we try to find images, logos or non text elements in the document-image by mean of an image segmentation. At this stage and if applicable, we provide two parts of the document image: the text part and the "non text" part of the document-image (images, logos ...). The text part of the document-image is enhanced by an original PDE's based model that we proposed. The "non text" document is enhanced by classical methods such as retinex processing. Then, we merge both parts of the document image by a poisson image editing. The effectiveness and the robustness of the proposed process are shown on numerical examples in real-world situation (images acquired from photophones and digicams).

Keywords: Document-image restoration, document scanning, photophones, digicams, denoising, rectifying perspective, segmentation, non uniform illumination correction, retinex, Poisson Image Editing.

1 Introduction

Computer vision based on documents recognition could be an interesting way to dematerialize informations to manage clients and company's internal documents. Thus it offers to enterprises wide fast access to business critical information while enhancing the achitecture in place. Typically the dematerialized document formats are PDF. Here, the problem could be separated at least in five steps: noise reduction, rectifying perpective, segmentation : text and non text parts of the document-image, text and "non text" enhancements and a merge of enhanced

T.-h. Kim et al. (Eds.): FGCN/DCA 2012, CCIS 350, pp. 331–341, 2012.

parts. In the computer vision approaches, low cost cameras (webcam, camera-phone, digicam ...) could introduce some distortions and noise artifacts, see [1] for an overview of document image degradation modeling.

Document-images are supposed to be obtained from a mobile device - a photophone more exactly, but could also come from any digital camera (digicam). In the following article, we will only suppose the device to be a photophone or a digicam like in most cases the problem occurs.

The image restoration images by PDE's based models starts to produce signifiant results thanks to the diffusion of document-images. This process removes noise while preserving important information for readability ([11,4,9,14]) or to separate the back to front ink interferences ([10]) . These works have shown that the readability could be improved up to 30% recognition rate of OCR by restoring the document images.

Generally speaking, an image u could be seen as the product of a reflectance v and the illumination effect I (see [7]). This model has been used in [8,5,6] to restore blurred barcode signals under non uniform illumination.

This paper provide a tool to scan a document with cameraphones or digicams. After the segmentation process, the text enhancement is based on new method based on an isotropic ([9]) or anisotropic ([14]) diffusion to estimate the luminance (or the log of the luminance) of a document-image.

Our methods can produce three kinds of documents: black and white, grayscale or color ones. In all cases, input images are color pictures. Producing color documents should be seen as a different workflow, involving mostly the same algorithms as in the grayscale processing.

The paper is organized as follows : section 2 gives a description of our method for scanning document-images with a photophone or a digicam. Section 3 presents the method that we used to rectify perspective distortions by mean of the Hough transform. Then, in section 4, we provide a method to deal with complex document-images (magazines or mixed document-images containing text and "non text" parts). Finally, some numerical results illustrate this work in Section 5.

2   Description

Most important image degradations are related to noise, poor contrast, Jpeg compression artifacts or even an inappropriate point of observation.

In figure 1, we show a flow chart of the processing sequence to be applied to restore document-images.

The input image (top of the flow chart) is the color Jpeg image sent by the photophone users. At the very bottom of this chart, output images are grayscale images, a black and white one (fax purpose) and optionally a thumbnail of the grayscale image. All other images shown on the chart are temporary images.

We can identify five major processing steps, which will be explained with much more details further in this paper:

- Denoising: if needed this processing step aims at reducing the noise of a color image. Here, we use for example the fast algorithm proposed in [3].

- Dewarping: if we can identify the document page borders in the image, we build a new image by cropping or by rectifying perspective of the denoised one. From this step, we can expect the document to fit a real quadrangle (see section 3).
- Document-image segmentation: if needed, at this step, we try to separate text and "non text" parts in the document-image. This segmentation is obtained by a constrained watershed (see [2]).
- Text and "non text" enhancements (if applicable):
  - Text enhancement : this processing step works as a poor contrast or non uniform illumination correction of the whole document. We refer to [9,14]) where we describe our method to enhance text in document image by PDE's based models.
  - "Non text" enhancement (images or logos) by a retinex processing (see [13]).
- The final document is obtained by the merge of both parts of the document (text and "non text" parts) by mean of a Poisson Image Editing Processing (see [12]).

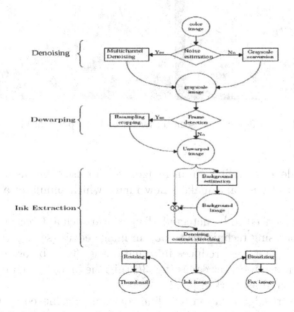

Fig. 1. Global flow chart of the image processing involved in the document image processings improvement. Images are represented like circles, while processing steps are associated with quadrangles. Decisions look as diamonds. A color image is provided as input (top of the chart), and one may expect three output images (very bottom of the chart): a grayscale one, a fax image (black and white) and optionally a thumbnail of the grayscale image. Major processing steps are denoising, dewarping, and text enhancement.

For the sake of simplicity, some processings have been expunged here. Indeed, some features are measured and collected all over the processing sequence to provide some user notifications about the input image quality. And so our ability to deal with it. These features come from the range of graylevels or the amount of noise in each color channel. They are all merged to give some clues about the input image quality.

3   Page Border Based Dewarping: A Way to Post-correcting the Observation Point

It is particularly relevant to produce straight documents as opposed to inclined ones (see fig.2). This step facilitates the photography acquisition to the end-users. Even more, sending well aligned documents to faxes is important to enhance the final document legibility.

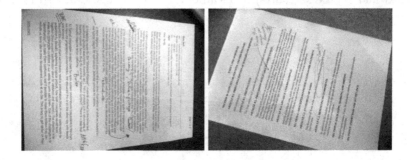

Fig. 2. Typical documents seen under an inclined point of view

When page borders are visible in an image, we can use them as a guideline to correct the point of view and make a new image which simulates a perfectly straight document.

First, page borders need to be detected. To perform such a detection we need some image preprocessing techniques to obtain image edges (see fig. 3).

As one can see, a first pass reduces information(fig. 3(a)) before extracting with filtering the most important edges (fig. 3(c)) in the image. From here, these edges are only delivered as marked pixels.

One way to convert edge location to a line equation is achieved by using the *Hough transform* algorithm. The following equation describes a line :

$$ax + by + c = 0 \qquad (1)$$

Where (x, y) are the coordinates of the points laying on the line whose parameters are (a, b, c). But our problem is to find parameters only knowing pixel edge locations. The *Hough transform* proposes a way to exchange the unknowns.

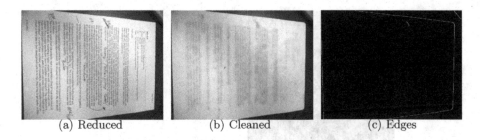

(a) Reduced   (b) Cleaned   (c) Edges

Fig. 3. Preprocessings before detecting page borders

Making the assumption that (x, y) are known there are two unknowns[1] which describe all lines that meet the point (x, y).

(1) is not well adapted (reasons are outside the scope of the paper), and typical *Hough transform* adopts a polar line representation.

So, a point (x_0, y_0) in the image gives a set of lines represented as a sinus curve in the Hough space. Our Hough space behaves as an accumulator space, meaning for each point label as edge we accumulate the associated sinus curves in the Hough space. Peaks appear in the Hough space which are the detected lines we are looking for. Because a point in the Hough space represents the parameters of a line in the image.

Figure 4 represents the detected image edges, the associated Hough space representation, and fitted lines.

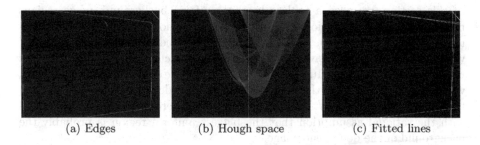

(a) Edges   (b) Hough space   (c) Fitted lines

Fig. 4. Hough transformation to detect lines

Several lines are detected but we still don't know which ones constitute the page borders. So all sets of four lines are tested if they are good candidates to represent the page borders. Unrealistic sets are immediately rejected and a score is given to the other ones. This score is built from the assumptions that the good lines have extremities closed two by two and they constitute a quadrangle big enough in the image. Figure 5 shows selected edges from previous line detection:

---

[1] (a, b, c) are related to each other, so only two unknowns remained.

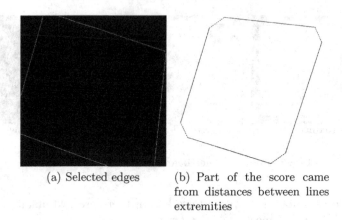

(a) Selected edges

(b) Part of the score came from distances between lines extremities

Fig. 5. Selected edges (fig.5(a)) lead to the computation of a score. This score is partly based on the cumulative distance between segments end points (dashed lines in fig. 5(b)).

When a frame is detected, we only need to perform the perspective correction of the image. Perspective correction is performed by using *bicubic* interpolation, and is a real perspective transformation (homography) hence respectfull of original document proportions.

4   Separation Text - Non Text in the Document-Image

In this section, we need a tool to localize uniform background image regions from previous ink extraction method. Such a tool should be a constrained watershed algorithm (see [2]). Here, images can be viewed as a topographical relief, which are flooded progressively (see figure 11). In practice, we consider gradients magnitude of the image. In figure 7, we describe the first step of this process, we remove the text from the document image in order to obtain only the non text part of the document. Figure 8, we apply a filtered constrained watershed with the rational assumption that the biggest uniform region is probably the background of the document-image.

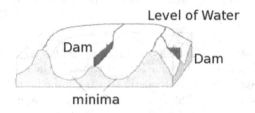

Fig. 6. Watershed principle

(a) Original	(b) Result of new background estimation (only dark ink- obtained by classical mathematical morphology tools)

Fig. 7. Original document is seen under some classical mathematical operations

(a) Segmentation obtained by an unconstrained watershed

(b) Segmentation obtained by a constrained watershed

(c) Segmentation obtained by a constrained watershed : The biggest uniform region is probably background

(d) Final segmentation obtained by a constrained watershed after an appropriate filtering

Fig. 8. Separation text-non text information in a document-image

5 Numerical Results

In this section, we present some simulation results showing the performance of the presented tool. We show the ability of the proposed process to successfully scan document-image acquired by camera in a tough environment. We show how the step of segmentation is important if we would like to scan complex document-images, for example document acquired by a photophone or a digicam from magazines or when we we have document-images containing text and images.

In all examples, the original images are acquired from a Sony Ericksson K800i (3.2 megapixels) or an Iphone 3GS.

Figure 10, figure 11 and figure 12 show examples of the dewarp-text enhancement by methods proposed in this paper. On the one hand, we can see that page corners are not necessary in the image, only edges are required to detect frames. On the other, even in strong perspectives distortions, our correction remains valid.

Figure 13 and figure 14 show the performance of our process to provide scanned quite complex documents. Here, after a segmentation which separates the text and images in the document-image, the texts in the document are enhanced by the method that we have proposed in [14]. As regards the "non text" part of the document, the images are enhanced by a retinex processing. Then a Poisson Image Editing (see [12]) in order to merge both parts and to reconstruct a coherent document. Moreover, in figure 14, the acquired document needs all processes, namely a dewarp, a segmentation to separate text and image in the document,

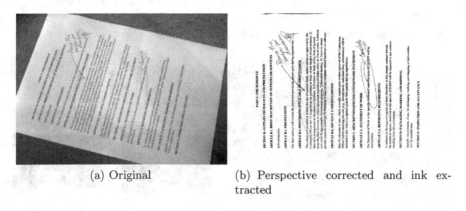

| (a) Original | (b) Perspective corrected and ink extracted |

Fig. 9. Example - Notice that page corners are outside the bounds of the image

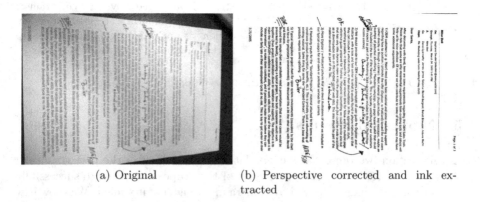

| (a) Original | (b) Perspective corrected and ink extracted |

Fig. 10. Original document is seen under some perspective which makes it slanted. Text lines become parallel in the corrected document.

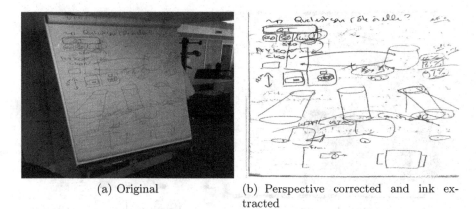

(a) Original   (b) Perspective corrected and ink extracted

Fig. 11. Original document is seen under a very strong perspective

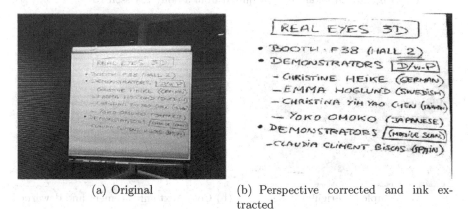

(a) Original   (b) Perspective corrected and ink extracted

Fig. 12. Original document is seen under a perspective

(a) Example 1 : original image   (b) Result without segmentation   (c) Result after segmentation

Fig. 13. Original image acquired from a Sony Ericsson K800i

(a) Example 3, original image   (b) Result with segmentation

Fig. 14. Original image acquired from a Sony Ericsson K800i

(a) Example 3 : original image   (b) Color text enhancement and dewarped

Fig. 15. Original acquired from a Casio Computer co. ltd-Digital still camera

an enhancement for each parts of the segmented document-image, then a Poisson Image Editing (see [12]) in order to merge both parts and to reconstruct a coherent document. This test is very interesting and our process has not only correctly cropped the document but the image enhancement gives a good result.

6   Conclusion

In this paper, we present a tool for scanning document-images. We have described five steps to obtain a correct scan. So far we have shown that our process remains robust even in rough environments and in low lightning conditions. As well as, the resulting process depends only on a few fixed parameters. Moreover, we proved that this process allows to estimate a scanning version of a document-image acquired from a photophone or a digicam in a robust and reproductible way. Our method allows end-users to take a photo with minimum constraints since our process correct some perspective distortion. It takes also into account complex document-images (mixed documents containing text and "non text" informations). After a segmentation of such documents, text and "non text" parts are originally and diffently enhanced. The final document is a merge of these parts by using a Poisson Image Editing process, and the resulting document could be provided to end-users as pdf documents like flatbed scanner documents. Results can be even better.

References

1. Baird, H.S.: The state of the art of document image degradation modeling. In: The 4th IAPR International Workshop on Document Analysis Systems, Rio de Janeiro, pp. 1–16 (2000)
2. Beare, R.: A locally constrained watershed transform. IEEE Transactions on Pattern Analysis and Machine Intelligence 28, 1063–1074 (2006)
3. Chambolle, A.: An algorithm for total variation minimization and applications. Special Issue on Mathematics and Image Analysis, J. Math. Imaging Vision 20(1-2), 89–97 (2004)
4. Drira, F., Le Bourgeois, F., Emptoz, H.: Document images restoration by a new tensor based diffusion process: Application to the recognition of old printed documents. In: 10th International Conference on Document Analysis and Recognition, Barcelona, pp. 321–325 (2009)
5. Dumas, L., El Rhabi, M., Rochefort, G.: An evolutionary approach for blind deconvolution of barcode images with nonuniform illumination. In: IEEE Congress on Evolutionary Computation, pp. 2423–2428 (2011)
6. El Rhabi, M., Rochefort, G.: Method of restoring a blurred image acquired by means of a camera fitted to a communication terminal. Realeyes3D SA (2009), patent http://www.wipo.int/patentscope/search/en/WO2009112710
7. Horn, B.K.: Robot vision. MIT Press (1986)
8. Kim, J., Lee, H.: Joint nonuniform illumination estimation and deblurring for bar code signals. Optic Express 15(22), 14817–14837 (2007)
9. Mahani, Z., Zahid, J., Saoud, S., El Rhabi, M., Hakim, A.: Text Enhancement by PDE's Based Methods. In: Elmoataz, A., Mammass, D., Lezoray, O., Nouboud, F., Aboutajdine, D. (eds.) ICISP 2012. LNCS, vol. 7340, pp. 65–76. Springer, Heidelberg (2012)
10. Moghaddam, R.F., Cheriet, M.: Rsldi: Restoration of single-sided low-quality document images. Pattern Recognition, Special Issue on Handwriting Recognition 42, 3355–3364 (2009)
11. Nwogu, I., Shi, Z., Govindaraju, V.: Pde-based enhancement of low quality documents. In: The Ninth International Conference on Document Analysis and Recognition, vol. 01, pp. 541–545 (2007)
12. Pérez, P., Gangnet, M., Blake, A.: Poisson image editing. ACM Transactions on Graphics (SIGGRAPH 2003) 22(3), 313–318 (2003)
13. Rahman, Z., Woodell, G.A.: Retinex processing for automatic image enhancement. Journal of Electronic Imaging 13, 100–110 (2004)
14. Saoud, S., Mahani, Z., El Rhabi, M., Hakim, A.: Document scanning in a tough environment: application to cameraphones. International Journal of Imaging & Robotics (IJIR), Special Issue on Practical Perspective of Dogotal Imaging for Computational Applications 9(1), 1–16 (2013)

Detection of Variations in HRV Using Discrete Wavelet Transform for Seizure Detection Application

P. Grace Kanmani Prince[1] and Rani Hemamalini[2]

[1] Electronics and Control Engineering Department,
Sathyabama University, Chennai
cog_grace@yahoo.co.in
[2] Electronics and Instrumentation,
St. Peter's University, Chennai
ranihema@yahoo.com

Abstract. During the seizure activity the heart rate variability of the patient differs from that of a normal person. In this paper statistical approach is used to calculate the HRV. The R peak is detected using discrete wavelet transform. Daubechies 6 (db6) is used as the mother wavelet. The statistical parameters of the R-R interval of a normal ECG and the ECG of a seizure patient are compared. The standard deviation, mean and variance of ECG of seizure patient are higher when compared to normal ECG. Hence variation in HRV can be used as one of the markers for seizure detection.

Keywords: Seizure, Heart Rate Variability, Discrete wavelet transforms, Daubechies 6.

1   Introduction

Heart rate variability reflects the regulatory function of the autonomous nervous system. The HRV is the measure of the interval between consecutive R peaks of the ECG signal [1]. The variation in the interval between the R-R peaks depends upon the pathological condition of the body. In most of the cases the heart rate of the person varies drastically during the time of seizure activity [2]. Along with EEG signals HRV can be used as an efficient marker in the automatic detection of seizure activity. Discrete Wavelet transform is used for extracting the R peaks from the ECG signal [3]. The mother wavelet which most likely resembles the ECG wave is the Daubechies 6 wavelet. It is decomposed into 8 levels and then processed to get the desired R peak from the ECG signal. Then the distance between each consecutive peak is calculated. The mean, variance and standard deviation of the R-R interval is calculated for a normal ECG and ECG of a patient during the seizure activity.

Section 2 covers the description of Heart rate variability. Section 3 deals with Discrete wavelet transform. Section 4 gives the steps for calculating the statistical parameters from HRV. Section 5 gives the results and comparison of the statistical parameters of the normal HRV and that of the HRV of the seizure affected patient. Section 6 gives the conclusion the paper.

T.-h. Kim et al. (Eds.): FGCN/DCA 2012, CCIS 350, pp. 342–348, 2012.
© Springer-Verlag Berlin Heidelberg 2012

2   Heart Rate Variability

ECG signal is composed of peaks and valleys which are represented by the P, Q, R, S and T for each heartbeat. The R peak is highest peak as shown in figure 1. Depending on the pathological condition of the body the time interval between the consecutive R peaks in the ECG signal varies. The sympathetic (SNS) and parasympathetic (PSNS) activities of the nervous system are reflected in the heart rate variability. The HRV is reduced when SNS activity is increased and PSNS activity is reduced [4]. HRV can be calculated using two main approaches. The first one is by statistical means and the second is by obtaining patterns of periodicity and extracting the frequency components [5]. Statistical methods are time domain approach. It is based on the time interval between the R peaks. The mean, variance and standard deviation of R-R interval is obtained in this method. The Heart Rate Variability changes considerably for a person who has a seizure. The statistical parameters are obtained from the ECG signal. Hence HRV can be used as one of the effective marker for detecting seizure activity.

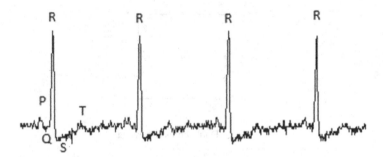

Fig. 1. ECG signal

3   Discrete Wavelet transform

Wavelet transform is advantageous when compared to Fourier transform because it gives the information about the time at which each frequency component is present in the signal. Whereas Fourier transform gives only the frequency information of the signal. Discrete Fourier transform uses filter banks. The filter banks uses high pass and low pass filter. Initially the signal is passed through high pass and low pass filters. The output of the low pass filter (LPF) is approximation coefficient and output of the high pass filter (HPF) is the first detail coefficient. The output of the high pass filter is again passed through HPF and LPF. The output at the second stage from the HPF is the second detail. The output of each filter is down sampled to reduce redundancy [6]. Usually down sampling is done by a factor 2. Hence the whole signal is split into different frequency bands. Figure 2 illustrates the concept of Discrete wavelet transform for two stages. It can be extended to any number of stages. In this particular application 8 level of decomposition is used.

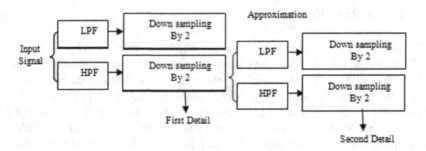

Fig. 2. Discrete wavelet transform

The frequency band of interest can be considered for further processing or analysis. The approximation and details are used for removal of base line wandering, denoising and detection of the R peak. The mother wavelet used here is Daubechies 6 since it closely represents the ECG signal. Figure 3 shows the shape of the Daubechies 6 wavelet [6].

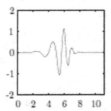

Fig. 3. Daubechies 6 wavelet

4   Steps Involved in Obtaining HRV

Discrete wavelet transform is used to obtain the HRV. Db 6 is used as the mother wavelet. The procedure for obtaining the R-R interval is given below

Step 1: The approximation and details of the ECG wave is obtained by 8 levels of decomposition.
Step 2: During the ECG recording the base line wandering may be present due to the movements of the electrodes. The base line wandering can be corrected by arithmetic processing of the approximation and details. It is given by $DS=(A-(A8+D8)$
    Where DS is the base line wandering removed signal, A is the original ECG signal, A8 is the approximation and D8 is the detail in 8th level.
Step 3: Denoising of the signal is done.
Step 4: Wavelet coefficient with eight levels of decomposition is obtained from the denoised signal.
Step 5: The coefficient which notably represents the R peaks is selected.

Step 6: Thresholding is done to eliminate the false peaks.
Step 7: The distances between the consecutive peaks are calculated.
Step 8: The mean, variance and standard deviation of the R-R intervals are calculated for the given ECG signals.

Comparison is done between the ECG signals of a normal person and seizure patients.

5   Results and Analysis

This section deals with the results obtained by using Discrete wavelet transform. The signals are collected from physionet database[7]. The results are obtained using Matlab programming. The figures below show the outputs produced at each stage of obtaining the heart rate variability of the ECG of the patient with seizure.

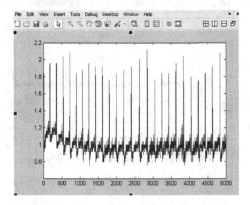

Fig. 4. ECG signal of a patient with seizure

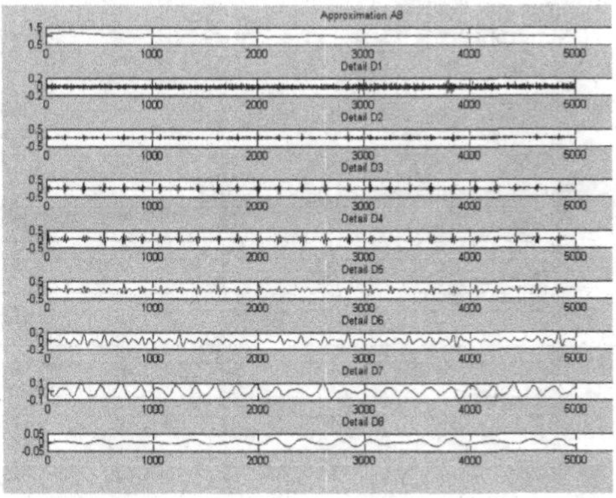

Fig. 5. Wavelet Coefficient Of Seizure ECG

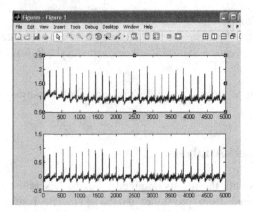

Fig. 6. Removal of base line wandering

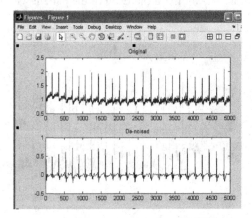

Fig. 7. Denoising

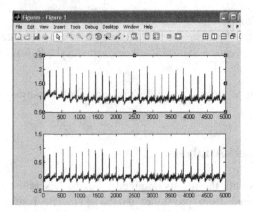

Fig. 8. Wavelet Coefficient Of Denoised Seizure ECG

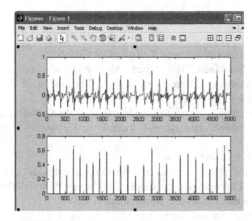

Fig. 9. R Peaks of Seizure ECG Signal

The figure 8 shows the extracted R peaks. The distances between the peaks are calculated. Mean, variance and Standard deviation are calculated and the comparison is made between the normal ECG and that of the patient having the seizure. The comparison table below clearly shows that the statistical data for the seizure patients ECG is higher than that of the ECG of the normal person.

Table 1. Comparison of Parameter Estimates of EEG signals

Parameter Estimates ECG Signals	Mean(μ)	Standard Deviation (σ)	Variance
Normal ECG1	0.5247	3.9726	0.2753
Normal ECG2	0.5368	3.9742	0.2882
Seizure ECG1	2.8452	8.4900	8.0950
Seizure ECG2	2.0643	9.3160	4.2614

6   Conclusions

The results prove that the statistical parameters such as mean, variance and standard deviation of the Heart rate variability of a seizure affected person are higher than that of the HRV of a normal person. Hence HRV also can be used as a marker for seizure detection together with EEG signal analysis. Discrete wavelet transform is one of the efficient means to denosie the ECG signal and to detect the R peaks from the ECG signal.

References

1. Nei, M.: Cardiac Effects of Seizures. Epilepsy Cur. (2009)
2. Niskanen, J.-P., Tarvainen, M.P., Ranta-Aho, P.O., Karjalainen, P.A.: Software for advanced HRV analysis. University of Kuopio Department of Applied Physics Report Series (2002) ISSN: 0788-4672
3. Vanisree, K., Singaraj, J.: Automatic Detection of ECG R-R Interval using Discrete Wavelet Transformation. International Journal on Computer Science and Engineering (IJCSE) (2011)
4. http://www.wikipedia.com
5. Gary, G.B., et al.: Heart rate variability: Origin, methods and interpretive caveats. Committee report, Phycophysiology. Cambridge University Press (1997)
6. Merry, R.J.E.: Wavelet Theory and Applications (2005)
7. http://www.physionet.org

Image Pre-processing and Feature Extraction Techniques for Magnetic Resonance Brain Image Analysis

D. Jude Hemanth and J. Anitha

Department of ECE, Karunya University, Coimbatore, India
{jude_hemanth,rajivee1}@rediffmail.com

Abstract. Image pre-processing and feature extraction techniques are mandatory for any image based applications. The accuracy and convergence rate of such techniques must be significantly high in order to ensure the success of the subsequent steps. But, most of the time, the significance of these techniques remain unnoticed which results in inferior results. In this work, the importance of such approaches is highlighted in the context of Magnetic Resonance (MR) brain image classification and segmentation. In this work, suitable pre-processing techniques are developed to remove the skull portion surrounding the brain tissues. Also, texture based feature extraction techniques are also illustrated in this paper. The experimental results are analyzed in terms of segmentation efficiency for pre-processing and distance measure for feature extraction techniques. The convergence rate of these approaches is also discussed in this work. Experimental results show promising results for the proposed approaches.

Keywords: Pre-processing, MR brain images, feature extraction, segmentation efficiency and convergence rate.

1   Introduction

Generally, real-time images collected from scan centre and simulated images collected from publicly available database are used for image classification and segmentation. These are raw images which are unsuitable for analysis due to the various types of noises present in the images. Hence, suitable pre-processing methodologies must be used to enhance the quality of the images. Literature survey reveals the availability of several pre-processing and feature extraction techniques for MR brain image analysis. The raw MR images normally consist of many artifacts such as intensity inhomogenities, extra cranial tissues, etc. which reduces the overall accuracy. Several researches are reported in the literature to minimize the effects of artifacts in the MR images. An analysis on filtering techniques such as Gabor & QMF filters for noise reduction is performed by Nicu et al (2000).

Fuzzy connectedness based intensity non uniformity correction has been implemented by Yongxin et al (2006). A sequential approach with fuzzy connectedness, atlas registration and bias field correction is used in this approach. The conclusions revealed that the proposed technique can be used only if the intensity variations between the images are of a limited range. Marianne et al (2006) have

T.-h. Kim et al. (Eds.): FGCN/DCA 2012, CCIS 350, pp. 349–356, 2012.

minimized the effects of inter-slice intensity variation with the weighted least square estimation method. The selection of weights for the least square method is the major disadvantage of this approach. Bo et al (2008) have proposed the noise removal technique using wavelets and curvelets.

Hybrid approaches involving Variance Stabilizing Transform (VST) are also used in this work. But this technique is applicable for images with Poisson noise. Tracking algorithm based de-noising technique is performed by Jaya et al (2009). Since the seed point for tracking is random in nature, this technique is not much efficient. A contrast agent accumulation model based contrast enhancement is implemented by Marcel et al (2009). This improves only the contrast of the image and the unwanted tissues are not eliminated. Rajeev et al (2009) have used the wiener filtering technique for noise removal in MR brain images. Apart from noise removal, several other pre-processing steps are also reported in the literature. This includes image format conversion, image type conversion etc. Rajeev et al (2009) also have used the combination of three modalities of MR images for further processing. All the above mentioned techniques remove only specific artifacts which is not sufficient for high classification accuracy and segmentation efficiency.

The next step in the automated diagnosis process is feature extraction. Feature extraction is the technique of extracting specific features from the pre-processed images of different abnormal categories in such a way that the within - class similarity is maximized and between - class similarity is minimized. Earlier research works report many feature extraction techniques employed for medical image processing. Arivazhagan et al (2003) have used 2D wavelet transform based textural features for classification. In this report, initially basic statistical features are used and then co-occurrence based textural features are used to improve the accuracy. But the effects of usage of different wavelets are not dealt in the report. A comparison of 2D wavelet transform based textural features and 3D wavelet transform based textural features is performed by Kourosh et al (2004). This work concluded that the combination of 2D and 3D wavelet based textural features yield better results than the 2D wavelet features. Hiremath et al (2006) have presented a feature extraction technique using the complimentary wavelet transformed image. The report claimed that the features extracted from all the four sub-bands are more efficient than the features from the only the approximation sub-band. All these techniques used the basic Discrete Wavelet Transform (DWT) which does not yield superior results.

An improved version based on wavelet packet decomposition is implemented by Hiremath et al (2006). The results revealed that the packet decomposition technique is more efficient than the DWT technique. Apart from extracting the features from the whole image, features are also extracted from local regions which are used for image segmentation applications. One such work is reported by Ryszard (2007). Pantelis et al (2007) have described a novel feature set which comprises the features such as short run emphasis, run length non-uniformity, etc. which are based on run length matrices. The drawback of this work is the low classification accuracy which shows that these features do not guarantee superior results. Ke et al (2008) have explored the merits of wavelet features for image classification. The technique of dimensionality reduction based on sub band grouping and selection have also been implemented in this work. A comparative analysis with the conventional algorithms is presented in this report.

In this work, emphasis is given to remove the extra-cranial (skull) tissues which often interfere with the brain tissues leading to the performance reduction of the system. Suitable morphology based techniques are used to remove the skull tissues. Next, an extensive feature set is extracted from these images and supplied as input to the automated system. The characteristics of the input images are reflected by these features which are necessary to enhance the efficiency of the system. These feature extraction techniques are performed in a different manner for the classification and segmentation techniques.

2 Brain Image Database

The image database used in this work is collected from M/s. Devaki scan centre in Madurai, Tamilnadu, India. The total number of images is 540 with representations from four categories such as Meningioma, Glioma, Metastase and Astrocytoma. The images are further categorized into training dataset and testing dataset. The images are gray level images with intensity value ranges from (0 to 255). These images are used for both classification and segmentation applications. Some samples of the MRI database have been displayed in Figure 1.

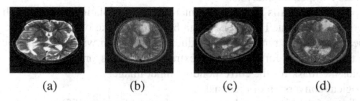

(a)   (b)   (c)   (d)

Fig. 1. Sample data set: (a) Metastase (b) Glioma (c) Astrocytoma (d) Meningioma

The ground truth tumor image is also available for all the 540 images. These ground truth are used as reference for the tumor segmentation applications.

3 Image Pre-processing

The raw images collected from the scan centre and the websites are not suitable for direct processing due to the various noises present in these images. In this work, emphasis is laid on the removal of extra-cranial (skull) tissues which often interfere with the brain tissues. The presence of these skull tissues has reduced the perofrmance of the automated system. Hence, suitable morphology based techniques are devised in this work to eliminate these extra-cranial tissues.

3.1 Framework of the Proposed Technique

The various steps followed in the extra-cranial tissue extraction are shown in this section. Different sequential steps with different parameters are implemented in this work to eliminate the skull tissues which are usually surrounding the brain tissues.

The procedual flow of this algorithm is detailed in the following three steps.

Step 1: Generation of mask

The first step after reading the image is the generation of a mask. Two basic morphological operations namely erosion and filling are used in this work to generate the mask.

a) Erosion:

The main function of this operation is to remove the pixels on object boundaries. The rule given below defines the operation of the erosion operation. "If every pixel in the input pixel's neighborhood is on, the output pixel is on. Otherwise, the output pixel is off". A specified neighborhood is used in this operation. The neighborhood for an erosion operation can be of arbitrary shape and size. The neighborhood is represented by a structuring element, which is a matrix consisting of only 0's and 1's. The shape of the structuring element used in this work is "ball" and the size of the structuring element is 5-by-5.

b) Gray to binary image conversion:

A suitable threshold (40-50) is selected and the pixels above the threshold value are made equal to 255 and the pixels below the threshold value are made equal to 0. These thresholds are selected based on trial and error method.

c) Connected component analysis:

It is a process that "fills" a region of interest by interpolating the pixel values from the borders of the region. This process can be used to make objects in an image seem to disappear as they are replaced with values that blend in with the background area. This function is useful for removal of extraneous details or artifacts. The resultant image yields the mask for the corresponding input image.

Step 2: Logical conversion of the mask

The indices of the binary mask image are changed from (0-255) to (0-1).

Step 3: Masking

The original input image is masked with the binary mask. The masking is achieved by performing the multiplying operation between the original image and the mask. The resultant image is free from the extra-cranial tissues which is evident from the output images.

4   Feature Extraction

The purpose of feature extraction is to reduce the original data set by measuring certain properties or features that distinguish one input pattern from another pattern. The extracted feature should provide the characteristics of the input type to the classifier by considering the description of the relevant properties of the image into a feature space. Eight different textural features are used in this work for image analysis. But, these features are estimated in a different manner for the classification and segmentation applications. Since image classification is performed between images, the features are estimated from the whole image. On the other hand, image segmentation is performed within the image and hence the features are estimated for each pixel. A neighborhood window of size 3×3 is chosen with the center pixel being the pixel of interest. The procedure is repeated for all the pixels to estimate the features.

In this work, eight textural features such as angular second moment, contrast, correlation, variance, entropy, Inverse Difference Moment, skewness and kurtosis are used for image classification and segmentation. The textural features are extracted from the pre-processed image which guarantees high success rate for the subsequent steps. The features used in this work are estimated from the following formulae.

Angular Second Moment (ASM):
The summation of the squares of gray levels of the image is known as angular second moment. It is also named as energy (or) uniformity. The energy is usually high when the intensity values are unequal.

$$f_1 = \sum_i \sum_j \{p(i, j)\}^2 \tag{1}$$

where $p(i,j)$ represents the input image.

Contrast:
The local contrast of an image is measured by this feature. It is expected to be low if the intensity values of the pixel are similar.

$$f_2 = \sum_{n=0}^{N_g-1} n^2 \left\{ \sum_{i=1}^{N_g} \sum_{j=1}^{N_g} p(i, j) \right\} \tag{2}$$

where N_g is the number of gray levels in the original image.

Correlation:
The linear dependency of grey levels on the neighboring pixels is represented by the correlation feature. The statistical relationship between the two variables is denoted by this feature.

$$f_3 = \frac{\sum_i \sum_j (ij)p(i, j) - \mu_x \mu_y}{\sigma_x \sigma_y} \tag{3}$$

where $\mu_x, \mu_y, \sigma_x, \sigma_y$ are the means and standard deviations of the input image in the row-wise and column-wise order.

Variance:
Variance is a measure of the dispersion of the values around the mean. The variance can also be defined as the measure of how far the gray values are spread out in the input image.

$$f_4 = \sum_i \sum_j (i - \mu)^2 p(i, j) \tag{4}$$

where μ is the mean of the whole image.

Inverse Difference Moment (IDM):
The details of the smoothness of the image are defined by the Inverse difference moment. The IDM is expected to be high if the gray levels of the pixel are similar.

$$f_5 = \sum_i \sum_j \frac{1}{1+(i-j)^2} p(i,j). \tag{5}$$

Entropy:

The randomness of a gray level distribution is denoted by entropy. The entropy is expected to be high if the gray levels are distributed randomly throughout the image.

$$f_6 = -\sum_i \sum_j p(i,j)\log(p(i,j)). \tag{6}$$

Skewness:

The measure of symmetry is given by this textural feature. This value can be either negative or positive. The value is usually zero if the image is exactly symmetrical.

$$f_7 = \frac{1}{\sigma^3} \sum_i \sum_j (p(i,j)-\mu)^3 \tag{7}$$

Kurtosis:

Kurtosis is a measure of whether the data are peaked or flat relative to the normal distribution.

$$f_8 = \frac{1}{\sigma^4} \sum_i \sum_j (p(i,j)-\mu)^4 - 3 \tag{8}$$

These features are commonly used for brain image analysis. These features are specifically found to be superior for image classification and segmentation applications.

5   Experimental Results and Discussions

The algorithms are implemented using MATLAB software with the processor speed of 1.66GHz and 1GB RAM. Sample results of the various stages of skull removal technique for the real-time dataset are shown in Figure 2.

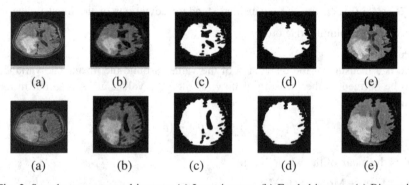

| (a) | (b) | (c) | (d) | (e) |

| (a) | (b) | (c) | (d) | (e) |

Fig. 2. Sample pre-processed images: (a) Input images, (b) Eroded images, (c) Binary images, (d) Images after connected component analysis, (e) Masked images

An analysis of the above results has clearly revealed the success rate of the pre-processing technique in removing the skull tissues. The difference is visible in Figure 2 (e). A quantitative analysis on these results is shown in Table 1.

Table 1. Quantitative analysis of image pre-processing technique

Image type	No. of ground truth skull pixels	No. of skull pixels removed by the technique	Segmentation efficiency (%)
Real-time images	4990	4878	98

The average values are shown in the results since there is a slight deviation in the number of skull pixels removed in each input images. The robustness of this technique is also revealed since this method is applicable for the simulated images and the real-time images. The convergence rate of this method is only 0.47 CPU seconds which is very much significant for real-time applications.

The textural features mentioned above are also calculated using the MATLAB software. These features are calculated separately for the image classification and segmentation process. The size of the feature set for the image classification is 1×8 for an image of any input size. These features are estimated for all the four categories and are tabulated in Table 2.

Table 2. Feature extraction results for image classification

Features	Metastase	Meningioma	Glioma	Astrocytoma
ASM	1.0022e+009	223000562	604422466	384652269
Contrast	8763781	2177178	6457236	3700147
Correlation	3.2290e+005	2.0014e+005	4.2467e+005	1.6320e+005
Variance	4.5537e+011	2.3593e+010	3.8371e+011	2.1467e+011
IDM	6.5249e+004	3.7115e+004	4.2941e+004	2.1614e+004
Skewness	3.1741e+010	8.5147e+009	1.3335e+010	2.8693e+010
Entropy	3.9759e+007	9.5895e+006	2.7925e+007	1.6630e+007
Kurtosis	5.5761e+012	1.3690e+012	2.7647e+012	4.7109e+012

The features extracted using this method is highly efficient which is validated from the experimental results. The distance measure of these feature values within the class is very minimum for any individual feature and maximum between the classes. Thus, this work has suggested suitable methodologies for image pre-processing and feature extraction for MR brain image analysis.

6   Conclusion

The significance of pre-processing and feature extraction methodologies is verified in this work. The accuracy level is significantly high for the proposed techniques. The time requirement is also significantly low which suggests the feasible nature of these techniques. Thus, these approaches can be used for practical medical applications where the accuracy and convergence rate are extremely important.

Acknowledgment. The authors wish to thank M/s. Devaki Scan Centre for their help regarding database collection and validation.

References

1. Nicu, S., Michael, S.L.: Wavelet based texture classification. In: 15th International Conference on Pattern Recognition, vol. 3, pp. 3959–3962 (2000)
2. Yongxin, Z., Jing, B.: Atlas based fuzzy connectedness segmentation and intensity non-uniformity correction applied to brain MRI. IEEE Transactions on Biomedical Engineering 54(1), 122–129 (2006)
3. Marianne, M., Russell, G., Jorg, S., Albert, M., Mark, S.: Learning a classification based glioma growth model using MRI data. Journal of Computers 1(7), 21–31 (2006)
4. Bo, Z., Jalal, M.F., Jean-Luc, S.: Wavelets, ridgelets and curvelets for Poisson noise removal. IEEE Transactions on Image Processing 17(7), 1093–1108 (2008)
5. Jaya, J., Thanushkodi, K.: Implementation of classification system for medical images. European Journal of Scientific Research 53(4), 561–569 (2011)
6. Marcel, P., Elizabeth, B., Guido, G.: Simulation of brain tumors in MR images for evaluation of segmentation efficacy. Medical Image Analysis 13, 297–311 (2009)
7. Rajeev, R., Sanjay, S., Sharma, S.K.: Brain tumor detection based on multi-parameter MR image analysis. Graphics, Vision and Image Processing Journal 9(3), 9–17 (2009)
8. Rajeev, R., Sanjay, S., Sharma, S.K.: Multiparamter segmentation and quantization of brain tumor from MR images. Indian Journal of Science and Technology 2(2), 11–15 (2009)
9. Arivazhagan, S., Ganesan, L.: Texture classification using wavelet transform. Pattern Recognition Letters 24, 1513–1521 (2003)
10. Kourosh, J.K., Hamid, S., Kost, E., Suresh, P.: Comparison of 2D and 3D wavelet features for TLE lateralization. In: Proceedings of SPIE, vol. 5369, pp. 593–601 (2004)
11. Hiremath, P.S., Shivashankar, S.: Texture classification using wavelet packet decomposition. Graphics, Vision and Image Processing Journal 6(2), 77–80 (2006)
12. Ryszard, S.C.: Image feature extraction techniques and their applications for CBIR and biometrics system. International Journal of Biology and Biomedical Engineering 1(1), 6–16 (2007)
13. Georgiadis, P., Cavouras, D., Kalatzis, I., Daskalakis, A., Kagadis, G.C., Sifaki, K., Malamas, M., Nikiforidis, G.C., Solomou, E.: Non-linear Least Squares Features Transformation for Improving the Performance of Probabilistic Neural Networks in Classifying Human Brain Tumors on MRI. In: Gervasi, O., Gavrilova, M.L. (eds.) ICCSA 2007, Part III. LNCS, vol. 4707, pp. 239–247. Springer, Heidelberg (2007)
14. Ke, H., Selin, A.: Wavelet feature selection for image classification. IEEE Transactions on Image Processing 17(9), 1709–1720 (2008)

Design of Circularly Polarized Microstrip Patch Antenna with Wide-Band Characteristic

Dong Hee Park

Dept. of Information and Communications Engineering
Korea National Univ. of Transportation, KNUT
50 Daehak-ro, Chungju-si, Republic of Korea
dhpark@ut.ac.kr

Abstract. A novel wide-band circularly polarized (WCP) microstrip patch antenna for wireless power transmission (WPT) at 5.2 GHz and 5.5 GHz is proposed. In particular, we are designed to be able to services for 5.2 GHz wireless local area network (WLAN) in wireless battery charging at 5.5 GHz. The designed antenna has two probes feeding, a corners-truncated and the two shorted diagonal slots in the square patch. As a result, this paper presents possibility for the design of microstrip patch antenna (MPA) with wide-band and CP characteristics with the general TLC substrate.

Keywords: wide band CP antenna, WPT antenna, CP patch antennas, slots antenna.

1 Introduction

The circularly polarized microstrip patch antennas, including single or double-feed patches, are widely used as effective radiators in many communication systems [1]. Also wireless power transmission (WPT) by microwaves has been studied several decades. The concept of WPT began with the ideas and demonstration by Tesla [2]. As the fundamental component of the WPT system, a rectenna is a receiving antenna attached to a rectifying circuit that converts microwave power into useful DC power.

Now the IEEE 802.11a use 5-6 GHz frequency band and WLAN applications are increasing very rapidly to replace short distance tethered communication links between devices, sensors, and computers. Such communication link can also be envisioned between wireless power sensors and the local area controller in a power distribution system [3].

Dual and circularly polarized (CP) antennas utilizing a circular patch antenna [4], dual band CP patch antenna [5] and wideband CP patch antenna for WPT [6] have been recently developed. Circularly polarized antennas will essentially help obtain the same dc voltage irrespective of the rotation of the rectenna. Most of the previous work on dual-frequency antennas and CP antennas has concentrated on optimizing the conversion efficiency of the microwave rectifier element.

As suggested in [4], they are introduced a new rectenna combining the advantages of dual-frequency operation and reception of CP radiation. The designed rectenna is able to

T.-h. Kim et al. (Eds.): FGCN/DCA 2012, CCIS 350, pp. 357–361, 2012.
© Springer-Verlag Berlin Heidelberg 2012

receive and convert microwave power into dc power at two industrial, scientific, and medical (ISM) frequency bands, 2.45 and 5.8 GHz. As in [5], when slots are etched close to the radiating edges, they do not change significantly the first resonant frequency and the radiation pattern of the patch. Furthermore they are extended to a dual-frequency CP antenna for the operation at 2.4 GHz and 3.2 GHz. As in [6], they are introduced a wide bandwidths CPMPA which can function as a rectenna for wireless battery charging at 5.5 GHz and data telemetry in the 5.2 GHz WLAN band. This solution has several drawbacks in terms of efficiently and noise performances because wide bandwidths are difficult to be achieved with planar structures.

In this paper, we introduce a wide-band circularly polarized MPA using Taconic TLC substrate which can function as a rectenna at 5.2 GHz for data and 5.5 GHz for battery charging. This is obtained by two probes feeding, a corners-truncated and the two shorted diagonal slots. As a result, this paper suggests that the dual band circularly polarized antenna can be designed to optimize for WPT as a WLAN antenna.

2   Antenna Design and Geometry

The geometry of the proposed dual band CP antenna along with its parameters is shown in Fig. 1. The antenna was initially designed and developed on Taconic TLC substrate having relative dielectric constant $\varepsilon_r=3$, loss tangent tan δ =0.003, height h_1=0.79 mm, and conductor's thickness t=18μm and fed by a coaxial probe.

The size of the patch was chosen to be suitable in the center frequency of 5.5 GHz. The outer dimensions of the square are 15.5 mm ×15.5 mm. The diagonal slots positioned along the left diagonal of the square patch generate the two modes. The optimum sizes of the slots are L_1=4.8 mm, W_1=0.2 mm. The corner truncation length D=1.6 mm is tuned to obtain wide AR bandwidth, while maintain the return loss bandwidth to overlap with the AR bandwidth. The feed point with a 50 [Ω] coaxial line is located in the central line of the patch with a distance of F_1=4 mm and F_2=4 mm from the

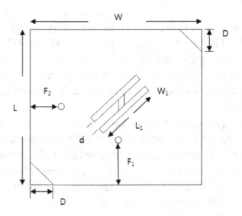

Fig. 1. Geometry of the proposed antenna: Top view

radiating edges. The antenna characteristics were optimized for wide-band return loss and circular polarization bandwidth by conducting a parametric study using Ansoft Designer tool.

3   Analysis and Results

Computed S11 (dB) data for the proposed antenna on TLC substrate have been shown in Fig. 2. These data are compared with the two shorted diagonal slots and without slots in the patch with truncated corners. In case of the two shorted diagonal slots, the bandwidth is about 360 MHz.

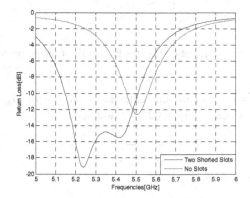

Fig. 2. Computed return loss versus frequency for the proposed antenna with two shorted diagonal slots and without slots

Computed current distribution of the proposed antenna is shown in Fig. 3. Clearly currents are concentrated at the edges of the slots. The two shorted diagonal slots create equal lengths for two separate current paths. These current paths correspond to two hybrid operating modes which result in wide-band characteristics. Computed radiation pattern data at 5.5 GHz are shown in Fig. 4.

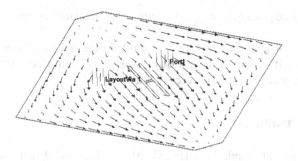

Fig. 3. Computed current distribution at 5.2 GHz

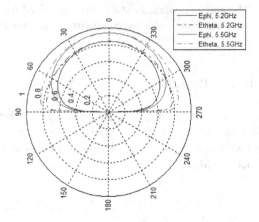

Fig. 4. Computed normalized radiation patterns E_Φ and E_θ of the proposed antenna at 5.2 GHz and 5.5 GHz. Φ=0o

Computed axial ratio data for this antenna are shown in Fig. 5. The axial ratio bandwidth extends, which is very good for a double-fed MPA.

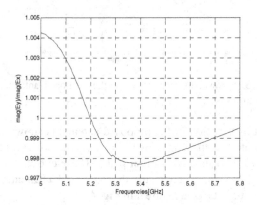

Fig. 5. Computed fields mag(Ey)/mag(Ex) of the proposed antenna   at 5.5 GHz

This particular geometry with its two shorted diagonal slots orientation results in right-hand CP. If a mirror image case is considered, left-hand CP will result with stringer field concentration along the other diagonal.

4   Conclusion

A novel wide-band circularly polarized MPA is introduced that can function as a WLAN antenna in the 5.2 GHz and as a WPT at 5.5 GHz. The designed antenna has two probes feeding, a corners-truncated and the two shorted diagonal slots in the square patch. The two shorted diagonal slots properly positioned along the diagonal of the square patch antenna create two hybrid operating modes which operate very close in frequency.

The future of researches of this paper is continuously required on the design of multi-band frequency a rectenna for near RF Network. As a result, this paper proposes possibility for the design of optimizing to wide-band or dual-band CP rectenna for near RF network.

Acknowledgement. The research was supported by a grant from the Academic Research Program of Korea National University of Transportation in 2012.

References

1. Wong, K.L., Wu, J.Y.: Single feed small circularly polarized square microstrip antenna. Electronics letter 33(22) (1977)
2. Brown, W.C.: The history of power transmission by radio waves. IEEE Trans. Microwave Theory Tech. MTT 32, 1230–1242 (1984)
3. Roy, J.S., Thomas, M.: Theoretical and experimental investigations on a new proximity coupled dual frequency microstrip antenna for the application in wireless communication. Microwave Review 13, 12–15 (2007)
4. Heikkinen, J., Kivikoski, M.: A Novel Dual-Frequency Circularly Polarized Rectenna. IEEE Antennas Wireless Propag. Lett. 2, 330–333 (2003)
5. Maci, S., Biffi Gentili, G.: Dual-Frequency Patch Antennas. IEEE Antennas and Propag. Magazine 39(6), 13–20 (1997)
6. Ali, M., Yang, G., Dougal, R.: A New Circularly Polarized Rectenna for Wireless Power Transmission and Data Communication. IEEE Antennas Wireless Propag. Litt. 4, 205–208 (2005)

Empirical Analysis of General Bayesian Network-Driven Online Recommendation Mechanism: Emphasis on User Satisfaction and Psychological Reactance

Dahee Chung[1], Kun Chang Lee[2,*], and Seung Chang Seong[1]

[1] SKK Business School, Sungkyunkwan University, Seoul 110-745, Republic of Korea
dahee0126@hotmail.com1, seongsc@gmail.com
[2] SKK Business School, WCU, Department of Interaction Science,
Sungkyunkwan University, Seoul 110-745, Republic of Korea
kunchanglee@gmail.com

Abstract. As Internet technology permeates into our daily lives, the importance of online recommendation grows quite rapidly. Needless to say, the success of the online recommendation mechanism depends heavily on how much users are satisfied by the recommendation results. Moreover, it is essential that users feel less psychological reactance about the recommendation results when it comes to the effectiveness of the online recommendation mechanism. To accomplish those two goals, we propose a new online recommendation mechanism on the basis of the General Bayesian Network (GBN). It is common that users have a large number of personal wants and needs in their minds when using the recommendation mechanism. In this case, GBN is very effective in selecting a small number of relevant factors and organizing a set of causal relationships among them. An advantage of GBN like this allows users to have much satisfaction about the recommendation results, and enjoy rich implications from them. We implemented the proposed GBN-driven online recommendation mechanism (GBNOREM), and tested with users who are suffering from minor health problems and therefore in need of proper menus at the right restaurants. Empirical results clearly revealed that the proposed GBNOREM can enhance users' perceived satisfaction about the recommendation results, while reducing the level of users' perceived psychological reactance.

Keywords: Online recommendation mechanism, General Bayesian Network, Health, Psychological Reactance.

1 Introduction

In the era of advanced Internet technology, there is no doubt that people are exposed to a lot more information. That is, the amount of choice has broadened, and depends on Internet technology. Despite its potential to enhance the public's satisfaction by presenting alternatives, increased choice also means that consumers are more likely to make wrong decisions. In response, online retailers like Amazon.com use their own

---

*Corresponding author.

T.-h. Kim et al. (Eds.): FGCN/DCA 2012, CCIS 350, pp. 362–368, 2012.
© Springer-Verlag Berlin Heidelberg 2012

recommender system, which helps users to reduce browsing time, and it supports their decision making. Through an effective recommender system, online retailers also improve customer satisfaction and loyalty [1]. Hence, recommender systems are not simply add-on features for e-commerce websites, but a crucial component of the online shop for both retailers and consumers [2]. Recently, a number of authors take into account recommender systems of various fields, such as movies, music, books and fashion. The domain of recommender systems has extended [3]. Particularly, studies of recommender systems on healthcare service have been actively conducted [4]. There is a growing interest in recommender systems that recommend healthy food and restaurants, personalized for the user. In addition, as "health" means both physical and psychological health, psychological views such as fatigue, stress and anger are considered to develop reliable recommender system for the healthcare domain.

Most previous studies on recommendation mechanisms have been focused on technical implementation, mathematical modeling and performance metrics. Hence, many researchers developed various approaches, such as collaborative filtering, content-based filtering and the heuristic method [5]. However, the more important thing is whether or not the users who use the recommender system accept and follow its recommendation. Hence, a non-technical issue like psychological reactance should be considered in order to improve a personalized recommender system [6].

The present paper examines the user's satisfaction with and psychological reactance level for the recommendation. The recommendation results are made by reasoning based on the General Bayesian Network (GBN), which is learned structure and parameters from data. The results are displayed in the following manner: First, we just show ingredients such as tomatoes, garlic and olive oil, which matched users' dietary requirements. Then users chose one of ingredients, depending on their preference. Finally, the recommender system showed appropriate restaurants considering users' locations. In other words, we try to reduce psychological reactance as much as possible. The proposed prototype named GBNOREM (GBN–driven online recommendation mechanism) was tested with valid surveys and experiments.

2   Theoretical Background

2.1   Online Recommendation Mechanism

In general, recommender systems consist of three components: (1) background data, which are used in the reasoning process; (2) input data, which the users provide to the system in order to get a recommendation and (3) an algorithm that combines background data and input data to generate recommendations [2].

Recommendation systems can be classified into three categories in terms of methods of generating recommendations [7]: (1) content-based recommender systems make recommendations that are similar to those already evaluated by the user, (2) collaborative filtering approaches generate recommendations based on a similar group of users' profiles and (3) hybrid recommendation systems combine two or more approaches in order to improve the quality of recommendations [3, 8].

In this aging society, people think that health is wealth, so the number people who require appropriate healthcare information and consider individuals' healthcare seriously is increasing. Also, the term "health" generally encompasses both a person's physiological and psychological status [9]. Hence, we try to consider users' psychological well-being as well as physical health when we make recommendations.

2.2   General Bayesian Network

A Bayesian Network (BN) is an approach that presents knowledge by integrating the Bayesian theorem with a graphical model, and is effective in explaining causal relationships. Each node in a Bayesian network means a random variable and is related to a probability function. [10] The main advantages of a BN: (1) it is available to handle situations when some input data are missing, (2) it can be used to understand causal relationships among variables of the problem domain and to predict the consequence of intervention and (3) as the BN model has both causal and probabilistic semantics, it is an appropriate representation for combining prior knowledge and data [11]. Especially, the GBN is an unrestricted BN, which treats a class node as an ordinary node, so we can find more accurate causal relationship among nodes. The GBN also provides effective analysis techniques, which are what-if and goal-seeking analyses. In addition, a Markov Blanket (MB), which represents a few relevant descriptive variables, can reduce the cost of data collection and reasoning time. Therefore, we propose recommender systems adopt the GBN.

2.3   Psychological Reactance

Online recommendation is one way to persuade people to buy or do something. Recommendation systems are apparently helpful to make decisions, but sometimes we feel that our autonomy is intruded upon by a recommendation [12]. That is, we experience psychological reactance. Psychological reactance was first defined by Brehm [13]. In general, people perceive that they have freedom of choice. If their freedoms are constrained or threatened, then individuals react against attempts to limit their free choices. Recent studies found that explicit messages generate more reactance than implicit messages [6]. Also, another study found the use of highly controlling language such as "should," "ought" and "must" enhance reactance [14]. Therefore, when we show results to users, we can only recommend essential ingredients. Then it has to be up to the users to make the final decision in order to lessen psychological reactance.

3   Experiments with GBNOREM

The General Bayesian Network–driven online recommendation system (GBNOREM) proposed in this study is a specific service that recommends proper food, menus and restaurants to people who are concerned about leading a healthy life.

3.1   GBNOREM System Design

Modeling General Bayesian Network

In general, there are two different methods that have been used to construct a BN: (1) the data-based method and (2) the knowledge-based method. Though the knowledge-based approach is helpful where the domain is unique and when data are scarce, it takes a long time to construct a network using this approach, and it cannot ensure the accuracy of the network. Hence, we adopt a data-based approach to construct a BN, using the data-mining tool WEKA (Waikato Environment for Knowledge Analysis). First, we surveyed 392 students who attended the lecture for management information systems. The survey included several questions about the respondents' physical and psychological status, such as level of fatigue, depression, anger, stress and diseases. Then, we mapped proper food ingredients, considering respondents' overall conditions. After that, we use these data to construct a GBN, learning the structure and parameters from the data. In addition, a K2 algorithm [15] in WEKA was adopted to construct the GBN, which showed high-prediction accuracy.

GBNOREM

(1) Data Handler: The data handler receives users' context data such as how they feel (e.g. tired or stressful), in addition to which diseases they are concerned about or suffer from chronically. When the users start this system, they fill out a questionnaire, which is intended to elicit information on their overall health conditions. Then the data handler passes information to the GBN inference engine.

(2) GBN Inference Engine: The GBN inference engine uses a GBN, which has been constructed before using a data-based approach, to predict and draw results. After the data handler passes information to the GBN inference engine, the engine calculates the target variable's posterior probabilities and returns the entry with the greatest probability as the predicted result.

(3) Recommendation Database: The database used in the GBNOREM contains information about restaurants near Sungkyunkwan University that offer various types of menus that include recommended   food ingredients such as tofu, tomatoes, olive oil and so on. The GBNOREM was developed using JAVA.

3.2   Experiment

A laboratory experiment was conducted to empirically test the effect of the GBNOREM on users' decision satisfaction, decision confidence, attitude toward the process and attitude toward the recommendation. For the experiments, a total of 12 college students were recruited. They included six females and six males and their average age was 25.83 years, with a standard deviation of 3.58. Participants were asked to respond to some questions designed to measure (on a seven-point likert-type scale) their responses to the three decision-confidence items and four items that assessed attitude toward the process, from Aldag & Power [16]. An established scale borrowed from literature including Bruner [17] and Li et al. [18] was used to measure participants' attitudes toward the recommendations. Also, to measure an individual's disposition of reactance and decision satisfaction, we employed the refined version of the Hong Psychological Reactance Scale [19, 20], and four decision satisfaction items from Fitzimons [21].

Table 1. Measurement Items

Construct	Item	Related literature
Decision Confidence	My choice is good one.	[16]
	I'm not sure my choice was appropriate	
	I'm not confident about my choice	
Decision Satisfaction	I'm satisfied with my choice	[21]
	I'm happy with my choice	
	I would like the same choice again	
	I thought the choice was good	
Attitude toward System	Using GBNOREM was fun	[16]
	I'm not in favor of GBNOREM because it is just another step toward depersonalization	
	Even otherwise interesting recommendation would be boring when presented by GBNOREM	
	I don't like GBNOREM	
Attitude toward Recommendation	Bad-good	[17] [18]
	Not appealing-appealing	
	Unpleasant-pleasant	
	Unattractive- attractive	
	Boring- interesting	

3.3   Results

Table 2 presents the value of decision confidence, decision satisfaction and attitude toward the system and recommendation, calculating the average of the related items based on the analysis of the questionnaire. The mean values are 5.33 (decision confidence), 5.52 (decision satisfaction), 5.25 (attitude toward system) and 4.87 (attitude toward recommendation). Therefore, most of the respondents rate the GBNOREM positively. Also, we analyzed the intraclass correlation coefficient (ICC) [22] using SPSS, which is the measure of the consistency of assessment made by different observers measuring the same target. The average measures of ICC are 0.716 (decision confidence), 0.902 (decision satisfaction), 0.802 (attitude toward system) and 0.887 (attitude toward recommendation). Meanwhile, according to a pairwise t-test conducted at the 5-percent significance level to compare the reactance level after experiencing the GBNOREM, the level of reactance decreased from 3.10, which is the value of general reactance propensity, to 2.14. This means that the GBNOREM provided recommendations in an efficient way and, finally, alleviated psychological reactance about the recommendations.

4   Discussion and Concluding Remarks

The main goal of this paper is to propose a new recommendation system, a General Bayesian Network–driven recommendation system (GBNOREM). The system applies a fresh approach to alleviating psychological reactance level. That is, the recommendation system doesn't make the ultimate decision but keep one's options open, so users can make the final decision. As a result, users experience less psychological reactance, as they maintain personal freedom to think and act as they choose.

Based on the statistical results presented in section 3.2, we found that overall, the GBNOREM performs well, because the recommendation of the GBNOREM is made by considering individuals' physical and psychological status, us a GBN. Also, results of this current study suggest that the GBNOREM can significantly alleviate psychological reactance. Generally, persuasive attempts are likely to fail if individuals experience an intrusion or restriction on their freedom of choice. Also, a recommendation may cause reactance if there is a gap between the recommendation and users' desires. [23] Hence, the GBNOREM lets users make the final decision. As a result, as the GBNOREM reduces differences between users' desires and the recommendations, it can alleviate psychological reactance.

The practical implications of this current study are as follows. First, the proposed GBNOREM used a General Bayesian network, which can be a robust inference engine that is especially useful in predicting an uncertain domain. Also, as the GBNOREM's recommendations are made considering users' psychological perspectives, it might be more acceptable for users. Secondly, the findings affect the way of designing recommendations. If we would like to develop a recommendation system, it is important to alleviate psychological reactance. This is because the objective of the recommendation is to make or stimulate people to do as recommended. Hence, in the GBNOREM, the last word belongs to the users, in order to alleviate reactance.

Acknowledgements. This research was supported by the World Class University (WCU) program through the National Research Foundation of Korea, funded by the ministry of Education, Science and Technology, Republic of Korea (Grant No. R31-2008-000-10062-0).

References

1. Hostler, E.R., Yoon, V.Y., Guimaraes, T.: Recommendation Agent Impact on Consumer Online Shopping: The Movie Magic Case Study. Expert Systems with Applications 39, 2989–2999 (2012)
2. Ochi, P., Rao, S., Takayama, L.: Predictors of User Perceptions of Web Recommender Systems: How the Basis for Generating Experience and Search Product Recommendations Affects User Responses. International Journal of Human-Computer Studies 68, 472–482 (2010)
3. Lee, Y., Huang, F.: Recommender System Architecture for Adaptive Green Marketing. Expert Systems with Applications 38, 9696–9703 (2011)
4. Kim, J., Lee, J., Park, J., Lee, Y., Rim, K.: Design of Diet Recommendation System for Healthcare Service Based on User Information. In: Fourth International Conference on Computer Sciences and Convergence Information Technology (ICCIT), pp. 516–518 (2009)

5. Bobadilla, J., Serradilla, F., Bernal, J.: A New Collaborative Filtering Metric that Improves the Behavior of Recommender Systems. Knowledge-Based Systems 23, 520–528 (2010)
6. Grandpre, J., Alvaro, E.M., Burgoon, M.: Adolescent Reactance and Anti-Smoking Campaigns: A Theoretical Approach. Health Communication 15, 349–366 (2003)
7. Vekariya, V., Kulkarni, G.R.: Notice of Violation of IEEE Publication Principles Hybrid Recommender Systems: Survey and Experiments. In: Second International Conference on Digital Information and Communication Technology and it's Applications (DICTAP), pp. 469–473 (2012)
8. Carrer-Neto, W., Hernández-Alcaraz, M.L., Valencia-García, R.: Social Knowledge-Based Recommender System: Application to the Movies Domain. Expert Systems with Applications 39, 10990–11100 (2012)
9. Danna, K., Griffin, R.W.: Health and Well-being in the Workplace: A Review and Synthesis of the Literature. Journal of Management 25, 357–384 (1999)
10. Hsu, F., Lin, Y., Ho, T.: Design and Implementation of an Intelligent Recommendation System for Tourist Attractions: The Integration of EBM Model, Bayesian Network and Google Maps. Expert Systems with Applications 39, 3257–3264 (2012)
11. Nadkarni, S., Shenoy, P.P.: A Causal Mapping Approach to Constructing Bayesian Networks. Decision Support Systems 38, 259–281 (2004)
12. Roubroeks, M., Midden, C., Ham, J.: Does it make a Difference Who Tells You what to do? Exploring the Effect of Social Agency on Psychological Reactance. In: Proceedings of the 4th International Conference on Persuasive Technology, Pervasive 2009, article no.15 (2009)
13. Brehm, J.W.: A theory of psychological reactance. Academic Press, New York (1966)
14. Miller, C.H., Lane, L.T., Deatrick: Psychological Reactance and Promotional Health Messages: The Effects of Controlling Language, Lexical Concreteness, and the Restoration of Freedom. Human Communication Research 33, 219–240 (2007)
15. Cooper, G., Herskovits, E.: A Bayesian Method for the Induction of Probabilistic Networks from Data. Machine Learning 9, 309–347 (1992)
16. Aldag, R.J., Power, D.J.: An Empirical Assessment of Computer-Assisted Decision Analysis. Decision Sciences 17, 572–588 (1986)
17. Bruner II, G.C.: Standardization & Justification: Do Aad Scales Measure Up? Journal of Current Issues & Research in Advertising 20, 1–19 (1998)
18. Li, H., Daugherty, T., Biocca, F.: The Role of Virtual Experience in Consumer Learning. Journal of Consumer Psychology 13, 395–407 (2003)
19. Hong, S.: Hong's Psychological Reactance Scale: A Further Factor Analytic Validation. Psychological Reports 70, 512–514 (1992)
20. Hong, S., Faedda, S.: Refinement of the Hong Psychological Reactance Scale. Educational and Psychological Measurement 56, 173–182 (1996)
21. Fitzsimons, G.J.: Consumer Response to Stockouts. Journal of Consumer Research 27, 249–266 (2000)
22. James, L.R., Demaree, R.G., Wolf, G.: Estimating within-Group Interrater Reliability with and without Response Bias. Journal of Applied Psychology 69, 85–98 (1984)
23. Fitzsimons, G.J., Lehmann, D.R.: Reactance to Recommendations: When Unsolicited Advice Yields Contrary Responses. Marketing Science 23, 82–94 (2004)

Evaluation of E-government Systems with Cognitive Mapping Simulation

Eunsung Lee

Graduate School of Business, Yonsei University, Seoul 120-749, South Korea
eunsung.lee@yonsei.ac.kr

Abstract. E-Government system performance must be measured by an exporting company prior to implementation in other countries. However, it is extremely difficult to perform this task due to the existence of a large number of factors to consider and analyze. The motivation of this study was to propose a new method to reduce this difficulty in measuring e-Government system performance. We adopted a cognitive mapping approach for this purpose, where a set of relevant factors that affect e-Government system performance were collected and the causal relationships among them were identified and analyzed to investigate the equilibrium results given certain input conditions. The e-Government system used for handling intellectual property in South Korea was used as a test-bed. Experiment results revealed that cognitive mapping simulation can yield statistically sound and practically rich results.

Keywords: E-government system, Cognitive map, Simulation, Monte Carlo Simulation.

1 Introduction

The emergence of the digital economy and the proliferation of the Internet and World Wide Web applications have significantly affected the administrative models of government. As Internet technology becomes more readily available, the reformulation of productive processes and reengineering of administrative processes have been increasingly involved in what are now known as electronic government projects (e-Government) in order to achieve greater efficiency, effectiveness, and accountability in government agencies' relationships with stakeholders. From static websites to direct citizen services, the transformation caused by e-Government has demanded a change in focus from administration to serving the citizenry and is being adopted across the globe.

However, little is known about the performance of e-Government systems, partially because of a lack of effective measures to evaluate e-Government performance. Heeks reports that the failure rates of e-Government projects are as high as 85%, and a more recent study conducted by Sauer and Cuthbertson (2003) reported that only 16% of Information Technology (IT) projects were considered successful. Due to high failure rates, more attention has been paid to the area of e-Government across the globe in recent years, particularly in regards to improving its performance.

T.-h. Kim et al. (Eds.): FGCN/DCA 2012, CCIS 350, pp. 369–376, 2012.
© Springer-Verlag Berlin Heidelberg 2012

Both the diversity of topics and the volume of articles dealing with e-Government have increased. Many e-Government studies have focused on the development and evaluation of a web site that interfaces between a government and its citizens. However, researchers concentrating on e-Government as a technology-led solution often overlook the context and nuances of governance, both of which make e-Government meaningful in the final analysis.

Conscious of the need to evaluate e-Government performance, this study starts with the belief that the adoption of an e-Government system should improve services to citizens. This means that when a country adopts a specific e-Government system, assessing its performance prior to adoption is crucial. We therefore propose a research question that remains unanswered in the current e-Government literature – "How do we predict the performance of the e-Government system when it is adopted in other countries and what is the best strategy to achieve the desirable performance?" – using the Korean Intellectual Property Office Net (KIPONet) as the target system. The research question is increasingly important with the need to adopt e-Government systems across the globe.

This paper aims to provide appropriate strategies to achieve desirable results in e-Government systems using the cognitive mapping simulation technique, where a set of relevant factors that affect e-Government system performance are collected and analyzed to investigate the equilibrium results given certain input conditions.

The current study is organized as follows:

- Section 1 provides an introduction to the issue and the proposed research.
- Section 2 addresses the theoretical background of FCM studies.
- Section 3 describes the adopted methodology, simulation results, and implications.
- Section 4 provides concluding remarks.

2   Theoretical Background

2.1   E-Government

Electronic government (e-Government) has been an important area of ICT applications over the last few years and has also received increasing attention by researchers. Government organizations no longer doubt the need to deliver their services online. Instead, the question that is more relevant is how well the electronic services offered perform, for instance, in comparison with those offered by other organizations. At the beginning of August 2011, the Web of Science captured 1,079 articles with the search word "e-Government."

Although almost all of these articles investigate e-Government systems in individual countries, few are country-independent or aimed at developing theory. For example, Rorissa et al. (2011) proposed a number of procedures to assess e-Government systems, expanding current frameworks by introducing techniques that account for the stages of development of e-Government services. Jansen et al. (2010) proposed the Contextual Benchmark Method, which measures how well the e-Government system offered by a particular organization performs in comparison with those offered by others.

Perhaps due to the nature of e-Government applications in dictating a boundary encompassing an individual country, most e-Government studies have been confined to analyzing a specific country's case in a broad, generic sense. Therefore, to the best of our knowledge, the present article is the first to analyze and predict the performance of an e-Government system (KIPONet in this instance) in a number of situations with the aim of helping other countries predict the expected performance of an e-Government system after adoption.

2.2   Cognitive Map

Since the pioneering work of Kosko (1986), Fuzzy Cognitive Maps (FCMs) have attracted a great deal of attention from various research communities. As a modeling methodology for complex systems, FCMs model the investigated causal system as a collection of concepts and relations among concepts originating from the combination of fuzzy logic and neural networks. Intuitively, an FCM is a signed, directed graph with feedback consisting of a collection of nodes and directed weighted arcs with interconnecting nodes, and can describe any system using a model with signed causality (indicating a positive or negative relationship), strengths of the causal relationships (that take fuzzy values), and causal links that are dynamic (i.e., the effect of a change in one concept/node affects other nodes, which in turn may affect other nodes).

FCM utilizes concepts to illustrate the different aspects of the model and behavior of the system while the concepts interacting with each other show the dynamics of the system (Stylios and Groumpos, 2004). An FCM can also be used to represent qualitative and quantitative data. Due to the way it is constructed, this model integrates the accumulated experience and knowledge on the causal relationships between factors and the characteristics and components of the system. It uses human experts who know the system and its behavior under different circumstances.

E-Government system performance is subject to a wide variety of factors, both qualitative and quantitative, that range from culture, IT infrastructure, and policy to users' personal attitudes and so on. Therefore, decision makers should assess an e-Government system based on both qualitative and quantitative factors. In this sense, it seems very timely and appropriate for FCM to be used to investigate the performance of e-Government systems under the assumption that it will be adopted in another country in which competitors' systems exist.

3   Methodology

3.1   Fuzzy Cognitive Mapping

This study proposes the integration of fuzzy cognitive mapping with a strategic planning simulation to predict the performance of an e-Government system such as

KIPONet when adopted in another country. The results can help decision makers understand the complex dynamics between a certain strategic goal and the related factors. The proposed FCM consists of three phases. The first is concerned with defining the concept nodes that represent the factors describing a target problem. The second phase determines the arrows indicating the causal relationships between the two concept nodes. The third phase analyzes the causality coefficients on each arrow indicating the positive or negative strength with which a node affects other nodes.

FCMs require defining the nodes representing the components or factors that make up the target problem. In this case, the strategic goal is to deliver desirable performance, and related factors of the target problem are identified through five rounds of in-depth interviews with four experts and three professors working in e-Government fields in the Republic of Korea.

Table 1. Nodes of the Target Problems

Node #	Description	Node#	Description
C1	Firm's overseas technical support capability	C11	Implementability in a short period
C2	Technological capability level compared to competitor's	C12	Strengthened notification service for customers
C3	Software quality compared to competitor's	C13	Full-scale online processing for international patents
C4	Price competitiveness compared to competitor's	C14	Cost savings in patent registration
C5	Application of international standard for business process	C15	S/W operation records
C6	Application of international standard for informatization	C16	S/W operation performance
C7	Integration of language and user interface	C17	S/W operation stability
C8	Security	C18	Benefit for cost
C9	Ease of use	C19	Increase in per capita productivity
C10	Level of technological originality	C20	User satisfaction

C18, C29, and C20 refer to the output nodes, and C1, C2, C3, C4, C10, C15, C16, and C17 denote the characteristics of KIPONet that a customer country would like to compare with the competitor's software. Therefore, the eight nodes should be dealt with appropriately because they could vary sharply according to the customer country's judgment and assessment of KIPONet. Henceforth, the FCM simulation process should represent the high volatility of the nodes.

3.2   Causal Relationships

First, to determine the strategy to attain the goal, the FCM should be built and then analyzed. Based on Table 1, the strategic goal to pursue is C18, C19, and C20: benefit for cost, increase in per capita productivity, and user satisfaction, respectively. The FCM showing the cause-effect relationships between the strategic goal and the related factors is constructed using the concept nodes identified above. The causal relationships were also determined through three rounds of interviews with two experts and one professor working in e-Government fields in the Republic of Korea. Figure 1 depicts the causal relationships used in the FCM simulation.

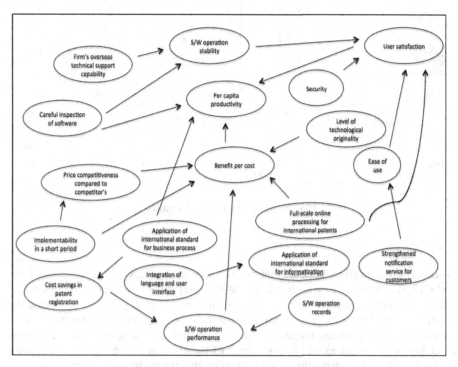

Fig. 1. Fuzzy cognitive map of the target problem

Second, on the basis of the cognitive map, a set of identified causality coefficients is organized in an adjacency matrix on which the WHAT-IF simulation is based. Multiplying the first concept node vector by the adjacency matrix repeatedly until we reach a state of equilibrium in which inference 'n' equals inference 'n-1', we can test the effect of eight volatile nodes on the output nodes in the cognitive map.

Third, the FCM results will be analyzed using the solver technique – identifying the maximum and minimum values of the output nodes and the values of the input nodes in the given circumstance – to determine the appropriate strategy to obtain the goal and predict KIPONet performance more accurately. Figure 2 shows the concept node vector and the adjacency matrix results.

		input																	output		
		C1	C2	C3	C4	C5	C6	C7	C8	C9	C10	C11	C12	C13	C14	C15	C16	C17	C18	C19	C20
input	C1	0	0	0	0	0	0	0	0	0	0	0	0	0	0	0	0	1	0	0	0
	C2	0	0	0	0	0	0	0	0	0	0	0	0	0	0	0	0	0	0	0	0
	C3	0	0	0	0	0	0	0	0	0	0	0	0	0	0	0	1	0	1	0	0
	C4	0	0	0	0	0	0	0	0	0	0	0	0	0	0	0	0	0	1	0	0
	C5	0	0	0	0	0	0	0	0	0	0	0	0	0	1	0	0	0	0	1	0
	C6	0	0	0	0	0	0	0	0	0	0	0	0	0	0	0	0	0	0	0	0
	C7	0	0	0	0	0	1	0	0	0	0	0	0	0	0	0	0	0	0	0	0
	C8	0	0	0	0	0	0	0	0	0	0	0	0	0	0	0	0	0	0	0	1
	C9	0	0	0	0	0	0	0	0	0	0	0	0	0	0	0	0	0	0	0	1
	C10	0	0	0	0	0	0	0	0	0	0	0	0	0	0	0	0	0	1	0	0
	C11	0	0	0	1	0	0	0	0	0	0	0	0	0	0	0	0	0	1	0	0
	C12	0	0	0	0	0	0	0	0	1	0	0	0	0	0	0	0	0	0	0	0
	C13	0	0	0	0	0	0	0	0	0	0	0	0	0	0	0	0	0	1	0	1
	C14	0	0	0	0	0	0	0	0	0	0	0	0	0	0	1	0	0	0	0	0
	C15	0	0	0	0	0	0	0	0	0	0	0	0	0	0	1	1	0	0	0	0
	C16	0	0	0	0	0	0	0	0	0	0	0	0	0	0	0	0	0	1	0	0
	C17	0	0	0	0	0	0	0	0	0	0	0	0	0	0	0	0	0	0	0	1
output	C18	0	0	0	0	0	0	0	0	0	0	0	0	0	0	0	0	0	0	1	0
	C19	0	0	0	0	0	0	0	0	0	0	0	0	0	0	0	0	0	0	0	0
	C20	0	0	0	0	0	0	0	0	0	0	0	0	0	0	0	0	0	0	1	0
C_i	$\dashv$	0	0	0.6	0.7	0.6	1	0.6	1	0.6	0	1	1	1	1	0	0	0	0	0	0
$C \times E$	$\dashv$	0	0	0	1	0	0.6	0	0	1	0	0	0	0	0.6	0	1	0.6	2.7	1.2	2.6
$\rightarrow$	(	0	0	0	1	0	1	0	0	1	0	0	0	0	1	0	1	1	1	1	1
C_i	$\dashv$	0	0	0.6	0.7	0.6	1	0.6	1	0.6	0	1	1	1	1	0	0	0	1	1	1
$C \times E$	$\dashv$	0	0	0	1	0	0.6	0	0	1	0	0	0	0	0.6	0	1	0.6	2.7	3.2	2.6
$\rightarrow$	(	0	0	0	1	0	1	0	0	1	0	0	0	0	1	0	1	1	1	1	1

Fig. 2. Summary of FCM results

3.3   Results

As described in Section 3.2, the eight nodes, such as C1, C2, C3, C4, C10, C15, C16, and C17, should be dealt with in relation to the competitor's software. The manner in which the adopting country will evaluate the eight nodes is very uncertain because the country will have its own unique culture, policy, IT infrastructure, user characteristics, and so on. Therefore, the proposed FCM is an appropriate simulation mechanism for situations of this sort. Each of the eight nodes should be represented by appropriate values depending on the situation that the customer country faces.

Let us suppose that a customer country is considering KIPONet as one of its e-Government system candidates. The customer will surely want to evaluate the expected performance of KIPONet by leaving the eight nodes at high volatility. In this sense, let us apply some random values to the eight uncertain nodes. When assigning random values to the eight nodes, the proposed FCM simulation yields results for output nodes C18, C19, and C20; the minimum and maximum values of C29 (benefit for cost) are -5 and 5, respectively, so its original value of 2.7 can be interpreted as large, meaning "Good". For C30 (increase in per capita productivity), the FCM simulation results show a minimum and maximum of -4 and 4, respectively, so its value of 3.2 is "Very Good". For C31 (user satisfaction), the FCM simulation results indicate that the minimum and maximum are -4 and 4, respectively, so its value of 2.6 indicates that user satisfaction would be "Good" when a customer country adopts KIPONet.

All of the 17 input nodes can be categorized into two groups: those that must be taken into consideration and those that can be ignored when planning a strategy for the best performance of the KIPONet adopted in the customer's country. Nodes C3, 4, 5, 8, 9, 10, 11, 13, 16, and 17 must be considered, while nodes C1, 2, 6, 7, 12, 14, and 15 have an insignificant influence on the overall performance and can be ignored. Among the nodes with significant influences on the output nodes, C3, 4, 5, 9, 10, 16, and 17 should be managed into higher values in order to produce a decent outcome, while C8, 11, and 13 are not higher values, and can thus stay at the status quo, so they should be managed in order to not be downgraded.

All nodes that influence performance have the same bearing on the output nodes, so they can be prioritized according to the level of immediacy and degree of control that the exporting company has when planning a strategy. Nodes C5 and C9 are controllable and have instant, positive influences on performance, and thus are the top priority. Nodes C3, 4, 10, 16, and 17 are semi-controllable because they are susceptible to competition and external environments, and thus are the second priority. Nodes 8, 11, and 13 are controllable, but do not further contribute to output, making them the lowest priority.

Based on the simulation results using the solver technique, maximizing the output node "Benefit for Cost" involves setting the values of C4, 10, and 16 at 1; maximizing the output node "Increase in Per Capita Productivity" involves setting the values of C3 and 5 at 1; maximizing the output node "User Satisfaction" involves setting the values of C9 and 17 to 1. On the contrary, minimizing "Benefit for Cost" requires taking the values of C4, 10, 11, 13, and 16 as -1; minimizing "Increase in Per Capita Productivity" requires taking the values of C3 and 5 as -1; and minimizing "User Satisfaction" requires taking the values of C8, 9, 13, and 17 as -1. Thus, the best strategy for the exporting company to implement in terms of the most desirable performance is to set the values of C3, 4, 5, 9, 10, 16, and 17 at 1, while the worst strategy, and the one that the exporting company should avoid, is to set the values of C3, 4, 5, 8, 9, 10, 11, 13, 16, and 17 to -1.

4   Conclusion

This study proposes a new method to assess the expected performance of e-Government software when adopted by other countries and consequently recommends the types of strategies to pursue or avoid. The main problem is in predicting the expected performance of the KIPONet, which has been successfully implemented and operated by the Korean Government since January 1999, in such an instance. This problem has remained unsolved because it requires significant levels of field knowledge and ample information about the adopting country, and also because there are a number of uncertainties and volatility in the relevant variables considered in the decision analysis.

To find a solution to the target problem, we used the Fuzzy Cognitive Mapping approach, in which the causal relationships among the qualitative and quantitative variables were analyzed and the solution mechanism was integrated with the solver technique. Experimental results showed that the proposed FCM could yield statistically significant and valid estimation results for the expected performance of the e-Government system when adopted in another country. The main advantages of the proposed FCM are as follows:

1. The customer country can simulate the performance of the e-Government system using the proposed FCM without spending a huge amount of money and time to collect questionnaire data prior to adoption of the system.
2. The proposed FCM can save decision makers time and cost in analyzing the economic efficiency of specific e-Government software programs, even under uncertain circumstances.
3. The FCM can be easily applied to the analysis of the cost-benefit ratio of other e-Government software programs.

We hope that this study will trigger further e-Government system performance assessment research.

References

1. Heeks, R.: Building eGovernance for development: a framework for national donor action: egovernment working paper series. EGovernment working paper series, p. 33. University of Manchester, UK (2001)
2. Jansen, J., de Vries, S., van Schaik, P.: The contextual benchmark method: Benchmarking e-Government services. Government Information Quarterly 27(3), 213–219 (2010)
3. Kosko, B.: Fuzzy cognitive maps. International Journal of Man–Machine Studies 24, 65–75 (1986)
4. Raghunathan, S.: Qualitative reasoning in quantitative modeling. IEEE Systems, Man, and Cybernetics, Part A: Systems and Humans 27(5), 683–690 (1997)
5. Rorissa, A., Demissie, D., Pardo, T.: Benchmarking e-government: A comparison of frameworks for computing e-government index and ranking. Government Information Quarterly 28(3), 354–362 (2011)
6. Sauer, C., Cuthbertson, C.: The State of IT Project Management in the UK. Oxford, Templeton College (2003)
7. Scavo, C.: World wide web site design and use in public management. In: Garson, G.D. (ed.) Public Information Technology: Policy and Management Issues, pp. 299–330. Idea Group Publishing, Hershey (2003)
8. Shapiro, C., Varian, H.: Information rules: a strategic guide to the network economy. Harvard Business School Press, Boston (1999)
9. Stylios, C.D., Groumpos, P.P.: Modeling complex systems using fuzzy cognitive maps. IEEE Transactions on Systems, Man, Cybernetics, Part A: Human Science 34(1), 155–162 (2004)

Author Index